Stephan Jaeger
The Second World War in the Twenty-First-Century Museum

Media and Cultural Memory/
Medien und kulturelle Erinnerung

Edited by
Astrid Erll · Ansgar Nünning

Editorial Board
Aleida Assmann · Mieke Bal · Vita Fortunati · Richard Grusin · Udo Hebel
Andrew Hoskins · Wulf Kansteiner · Alison Landsberg · Claus Leggewie
Jeffrey Olick · Susannah Radstone · Ann Rigney · Michael Rothberg
Werner Sollors · Frederik Tygstrup · Harald Welzer

Volume 26

Stephan Jaeger

The Second World War in the Twenty-First-Century Museum

From Narrative, Memory, and Experience to Experientiality

DE GRUYTER

An electronic version of this book is freely available, thanks to the support of libraries working with Knowledge Unlatched. KU is a collaborative initiative designed to make high quality books Open Access. More information about the initiative and links to the Open Access version can be found at www.knowledgeunlatched.org

 Knowledge Unlatched

The Open Access book is available at www.degruyter.com

ISBN 978-3-11-077770-3
e-ISBN (PDF) 978-3-11-066441-6
e-ISBN (EPUB) 978-3-11-066133-0
ISSN 1613-8961

This work is licensed under the Creative Commons Attribution-Non Commercial-No Derivatives 4.0 Licence. For details go to http://creativecommons.org/licenses/by-nc-nd/4.0/.

Library of Congress Control Number: 2020901137

Bibliographic information published by the Deutsche Nationalbibliothek
The Deutsche Nationalbibliothek lists this publication in the Deutsche Nationalbibliografie; detailed bibliographic data are available on the Internet at http://dnb.dnb.de.

© 2021 Stephan Jaeger, published by Walter de Gruyter GmbH, Berlin/Boston
This volume is text- and page-identical with the hardback published in 2020.
Cover Image: Installation 'bomb hail,' aerial bombs, missiles, and shells, permanent exhibition Militärhistorisches Museum der Bundeswehr, © MHM/Andrea Ulke, 2019.
Printing and binding: CPI books GmbH, Leck

www.degruyter.com

For Priya

Acknowledgements

This book is the result of more than nine years of research into the narratives and representations of war and history museums, which originated in the summers of 2009 and 2010. While visiting museums in Berlin, London, Warsaw, and Kraków and looking for patterns in representations of the Second World War in different historiographical media, I became fascinated with visitors' 'readings' of museum space in contrast to readers of text and viewers of film. I realized the potential in using aesthetic and narratological reading techniques to analyze the reception of exhibitions as well as the constructive and performative nature of collective memories. This eventually led me to conduct fieldwork in 157 different museums and independent exhibitions on both of the world wars, the Holocaust and other genocides, human rights, war and military history, and some more general history museums and exhibitions. These exhibitions were located in fifteen countries, and the fieldwork was conducted between July 2010 and August 2019.

The research for this book was generously supported through an Insight Grant by the Social Sciences and Humanities Research Council of Canada and through several internal grants facilitated by the University of Manitoba. This book would not have been written in this form without the help of a number of people. This includes curators and staff in the various museums in which I conducted my field research. I would like particularly to thank Gorch Pieken, Andrea Ulke, Monika Bednarek, Klaus Hesse, Thomas Lutz, Dean Oliver, Jeff Noakes, Mélanie Morin-Pelletier, and Anna Muller in this regard. All twelve core museums analyzed in this book were graciously willing to assist me with numerous questions and allowed for the reproduction of photographs from their exhibitions.

I presented ideas that made it into this book at around twenty conferences and guest lectures, and in doing so received valuable feedback from discussants and anonymous peer reviewers of my museum research. The ideas received over the years from the German Studies Association (GSA) "War and Violence" interdisciplinary network, which I co-chaired between 2013 and 2017, were invaluable. I also cannot thank my colleagues enough at the University of Wisconsin-Madison and at the Universität Trier, where each I spent long spans of my year-long research leave in 2017–2018 and found the quiet and inspiration to finally write the majority of this manuscript. A particular thanks goes to Sabine Gross, Marc Silberman, Wolfgang Klooß, Ralf Hertel, and Herbert Uerlings.

It would be impossible to name all of my colleagues, friends, and family members who helped enable the completion of this project. In particular, I

∂ OpenAccess. © 2020 Stephan Jaeger, published by De Gruyter. [CC BY-NC-ND] This work is licensed under the Creative Commons Attribution-NonCommercial-NoDerivatives 4.0 License.
https://doi.org/10.1515/9783110664416-001

want to thank Adam Muller, Susanne Vees-Gulani, Jörg Echternkamp, and Kathrin Maurer for their support, ideas, and encouragement. Additionally, without the supportive atmosphere from all my colleagues in my home department, the Department of German and Slavic Studies at the University of Manitoba, the completion of this project would have taken much longer. Especially inspiring to me were the discussions with my graduate students, in particular Erin Johnston-Weiss, Emma Mikuska-Tinman, Esther Hein, and Olurotimi K. Oni. Emma Mikuska-Tinman and Erin Johnston-Weiss were absolutely instrumental in proofreading and editing this manuscript in its various stages.

My gratitude goes to Astrid Erll and Ansgar Nünning for agreeing to publish this book in their Media and Cultural Memory series and to Manuela Gerlof, Lydia J. White, Stella Diedrich, and all the De Gruyter staff for their support and efficiency in making this publication possible.

Finally, this book is dedicated to my life partner Priya. Without her patience and unwavering support whenever this endeavor seemed to take over our lives, I could not have completed it.

Contents

Abbreviations —— XI

List of Illustrations —— XIII

Prologue —— 1

Chapter 1: The Second World War in the Twenty-First-Century Museum —— 8
1.1　　　The Museum between History and Cultural Memory —— 8
1.2　　　The Second World War between National and Transnational Memory —— 13
1.3　　　Museum Types and the Second World War —— 21
1.4　　　Selection of Museums Analyzed —— 32

Chapter 2: The Medium of the Museum —— 40
2.1　　　Museum Space and the 'Ideal' Visitor —— 40
2.2　　　Experientiality —— 47

Chapter 3: Restricted Experientiality —— 61
3.1　　　The Canadian War Museum in Ottawa —— 62
3.2　　　Warsaw Rising Museum —— 77
3.3　　　The Imperial War Museum in London —— 88

Chapter 4: Primary Experientiality —— 94
4.1　　　The National WWII Museum in New Orleans —— 95
4.2　　　The Oskar Schindler's Enamel Factory in Kraków —— 107
4.3　　　The Bastogne War Museum —— 116

Chapter 5: Secondary Experientiality —— 128
5.1　　　The Bundeswehr Military History Museum in Dresden —— 129
5.2　　　The Imperial War Museum North in Manchester —— 150
5.3　　　The Topography of Terror in Berlin —— 160

Chapter 6: The Transnational —— 172
6.1　　　The German-Russian Museum in Berlin-Karlshorst —— 172
6.2　　　The Museum of the Second World War in Gdańsk —— 182
6.3　　　The House of European History in Brussels —— 203

Chapter 7: The Holocaust and Perpetration in War Museums —— 221

Chapter 8: Total War, Air War, and Suffering —— 265

Chapter 9: Art in Second World War Museums —— 292

Conclusion —— 306

Bibliography —— 314

Index —— 341

Abbreviations

BWM = Bastogne War Museum in Bastogne, Belgium
CWM = Canadian War Museum in Ottawa, Canada
DRM = Deutsch-Russisches Museum (German-Russian Museum) in Berlin-Karlshorst, Germany
HEH = House of European History in Brussels, Belgium
IWM = Imperial War Museum
IWML = Imperial War Museum in London, United Kingdom
IWMN = Imperial War Museum North in Manchester, United Kingdom
MHM = Militärhistorisches Museum der Bundeswehr (Bundeswehr Military History Museum) in Dresden, Germany
MIIWŚ = Muzeum II Wojny Światowej (Museum of the Second World War) in Gdańsk, Poland
New Orleans WWII Museum = The National WWII Museum in New Orleans, USA
OSF = Fabryka Emalia Oskara Schindlera (Oskar Schindler Enamel Factory) in Kraków, Poland (permanent exhibition *Kraków – czas okupacji 1939–1945* = *Kraków under Nazi Occupation 1939–1945*)
ToT = Topographie des Terrors (Topography of Terror) in Berlin, Germany
USHMM = United States Holocaust Memorial Museum in Washington, D.C., USA
WRM = Muzeum Powstania Warszawskiego (Warsaw Rising Museum) in Warsaw, Poland

List of Illustrations

Fig. 1: Section "War of Annihilation" with "Toy car dug out from under the rubble." Permanent exhibition. Muzeum II Wojny Światowej (Museum of the Second World War), Gdańsk (Photo: Author, 2017). —— 2

Fig. 2: Destroyed Gama toy tank opposite to parade of war toys. Permanent exhibition. Militärhistorisches Museum der Bundeswehr (Bundeswehr Military History Museum), Dresden (Photo: Author, 2013, courtesy of Militärhistorisches Museum der Bundeswehr). —— 4

Fig. 3: Entrance area in exhibition "Germans in Warsaw." Muzeum Powstania Warszawskiego (Warsaw Rising Museum), Warsaw (Photo: Author, 2013, courtesy of Muzeum Powstania Warszawskiego). —— 18

Fig. 4: Opening section of gallery "Forged in Fire: The Second World War, 1931–1945." Permanent exhibition. Canadian War Museum, Ottawa (Photo: Author, 2015, courtesy of Canadian War Museum). —— 65

Fig. 5: "The Air War" section with subsections "Terror from Below" and "Bomber Command" in background, gallery "The Second World War: 1931–1945." Permanent exhibition. Canadian War Museum, Ottawa (Photo: Author, 2015, courtesy of Canadian War Museum). —— 68

Fig. 6: Part of section "Airdrops." Permanent exhibition. Muzeum Powstania Warszawskiego (Warsaw Rising Museum), Warsaw (Photo: Author, 2013, courtesy of Muzeum Powstania Warszawskiego). —— 82

Fig. 7: "Make Do and Mend" cabinet. *Family in Wartime* exhibition. Imperial War Museum, London (Photo and © Imperial War Museum). —— 92

Fig. 8: Immersive film theater in ruins, room "Into the German Homeland" in "Road to Berlin" exhibition. The National WWII Museum, New Orleans (Photo: Author, 2017, courtesy of The National WWII Museum). —— 99

Fig. 9: Immersive bus stop in the ruins of Cologne. Advertising for The National WWII Museum, Canal Street, New Orleans (Photo: Author, 2017). —— 102

Fig. 10: Section "Generalgouvernement." Permanent exhibition. Fabryka Emalia Oskara Schindlera, Kraków (Photo: Author, 2013, courtesy of Fabryka Emalia Oskara Schindlera). —— 113

Fig. 11: Meeting historical people in transparent plexiglass panels in Kraków's Old Market Square in 1944. Permanent exhibition. Fabryka Emalia Oskara Schindlera, Kraków (Photo: Author, 2013, courtesy of Fabryka Emalia Oskara Schindlera). —— 115

Fig. 12: Narrative characters "See the War through our Eyes." Permanent exhibition. Bastogne War Museum, Bastogne (Photo: Author, 2016, © Bastogne War Museum). —— 118

Fig. 13: Scenovision 2: "The Offensive: In the Woods near Bastogne: At the Dawn of 16 December 1944 …." Permanent exhibition. Bastogne War Museum, Bastogne (Photo: Author, 2016, © Bastogne War Museum). —— 122

Fig. 14: Front façade of main museum building with Libeskind wedge. Militärhistorisches Museum der Bundeswehr (Bundeswehr Military History Museum), Dresden (Photo: Author, 2012). —— 130

ə OpenAccess. © 2020 Stephan Jaeger, published by De Gruyter. This work is licensed under the Creative Commons Attribution-NonCommercial-NoDerivatives 4.0 License.
https://doi.org/10.1515/9783110664416-003

Fig. 15: General Kurt G. A. P. Hammerstein-Equord and Adolf Hitler 'looking at each other.' Permanent exhibition. Militärhistorisches Museum der Bundeswehr (Bundeswehr Military History Museum), Dresden (Photo: Author, 2013, courtesy of Militärhistorisches Museum der Bundeswehr). —— **138**

Fig. 16: Outside view of Imperial War Museum North, Manchester (Photo: Author, 2018). —— **150**

Fig. 17: Scene from the Big Picture Show "Children and War." Permanent exhibition. Imperial War Museum North, Manchester (Photo and © Imperial War Museum). —— **157**

Fig. 18: Part of section "The 'Volk Community.'" Interior permanent exhibition. Topographie des Terrors (Topography of Terror), Berlin (Photo: Author, 2017, courtesy of Topographie des Terrors). —— **164**

Fig. 19: Right half of section "Poland: 1939–1945." Interior permanent exhibition. Topographie des Terrors (Topography of Terror), Berlin (Photo: Author, 2017, courtesy of Topographie des Terrors). —— **168**

Fig. 20: Room "Soviet Prisoners of War." Permanent Exhibition. Deutsch-Russisches Museum (German-Russian Museum) Berlin-Karlshorst (Photo: Author, 2013, courtesy of Deutsch-Russisches Museum). —— **176**

Fig. 21: Section "Leningrad." Permanent Exhibition. Deutsch-Russisches Museum (German-Russian Museum) Berlin-Karlshorst (Photo: Author, 2017, courtesy of Deutsch-Russisches Museum). —— **180**

Fig. 22: Outside view of Muzeum II Wojny Światowej (Museum of the Second World War), Gdańsk (Photo: Author, 2017). —— **185**

Fig. 23: Corridor between Nazi Swastikas and Soviet Hammer and Sickle Flags. Permanent Exhibition. Muzeum II Wojny Światowej (Museum of the Second World War), Gdańsk (Photo: Author, 2018). —— **190**

Fig. 24: Floor plan of floor 3 "Europe in Ruins." Permanent Exhibition. House of European History, Brussels (Photo and © House of European History). —— **207**

Fig. 25: "World War II" gallery. Permanent Exhibition. House of European History, Brussels (Photo: Author, 2017, courtesy of House of European History). —— **210**

Fig. 26: Section "Memory of the Shoah." Permanent Exhibition. House of European History, Brussels (Photo: Author, 2017, courtesy of House of European History). —— **215**

Fig. 27: Section "Poles in the Face of the Holocaust" between "Road to Auschwitz" section (background) and "People like us" installation (foreground). Permanent Exhibition. Muzeum II Wojny Światowej (Museum of the Second World War), Gdańsk (Photo: Author, 2018). —— **251**

Fig. 28: Atrium and "Witnesses of War" exhibition. In center, installation of V2 rocket and V1 flying bomb. Imperial War Museum, London (Photo and © Imperial War Museum). —— **279**

Fig. 29: Cluster of V2 rocket, dollhouse, Sojus 29, and art installation *Galilei's Monologue*. Permanent Exhibition. Militärhistorisches Museum der Bundeswehr (Bundeswehr Military History Museum), Dresden (Photo: Author, 2014, courtesy of Militärhistorisches Museum der Bundeswehr). —— **281**

Fig. 30: Cabinets "Battle of Britain" and "Luftwaffe Personnel." Permanent exhibition. Militärhistorisches Museum der Bundeswehr (Bundeswehr Military History Museum), Dresden (Photo: Author, 2013, courtesy of Militärhistorisches Museum der Bundeswehr). —— **283**

Prologue

In the traditional war museums of the twentieth century, models of war toys such as tanks were often used as artifacts to depict real war machines in miniature. Second World War exhibitions[1] in the twenty-first century, however, take a markedly different approach to these objects. A brief look at three recent examples of toy tanks and vehicles in war museums – all related to aerial warfare – indicates a clear shift away from the imitation of military equipment and toward the display of stories concerning the cultural impacts of war. War toys have become much more closely related to the fate of civilians. These examples also indicate the multitude of aesthetic, emotional, didactic, narrative, meta-representational, and experiential functions that constitute the dimensions of representing the Second World War (and war in general) in the contemporary museum.

My first example is a toy truck on display in the Museum of the Second World War (MIIWŚ) in Gdańsk, Poland (opened in 2017). It can be found in a room in the section "War After All" that marks the beginning of Germany's 'total' warfare against Poland. The object's description reads: "Toy car dug out from under the rubble of a house destroyed in the German bombing of the town of Kalisz in September 1939" (see fig. 1). There is no indication as to whether the pick-up truck served a military or civilian function. It seems to be largely intact. Its color has possibly darkened, and if it ever had rubber tires, they are now gone. This toy is located in a small display case and is the only artifact in the room. It neither serves a meta-function reflecting on the relation of toys to war nor on the memory- and myth-making function of toys; there are also no elements of reenactment. The toy truck appears to symbolize childhood innocence and hope for a better future. The object's description emphasizes that the toy came out of the rubble almost uncharred. It survived the air-raid by the enemy and lives on, even if only as part of an artificial museum-display. Metonymically, it seems as if the Polish nation has risen completely intact out of utter disaster.[2] The narrative trope of emerging from the rubble makes this display particularly powerful, and it can presumably elicit emotions of pride and identification with the Polish national journey. The fact that the museum uses

---

[1] Note that this book, though otherwise written in American English, uses 'exhibition' throughout; 'exhibit' is only used, as is common in British English, to signify a single object or a limited arrangement of objects in an exhibition.

[2] This is the design by the museum's original leadership. But in a subtle way its more humanist agenda fits the nationalistic agenda of the new leadership (see chapter 6.2 for further details).

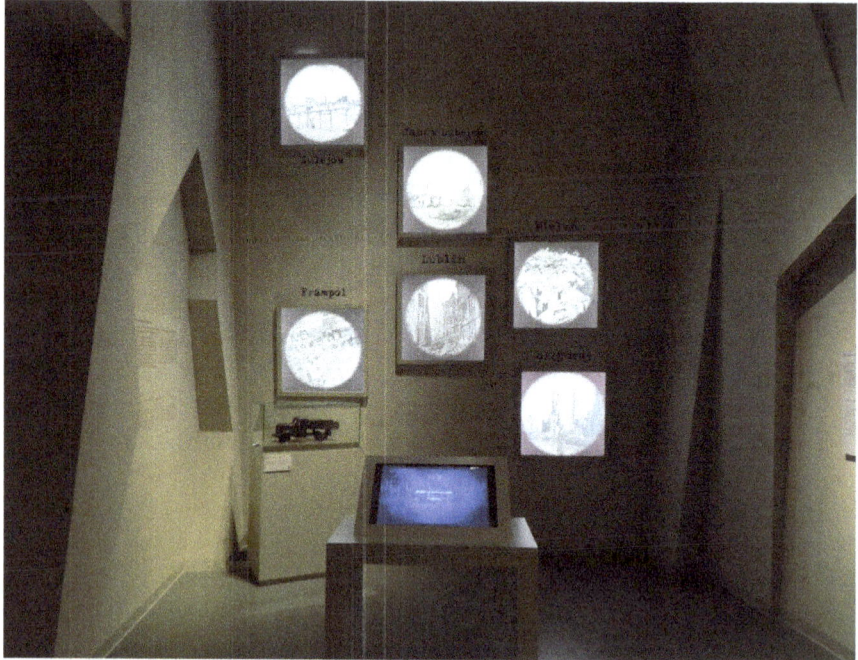

Fig. 1 Section "War of Annihilation" with "Toy car dug out from under the rubble." Permanent exhibition. Muzeum II Wojny Światowej (Museum of the Second World War), Gdańsk (Photo: Author, 2017).

a toy as the only artifact in this room intensifies the message of the innocent being illegally targeted.³

In the Second World War section of the House of European History in Brussels (opened in 2017), the visitor encounters what appears to be a similar display to that in Gdańsk. In a vertical display cabinet, the museum exhibits three charred military toys from Dresden – the figurines of an anti-aircraft gun, a truck, and a tank – and a fragment of a sculpture taken from the ruins of Warsaw in 1945.⁴ The anti-aircraft gun, truck, and tank are war toys unambiguously meant for civilian use. At the same time, unlike the truck in Gdańsk, the toys do not appear to have arisen from the rubble. While their shapes are more or

---

3 Toys, games, and the topic of children and war are, however, present throughout the Gdańsk Museum of the Second World War. The museum allows the visitor to have considerably more open interpretations in other sections, regarding what a toy or war toy means in specific historical circumstances.

4 For the position of this cabinet see fig. 24 (at the beginning of section 3 on the floor map).

less recognizable, they are damaged or even destroyed. Whilst there are precise captions to identify these objects, the museum's tablet[5] relating to the display provides no additional information. The survey text for the section explains that the concept of 'total war'[6] "was particularly brutal in Central, Eastern and Southern Europe." The display is more interpretatively open than in Gdańsk, since the visitor can read the artifacts in at least two ways. The first is that in war, there is total destruction on all sides: none of the artifacts can be repaired; they are fragmented or dysfunctional forever. Along these lines, the war toys can be read metaphorically as representing the suffering of all children, and even possibly as condemning various parties for the suffering of children. The second reading is that the destruction of Warsaw points to German perpetration and highlights that it occurred prior to the bombing of Dresden, so that the artifacts at least partially express German responsibility for the resulting destruction of the city. Neither reading is made explicit by supplementary text; the readers must make these connections themselves.

The third war toy, a toy tank made by the company GAMA, is exhibited in the Bundeswehr Military History Museum (MHM) in Dresden (re-opened in 2011). The toy tank was damaged on February 13, 1945, and was later discovered on Dresden's Weberstraße. The description notes that today, a shopping center is located on the site of the findings and that mechanical GAMA tanks, which sent out showers of sparks, were among the most popular toys in the Third Reich. The exhibition also informs the visitor that such toy tanks were reproduced in West Germany in the 1950s. The museum's toy tank can be found at the very end of a large horizontal glass-display cabinet, located where the "War and Play" section leads into one of architect Daniel Libeskind's voids.[7] Opposite the tank is a parade of toys: soldiers and vehicles from the seventeenth century to the present, from tin soldiers, to Lego soldiers, to space warriors – all of which seem to be marching against the burnt-out tank (see fig. 2). In contrast to most of the museum's displays, the individual objects here are not referenced with exact source material. Neither are they set up in chronological order, emphasizing the anthropological and experiential message of the installation. They create an aesthetic impression of the power of children playing war. This is supplemented by a paragraph from the childhood of German writer and satirist Erich Kästner, who was born in Dresden, in which he expresses his love of playing at all kinds of war. The museum description notes that there is no need for historical accuracy

---

5 For the museum's use of tablets that provide text and contextual information in twenty-four languages, see chapter 6.3.
6 See also chapter 8.
7 See also chapter 5.1.

Fig. 2 Destroyed Gama toy tank opposite to parade of war toys. Permanent exhibition. Militärhistorisches Museum der Bundeswehr (Bundeswehr Military History Museum), Dresden (Photo: Author, 2013, courtesy of Militärhistorisches Museum der Bundeswehr).

in play: "The child alone, almighty and godlike, determines the course and outcome of the war. The omnipotence experienced in play contrasts with children's experiences of helplessness in real war." The visitor who reflects upon the installation can experience some of the fun of playing as well as the sobriety of the real war as symbolized by the burnt-out tank. The artifact is even more powerful since its destruction replicates exactly how a real tank is destroyed in combat. That the tank is a concrete artifact from firebombed Dresden intensifies its authenticity and the perception that it stands metonymically for the real war. The installation creates an experiential stage for visitors to connect the past with their present attitudes or those from their childhoods. Would one allow one's child to play such war games? Did one love playing such games as a child? What are the repercussions of reality overlapping with a game scenario? The tank is ambiguous, oscillating between being a 'victim' of the Allied fire bombings and a 'perpetrator' metonymically pointing to German atrocities, between being a symbol of defeated evil and a symbol of such evil's afterlife in post-war West Germany, and between play and reality. The museum also avoids a clear assessment of whether war toys should be approached critically or not.

To better understand the museums' staging of toys, the theoretical concepts of historical authenticity and of '*in situ*' and 'in context' displays are helpful. Eva Ulrike Pirker and Mark Rüdiger define historical authenticity in two ways: as witnessing and as experiencing the past (2010, 17). All military history museums aim to generate authenticity, but the form of authenticity varies between degrees of reconstructive authenticity based on material and human witnesses and simulative authenticity (Jaeger 2017b, 165). On the one hand, authenticity of witnessing can be achieved through first-hand accounts, historical places, or objects from the past. On the other hand, historical authenticity can be reproduced through simulations of the past. These simulations can be achieved through the use of replicas, historical reenactments, and through the evocation of authentic feelings that relate to the mood or atmosphere of the past. A second theoretical paradigm stems from Barbara Kirshenblatt-Gimblett who distinguishes between '*in situ*' and 'in context' displays. Both allow for different kinds of performativity and creation of space in displaying objects in museums. "In-context displays [...] depend on the drama of the artifact. Objects are the actors and knowledge animates them" (1998, 3). They are often set into a larger narrative such as "a story of evolution or historical development. The performative mode is exposition and demonstration. The aesthetic is one of intelligibility" (1998, 3). In contrast, she describes '*in situ*' displays as immersive and environmental. They privilege the experience of the past through dioramas, live displays, and the display of humans: "they recreate a virtual world into which the visitor enters" (1998, 4).

At first glance, all three examples of war toys fall under Pirker and Rüdiger's first category of the authenticity of witnessing in their role as historical artifacts that draw the visitor closer to the realness of the past. At the same time, they all seem to be 'in context' displays, since none of them are meant to recreate the space of a virtual past world. However, upon closer examination, each example establishes something that seems to simulate authenticity in the staged museum space as well as allowing the visitor to be immersed in past structures and to emotionally connect with the past. The Gdańsk Second World War Museum uses its toy artifact to establish a metonymic-narrative experience. The authenticity of the original artifact is only a stepladder for emotionalizing visitors toward the museum's narrative argument of Poland rising from the rubble.[8] The artifact

---

[8] See also the discussion about the Warsaw Rising Museum in chapter 3.2.

is staged as the lone survivor among photographs of destruction,[9] making it so that the museum simulates a sense of resistance and survival against a criminal 'war of annihilation.' It remains ambiguous whether the uncharred truck refers to the historical will to survive or whether it explicitly connects the visitor's present to the past through contemporary narratives and cultural memory. Similarly, the historical authenticity of the destroyed toys in the House of European History leads to a metaphorical experience that emotionally draws the visitor into the meaning and effects of total warfare. In their function as witnesses of authenticity, they simulate a universalization of warfare within the narrative context of the museum. Finally, in the Bundeswehr Military History Museum's toy parade and tank installation, the visitor is confronted with a temporalized scenario that requires individual interpretation in order to decide how toy war and real war overlap and what these potential overlaps mean. It is a meta-representational display that challenges visitors to immerse themselves reflectively in it and therefore allows for a structural (non-mimetic and non-historical) temporalization of past and present. The burnt-out tank as a witness to and creator of historical authenticity is an important vehicle for the installation to maintain its effect of historical reality. The scene between tank and toy parade performed here creates a structural experience of war, challenging visitors to reflect upon what relates to the past and what relates to their individual and collective memories in the present, upon what is real and what is re-imagined.

Generally, all three cases cannot be understood without considering the narrative techniques of meaning and memory production employed in each exhibition. None of them create a direct immersive experience, but all three trigger different emotional or aesthetic responses to structural or symbolic understandings of the past through the lens of the visitor's present. A structural response by the visitor – as seen, for example, in the installation in Dresden – first creates an aesthetic response with various potentialities that exceed the intent of the museum curators and architects. At the same time, the display supersedes a mimetic re-production of possible past experiences (by individuals or collectives). Consequently, neither mimetic immersion nor mere explication of context can grasp the aesthetic effect on the visitors in the examples provided. This means the dichotomy of '*in situ*' and 'in context' display, while helpful, is insufficient on its own. The visitor – entrenched in her or his own cultural memory and possibly challenged to reflect on its implications and biases – becomes a mediating con-

---

9 Aside from the truck, the room only contains enlarged vignette-like photographs of bombed cities, an enlarged series of photographs of a German massacre of Polish prisoners, and a computer station providing further photographs and brief textual context about the bombed Polish cities.

sciousness in the museum space, activating different potentialities of artifacts, space, and constellations. To understand this process, this study has utilized and further developed the concept of experientiality for the medium of the (history) museum. This has the potential to advance the analysis of how exhibitions emotionalize the visitor; how they create proximity or distance to the historical subject-matter; how they balance or blur the historical understanding of the past with the cultural memory of the present; how they produce or steer ethical statements and narrative structures; and how they allow for reflection on methods of representing the past. Finally, experientiality is significant for how museums represent and simulate specific historical events of the Second World War in general. None of the toys analyzed – although all stem from the Second World War and relate to the destruction of aerial warfare in particular – seem to create an understanding or experience for the visitor that is specific to that war. The theme of war toys – often connected to the innocence of children – seems too universal to achieve historical specificity. Consequently, this tension between historical specificity and anthropological or universal arguments will be another core subject addressed in this study.

Chapter 1:
The Second World War in the Twenty-First-Century Museum

1.1 The Museum between History and Cultural Memory

The core question of this book is how Second World War museums and exhibitions can help prototypical visitors from diverse cultures comprehend or experience the past in the twenty-first century. As the prologue has shown by example of war toys, there are multifaceted ways to involve the visitor in an exhibition, whether it allows for historical understanding or for universal emotional reactions that bring the past closer to the present. As the living memory of the Second World War fades, the museum has become an increasingly significant medium to connect past and present (see e.g. Finney 2017). In other words, it has become a medium of remembrance (see e.g. Makhotina and Schulze-Wessel 2015, 8–9; Thiemeyer 2015). The German philosopher Herrmann Lübbe argues that the increasing musealization of the late twentieth century is a reaction to the acceleration of progress in human society (1982, 2000; see also Koselleck 2004 [1979], 258–263). That is to say, Lübbe argues that the quicker society changes, the more it creates forms and institutions to save artifacts and structures from the otherwise would-be-forgotten past. Consequently, the loss of familiarity with the well-known can be compensated for by musealization. The museum functions as one of the institutions that allow the present to be connected with the past, which for Lübbe enables the process of progress toward the future to actually occur. Even if one objects to the 'progressive' nature of this development,[1] the trend toward temporalization of the past, present, and future seems to have further intensified in the first two decades of the twenty-first century.

Jan Assmann's distinction between communicative (social) and cultural memory (1992, 48–66) helps us to understand the role of the museum when communicative memory becomes increasingly ritualized, materialized, and institutionalized. Astrid Erll points out that memory occurs as both individual and collective processes: "[W]e have to differentiate between two levels on which cul-

---

[1] See especially Andreas Huyssen's critical reading of Lübbe (2003, 22–24). Instead of Lübbe's compensatory argument, Huyssen argues that it is important to accept a fundamental shift in structures of feeling, experience and perception. He points out the moral and political nature of the discourse of musealization and how the museum can easily lose "its ability to guarantee cultural stability over time" (Huyssen 2003, 24).

∂ OpenAccess. © 2020 Stephan Jaeger, published by De Gruyter. [CC BY-NC-ND] This work is licensed under the Creative Commons Attribution-NonCommercial-NoDerivatives 4.0 License.
https://doi.org/10.1515/9783110664416-005

ture and memory intersect: the individual and the collective or, more precisely, the level of the cognitive on the one hand, and the levels of the social and the medial on the other" (2010, 5). The collective level "refers to the symbolic order, the media, institutions, and practices by which social groups construct a shared past" (Erll 2010, 5). It is important to note that 'memory' functions metaphorically when used in collective concepts such as cultural memory or Pierre Nora's *lieux de mémoire*; societies or groups cannot literally remember. In this way, the museum functions as a composite multisensory medium that assembles other media within the museum space. It can reinforce a ritualized or institutionalized form of memory, or it can challenge visitors to distance themselves from the historical material and narratives it represents. Consequently, the museum can mirror the stored cultural memory of its time, or it can shape the formation of new memory patterns. It can work to enhance the functional and storage aspects of cultural memory (A. Assmann 2016 [2006], 38–42). Visitors can either learn about the past, develop their own war memories, or be steered toward preconceived narratives that comprise master narratives and cultural memory politics.

Contemporary museum and heritage studies researchers as well as museum practitioners, have advocated for a social justice approach in museums based on dialogue and debate: "[a] courageously reflective practice [...], based upon a radical transparency and trust, and practiced both inside and outside of the museum" (Lynch 2013, 11; see also Kidd 2014). For the representation of a historical theme such as the Second World War, this raises the complex question of how museums represent historical research, how they react to their influential role as carriers of cultural memory (A. Assmann 2007, 154), and whether they find ways to integrate pluralistic perspectives into their exhibition narrative. How have different communities constructed the cultural memory of the Second World War? Following memory trends in Holocaust (and later in Second World War) remembrance,[2] there has been an increasing convergence of history and memory in Second World War museums since the 1980s (A. Assmann 2016 [2006], 32). Visitors can certainly learn a lot about historical knowledge and facts; however, these museums also affect the visitors' personal memory and

---

[2] The tendency of history and memory to converge must be differentiated from earlier memory studies. In Maurice Halbwachs's social concept of collective memory, the relation of memory to history is sequential (1992 [1925]). History starts when living memory of the past ends. Pierre Nora picks up Halbwachs's differentiation: "(...) Maurice Halbwachs has said, that there are as many memories as there are groups, that memory is by nature multiple and yet specific; collective, plural, and yet individual. History, on the other hand, belongs to everyone and to no one, whence its claim to universal authority" (Nora 1989, 9).

the cultural memory of nations and other groups. Second World War representation in museums has partially followed Holocaust representation in emphasizing individual experiences and memories to express the authenticity of witnessing and the irreducible plurality and diversity of those experiences (A. Assmann 2016 [2006], 33). Here, memory studies enhances history writing within the museum by emphasizing emotion and individual experience, by highlighting the function of history as a form of remembrance, and by adding an ethical orientation (A. Assmann, 2016 [2006], 34).

Actual events are less relevant to memory studies than what people feel and think occurred. Consequently, today, most museums representing the Second World War are hybrids of factual and contextualizing historical research on the one hand, and carriers of perceptions and memories on the other. These museums often conduct research to understand the content of represented events and to argue in an evidentiary mode that certain facts are true and certain historical events happened. Ultimately, they reflect the historical knowledge and the cultural memory of their time. This study analyzes the semiotic, aesthetic, and narrative techniques of Second World War representations in permanent exhibitions. Every museum analyzed here would likely argue that they represent historical facts. Some stress methods of oral history – see e.g. especially the New Orleans WWII Museum – and therefore highlight the convergence of history and memory. At the same time, many museums increasingly exhibit and narrate individual stories and give room to multiple and diverse voices. Whereas some of these voices can develop individualized aesthetics for visitors willing to engage with them, most voices are used as examples for historical groups and arguments. Thus they function less as individual memory than as individual carriers of a collective consciousness, which is part of the museum's memory construction.

Museums can mimetically simulate the past. They can either simulate historical perspectives of individuals, collectives (most commonly), or historical structures. Understanding and representing concepts and instances of violence, atrocities, death, genocide, trauma, loss, perpetration, victimhood, and guilt, among others, methodologically challenge museums to involve the visitor in the past reality of war as well as its current perception. This relates to the concept of 'difficult knowledge,' whereby museums challenge visitors to push beyond the preconceived boundaries of their collective selves (Lehrer et al. 2011; Simon 2004, 2011; Rose 2016; see also Macdonald 2008 for the concept of 'difficult heritage'). This study explores the ways in which contemporary museums bridge the gap between the present and the past by employing the aura of authentic objects, the medium of text, techniques of reenactment, the creation of scenes (both dioramas and scenes the visitor appears to populate), photography, audiovisual material, digital sources, scenography simulating past spaces and atmospheres, effects of light and color, and works of art. Different agents or factors influence the mediation between the visitor and the past: rituals and traditions of cultural memory; the authority of eyewitnesses, and, at the end of living memory, their narratives and voices in text and video testimonies; material objects; the selection and construction decisions made by curators, architects, designers, and museum management; and the influence of governments and lobbying groups pursuing active memory politics. At the same time, this study argues that it is crucial to understand the representational potentiality of an exhibition space not only beyond the intentions of its makers and but also beyond the explicit experiences of those who have witnessed the past. Museums either create a spatial structure that visitors can activate by following multiple paths, or museum makers use particular techniques to restrict such visitor mediation in favor of steering visitors toward specific narratives, meanings, moral judgments, and emotions.

This book contributes to research on Second World War representation, memory studies and museum studies in two distinct ways. First, this study is the first to systematically analyze on a global scale – by example of the European theater of the Second World War – how museums allow contemporary visitors to comprehend and experience the history of the war. Unlike the most prominent Holocaust exhibitions in Washington, London, or Jerusalem, which have been researched extensively (Holtschneider 2011; Hansen-Glucklich 2012; Schoder 2014; Bernard-Donals 2016) or representations of National Socialist ideology (Macdonald 2008, 2013; Paver 2018) and the history of the Holocaust in memorial sites (Lutz 2009; Kleinmann 2017; Luhmann 2018),[3] most current Second World War exhibitions have received relatively minor systematic scholarly attention. In the German-speaking world, the major exception to this is Thomas Thiemeyer's descriptive and comparative media history (2010a), in which he analyzes exhibitions in France, Germany, Belgium, and Britain from the first decade of the twenty-first century.[4] He focuses on national differences and differences in political frameworks and representational forms between exhibitions on the two world

---

[3] See chapter 8 for the discussion of the representation of the Holocaust in Second World War exhibitions.

[4] Consequently, the overlap with this book is limited to the discussion of the Imperial War Museum North and a prospective discussion of the Bundeswehr Military History Museum. The exhibitions in the Imperial War Museum in London, the German-Russian Museum, and the Mémorial de Caen have changed since Thiemeyer conducted his study.

wars (see also Thiemeyer 2013, 2019).[5] The debates and controversies surrounding post-Soviet public memory of the Second World War in Eastern Europe and former Soviet states have led to numerous studies about museums and memorial sites, which often emphasize a singular national cultural memory context (e.g. Heinemann 2017; Makhotina 2017).[6] More recently, a number of studies have analyzed the impact of memory politics and cultural diplomacy on contemporary exhibition design, especially in relation to transnational museums dealing with the Second World War[7] (e.g. Kaiser 2017; Clarke and Duber 2018; Hackmann 2018; Clarke and Wóycicka 2018; Siddi and Gaweda 2019).

Second, in relation to narrative, memory, and experience, this study develops the concept of experientiality (on a sliding scale between mimetic and structural forms). This contributes to existing theories regarding methods used for the reading of history museums. It also provides a textual-spatial method for reading exhibitions and understanding the experiences of historical individuals and collectives. The experientiality created through the interaction between the museum space and the ideal museum visitor helps us comprehend the representational and performative potential of each exhibition, even if an actual visitor can only realize parts of it. Other dimensions and categories – such as the function of museum objects, the use of space and architecture, the function of visual media, and multimedia elements – will be analyzed in terms of their relationship to narrative, memory, and experience. It is crucial to note that these categories do not automatically determine the following: whether an exhibition has the effect of openness or closure; whether it creates debate or manipulates the visitor into believing a single narrative; or whether it forces visitors through a pre-fabricated experience or helps them reflect upon their own position by employing an experiential approach. Simply identifying one particular representational technique as constructing the collective role of a country or a group in war – as victims, perpetrators, resisters/upstanders, collaborators, bystanders, victors, or losers – unnecessarily reduces the complexity of contemporary Second World War representation. This study also attempts to avoid judgment about which method is 'better' for representing the Second World War. Whereas there are cer-

---

[5] See also for the representation of war in the museum also the edited collections by Hinz 1997 and Muchitsch 2013, and specifically for the Second World War Kjeldbæk 2009 and Echternkamp and Jaeger 2019a.
[6] See also the individual studies in the edited collections in Kurilo 2007; Troebst and Wolf 2011; Makhotina et al. 2015; and Bogumił et al. 2015, who assemble individual case studies focusing on specific Eastern European and German museums and memorial sites.
[7] See chapter 6.

tain ethical or critical standards that can be described and assessed,[8] the objective of this study is to explore the range of representational possibilities and their potential cognitive, ethical, emotional, and aesthetic effects on the visitor.

In this introductory chapter, I first discuss the relevance of the Second World War in memory discourses and remembrance politics. I place particular emphasis on the tension between the national and the transnational, exploring transnational, multidirectional, and agonistic modes of memory (chapter 1.2). I then differentiate between different types of museums and contextualize different representational modes within current museum scholarship (chapter 1.3). Finally, I explain the selection of the twelve museums in six countries that form the center of this study's analysis and elaborate on my fieldwork (chapter 1.4).

1.2 The Second World War between National and Transnational Memory

The last three decades have led to an immense global memory and museum boom. History museums play a strong role in this, as they attract a mass audience (Beier-de Haan 2005, 7). Narrowing the scope down to museum representation of war, and particularly of the Second World War, confirms the general trend. Although the war ended seventy-five years ago, and most of its eyewitnesses have passed away, it is nevertheless a constant topic of public discourse and debate. The number of new museums and memorial sites representing and commemorating aspects of the war has multiplied in the twenty-first century. The 2016-edition of the French-authored military guidebook *1939–1945: guide Europe* lists 1,500 museums and memorial sites of the Second World War across Europe (Hervouet et al. 2016). The actual number of memorial sites is much higher; the book's selection is clearly French-focused and consequently includes only a fraction of museums and memorial sites in other countries. What makes the Second World War – and the Holocaust as often inextricably related – most interesting in comparison to other conflicts and historical events is that it is engrained in virtually every country's cultural memory and continues to be relevant for groups and nations in the present, even at the end of its living or communicative memory (see e. g. Flacke 2004; Echternkamp and Martens 2010 [2007]; Bragança and Tame 2016; Echternkamp and Jaeger 2019b).

---

[8] For example, following the *Beutelsbacher* consensus of 1976, German historical museums and memorial sites began to slowly commit themselves to a prohibition on 'over-emotionalization,' that is, to adopt a pedagogical model independent from indoctrinating visitors and/or from overwhelming them emotionally (Thiemeyer 2019, 33).

Take, for example, two recent controversies related to competing cultural memories of the Second World War. The first, between Japan and South Korea (as well as other nations occupied by Japan), concerns the commemoration of the so-called 'comfort women' – girls forced into sexual slavery by the Imperial Japanese Army in its occupied territories (Kimura 2016) – and actively influences contemporary foreign relations between these countries. The second is the debate concerning the Memorial to the Victims of the German Occupation by the sculptor Imre Párkányi Raab, erected in Budapest in July 2014. The monument represents 'innocent' Hungary through a bronze statue of the Archangel Gabriel over whom a bronze eagle (representing Nazi Germany) towers. The memorial has triggered a protest movement, which has manifested itself in the hundreds of spontaneous remembrance notes and objects located opposite the memorial (see also Arnold-de Simine 2015). The latter case demonstrates – similarly to the controversies around the Gdańsk Museum of the Second World War in 2016–2017 (see particularly Machcewicz 2019 [2017])[9] – that the memory battles over the Second World War and its interpretations in Europe today have become a mirror for the tensions in some European countries between European-oriented democracies and authoritative nationalism.

Whereas the First World War might have had a renaissance through its centennial activities from 2014 to 2018, it only fulfils a function of defining national identity and cultural memory in certain countries, including Belgium, France, Britain, and Commonwealth countries such as Canada and New Zealand (see e.g. Kavanagh 1994; Beil 2004; Winter 2006; Wellington 2017, 261–318; Shelby 2018). Other wars are remembered on specific occasions or in specific countries in the form of founding myths. Only the memory of the Second World War, however, is constantly present in the popular imaginary as a global and total war, providing a multitude of narrative and remembrance possibilities. One can argue that for Western European countries the Second World War and the Holocaust "became crucial elements in a strategy to construct a sense of Europeanness" (Berger 2010, 134), while at the same time it is also clear that the universalization of memory and top-down politicization of the war by the European Union can be problematic (Berger 2010, 135; see also Tekin and Berger 2018, 2–6). The West German / contemporary German way of working through responsibility for the Holocaust is distinct from that of other nations, even those that must integrate collaboration into their memory processes (Kaiser et al. 2014, 143; Kaiser 2017, 528–529).

---

[9] See also chapter 6.2.

1.2 The Second World War between National and Transnational Memory

The Second World War can be represented from different national perspectives as the 'good war' (e.g. Terkel 1984). It can also be represented as a human catastrophe, or one can single out the Holocaust as an exemplary event that is either separate from or closely interwoven with the Second World War. Importantly, the war's global impact also adds perspectives from Asia-Pacific (see e.g. Chirot et al. 2014). The war allows for the representation of individual and collective heroics and valor. From the perspectives of countries that belonged to the Axis powers, perpetration and victimhood are complex issues. As a total war, it involved whole civilian populations as supporting the war effort and/or as civilian targets.[10] The long phases of occupation and perpetration of wartime atrocities allow for a strong focus on resistance and collaboration (Flacke 2004). Finally, the history of post-war Eastern Europe in which the Soviet Union made the Eastern bloc states its satellites (often seen and narrated as a second occupation), prolonged the war in the eyes of many countries. Consequently, following a more universal, liberal phase of cultural memory, this has become a major driving force of memory politics in Eastern Europe (see e.g. Bogumił et al. 2015; Makhotina et al. 2015; Chu 2019).

Wars are usually instances of state-organized violence. Historically, traditional military museums or war museums have displayed military trophies and emphasized valor and heroism, establishing identification with a particularly national perspective and memory (Westrate 1961; Kavanagh 1994, Zwach 1999; Thiemeyer 2010a, 95–102; Thiemeyer 2019, 30–34). Rosmarie Beier-de Haan uses the cosmopolitan theory of 'Second Modernity'[11] to identify three trends found in national historical museums and large historical exhibitions in the early twenty-first century. First, the process of globalization reduces the orientation toward nation states and national identity in exhibitions. Similarly, Daniel Levy and Natan Sznaider – regarding Holocaust memory – see a global trend toward "a shared consciousness and cosmopolitan memories that span territorial and linguistic borders" (2002, 91). Second, Beier-de Haan sees a stronger focus on individual rather than collective memory. Finally, she notices the reduction of academic or scientific knowledge in relation to experiential knowledge (Beier-de Haan 2005, 232–233). In other words, cultural memory partially replaces historical analysis and truth-claims. This third assertion clearly influences worldwide trends in today's Second World War exhibitions. The second trend is also observable: museums have begun to represent more individual voices, although many exhibitions continue to use them to construct collective perspec-

---

[10] See chapter 8.
[11] Developed by the sociologist Ulrich Beck in the 1990s.

tives and narratives. Most interesting is Beier-de Haan's first trend, since Second World War exhibitions in almost all national contexts display an inherent tension between a focus on national perspectives, history, and identity and on transnational, global, or universal themes.

Even in explicitly transnational or comparative exhibitions, Second World War representation is almost always connected to the nation state or at least to national perspectives, sources, and themes. In other words, their memory seems connected to an antagonistic mode of memory (Erll 2009, 41–42). At the same time, cultural memory patterns of the Second World War tend to show structural affinities between different cultural memories. This allows for a comparative approach and discussion of transnational and universal memory patterns (François 2004). It also has the potential to overcome antagonistic memory patterns. This is not only evident through a focus on national artifacts, stories, and sources, but also through the high degree of generalization regarding other nations.[12] When, for example, Western European museums speak more precisely of German perpetrators, they mostly refer to Hitler, major SS leaders, and the collective of Nazis or Germans; no war museum – even today – discusses the debates surrounding the guilt and perpetratorship of other nations in-depth (see e.g. Thiemeyer 2013, 291–298; Thiemeyer 2019, 37–38).[13] If a museum highlights an enemy perpetrator – such as in the "Germans in Warsaw"[14] exhibition (see fig. 3) of the Warsaw Rising Museum– they are enshrined as one-dimensionally evil. Further analysis on what motivated such evil is not provided. Regarding victimhood, museums first exhibit their own group or national suffering as well as the targeted victims of the Nazi (or Japanese) enemy. Several of the museums

---

12 Comparative exhibitions reflecting primarily on memory patterns are rare. Exceptions in the form of special exhibitions relating to the Second World are *Myths of the Nations: 1945 – Arena of Memories* (*Mythen der Nationen: 1945, Arena der Erinnerungen*), curated by Monika Flacke, which could be seen in the *German Historical Museum* (Deutsches Historisches Museum) in Berlin from October 2, 2004 to February 27, 2005 (Flacke 2004; see also Jaeger 2015a, 151–152); and most recently the exhibition *[War. Power. Meaning:] War and Violence in European Memory* (*Krieg. Macht. Sinn: Krieg und Gewalt in der europäischen Erinnerung*; the main title is also a play on words, since it can also be read as 'war makes sense'), which took place in Ruhr Museum in Essen from November 12, 2018 to June 10, 2019 as part of the EU-funded project UNREST (see the "Conclusion" below; see also Berger et al. 2019; Berger and Kansteiner 2019; Cento Bull et al. 2019, 620; Fernández-Maya 2019). The permanent exhibitions analyzed in this study that most obviously depict memory patterns of war are the Bundeswehr Military History Museum, the House of European History, and, to a slightly lesser degree, the Imperial War Museum North.
13 See chapter 7 for a further discussion on the representation of perpetrators and perpetration in Second World War exhibitions.
14 See chapter 3.2 and chapter 7.

1.2 The Second World War between National and Transnational Memory — 17

in this study seem to overcome the national in different ways: by diversifying what comprises the national (Oskar Schindler Factory); by universalizing certain elements of the war, pinpointing anthropological and universal elements, primarily within the context of national history (Bundeswehr Military History Museum, partially the Topography of Terror); by depicting a multi-national, partially global scenario that is merely supplemented by a national perspective (Bastogne War Museum); and by explicitly displaying artifacts, images, and narratives from multiple nations simultaneously, which happens in different ways in the German-Russian Museum, the Gdańsk Museum of the Second World War, and the House of European History – the three museums that will be discussed as explicitly transnational museums in chapter 6.

Any museum exhibition about the Second World War attempting to break up the dominant perspective of a nation state must find other ways of structuring the history and memory of warfare to highlight regional, transnational, European, global, anthropological, or universal tendencies. The category of 'transnational memory' seems the most useful for analyzing Second World War museum representation. Transnational history and memory refer to a broad range of phenomena surpassing national boundaries (Tyrrell 2009, 454). They allow museums to go beyond the national without abandoning the idea of its importance: "Nation is therefore constitutive to the definition, not as its center, but as something that has to be overcome, implying that transnational is a category, covering everything that is not contained primarily within the nation state" (Jarausch 2006). The idea of the transnational can offer fresh perspectives, "a set of questions to be asked about the past that cut across the nation-state" (Jarausch 2006). Methods such as connected history, entangled history, *histoire croisée*, translocal history, and world history (Pernau 2011, 36–84), entangled memory (Feindt et al. 2014), traveling memory (Erll 2011), multidirectional memory (Rothberg 2009) and agonistic memory (Mouffe 2012; Cento Bull and Hansen 2016), allow for the sketching, creation, and performance of non-nation-state paths.

Thus, there is first a type of transnational memory in museum representation leading to a progressive, all-encompassing transnationality in which nations move toward the transnational while nation-states potentially maintain a certain relevance. A second, open type of the transnational allows for multiple voices and perspectives, creating transnational constellations, which makes it possible to see comparative perspectives between national or regional narratives.[15] Trans-

---

[15] Narratologically, this can be analyzed through approaches of multiperspectivity. An open multiperspectivity allows for tensions between different viewpoints in a museum narrative versus a closed one in which different voices and perspectives are recognizable but eventually syn-

Fig. 3 Entrance area in exhibition "Germans in Warsaw." Muzeum Powstania Warszawskiego (Warsaw Rising Museum), Warsaw (Photo: Author, 2013, courtesy of Muzeum Powstania Warszawskiego).

national techniques of representation provide opportunities for the expression of structures and constellations that transcend the national. The question in analyzing historical exhibitions is thus whether the historical specificity of a nation or other group is maintained, or whether it disappears into a universal more abstract concept that surpasses the idea of the nation-state altogether. In other words, the contrast between the first and second type of transnational represen-

---

thetized. For multiperspectivity in historiography see Jaeger 2000, for the narratological concept in general Nünning and Nünning 2000.

1.2 The Second World War between National and Transnational Memory — 19

tation is that in the former, the development of a transnational perspective leads to a closed perspectival structure (i.e. there is a distant bird's eye perspective that synthesizes different national voices); whereas in the latter, an exhibition can create co-existing tensions between the transnational and the national.

In this study, a concept that is particularly relevant to transcending or diversifying the national is the European (Pakier and Stråth 2010; Macdonald 2013), evident in the conceptual discussions about the development of the House of European History in Brussels.[16] Stefan Krankenhagen describes how Europe is imagined as "a common historical and experiential space whose abundance is ostensibly captured by the unique characteristics of the continent" (2011, 270). There is a need to legitimize Europe as a cultural-historical process, which can be one goal of such a museum: "Thus, from the many histories of Europe, there emerges the ordered and ordering image of a European 'unity in diversity,' of an imagined property of Europe as the legitimation of its present and future political composition" (Krankenhagen 2011, 270).[17] Cris Shore has identified three features of Europe's new iconography: the teleological orientation of the concept based on the nineteenth-century conception of history; the fact that the symbols of the new Europe replicate those of the old nation-states; and the paradox regarding the construction of a European cultural unity that is simultaneously present and still to be created (2000: 50–53; see also Krankenhagen 2011, 270–271). For contemporary Second World War representation, the challenge lies particularly in this second feature. The nation-state is the very foundation upon which the concept of the transnational is built. The teleological orientation of Europe highlights the problem of whether Europe – in the sense of the first type of transnational representation – is simply replacing the nation-state as a larger conglomerate in a progressive, linear narrative, and thereby threatening the existence of its nation-states: "The distinction between Eastern and Western Europe within an extended EU makes it much more difficult to anchor the history of European integration in museums located in the new member states" (Kaiser et al. 2014, 148). Consequently, the memory of the experience of National Socialism and fascism and the belief in the singularity of the Holocaust could change in the long-run as a consequence of the opening of the European Union to the East (Kaiser et al. 2014, 149).

Anna Cento Bull and Hans Lauge Hansen identify this universalizing tendency as a cosmopolitan mode of memory that contrasts to the increasing trend to-

---

16 See chapter 6.3.
17 Sharon Macdonald has provided a very convincing analysis of the diverse processes for discussing a dynamic and differentiated European memory and consciousness, which recognizes commonalities and diversity, thus allowing for a "'multiperspectival' history" (2013, 40).

ward an antagonistic mode of memory, as discussed above. Similar to the second type of transnational memory, they propagate a third mode of the memory, the 'agonistic memory' (2016). This is based on Chantal Mouffe's discussion of an "agonistic approach to the future of Europe" (2012, 629), wherein she argues for a "pluralization of hegemonies" (2012, 639). Mouffe criticizes an all-encompassing European integration that is blind to "the process of the creation of collective identities" (2012, 630) and argues that, in an agonistic approach, an affective dimension needs to be considered next to a rational one. Consequently, European integration is unable to integrate regional and national forms of identity into its (cosmopolitan) framework without acknowledging necessarily conflicting views. Mouffe therefore argues against a cosmopolitan approach that organizes the unification of the world around a single model and that therefore does not know 'otherness.' In her agonistic model, a "multipolar world would acknowledge diversity and heterogeneity without attempting to overcome them through the imposition of a supposedly superior and more advanced form of political organization" (2012, 639).

Consequently, Cento Bull and Hansen define agonistic memory through four features. First, it avoids setting up 'good' against 'evil' by acknowledging the human capacity for evil within specific historical circumstances. Second, it relies on testimonies from all kinds of historical actors, including victims and perpetrators, to understand their experiences and motivations. Third, it recognizes how important affect and emotions are and advocates for empathy toward victims. Finally, it is attentive to historical context, the socio-political struggles, and the individual and collective narratives that led to perpetration of mass crimes (2016, 399).

Similar to the concept of agonistic memory, Michael Rothberg's multidirectional memory is closely connected to the second, open type of the transnational, which relies on constellations. Rothberg argues against collective memory as competitive memory, "a zero-sum struggle over scarce resources," and develops a multidirectional memory that relies on "ongoing negotiation, cross-referencing, and borrowing" (2009, 3). Rothberg directs his argument particularly against a nation-centered model of memory "in favor of a more open-ended sense of the possibilities of memory and countermemory that might allow the 'revisiting' and rewriting of hegemonic sites of memory" (2009, 310). Following his definition of multidirectional memory, the Second World War remains a memory discourse that almost inevitably seems to return to competitive memory, group identities, and national claims, as can be seen in metaphors such as Claus Leggewie's and Anne Lang's "battlefield of European memory" (2011) and Paweł Machcewicz's "war that never ends" (2019 [2017]). Thus, this concept is interesting for museums exhibiting the Second World War, since – if they intend to operate transnationally – they can create constellations and associations between different war histories and memories. They can also create networking effects with various potential paths for the museum visitor, as discussed above.

At the same time, it is crucial that museums using transnational, agonistic, or multidirectional memorial strategies carefully maintain the historical specificity of different memory communities. Performing a circulating memory of different cultural signs, including ones that claim a strong national (or other group) identity, allows for simulated structural experiences of particular tensions in European Second World War memory. Consequently, this process can create secondary experientiality.[18] Rothberg's anti-competitive idea of multidirectional memory can therefore work on a micro-scale within actual museum exhibitions and in the circulating dialogue between different exhibitions. However, the dynamic re-writing of European Second World War memory will not eradicate nation-centered perspectives. Nevertheless, in twenty-first-century European museums, its temporalized model increasingly simulates multidirectional and agonistic memories that can display dynamic tensions between the national and the transnational, between the historical and the universal (see also Jaeger 2017a, 24–26).

1.3 Museum Types and the Second World War

In categorizing history and war museums, a variety of types are recognizable in relation to Second World War representation. In particular, there are (1) history museums, often object-based, (2) narrative history museums, (3) memorial museums, (4) memorial sites, (5) documentation centers, (6) experiential museums, (7) ideas museums, and (8) collector museums. These eight categories do, of course, overlap in actual institutions. Nevertheless, these categorizations remain useful for this study to help understand the different frameworks in which museums are created.[19]

The first type, a typically artifact-based history museum,[20] is particularly concerned with interpretation, contextualization, and critique (Williams 2007,

---

[18] See chapter 2.2.
[19] Other factors will be considered within this study, such as the differences between public and private institutions, local, regional, and national institutions, and the differentiation between permanent exhibitions and special exhibitions.
[20] Whether artifacts are displaced to auratically connect to the past or whether they are mere illustrations overshadowed by an often-didactic text depends on the style of the history museum (Grütter 1994, 82).

8). Gottfried Korff explains the expositional function that makes museums places of display: as sites of interpretation, they surpass simply acting as sites of preservation (1999, 270). The authentic object can stand in a synecdochic relationship to the past. Its 'thing-connectedness' transfers the cultural energy of the past to the visitors,[21] while allowing them to experience distance and alienation from that same past (Korff 1999, 269; for world war museums, see Thiemeyer 2010a, 263–274). History museums can either focus on artifacts and/or images, or more strongly on textual contextualization and commentary. Consequently, they operate closely to Kirshenblatt-Gimblett's 'in context' displays, using exposition and demonstration as their performative modes (1998, 3). Nevertheless, it is clear that in order to allow the visitor to develop a synecdochic relationship with the past, the modern museum does not merely assemble artifacts in display cases, but stages the past (Beier-de Haan 2006, 192). If the staging of objects transforms into staging a scenography of the whole exhibition, the object-based history museum could quickly become a narrative history or an experiential museum (Korff 1989, 70); 'in context' style could shift to a more immersive 'in situ' style (Kirshenblatt-Gimblett 1998, 3–4).

Second, there are narrative history museums, which are less interested in exhibiting a museum collection than in narrating specific stories through media such as original artifacts, images, or stories (Majewski 2011, 152). Narrative museums tend to gravitate more closely toward either history or memorial museums. For example, in Poland, a new genre of 'narrative museum' was developed in the first decade of the twentieth century, which differentiates itself from matyrological and monographic museums (Majewski 2011, 151–152). The main function of these museums is not the collection, preservation, and exhibition of artifacts, but rather the narration of specific stories through a diverse number of media. The United States Holocaust Memorial Museum in Washington, DC (USHMM), which opened in April 1993 (e.g. Majewski 2011, 152), is often considered to be the archetype of narrative museums. Its founding director Jeshajahu Weinberg has emphasized the importance of narrative within the museum:

> The museum's primary objective is to communicate to visitors a particular chapter of history. To this end, the USHMM draws upon thousands of artifacts. But it uses these artifacts only inasmuch as they constitute building blocks that help compose the historical story line as a visual continuum. This approach is essentially an attempt at visual historiography, and thus, the USHMM can be called a 'narrative museum.' (Weinberg 1994, 231)

---

21 Thiemeyer highlights that artifacts can be represented as authentic through either critical historical analysis and contextualization of the historical source, or through staging the artifact's aesthetic effects (2010a, 265–266).

In other words, in a narrative museum, artifacts, images, and scenography are functional. They work primarily to establish "a historical story line as a visual continuum." The emphasis on the concept of storyline and continuum in Weinberg's statement is significant. It suggests a linear, progressive narrative and the possibility that many stories and voices will be contained within one larger story. Put differently, despite the acceptance of the narrative structure of history,[22] Weinberg's statement implies the telling of one 'great story' in a single master narrative (Berkhofer 1995, 40–44). This seems less inspired by postmodern theory highlighting multiple stories than by nineteenth-century historiography, which championed such master narratives (White 1973). It also counterbalances a more recent trend in museum studies, and the representation of the Second World War in particular, to highlight the individual stories of historical people (Thiemeyer 2019, 29), or at least demonstrates the objective of containing all stories within a larger frame. Weinberg also attributes the success of the USHMM to its capacity to evoke emotions among its visitors. This corresponds with Majewski's observation that narrative museums often use specific staging techniques to advance their narrative message (2011, 152).[23] The evocation of emotions is achieved through narrative rather than through individual exhibits, and because "[the museum] succeeded in demonstrating the universal character of the lessons to be learned from the Holocaust" (Weinberg 1994, 239). One of the critical questions emerging from this claim is whether the visitor still has, or even should have, freedom of interpretation and different emotional reactions to the narrative being presented.

A narrative museum, however, can mediate a multitude of messages and ideologies. Here, it is telling that two of the museums that took cues from the USHMM and aimed for a similar form with which to frame their master narratives – the House of Terror (Terror Háza) in Budapest (2002) and the Warsaw Rising Museum – have completely different agendas than their American model. Instead of Weinberg's claim of universality, they aim to re-establish national identity narratives. A matyrological museum – in Poland, originally exhibitions in the German concentration and extermination camps as well as in prisons and other memorial sites – can be easily integrated in the concept of a narrative museum. This is demonstrated through the discussions surrounding the Gdańsk Museum of the Second World War and the contemporary Polish memory debates

---

22 See the insights of the linguistic turn by philosophers and historical theorists such as Arthur Danto, Hayden White, Roland Barthes, and Paul Ricœur (e.g. White 1973, 1978; 1987; Ricœur 1984–85 [1983–1985], Rüth 2005, 16–52; Munslow 2007; Jaeger 2009).
23 See also Bogunia-Borowska 2016, 240.

about the war in general.²⁴ Nationalism and universality are not necessarily opposites, as this study discusses in detail in relation to the narrative structure and message of the House of European History in Brussels.²⁵ The basic structure of a narrative history museum is ideally suited to merge with the third type of museum discussed here, the memorial museum.

Paul Williams systematically defines the memorial museum as a compound of a physical memorial museum and a history museum. He identifies this type of museum as one that is "dedicated to a historic event commemorating mass suffering of some kind" (2007, 8). In other words, a memorial museum prioritizes the perspectives of victim groups and individual victims. This type of museum coalesces history and commemoration, which also means that a moral framework supplements the historical narration of atrocities. Williams emphasizes that recent memorial museums across the globe, which "find themselves instantly politicized [...] reflects the uneasy conceptual coexistence of reverent remembrance and critical interpretation" (2007, 8). In the French museum context, the term 'mémorial' is also used; however, this usually implies that memory becomes subject matter for the history museum, which also uses a commemorative mode (see also Peschansky 2011 [2010]).²⁶ Though sometimes read as identical to William's 'memorial museums,' the documentary and educational approach in a memorial museum is subordinated to its commemorative function, whereas *mémorials* usually strike a more balanced approach between commemoration and historical museums. As can be also seen in recent comparative educational strategies of the USHMM, memorial museums are intended "to translate the suffering of the past into ethical commitments" (Sodaro 2018, 4). Amy Sodaro argues that they aim to create "a more democratic, inclusive, and peaceful culture and to put the violence of the past to use in creating a better future" (2018, 5). This objective connects the memorial museum to the sixth museum type of museum – the ideas museum – discussed below.

Ethical temporalization is clearly evident in the USHMM. Michael Bernard-Donals reads it as a form of "monumentalization" and "memorial space" (2016, 18–19) emphasizing the tension between the permanent exhibition and what visitors see in the exhibition's representations. For him, this depends less on the actual exhibition than on the museum's rhetorical and discursive genesis, where the museum attempts to produce ethical behavior in its visitors

---

24 See chapter 6.2.
25 See chapter 6.3.
26 Another French term weighing history slightly stronger than commemoration is 'historial,' as used for the Historial of the Great War (Historial de la Grande Guerre) in Péronne (Becker 2008, 31–32).

that surpasses its master narrative (2016, 184). Bernard-Donals argues that the memorial museum is also an ideas museum that does not just preserve memory, but also orientates visitors bearing witness toward their involvement in the present and future (2016, 19). The risk of using the past primarily as a basis for the social justice education of the visitor is that such museum missions seem to require a fairly linear progressive narrative that is far more based on cosmopolitan memory than on agonistic memory. In other words, there is the danger that the visitor is simply asked to accept a given social justice model, instead of working through aesthetic and critical experiences of the past to develop a position on contemporary memory discourse.

To understand all modes of representing the Second World War in the museum, it is important to consider the term 'memorial museum' in a broader sense: Steffi de Jong argues that memorial museums "have both a memorial function of remembering and honouring the dead and a didactic function of transmitting historical knowledge" (2018a, 25). This allows for the analysis of museums that do not only commemorate the victims of atrocities, but also present the war either heroically[27] or in terms of the sacrificial valor of soldiers to be commemorated – as will be seen in this book's discussions of the New Orleans WWII Museum and the Canadian War Museum in particular. On the other hand, as seen in the USHMM, narrative museums can imply a universal vision for human rights, peace, a United Europe, or freedom emerging from their historical narratives. A memorial museum with a strong historical master narrative can therefore use representational techniques such as repetition, story-telling, and a linear, progressive design to create a nationalist, military, liberal, humanist, or transnational museum. It can also reinforce ideologies and myths. The memory struggles concerning the Second World War and the Holocaust make it particularly crucial for us to understand how narrative techniques can shape the story or stories of the war and how they shape the museum space to which the visitor reacts.

The fourth type of exhibition under consideration is the memorial site. This term is particularly theorized in Germany as *Gedenkstätten* (Lutz 2009, 40–45; Stiftung Topographie des Terrors 2001) and in the English-speaking world more positively as heritage site (see e.g. Jackson and Kidd 2011a). The English concept has undergone intensive discussion regarding how exhibitions can transform the authority and authenticity of heritage into a performative, multilayered endeavor for the museum visitor; one that is not simply affirmative of

---

[27] For a heroic perspective see for example the exhibitions in the Museum of the Great Patriotic War in Moscow that opened in 1995.

the past, but "places increased emphasis on heritage as a *process*" that can reveal a multiplicity of narratives (Jackson and Kidd 2011b, 2). All memorial sites that feature exhibitions relate to physical locations that refer to the past. In the German context, the term *Gedenkstätten* is further specified, referring to educational places[28] with independent exhibitions that document past atrocities that occurred on those particular sites. The concept relates first of all to sites of victimhood for those persecuted by the Nazi regime between 1933 and 1945.[29] However, the East German past in particular has recently led to a considerable expansion of the concept, commemorating victims persecuted by the GDR regime. These sites feature historical exhibitions with strong documentary claims and educational mandates; in other words, their social justice mandate is less pronounced than in memorial museums, and the past, mediated by guides and educational programming, is supposed to speak for itself. At these authentic[30] sites of atrocity, the commemoration of victims, historical information, and education overlap. Whereas a heritage context can clearly tell a positive story of heroic deeds, a worthy past, and group identity, German *Gedenkstätten* – similar to memorial museums – relate to atrocities and to the story of the victims in particular (see e.g. Kaiser 2001). Despite the differences between memorial sites and memorial museums, both seek to educate and ensure that atrocities and their contexts cannot be forgotten.[31]

The fifth type of museum relevant to this study, closely related to the concept of educational memorial sites, is the documentation center. This term is almost exclusively used in the German-speaking world,[32] particularly in relation to exhibitions and sites that document Nazi perpetration and perpetrators.[33] Their em-

---

[28] In German *Lernorte* (Raupach-Rudnick 2001, 9).
[29] In the German context, *Gedenkstätten* – by 2009 there were almost 100 (Lutz 2009, 45) – include, among many others: the House of the Wannsee Conference, the German Resistance Memorial Center, and the Plötzensee Memorial Center, all in Berlin, and the memorial sites (*Gedenk-* and *Mahnstätten*) at different concentration camp sites in Germany, such as Dachau, Bergen-Belsen, Buchenwald, Ravensbrück, and Sachsenhausen.
[30] See also Hoffmann 2002 for a critical discussion of the concept of authenticity regarding *Gedenkstätten* / memorial sites.
[31] Consequently, the German language often designates memorial sites as *Mahnstätten*, places to warn about the developments of history.
[32] The American and Canadian equivalent would be the education center; however, when these institutions offer the exhibiting function of a museum, they are usually more closely related to a narrative history or a memorial museum, such as the Illinois Holocaust Museum and Education Center in Skoke (permanent exhibition from 2009).
[33] Similar to the previous concept of *Gedenkstätten* (memorial sites), crimes by the GDR dictatorship are also represented in documentation centers.

phasis again relies on information, education (*Bildung*), and establishing evidence through documentation. They imply the possibility of establishing objectivity and evidentiary historical truth, and they are usually structured chronologically with thematic sections complementing their factual representations. Its most prominent examples in Germany are the Topography of Terror (Topographie des Terrors) in Berlin (2011),[34] the Documentation Centre for the History of National Socialism (NS-Dokumentationszentrum) in Munich (2015), and the Documentation Center Nazi Party Rallying Grounds (Dokumentationszentrum Reichsparteitagsgelände) in Nuremberg (2001).[35]

Sixth, there is the ideas museum (Busby et al. 2015), which highlights a concept – such as human rights, tolerance, peace (Apsel 2016), anti-war, and innocence – rather than historical events or periods. Positive 'ideas museums' tend to focus primarily on the present and future; they emphasize the idea of learning about the past to influence their visitors' future behavior and actions. Here, the concept is divided in two ways, similar to the contrast between cosmopolitan and agonistic memory (Mouffe 2012; Cento Bull and Hansen 2016). On the one hand, ideas museums can follow a strong, linear and progressive narrative; they merge with the narrative museum to set both a pre-determined ethical and educational goal and a strong master narrative. When this is the case, ideas museums are based on a value system; their historical context serves to influence present and future behavior. On the other hand, ideas museums can emphasize the critical education of their visitors. Angela Failler and Roger I. Simon phrase this as follows:

> What is difficult about difficult knowledge in these instances is not just becoming aware of the 'terrible facts' but also, more precisely, figuring out what to do with such knowledge and imagining how to learn from it, especially when it triggers our fears, defensiveness, aggression, or feelings of hopelessness, threatening to undo our fundamental frameworks for making sense of ourselves and the world around us. (2015, 174)[36]

---

[34] See also its detailed discussion in chapter 5.3.

[35] Sometimes the term documentation center is used to describe learning and research institutions within memorial sites. For example, the Rhineland-Palatinate National Socialist Documentation Centre (NS-Dokumentationszentrum Rheinland-Pfalz) is part of the Osthofen concentration camp memorial site (Gedenkstätte KZ Osthofen). Specific perpetrator sites are also the former SS castle Wewelsburg 1933–1945 Memorial Museum (Erinnerungs- und Gedenkstätte Wewelsburg 1933–1945; reopened in 2010) – that was also the location of an adjacent satellite camp of the Sachsenhausen concentration camp – and the Nazi Documentation Center Ordensburg Vogelsang (Vogelsang NS-Dokumentationszentrum) in North Rhine-Westphalia (2017).

[36] George Jacob notes that ideas museums – unlike museums exhibiting historical and cultural objects – "have no obvious claim to the uniqueness or superiority of their content or to the physical protection of this information" (2015, 248). Consequently, engaging the visitor in difficult

Difficult knowledge can be defined as knowledge that does not fit into traditional discourse. In regard to trauma it presents "the psychic difficulty of learning from traumatic experiences of others" (Britzman 2000, 28). Difficult knowledge forces visitors to challenge their own experiences, transcend the boundaries of their collective selves, and potentially reconceive their relationships with their own identities and the identities of others (Lehrer and Milton 2011, 8). In this way, the ideas museum can change the visitors' understanding of past and present discourses and, potentially, their future actions, without didactically telling visitors how they should think, feel, or act. Simon argues that a recipient's attentiveness to testimony is twofold: informational and (self-) reflexive (2006, 197). Instead of highlighting master narratives and collective stories, he sees transformative possibilities within the visitor's experience of personal and local memories (Simon 2004, 198–199).

Ideas museums – especially those that focus on negative, historical ideas – need to combine past, present, and future in their exhibitions, so that visitors, with their own prejudices and memory, engage with the museum exhibition. In terms of representing the Second World War and its atrocities, this means that an ideas museum is usually hybridized with a history or memorial museum. It also focuses on specific historical events or periods that often serve related memorial functions and are linked to sites of commemorative significance (i.e., the museum is embedded within an authentic space / memorial site where past atrocities have taken place). An ideas museum cannot simply abandon the representation of the past when educating audiences and expressing hope in and beyond the past, nor can a history museum eliminate the expression of futurity. Ideas and history remain inseparably intertwined (Jaeger 2015b, 230). This type of museum can also connect to a documentation center if the latter prioritizes learning from historical contexts to understand comparable contexts in the present and future. The Munich Documentation Centre for the History of National Socialism describes itself through the link between past and present: "[it is] a place of education and remembrance documenting and addressing the crimes of the Nazi dictatorship and their origins, manifestations and consequences right up to the present day. [...] The key questions that the documentation center poses to visitors are: 'What does this have to do with me?' and 'Why should this still concern me today?'"[37]

---

knowledge production could replace this lack of authentic objects. However, Jacob also seems to underestimate the strength of storytelling, which usually helps ideas museums to create a unique space.

37 https://www.ns-dokuzentrum-muenchen.de/en/documentation-center/about-us/, accessed 13 October 2019.

The temporalization of the past, present, and future allows museums to shape memories that can move toward the future by simultaneously overcoming historical specificity and maintaining it. Temporality is extremely important in museums, since the exhibition is nothing more than a spatial and temporal blueprint; the visitor, situated in the present, is required to actualize the potentialities of the museum space. Creating a dynamic relationship between past, present, and future usually requires an ideal, since otherwise they merely confirm the interpretation or master narrative of an exhibition. Such an approach is affirmed by art historian and museologist Michael Fehr, who argues for a paradigm shift: museums increasingly need to reflect upon their own space in the present, rather than functioning as documentary-realistic containers for the past (2005, 172; 2010). Museums must accept and embrace that they are constructing new, individualized realities within their unique spaces. They are situated between a documentary paradigm and a simulative, performative paradigm through which they create, rather than simply reconstruct past realities. This allows them to deal with more complex temporalities.

Seventh are experiential museums. Particularly in the Anglo-American world, there is a tendency toward experiencing the past via empathy or reenactment of the past (Agnew 2007) in museums with a strong emphasis on the master narratives and scenography of an exhibition (Arnold-de Simine 2013, 44–53; Jaeger 2019, 54–55). This is in contrast to traditional war museums, which emphasize objects and artifacts. Experience can become the dominant mode, making it so that the visitor mainly experiences simulated scenes and atmospheres of the past, while lacking the cognitive distance to understand historical processes and contexts. As this study documents, all Second World War exhibitions create experiences in different forms – yet a museum whose primary mode is experiential emphasizes the emotional over the cognitive function. Here, it is important to differentiate between approaches that mainly create proximity to collective experiences of the past and ones that use empathy and reenactment of the past to trigger critical thinking and reflexive modes in the visitor – in other words, that mobilize difficult knowledge. Vanessa Agnew further elaborates on this distinction: on the one hand, there are reenactments that rely on the notion that the past has been mastered, which means that they are neither explaining historical processes nor interrogating historical injustices for such a theatrical reenactment of history. This collapses temporalities and privileges experience over events and structures in order to maintain historical depth (2007, 301–302). On the other hand, she notes that "[r]ather than eclipsing the past with its own theatricality, reenactment ought to make visible the ways in which events were imbued with meanings and investigate whose interests were served by those meanings" (Agnew 2004, 335).

In terms of museum representation of atrocities, Paul Williams and Alison Landsberg have argued that experiential forms can uncover power structures and representational and ethical challenges. This is also the goal of empathetic techniques in the museum. The demand for an imaginative investment by the visitor leads to different concepts of secondary witnessing of trauma, which Landsberg uses to develop the concept of 'prosthetic memory.' This implies that mass media such as film and experiential museums can create sensuous and bodily memories that do not come from lived experience, but rather from engagement with mediated representations (Landsberg 2004, 2015). Discomfort in inhabiting the experiences of others is often connected to physicality: "that we remember not so much in a cognitive, declarative fashion, but in one that is bodily and sensory" (Williams 2007, 98). Consequently, Williams argues that the depiction of trauma must occur through an experiential return to the event. He concludes "that in order for visitors to grapple with what others endured, the idea of an event must be 'burned in'" through visual depictions and experiential installations (2007, 98). Williams highlights the "pain of looking" in memorial museums that transcends from the victims' "agonizing experiences" to the visitors' "discomfort at having to see" (62). He points out that "[w]hile the act of looking is typically understood as a necessary burden in order to appreciate what is at stake, the viewer's actual response may be more self-consciously rooted in the shortfall of his or her emotional reaction" (Williams 2007, 62; see also Landsberg 2004). However, even if one does not go as far as Williams, empathy remains a useful and important tool in museum representation to help understand how museums mediate and reflect upon the gap between the historical past and the visitor's present. Virtually every historical exhibition, even ones that highlight their distance from the historical persons depicted, allows for a certain amount of empathy. The simulated experiencing of other perspectives is crucial in allowing the visitor to understand the past. Cognitive and emotional functions of museum representation are clearly present in different museum types; to understand their impact, it is important to analyze how they either open meaning and allow for different forms of reflection, or represent one version of historical truth and reality that visitors cannot challenge because they are either emotionally overwhelmed or cognitively under-informed.

Finally, there are collector museums (type 8) which focus particularly on displaying authentic artifacts such as weapons, uniforms, military equipment, and insignias (see also Thiemeyer 2010a, 275–282). Today, collector museums representing the Second World War primarily display military memorabilia stemming from veterans (and possibly civilians) who experienced the war, and their families.³⁸ Some resemble a basement full of memorabilia.³⁹ Others are more deliberately designed, such as the Bastogne (Sous-Lieutenant Heintz) Barracks, which – though still hosting military operations – has functioned as an interpretation center for the Second World War since 2010 (Jaeger 2019, 56). Their educational value is completely oriented toward reconstructing authenticity and documenting unquestioned facts, possibly supplemented by the function of commemorating war veterans from specific regions or units. Collector museums particularly appear in battleground regions that attract significant tourism, for example, in the Normandy region for the D-Day landings or the Ardennes for the Battle of the Bulge. These museums often sell uniforms, insignia, and presumably authentic objects.⁴⁰ Their narrative structure is – at best – chronological. At times, such in the Bastogne Barracks Interpretation Center, collector museums reconstruct authentic scenes through the use of dioramas.

In relation to the representation of the Second World War as discussed in this study, the eight types of museum are relevant to varying degrees: types 1 (historical), 2 (narrative), 3 (memorial), 5 (documentation center), and 7 (experiential) are the primary types of the institutions in question. Memorial sites are less relevant; at the same time, almost all these museums connect with some authentic aspects of their actual sites or locations. This study does not directly focus on ideas museums, since the historical theme of the Second World War offers a wide variety of themes and perspectives and serves as its focal point. But ideas museums will be discussed where historical museums relate to the past, present, and future. The concept of ideas museums will also be considered in terms of how history museums representing the Second World War reflect on conceptual themes such as violence, genocide, or peace, overcoming a narrow historical focus. Finally, specific collector museums are not the direct focus of this study either. All museums analyzed either imply different interpretations, narratives, or understandings of the war with a national, transnational, or global focus that goes beyond a mere appreciation of authentic reconstructions – as

---

38 Before the advent of military history museums, army and military museums in particular, highlighted the 'custodial' function and almost seemed like armories (Westrate 1961, 5–6). Westrate also discusses the educational, commemorative, and entertainment functions of military museums (1961, 5–8).
39 An excellent example for a random display of items related to the Battle of the Bulge and its local events around the city of Clervaux, Luxembourg, is the Musée de la Bataille des Ardennes in Clervaux (visited in May 2016).
40 For example, during a visit in July 2014, the Bastogne Ardennes 44 Museum offered an original Wehrmacht artillery uniform, a Wehrmacht parade dagger, many original grenade shells, a US razor, a US foxhole lighter, and hundreds of other original pieces of memorabilia for purchase.

seen, for example, in dioramas. However, to understand the concept of primary and secondary experientiality[41] for all museums, it is vital to consider some ideas that make collector museums popular with regard to their claim of creating historical authenticity.

Although the conceptual definition of museum types is useful, the analysis of exhibitions ultimately proves more dynamic than assigning each museum a type. Nevertheless, these typologies help us in understanding how a museum blends cognitive, affective, ethical, political, and commemorative functions. All museums have didactic and educational goals, but whether they refer to cognitive, affective, ethical, or aesthetic capacities strongly varies. This differs in terms of whether a museum aims for interpretative openness or moral or ideological closure, and how it creates effects of proximity and distance with historical individuals, groups, and events. As discussed below, depending on both their governance structure and their political and societal contexts, museums also vary in their curatorial freedom and how much they must adhere to visitor numbers. Silke Arnold-de Simine emphasizes the tasks of the museum today and the different roles of private and public institutions:

> Museums – especially but not exclusively those that are privately funded – need their customers to approve of the exhibition rather than feel challenged beyond their comfort zone. State-funded museums, on the other hand, perform a public role of remembrance in which they are expected to represent a broad social or at least political consensus, producing narratives that form an integral part of national identity politics (2013, 2).

In other words, the institutional structure can strongly influence whether an exhibition is designed to produce new ideas and critical thinking, or whether it reproduces the status quo of a specific memory narrative.

1.4 Selection of Museums Analyzed

This study performs a detailed analysis of twelve permanent exhibitions in six countries that opened in the twenty-first century. The typical military or army museum representing military weaponry, technology, heraldry, etc. without a strong cultural narrative, which represents war as heroic or at least uncritically, is not discussed in this study.[42] Reconstructive museums that put the visitor in

---

[41] See chapter 2.2.
[42] The Military History Museum (Heeresgeschichtliches Museum) in Vienna and Royal Army Museum of Military History (Musée royal de l'Armée et d'Histoire militaire) in Brussels still

the passive position of observing and admiring a reconstructed scene, an authentic artifact, or a collection of original artifacts do not develop a strong potential for experientiality.

The twelve museums and their most recent permanent exhibitions analyzed in study are as follows: in Germany, the Bundeswehr Military History Museum (Militärhistorisches Museum der Bundeswehr) in Dresden (MHM) from 2011,[43] the Topography of Terror (Topographie des Terrors) in Berlin (ToT) from 2010, and the German-Russian Museum (Deutsch-Russisches Museum) in Berlin-Karlshorst (DRM) from 2013; in Belgium, the Bastogne War Museum in Bastogne (BWM) from 2014 and, as a European example, the House of European History in Brussels (HEH) from 2017; in Poland, the Warsaw Rising Museum (Muzeum Powstania Warszawskiego) in Warsaw (WRM) from 2005, the Oskar Schindler Factory (Fabryka Emalia Oskara Schindlera) in Kraków (OSF) from 2010, and the Museum of the Second World War (Muzeum II Wojny Światowej) in Gdańsk (MIIWŚ) from 2017; in Britain, two branches of the Imperial War Museum, the Imperial War Museum in London (IWML) from 2000 to 2014 and the Imperial War Museum North in Manchester from 2002; in Canada, the Canadian War Museum in Ottawa (CWM) from 2005; and in the United States, the National WWII Museum in New Orleans from 2000 to 2018. The Mémorial de Caen in France, which was founded in 1984 and considerably revised in 2009 and 2010 serves as a backdrop, particularly in the chapters on the representation of the Holocaust and the Air War.

All exhibitions analyzed in this study function as regional or national focal points for Second World War narration, although their actual numbers of visitors vary widely between roughly 40,000 a year in the German-Russian Museum and 1.3 million in the Topography of Terror. Most institutions are either publicly funded or, if they are privately funded like the New Orleans WWII Museum, function

---

are predominantly designed as exhibitions fully based on assembling and displaying original military artifacts. The Brussels museum uses modern museum design techniques to depict the Second World War in its *Halle Bordiau* – the exhibition is currently being expanded –, however, it still looks like a traditional war museum that does not tell a story but mainly displays historical war scenes and focuses on equipment, with a certain emphasis on heroic commemoration. Another example is the International Museum of World War II located in Natick, Massachusetts. Its permanent exhibition, currently being redeveloped (a move to Washington, D.C. is under discussion), is fully based on its collection of authentic military documents, artifacts, and memorabilia.

[43] Note that the dates provided in this list are the opening years for the new or redesigned permanent exhibitions. Several institutions are constantly redesigning parts of their permanent exhibition or expanding it, especially the Imperial War Museum in London and the National WWII Museum in New Orleans.

as a national hub for telling a national or transnational story as well as reflecting and influencing cultural memory. Each exhibition constructs and simulates human experiences of war within different memory contexts. All exhibitions analyzed have been either redesigned in the twenty-first century or opened in new museum institutions and buildings since 2002, the large majority since 2010. Half of the permanent exhibitions are the inaugural exhibitions for a new institution or museum sub branch (in Brussels, Gdańsk, Kraków, Manchester, New Orleans, and Warsaw), another four have a new building (in Bastogne, the Topography of Terror in Berlin, Dresden, and Ottawa), even if the actual institution had preceding permanent exhibitions.

All six countries in which the museums are located have recently founded or reopened major state-sponsored permanent exhibitions about the Second World War, attracting considerable national and international media attention. One could theoretically include a large number of countries that participated in the Second World War and consider other regions such as Asia-Pacific,[44] the Middle

---

44 There is obviously endless material on the memory debates about the Second World War in the Asian-Pacific theater, particularly in East Asia and South-East Asia, and regarding the relationship of Japan to China, Korea, and the Philippines, and the American campaign in Asia. Specific Japanese atrocities such as the Nanjing Massacre and the fate of the 'comfort women' in Japanese-occupied territories have received worldwide attention. The British and Allied Campaign in Burma and the colonial past of Western powers in general could have been further topics. I decided to only include the Asian-Pacific theater in the discussion in this book if it was crucial to understand the exhibition designs and representations in Europe and North America, such as in the discussion of the American master narrative of the war or in the discussion of the depiction of aerial warfare and nuclear bombing in the museums (see chapters 4.1 and 8 in particular). Whereas several well-known museums such as the Memorial Hall of the Victims in Nanjing Massacre by Japanese Invaders (founded 1985, renovated 1995) have been redesigned in the late twentieth century, there is also a larger number of smaller or more local museums that opened in the twenty-first century such as, in Japan, the Shokeikan Museum for Wounded Soldiers in Tokyo (2006) and the Okinawa Prefectural Peace Park (2000; see Allen and Sakamoto 2013, 1051–1053). In 2019, the Hiroshima Peace Memorial Museum (founded 1955, renovated 1994) reopened its Main Building and redesigned permanent exhibition (the East Building with parts of the permanent exhibition was reopened in 2017); the museum focuses, however, clearly on the aftermath of the bombing, the universal destruction of nuclear bombs, and on commemorating the victims, not on understanding the historical context of the war. Scholars reflect in particular on the political discourses, cultural memory, and master narratives purported by museums in Japan, China, and South Korea (see e.g. Allen and Sakamoto 2013; Denton 2014; Hatch 2014; Yoshida 2014; Lee 2018). Jooyoun Lee demonstrates in her analysis of major Japanese war and peace museums that these "not only produce knowledge of the nation's past, but also trigger the emotions of contemporary people to connect them to the war dead, by exhibiting personal stories, photographs, and belongings of the deceased and thereby generating an affective identity that transcends time and space" (2018, 8). The debates about victim-

East, Australia (see e.g. Allen 2015), Scandinavia (see e.g. Kjeldbæk 2009; Stugu 2011), or other Eastern European countries besides Poland[45] to discuss representational techniques; however, the close reading of the different exhibition spaces and their potentialities for an 'ideal visitor'[46] requires concentrating on a reasonable number of museums. First, this prevents this study from getting lost in generalities that simply repeat the museums' curatorial and architectural mission statements. Second, it allows for a focus on the intricacies of a specific set of national and transnational variations on cultural memory of the war.

The six countries in this study were selected for specific structural reasons that could be transferred to other arenas of memory and explain similar representational techniques and variations in other regions and countries. They function as models for the analysis of Second World War exhibitions due to their specific roles in the war. European memory is the core of this study; the comparison to North America is needed to demonstrate the markedly different memory of a continent that did not experience the war directly on its own soil. The European Union has tried to define a shared collective memory and identity coming out of the Second World War, which has been contested in national memory frameworks. Germany is the aggressor or perpetrator nation, dealing with questions of collective guilt and how, simultaneously, to represent its own suffering. Great Britain is a victor and survivor country for which war in general and more recently the Second World War, has been an important identifier for the nation as defenders and liberators of the world. Poland perceives itself as a country in a victim position (albeit with issues of collaboration and antisemitism) that was able to begin the redevelopment of a national master narrative only after the Soviet dictatorship, which had partly overshadowed the memory of the Second World War. It has become the model for countries in which memory politics, particularly related to the Second World War, have become a highly debated part of national identity between a more European-oriented model and a nationalist narrative. Belgium functions as example of a victim and occupied country that relied on others for its survival as a state.

Canada is a victor/savior from outside of Europe in which post-war representation and collective memory have led to the formation of a strong national identity, including Canada's post-war role as an international peacekeeper and diplomatic mediator. The United States has a similar master narrative, but the narrative emerges from an already self-affirmed perspective of identity and

---

hood, suffering, and perpetration provide for interesting comparative insight if one juxtaposes the memory battles of Japan and Germany.
45 See also Kurilo 2007; Makhotina et al. 2015; Bogumił et al. 2015, among others.
46 See chapter 2.1.

strength in fighting the 'good' war to save the world from evil. The analysis of US American and Canadian museums also allows for the discussion of whether there is a unique North American perspective in Second World War museum representation and in which ways the North-American memory has been more stable throughout the last seventy years than its European counterpart.

This study focuses on permanent exhibitions since they are the better reflections of the long-term processes of cultural memory and group narratives that shape the representation of the Second World War on a national or transnational level. The study excludes explicit Holocaust memorial museums and Holocaust educational centers as well as memorial sites, as discussed above as type (4), which create exhibitions through the lens of a historic place and its events. The Topography of Terror has been included to serve as an example of an institution that is almost exclusively focused on the depiction of perpetration. It also works as a model for generating structural experiences of the war. The twelve museums analyzed include five museums in which the Second World War is prominently displayed but as part of a more all-encompassing history, including four military history museums – the Bundeswehr Military History Museum, the Canadian War Museum, the Imperial War Museum in London, and the Imperial War Museum North – and one history museum – the House of European History. The other seven museums exclusively represent the Second World War, even if this is done in numerous forms and from various thematic angles.

In sorting the twelve museums by the main typology to which each museum adheres, only the Bundeswehr Military History Museum and German-Russian Museum primarily function as object-based history museums, although they also have narrative and experiential qualities. The Gdańsk Museum of the Second World War, the Warsaw Rising Museum, the Canadian War Museum, the House of European History, and the Bastogne War Museum are predominantly narrative history museums. Whereas the New Orleans WWII Museum is first and foremost a 'memorial museum' for United States veterans and the collective effort of the USA in the war, it also features elements of an object-based and a narrative history museum with strong experiential components. Similarly, the Warsaw Rising Museum and the Canadian War Museum partially function as memorial museums for the insurgents of the Warsaw Uprising and Canadian war veterans respectively. The House of European History is on the borderline between an object-based and a narrative history museum, while the Bastogne War Museum and the Warsaw Rising Museum both also feature strong experiential aspects. In addition to the Oskar Schindler Factory, the Imperial War Museum in London and Imperial War Museum North could also be described as experiential with regard to their Second World War sections. Both branches of the Imperial War Museum also have elements of object-based and of narrative history museums. The most comprehensive museums are the Gdańsk Museum of the Second World War, the Bundeswehr Military History Museum with its German-based but universally anthropological focus, and – although more restricted to the American point of view – the New Orleans WWII Museum. The German-Russian Museum focuses on the German-Soviet war. Three museums – the Oskar Schindler Factory, the Warsaw Rising Museum, and the Bastogne War Museum – focus on a specific place, event, or battle, but all represent an overarching story that seems to surpass the official local focus in different ways. The Warsaw Rising Museum creates a national narrative out of the local historical event. The Oskar Schindler Factory produces a microcosm of the German occupation of Poland through its spatial representation of Kraków between 1939 and 1945. The Bastogne War Museum in particular combines local, national, and global aspects of the war. Finally, the Topography of Terror deals with the whole range of atrocities committed during the Second World War, but with a focus on German perpetration.

Thomas Thiemeyer has differentiated between the three layers of the exhibition creators, the actual exhibition, and the museum visitor (2010b, 82; Heinemann 2017, 57–60). He also differentiates between the analysis of current and past exhibitions. For Thiemeyer, the latter is based on the study of sources and empirical research in the field (2010b, 82). For the former, I talked to museum staff, researchers, and curators and used libraries and archives when appropriate.[47] Planning papers and protocols, institutional annual reports, reviews and interviews in the press, and museum websites have been analyzed and are discussed / referenced when they contribute to the representational and aesthetic analysis of the resulting museum and its effects on the visitor. For the fieldwork component, to select the twelve museums in question and to have a sufficient comparative insight into the design, representational, narrative, and remembering techniques, and the experiential effects in Second World War museums, I visited 157 different museums and independent exhibitions on both world wars, the Holocaust and other genocides, human rights, and war and military history (and some more general history museums and exhibitions) in fifteen countries between July 2010 and August 2019. All twelve core museums for the project were visited on at least two different research trips, for a minimum of five days and a maximum of twenty-one days; the average was nine days of field-

---

[47] These were not formal interviews; when an oral or non-published comment or information is cited in this study, it is explicitly referenced and I have received permission to do so.

work in each museum.[48] The close reading of multi-dimensional museum spaces was prepared through the creation of a list with analytical research questions that allow for the comparison of these museums. This method relates to ethnographic research and its (self-) reflexivity, which sees the museum as stage for 'performances' by staff and visitors, as well as a field- or discourse-specific understanding of perspectives and prejudices that accompany any production of meaning within discursive frames (Gable 2005, 2010; Bal 1996; Scholze 2004, 2010). However, this study highlights a more literary form of close reading of the potentialities of semiotic meanings and of cognitive, aesthetic, ethical, and emotional effects that an exhibition can have on different visitors. It relates to the concepts of narrative, experience, and memory in Second World War exhibitions, while considering the specificity of the medium of the museum in its multi-dimensional setting and addressing the visitor through multiple senses.

This methodology is further reflected throughout the second chapter of this book. In its first half, I discuss the concepts of museum space and the ideal visitor in relation to representational techniques such as staging and distantiation. The second subchapter discusses the relation between historical experiences of individuals as well as constructed collective experiences from the past and the visitor experience in the present. From there I develop the concept of experientiality and a sliding scale between primary and secondary experientiality. The actual discussion of the twelve museums is divided into four main chapters that provide the primary theoretical angles used to understand each specific exhibition: restricted experientiality (Canadian War Museum, Warsaw Rising Museum,

---

48 Since some exhibitions, such as Gdańsk Museum of the Second World War, the New Orleans WWII Museum, and the Bundeswehr Military History Museum are constantly evolving or changing, it is important to note the first and last visit for each of the twelve core museums, in alphabetical order: Bastogne War Museum: July 2014 & June 2018 (eight days of fieldwork in three different visits); Bundeswehr Military History Museum: March 2012 & August 2019 (twenty-one days of fieldwork in ten different visits); Canadian War Museum: August 2012 & June 2015 (eleven days of fieldwork in two different visits); Gdańsk Museum of the Second World War: July 2017 & April 2018 (seven days of fieldwork in two different visits); German-Russian Museum: July 2013 & December 2017 (eight days of fieldwork in six different visits; the previous permanent exhibition was analyzed in 2009 and 2011 as well); House of European History: June 2017 & May 2018 (six days of fieldwork in two different visits); Imperial War Museum in London: August 2013 & August 2017 (ten days of fieldwork in four different visits; one visit before actual project started in June 2009); Imperial War Museum North: August 2013 & May 2018 (seven days of fieldwork in two different visits); New Orleans WWII Museum: June 2014 & May 2017 (ten days of fieldwork in two different visits); Oskar Schindler Factory: June 2010 & December 2013 (six days of fieldwork in two different visits); Topography of Terror: December 2010 & August 2019 (twelve days of fieldwork in eight different visits); Warsaw Rising Museum: July 2010 & December 2013 (five days of fieldwork in two different visits).

Imperial War Museum in London), primary experientiality (New Orleans WWII Museum, Oskar Schindler Factory, Bastogne War Museum), secondary experientiality (Bundeswehr Military History Museum, Imperial War Museum North, Topography of Terror), and the transnational (German-Russian Museum, Gdańsk Museum of the Second World War, House of European History). The second half of the book consists of three chapters on specific thematic angles of contemporary representation of the Second World War in war museums: first, Holocaust and perpetration; second, total war, aerial warfare, and suffering; and finally the use of art in Second World War exhibitions. The book closes with a synopsis of the results and the discussion of future approaches for museum representation of the Second World War and its scholarship.

Chapter 2:
The Medium of the Museum

2.1 Museum Space and the 'Ideal' Visitor

How do history museums approach the past? Aleida Assmann – partially drawing on the museum analysis of Rosmarie Beier-de Haan – differentiates between three types of historical representations of memory: narrating, exhibiting, and staging (2007, 149–153).[1] Narrating refers to the narrative semantics of a historical representation that ascribes meaning, importance, and direction to the narrated events. Exhibiting refers to the placement of historical texts, images, and objects in space, which is far less sequential and causal than narrating and allows for effects of simultaneity. Finally, staging the past is divided into the categories of media staging, particularly through film and moving images, and spatial staging, which Assmann mainly relates to authentic heritage spaces that allow for imaginative re-experiencing or performative simulations of the past. However, Assmann's analysis is not specific enough to help us understand the particularities of the medium of the 'museum' (or exhibitions in museum space). In her chart – which is divided into basic representational modes, media, and format – the museum as a 'format' only appears to be connected to the mode of exhibiting, whereas 'medial staging' relates to documentary and historical film, and 'spatial staging' to memorial sites and reenactments of history (2007, 154).

While Assmann's typology, terms and structural descriptions of 'staged' public history are slanted toward the production sites of narratives, museum exhibitions, or performances, narratologists have broadened the subject-matter of narratology to cultural representations in general (see e.g. Nünning and Nünning 2010). Ansgar Nünning has shown how the focus on world-making allows for the discussion of historiographic narrative in the much wider contexts of media and discourse theory, if one, for example, sees "events, stories, and storyworlds as discursively created, medially represented, culturally specific and historically mutable constructs" (Nünning 2010, 206). To apply this to an understanding of representational forms and storyworlds of history museums and the specifics of the museum as medium the potential visitor must be taken into account – at least as much as the motivation and intentional design of the exhibition creators. The question of whether museums can be read like a text has caused considerable debate, particularly among narratologists and semioticians on the one hand, and museum stud-

---

[1] In German *erzählen*, *ausstellen*, and *inszenieren*.

 OpenAccess. © 2020 Stephan Jaeger, published by De Gruyter. [CC BY-NC-ND] This work is licensed under the Creative Commons Attribution-NonCommercial-NoDerivatives 4.0 License.
https://doi.org/10.1515/9783110664416-006

ies scholars and museum practitioners on the other. In comparison to a more general reader response theory that relates to textual media, one must here ask what specific role the visitor has in history museums' representations, narrations, staging, and simulations of the past? What does it mean when the visitor moves through space and spatial arrangements, in comparison to the reader of a book who must imagine the spaces being narrated?

Space in museums can also be described through a narratological approach that has recently emerged: 'narrative geography.' Marie-Laure Ryan, Kenneth Foote, and Maoz Azaryahu define space as denoting "certain key characteristics of the environments or settings within which characters live and act: location, position arrangement, distance, direction, orientation, and movement" (2016, 7). Regarding this concept, the museum functions as a core example for spatial narrative media. However, its discussion does not explain the specificity of museum narratives in space, beyond the general observation that museums speak to the visitor's different senses. After the authors explain numerous possibilities of how narrative can play a role in spatial museum design, their chapter on "museum narrative" goes on to explore fairly broad spatial storylines in narrative-based museums, narrative architecture in history museums, and the framing of museum narratives through beginnings and endings. Finally, Ryan et al. argue that the museum's main characteristic in terms of narrative geography can be found in its difference from landscape narratives: "the possibility to design the exhibit along a circulation path that accords with a storyline and narrative progression" (2016, 203). However, even if memorial sites deal with the physical conditions that they find in pre-existing buildings or landscapes, the complexity of museum representation is clearly restricted through numerous discursive and political conditions. The complexity of demands made by the architectural design, the design firm itself, museum stakeholders, marketing pressures, lobbyists who want their themes represented, local and national politicians, and the press are such that one wonders how free museums actually are to narrate space. A narratological theory of space derived mainly from categories that have been developed for the literary analysis of fictional texts seems to fall short in explaining narrative and space within the museum.

To explain the relationship of museum and space, Daniel Tyradellis identifies exhibitions with "thinking in space" (2014, 134–159). Kirshenblatt-Gimblett notes that "[e]xhibitions are fundamentally theatrical, for they are how museums perform the knowledge they create" (1998, 3). Similarly, Heike Buschmann follows Michel de Certeau in reading 'space' as the result of the interaction between a person and the structural condition provided in the three-dimensional 'place' (2010, 162–163). This acknowledges that the museum needs the entity of the recipient to actualize or perform its space, and furthermore, that it is necessary to understand the role of the visitor in space and to illustrate the poietic and performative nature of museum exhibitions, in analyzing how exhibitions represent the past. Poiesis – a prominent concept in the historiographical theories of Hayden White (1987: 42; see also Jaeger 2011, 33–34) and Paul Ricœur (1984–85, I: 52–87) – means that the past only becomes reality through the act of representation or narration. This is particularly evident in the medium of the museum, where the museum first creates a spatial arrangement of objects, images, texts, and scenes; and secondly, it requires the (active) perception of visitors to complete the process of experientiality and fill the shell of the exhibition. This second element surpasses White's and Ricœur's use of the term, wherein they emphasize the poietic potential of historiographic narrative.

To understand this aspect of the museum visitor's role, Mieke Bal's comparison between visitors of the theater and of art exhibitions proves helpful: "Instead of standing still *in front of* an imaginary stage, as in theater, the visitor now walks *through* a forest of objects. And instead of being a spectator of the play, she is now a co-narrator, fulfilling in her own way the script that predetermines the parameters within which the story can be told" (2008, 20, see also 1996, 2–4). Bal's approach emphasizes the dynamics that a museum visitor can perform in space, by zooming in and out like a film camera, from long shot to a close-up and vice versa (2008, 26).[2] Similarly, Rosmarie Beier-de Haan's discussion of staging as an integral part of 'new museology' helps in defining the specifics of the museum as medium. Traditionally, museums have tried to create exhibitions that positioned the visitor as a detached observer (2006, 192). As part of 'new museology,'

> [v]iewers are now drawn into the ensemble of exhibited objects, no longer able to assume the position of detached museum-goers hovering above or outside the exhibition. The viewers and their potential perceptions are now taken into account; they become part of the ensemble and are challenged to express their own perceptions, judgments, and emotions. (Beier-de Haan 2006, 192–193)

Suzanne MacLeod also points out both how the visitor's individual use and experience of space surpasses any intentional approaches that architects, interior designers, and curators in developing specific effects of space and architecture:

> In the museum then, a range of users – professionals, researchers, families, tourists, organized groups, repeat visitors and so on – must also be recognized as continually remaking the architecture of the museum through the uses to which it is put. Such uses are, to a great extent of course, closely controlled by the individual and organizational visions of museum

---

2 See the discussion of 'historical distance' below.

space dominant at any particular moment. This said, most of us could probably call to mind a memory of a museum space suddenly transformed through the uses to which it was put, even if it did return to its established character with its requisite spatial practices soon afterwards. (MacLeod 2005, 20)

In the museum context, design (the planning and building of a museum space) and reception (by the visitors who fill the space with their own expectations, decisions, and reactions) cannot be completely isolated from one another. Another concept utilizing space is assemblage theory. It surpasses the agency and intentional authorship of the museum planners and of the visitor and looks at assemblages or clusters that constitute discursive meanings in which the museum emerges (Macdonald 2013, 5–7). Adam Muller highlights the "dynamic interaction / intersection of overlapping clusters of objects, spaces, ideologies, memories, feelings, structures, histories, and experiences" (2019). Understood as 'assemblages,' these clusters are dynamic, open systems that lie partially beyond the scope of formal agency, such as that exercised by curators and museum administrators. External conditions, like a military's engagement in a contemporary war, or the European migrant 'crisis,' can completely change the perception of a pre-conceived exhibition design. Emma Waterton and Jason Ditmer combine assemblage and affect theory in their analysis of the Australian War Memorial in Canberra, conceptualizing it in terms of: "how designed museum spaces, exhibitions, landscapes, lighting, sound and visiting subjects, along with the predictive power that some of these are afforded, work together in the here-and-now to produce a range of possibilities" (2014, 136). Unlike Muller, they center their analysis – based on ethnographic visitor observation in actual museum spaces – around the interior spaces and scenes of an exhibition and stress an element of the 'unforeseeable' in the shifting actualities of the museum space during visitors' interactions with it (Waterton and Ditmer 2014, 136).

In reality, different visitors will react differently to each museum display, based on, among other things, their background, their intentions and interests, and the conditions of the actual visit (Hooper Green 2006; Falk 2009; Kirchberg 2010; Falk and Dierking 2012; Schröder 2013). Whereas empirical visitor analysis can certainly demonstrate important patterns that help museums understand an exhibition's effects, this study utilizes an aesthetic response theory[3] in analyzing the semiotic and aesthetic potentialities of the museum space that an 'ideal' visitor can evoke, even if an actual visitor will only realize parts of it. Jennifer Hansen-

---

[3] For its origins in literature analysis, see Iser 1978 (1976). See also Wolfgang Iser's discussion of the necessary interaction between mimesis and performance and the concept of 'staging' as an anthropological category (1993 [1991], 281–303).

Glucklich uses the concept of the 'ideal visitor' as a way of understanding the "a visual language" each museum creates, "inscribed in its architecture, exhibits, objects, and spaces, to construct a particular visitor to its unique space. This visitor, like the novelist's 'ideal reader,' does not exist empirically. Rather, he or she is an ideal composite – fashioned through the language of the museum and made sympathetic to the salient worldview of the museum's host culture" (Hansen-Glucklich 2014, 10).

While this is a very useful description of the ideal reader/visitor concept, my approach is considerably more focused on the potentialities of an exhibition's spatial language than on the intended ideal visitor imagined by museum planners. Even if a museum intends to have their visitors react in a certain way, an approach that relies on the method of 'thick description,' can consider the performative nature of exhibition more precisely.[4] In the context of representations of the Second World War, Zuzanna Bogumił et al. recently utilized such an approach to understand the representation of the 'enemy' in three city museums in St. Petersburg, Warsaw, and Dresden (2015). They provide a 'close reading' of the politics and poetics of display, power relations, agency, semiotics, narrative, aesthetics, and the construction of knowledge (2016, 14–15).[5]

In summary, beyond Bal and Hansen-Glucklich's 'ideal visitor,' it seems important to consider the specificity of the medium of the museum in space, and its performative and poietic nature – as distinct from text. Newer empirical visitor studies can function as complex identity studies or consider the actualities of individual and, consequently, varying museum experiences. In contrast, the aesthetic, response-based 'ideal visitor' approach allows us to understand both the different potential interpretations an exhibition holds and the techniques it employs to foreclose certain kinds of interpretation, manipulating its visitors toward accepting a specific interpretation and meaning of the past. On the one hand, such an analysis might confirm strategies and storylines that were implied by the creators of a museum. On the other, it can go beyond such agency and intentionality and in doing so, demonstrate the structural potential of an exhibition space to be read in specific or in various ways.[6]

---

4 This method was developed by cultural anthropologist Clifford Geertz [2017 [1973]) and applied to museum studies in the wake of the discussion of 'new museology' (Vergo 1989; Macdonald and Fyfe 1996; Macdonald 1998; Witcomb 2003; Beier-de Haan 2005).
5 In general, see also Gable 2005, 2010; Scholze 2004, 2010, for ethnographic and semiotic close readings of history museums.
6 Charting the paths and interpretations of actual visitors goes beyond this study and its methodology, yet such approaches can easily connect to this one, as Waterton and Dittmer do, in their

In order to further understand the difference between the museum and other media and to reflect on the main representational parameters of historical (Second World War) exhibitions, it is useful to follow Thiemeyer's utilization of Marshall McLuhan's theoretical framework of hot and cool media (Thiemeyer 2010a, 247). Hot media – a category under which McLuhan also includes photography – are so detailed that the visitor only passively perceives the singular version of the past being represented. In contrast, cool media have little visual information and require the active engagement of a visitor using their own imagination (McLuhan 1965 [1964]). The latter allows for distance between recipient and historical subject matter; the former seduces the visitor into following a pre-described path to understanding the past. At first glance, the medium of the museum, and in particular historical museums, seems to be a cool medium. This is due to that fact that visitors can choose their own paths through the museums, select what texts, images, objects, and installations they focus on. Depending on their background and expectations, there will be infinite ways of performing actual museum visits.

Yet, upon closer examination, this shows that the museum is a composite medium assembling and combining other media and potentially speaking to several of the visitor's senses; curatorial strategies can make the museum a hot medium that shapes narratives and experiences in specific, predetermined ways, as much as they can keep visitors at a distance and allow for reflection and contemplation. As a hot medium, the museum can steer and manipulate the visitor's emotions. As a cold one, it allows the visitor distance and relies on the visitor's participation. Thiemeyer is strongly critical both of experiential approaches that pretend to mimetically imitate the past and the suggestion of authenticity via sensual evidence. Consequently, he highlights the value of actual objects and the need for critical contextualization of images and objects (2010a, 248–253, 264–266; see also Jaeger 2019, 54–55).

Unlike Thiemeyer, Williams sees cool media as mainly illustrative. However, he similarly affirms that, "we can call those objects that may lack self-evident attachment to the narrative at hand, but possess a high emotional quotient and hence lend themselves more easily to emotive spectacle, 'hot'" (2007, 33). Therefore, as soon as a museum constructs an emotional path for the visitor,[7] the visitor becomes passive in experiencing such a spectacle. Péter Apor demonstrates this in his analysis of the permanent exhibition (from 2002) in the House of Terror in Bu-

---

use of ethnographical methods in observing themselves and other visitors in experiential spaces in the Australian War Memorial (2014).
7 Often toward the political or didactic message that underlies the exhibition, via simulated authenticity, reduced visitor flexibility, and high narrativity. In other words the museum highlights one master narrative.

dapest (2014).⁸ Apor notes "the dominance of audiovisual spectacle and the disorderly mixture of original and replica, authentic and scenery" that overwhelms the visitor emotionally (2014, 332). This also prevents the visitor from having interpretative freedom. The emotional feeling of "the authenticity of the experience of the past [is] irrespective of the authenticity of individual objects" (Apor 2014, 338). In contrast to such an emotional overwhelming of the visitor, the majority of recent theoretical approaches highlight the representational potential of the museum in forcing visitors out of their comfort-zone, showing its cool media qualities (e.g. Arnold-de Simine 2013, 2; Thiemeyer 2010a, 249; Crane 1997, 33).

In providing a close reading of the performative space of an exhibition, it is useful to employ the concept of distantiation and historical distance, as developed by Mark Phillips. Traditionally, historical practice has been defined by historical distance as "a position of detached observation made possible by the passage of time" (2011, 11). Distantiation is a tool to gauge how close or far a visitor is brought to the historical processes and experiences of the past.⁹ Phillips sees four distinct but overlapping modes as a constitutive part of every representation of history for historical authors and readers: "whatever its genre, [it] incorporates elements of *making, feeling, doing,* and *understanding* – or (to alter the terms) questions of formal structure and vocabulary, affective impact, moral or ideological interpellation, and underlying intelligibility" (2013, 6). In this way, historical distance does not merely imply detachment or separation between past and present; it can be seen in relational terms on a sliding scale, "into a continuous gradation made up of all positions from near to far" (Phillips 2013, 6). Historical distance works as a descriptive tool to demonstrate how human beings operate in the world "in relation to gradations of time, space, affect, or to the rewards and pressures of community" (2013, 12).¹⁰

For the analysis of the spatial language of exhibitions and their representational effects on the potential museum visitor, Phillip's concept of distantiation proves useful in numerous ways – even if he shapes his concept mainly to describe the historian's authorial perspective and the structure of text. How do war museums create proximities and distances between the past and the visitor in the present?¹¹ If one takes aerial warfare in the Second World War, for example, how does a museum create emotional proximity or distancing when repre-

---

8 The House of Terror represents the fascist and communist regimes in twentieth-century Hungary in an experiential way, generally highlighting Hungarian victimhood.
9 For the function of narrative in this process see Bal 2008, 26.
10 For its relevance for memorial museums see also Williams 2007, 258.
11 For the application of Phillips's own approach to museums see also his analysis of the Canadian Museum of Civilization (now Canadian Museum of History) in Ottawa (2013, 211–218).

senting past events and exhibiting historical objects? Do visitors empathize, sympathize or identify with individuals or collectives from the past? Or is it more likely that they will feel an unbridgeable gap to such experiences? The range of historical distance is as wide ideologically as it is emotionally. Is the visitor led into confirming or questioning frames and traditional narratives of the Air War? Can the visitor's interaction with the museum create an ideological rethinking of her or his own position, or does it confirm or reinforce the knowledge and prejudices she or he had before the visit? Cognitively, visitors can be so close to the past events of the Air War that an understanding of the overall historical processes is impossible. Furthermore, their understanding of the past can be steered toward a predominantly historical understanding (proximity) with a high degree of historical specificity, toward a predominantly anti-historical understanding of universal suffering in the Air War, or toward the heroism and sacrifices of the pilots and aircrew members. The latter creates distance on the cognitive level, but possibly highly affective and/or ideological proximity. To further understand the dynamics of a performative museum space in which the visitor operates according to different distantiation techniques, the second half of this chapter discusses how constructed or performed experience of the past – the Second World War and its historical agents – can overlap with present experience. It also examines how this leads to a sliding scale between primary and secondary experientiality.

2.2 Experientiality

The concept of experientiality in history museums helps immensely in understanding the narrative, experiential, and representational possibilities and limitations of the medium of the (history) museum. It allows us to understand the natural difference, but also the dynamic overlap, between the visitor's experience as part of the performative nature of the museum and the historical experience of individuals and collectives. This subchapter explains two conceptual differences: first, the difference between experience and experientiality, and second, the difference between primary and secondary experientiality. With the advent of cognitive theory in narratology (for museums see Fulda 2005; Lippert 2009, 2010; Jaeger 2019), experientiality has become an important category in the discussion of the representation and narration of history. When representing the past one never discusses experiences of the 'real' past, but instead, in the words of Jonas Grethlein, the "experiences of experiences" (2010, 220). Monika Fludernik introduced the term experientiality into narratological research by defining narrativity as representation of experientiality (1996, 20–43). 'Natural' narratives cognitively correspond to human experience. Experientiality is "the quasi-mimetic evocation of 'real-life experience'" (Fludernik 1996, 12). Fludernik's emphasizes that the most important cognitively relevant factor for experientiality is "the presence of a human protagonist and her experience of events as they impinge on her situation or activities" (1996, 30). The protagonist reacts emotionally and physically to the experiential situation. Consequently, experientiality always implies an anthropomorphic experiencer, the protagonist's consciousness (Fludernik 1996, 30).

Regarding historiography, Fludernik argues that "[t]he experientiality of the source is [...] sublimated and transformed into collective experience as the historical object of analysis" (Fludernik 2010, 41–42). Originally, Fludernik strictly differentiated historiography from fiction and 'life-writing,' and maintained that:

> historical narrative displays a *degré zéro* of narrativity since the purpose of historical narrative is not to portray the experience of individual characters that will allow readers to make sense of life by vicarious projection into the situation of a fictional protagonist, but the function of history is to provide an argument about what happened and why it did so, and how this relates to the present-day situation. (2001, 93, see also 1996, 328)

Fludernik has softened this differentiation in her later research, but has continued to maintain that historiographic narrative can merely express experience, not experientiality (2010, 70). There is no doubt that any form of historical experience is mediated and constructed. Museums, on the one hand, construct, simulate, and stage the past. On the other, visitors complete the museum experience with their own individual perceptions, selections, and routes through the museum space. This means that Fludernik's argument for scholarly historiography, in which the historian synthesizes knowledge in such a way that the experience is always mediated and secondary, does not work for the museum. The museum creates a different hybrid between historical experience and visitor experience, making "the quasi-mimetic evocation of 'real-life experience'" (i.e. experientiality) a particularly interesting concept with which to describe the representational potential of exhibitions.

In order to express historical experiences, museums can quote ego-documents from diaries, autobiographies, letters, interviews, and other sources. These are usually arranged in an argumentative or aesthetic ensemble and have a predominantly illustrative function. The term 'experientiality,' however, becomes useful when the idea of experiential consciousness is present in the act of reception. Researchers working with Fludernik's concept of experientiality have criticized it for seeming too rooted in narrative structure and underestimating the act of reception and the reader (Caracciolo 2014, 47–48). The interaction of narrative and reception needs to be considered in order to make this concept useful to museums. If one recognizes that historiography always produces constructed, simulated experiences, Fludernik's "quasi-mimetic evocation of real-life experience" shifts from the individual to the collective. A collective perspective is always a retrospective construct, since humans can feel like they are part of the collective, but they can never have a collective perception in the present moment.

Consequently, in the museum, the visitor becomes significant as a mediator – an anthropomorphic experiencer – for experientiality. An exhibition constructs a simulation effect, with the result that the visitor experiences the past as a collective human consciousness. This can include experiencing the collective effort of Canadians on the home front, the German's collective fascination with ideas of National Socialism, the fear of Belgian civilians under occupation, or the will to resistance in any occupied country. Since historiography, including museum representations of history, cannot reproduce the past or past worlds as such, this means that all primary 'quasi-mimetic' effects are constructed and simulated. The visitor reacting to the exhibition's spatial-temporal semiotic structure overlaps with historical entities who experienced the past as either individuals or constructed collectives. The ability to simulate experientiality is particularly interesting since museum visitors enter a space and scenery, taking over the role of an entity who has had a real life experience, which Fludernik primarily sees in fictional characters and real-life individuals (such as the writers of an autobiography). At the same time, there is no need to equate the visitor experience with any historical experience, since an exhibition clearly cannot equate the two. Therefore, experientiality becomes the analytical concept with which to examine the representational and narrative potential of an exhibition.

If a museum such as the Oskar Schindler Factory in Kraków creates a scene like that of a film-set, there are nevertheless no fictitious characters. However, visitors become like space and time travelers; they possess and express the consciousness needed to perform the experientiality of the museum.[12] Even if a museum has a strong master narrative, as exemplified by the Warsaw Rising Museum, it still requires the visitor to generate experientiality in the space of the exhibition – in this case, the visitor is steered toward feeling empathy with the insurgents of the Uprising.[13] There is experientiality here, but it is restricted by a strong ideological narrative. Therefore, even if experientiality originates in the exhibition's construct of text, narrative, and space, as designed by curators, interior exhibition designers, and architects, the concept of the 'ideal' museum

---

12 See also chapter 4.3.
13 See also chapter 3.2.

visitor as mediating consciousness is needed to understand exhibitions' experientiality. Consequently, the need for analyzing the impact of reception in the museum is more intense than in other historiographical media. Whereas in fiction, an analysis could ignore the reader's responses and fully focus on the production and constructive nature of a text, the analysis of experientiality between exhibition and visitor is mandatory for understanding the representational effects of an exhibition. Experientiality, as developed by Fludernik for non-historiographical forms of narrative, becomes a particular important category for historical museums. An exhibition – as with any historiographical representation – can quote from the historical sources of ego voices: those of individuals who express their own experience of historical events autobiographically. In contrast, primary and secondary experientiality in a museum are always simulated. This differentiates experience and experientiality.

Daniel Fulda was one of the first researchers to apply insights from natural and cognitive narratology to the medium of the museum by analyzing the narrative of the *Wehrmacht Exhibition* (*Wehrmachtsausstellung*).[14] He uses the concept of narrativity in cognitive narratology to demonstrate the experiential potential of narrative exhibitions: "Cognitive narratology not only describes narrativity within the structure of artifacts but goes beyond this to investigate the way that such artifacts are cognitively processed, with the consequence that entire worldviews emerge within the consciousness of their recipients" (2005, 181). Fulda explains the scandal of the exhibition (see also Thiele 1999) by its lack of narrative contextualization. "[I]ts decontextualizing and singularly instrumental narrative structure" (2005, 186) could easily be countered with visitors' personal, autobiographical stories. What Fulda identifies as "singularly instrumental narrative structure" closely relates to the term 'restricted experientiality' as used in this analysis, though one can argue that exhibitions with restricted expe-

---

14 The full title of the traveling exhibition is *War of Annihilation: Crimes of the Wehrmacht 1941 to 1944* (*Vernichtungskrieg: Verbrechen der Wehrmacht 1941 bis 1944*). It was organized by the Hamburg Institute for Social Research (Hamburger Institut für Sozialforschung) and shown in more than thirty German and Austrian cities between 1995 and 1999. The public debates and conflicts about the photography-based exhibition on war crimes of the Wehrmacht led to the intense debate about German perpetration and led German cultural memory of the war toward the universal acceptance that the Wehrmacht as an institution was heavily involved in the crimes and atrocities in the Second World War. The exhibitions of the Bundeswehr Military History Museum, the Topography of Terror, and the German-Russian Museum would not be possible without the transformation of public memory as result of the *Wehrmacht Exhibition* during World War II (see Mösken 2007; Thiemeyer 2019, 35–38; and Nugent 2014 for an empirical visitor studies approach by analyzing the exhibition's visitor books).

rientiality generally rely openly on a single dominating narrative structure.¹⁵ Consequently, Fulda follows Fludernik's equation of narrativity and experientiality more closely than my study does. He is more interested in the potential of narrative in general, for which the exhibition functions as a case-study than in exploring the specificity of the medium 'museum.'

To understand the decisive second distinction between primary and secondary experientiality, it is first important to explain the concept of simulation, since it leads to the core of experiential challenges in the museum. Museums in general fail to represent the 'real' past; Jay Winter argues that war museums by definition fail to represent war, "because there was then and is now no consensus as to what constituted the war" (2013, 23). They can only "represent the traces and trajectories of collisions that happened a long time ago. They never describe war; they only tell us about its footprints on the map of our lives" (Winter 2013, 23). Whereas a novel or feature film would allow the visitor to dive imaginatively into a fictional world, in a museum, the visitor mainly remains safely in a visitor position. Museum buildings are not a natural environment for representing war. Visitors pay admission; they know they can come and leave at their leisure; they decide how much time to spend in the galleries; they make decisions concerning what texts, images, artifacts, and scenographic installations they actually pay attention to and choose how long they linger in certain exhibition sections. Consequently, the representational act of 'simulating' a specific historical scene or experience always pretends to act out an impossible illusion of 'imitating' the past. This never goes as far as Jean Baudrillard's postmodern thesis about the disappearance of the real or authentic in today's media age, wherein everything becomes a simulation (1994 [1981]).¹⁶ History museums can never reproduce historical experiences and atmospheres, which ensures that the visitor can only experience the 'original past' as a simulation, an illusion of a presence, or by assuming the museum stages an illusionary proximity to the past. The mimetic relationship to the past remains critical in any museum simulation of the Second World War.

---

15 Fulda reads the revised *Wehrmacht Exhibition* (2001–2004, renamed *Crimes of the German Wehrmacht: Dimensions of a War of Annihilation 1941–1944* = *Verbrechen der Wehrmacht. Dimensionen des Vernichtungskrieges 1941–1944*) as still lacking narrative, since it did not offer insight into a continuous sequence of events, but he interprets its deep structure as narrative "since it contextualizes at every turn" (2005, 188).
16 For a detailed summary of the rhetorical concept of 'simulation' (*simulatio*) from antiquity to its postmodern understanding, see Dotzler 2010 [2003].

As discussed above,[17] visitors can be temporarily overpowered by media and forget that they are experiencing a simulated historical scene as a virtual reality. They imagine the historical scene and suspend their reflective judgments. This helps us to understand Alison Landsberg's concept of 'prosthetic memory,' which implies that mass media such as film and experiential museums can create sensuous, bodily memories that do not come from lived experience, but from engagement with mediated representations (2004).[18] In Landsberg's theory, there is clearly a mimetic connection to the past that allows visitors to experience secondary memories. For example, Landsberg argues that in the United States Holocaust Memorial Museum, visitors, realizing that they are walking on actual cobble stones from the Warsaw Ghetto, are enabled to forget the distinction between safe museum space and their own bodily reaction – connecting them empathetically to history (2004, 132). Even authentic objects from the past, observed from a distance, draw visitors through "their very materiality [...], their seductive tangibility" into a "lived relationship with them" (Landsberg 2004, 132). The concept of simulation helps to understand Landsberg's concept in a wider context; there is no need for mimetic equivalency, but the resemblance of present and past with a "seductive tangibility" allows – in Landsberg's case – for forms of secondary witnessing of past traumas.

When representing war and atrocities, the representation of trauma works as a powerful example to further understand the difference between primary and secondary experientiality. Can a visitor really empathize with the trauma and anxiety of historical groups? How can the presumably 'safe' museum relate to the realness of trauma that exists beyond representation through a historiographical and objectifying narrative, without taking "the trauma out of trauma?" (LaCapra 2016, 377). Dominick LaCapra argues that structural trauma can express transhistorical absence and is an anxiety-producing condition of possibility (2001: 84–85; see for trauma in the war museum also Jaeger 2017c, 146–147). To circumvent postmodernist skepticism, trauma must be viewed as "existing outside conventional forms of perception, representation and transmission," with the Holocaust in particular as the central traumatic event in the twentieth century and "the last example[] of the 'real'" (Arnold-de Simine 2013, 35). LaCapra identifies two secondary experiences of trauma: vicarious and virtual experiences (2004: 125). Vicarious experiences can lead to confusing one's participation in the traumatizing events through identification with the victim, whereby one

---

[17] See also chapter 1.3.
[18] See also Bedford 2014 for practical techniques to evoke and imagine the past through stories, aesthetic experience, immersive environments, and unique artifacts for the museum visitor.

becomes a surrogate victim. In the museum context, this is most likely to occur at authentic places of historical, traumatic events, such as a memorial site at a Nazi concentration camp. However, as demonstrated, for example, by Julia Rose's concept of Commemorative Museum Pedagogy for representing difficult knowledge in museums, such surrogate victimhood is to be avoided through the development of ethical standards of representation (2016, especially 99–134). In LaCapra's concept of the virtual experience of trauma, one may imaginatively put oneself in the victim's position, while respecting the difference between self and other and recognizing that one cannot take the victim's place or speak in the victim's voice: "Such virtual experience may be connected with what I have termed empathetic unsettlement, which, I would argue, is desirable or even necessary for a certain form of understanding that is constitutively limited but significant" (LaCapra 2004, 125). LaCapra sees empathetic unsettlement as "a barrier to closure in discourse" that creates a certain discomfort in 'inhabiting' the experiences of others (2001, 41).

The challenge in simulating history in the museum is to understand whether, or to what degree, a given museum representation pretends to simulate possible realistic perspectives that historical people in the past could have had, or whether the simulation relates to structures that do not have a direct equivalent in the past but contribute to the understanding of past structures and atmospheres or memory patterns at a later stage. This leads to an understanding of primary and secondary experientiality on a sliding scale. In all of their forms, primary and secondary experientiality are simulations; both pretend, in different ways, to bring the visitor close to the past. Visitors are – presumably – aware that they are not experiencing the past as historical contemporaries experienced it; yet museum techniques can help to simulate historical experience and create experientiality with the effect that the visitor understands and possibly feels how an individual or collective human consciousness might have perceived and experienced the past. Primary experientiality in a museum can therefore be defined as a simulation of actual historical events or of historical situations that demonstrates how members of a group could have experienced the past as such. It includes forms of empathy and reenactment that claim to mimetically bring the visitor close to historical experiences.

In contrast, secondary experientiality produces the effect of a collective historical experience without any equivalent that could be mimetically approached in the past; it is a simulation of abstract structures. Before I provide a range of examples for primary and secondary experientiality as well as hybrid forms that oscillate between both, it seems useful to provide one more detailed example. The 101st Airborne Museum Le Mess in Bastogne, features a basement shelter installation behind a steel door. The visitor finds a wooden stool and bench to sit on and experiences a 'live' air-raid, while watching a static diorama of a family, depicted through mannequins, hugging each other and apparently trying to survive the air-raid.[19] Visitors experience a combination of light, vibration, and sound effects; they seem to be joining the family in experiencing the raid in a small, almost claustrophobic space. The light is shaky and at times it is completely dark. One hears coughing, shouting, and crying. The museum does everything to make this experience mimetically close to the historical one many people might have had on Christmas night in 1944, when Bastogne was bombed by the Germans. The bodily effects that the exhibit elicits, such as hearing the extreme noise in a small space, certainly makes it an uncomfortable experience that might allow the visitor to shift in part from an observational perspective to an experiential one. The exhibition simulates a primary experience, i.e. it creates the effect of primary experientiality of how a collective could have experienced an air raid in the Second World War. There is a clear historical referent; it is also clear that, unlike in a fictional or autobiographical account, the installation does not refer to one specific experience by one character or person in an air raid shelter, but to the collective experience of all civilians in Bastogne.[20]

Exhibitions that follow a mimetic pattern of creating experientiality are often highly focused on the reconstruction of presumably authentic scenes, which is usually connected to the belief in the authenticity of original objects and carefully / accurately arranged uniforms and weapons. Most often, visitors see dioramas with mannequins arranged into a particular war scene, which could either be a specific historical moment in war or a scene serving as example for a typical scene or activity in the war, such as a field hospital scene (see e.g. Jaeger

---

19 The museum praises itself as "a realistic authentic war museum" (http://www.101airbornemuseumbastogne.com/, accessed 13 October 2019). I visited the museum on July 4, 2014.
20 The Airborne Museum 'Hartenstein' in Oosterbeek near Arnhem, tells the story of the Battle of Arnhem as part of the Allied operation Marketgarden in September 1944. In 2009, on the sixty-fifth anniversary of the Battle of Arnhem, the museum opened the new *Airborne Experience* in its basement. The visitor walks through a number of dioramas and between large poster walls of the battle, supported by audio-visual means, including a mission briefing, and entering and exiting of a glider. Since the exhibition lacks narrative features that enhance the perspective of the visitor as a young British parachutist, the potential for primary experientiality is limited. This means that the installation remains static and the visitor a passive observer. During a visit in August 2019, most visitors were moving quickly through the different scenes, without engaging with the potential experiential perspectives that the *Airborne Experience* wants to create: "The underground Airborne Experience showcases the war in all its intensity. Here you will feel the impact of the violence on the young boys who were desperately fighting for their lives" (https://www.airbornemuseum.nl/en/exhibitions/airborne-experience, accessed 13 October 2019).

2017b, 167–168). This representational technique remains mostly static; the visitor is a passive observer. On the one hand, such representations are typical of older museum exhibitions that predate the digital age. On the other, they are typical of collector museums up to today (see also Jaeger 2019, 55–58). For example, the Overlord Museum in Normandy near Omaha Beach[21] is completely based on dioramas, although it only opened in June 2013. If the viewer is simply an observer of a diorama that pretends that a reconstructive view of history is possible, the scene is usually static and the visitor cannot therefore become directly part of it. Often, such reconstructive scenes are connected to the desire for authenticity, of being physically at a historically authentic space. This could be the case when a visitor enters the Imperial War Museum's Cabinet War Rooms (now Churchill War Rooms) in London, from where Churchill orchestrated British activities in the Second World War. There is nothing experiential here, except for the feeling of authenticity based the Cabinet War Rooms' function as an 'auratic' place in the mode of witnessing authenticity (Pirker and Rüdiger 2010, 17; Sabrow and Saupe 2016). How it is refurbished or reconstructed is probably of secondary interest to the primary feeling that one is standing in the 'real place.'

Whereas older exhibitions try to reconstruct historical scenes and spaces to allow the visitor to enter history, most museums today avoid this static form of immersion. The more dynamic the representation is, the more likely it is that its exhibitions produce experientiality. Astrid Erll and Ann Rigney differentiate accordingly, in their approach to mediation and remediation, between 'immediacy' that expresses the experience of the presence of the past and 'hypermediacy' that reminds the recipient of the medial and constructed character of the medium, potentially producing self-reflexivity (2009, 4). In all cases of immersion into history in the museum, the visitor will need a certain amount of imagination to connect past and present. For variations of primary experientiality, the visitor can be made fully aware of the artificiality of the setting and more emotionally steered toward a certain perspective that usually reproduces the collective gaze of a group. This often happens in theatrical settings, which allow the visitor to enter a scene designed through interior architecture, as can be seen in detail in the analysis of the Oskar Schindler Factory later in this study.[22] For example, visitors enter the staged Old Market Square of Kraków in 1944. They walk between transparent plexiglass panels, which are spread throughout the room and that tell different stories of historical people in Kraków representing typical groups and types from that era. The reduction of mannequins to transparent fig-

---

21 Visited on June 20, 2015.
22 See chapter 4.2.

ures in space is part of the negation of a simplistic mimetic model of experience and allows for the creation of a stronger primary experientiality (in which the visitor plays a role). Visitors can explicitly feel the distance between themselves and the historical place and time, creating a potential for reflection. This allows visitors to consider what they know about the historical persons represented in the exhibition and what they stand for. In contrast, the reconstruction of an allegedly correct or at least probable past might help the visitor to remember specific historical facts or scenes that model specific types of war activities, which makes it easier to understand the different elements of war. However, visitors in this case remain passive, observing constructed examples of the war, authenticated through the sheer mimesis of objects or by the authenticity of the space. This often confirms myths and stereotypical patterns of cultural memory. Immersing a visitor directly into a scene of the past is closer to a playful trick whose function is to attract higher visitor numbers via entertainment, rather than bringing them closer to experiencing the war and empathizing with real historical people. Consequently, such reconstructive approaches are unlikely to create primary or secondary experientiality for the visitor; they simply mirror the past without integrating visitors and do not require their imagination.

Secondary experientiality is produced if an exhibition creates structural experiences in which the museum visitor cannot simply empathize with the role of an individual as part of a historical collective. It constructs an experiential space that is clearly differentiated from a past reality as a construct of traces and forces of the past, which only comes into being in the poietic act of museum representation. There is no direct referent in the past if a museum simulates the effect of force, power, and violence in war, as will be analyzed in detail below for the Bundeswehr Military History Museum in Dresden.[23] If a museum stages the suffering of civilians in the Second World War, such as the Gdańsk Museum of the Second World War, secondary experientiality can be felt; however, no referent to 'the' experience of civilians or to 'the' experience of German behavior in the last days of the war exists.

Because primary experientiality is as simulated as secondary experientiality, I argue that almost all museums today construct their own simulated historical, poietic worlds (see also Jaeger 2011, 31–33)[24] and thereby their own experientiality, although they vary in their representational strategies. To understand these strategies, it is crucial to examine the varying degrees of primary and secondary

---

23 See chapter 5.1.
24 See also Jaeger 2011, 44–46 for initial thoughts on the poietic character of exhibitions by example of the Oskar Schindler Factory.

experientiality. Examples of these strategical variations include historical distance between visitor and museum content, focus on individual voices and collective perspectives, and use of narrative and scenography. A museum can expand the notion of time and space, which leads to a dynamic relationship between history and memory and additionally involves visitors in terms of their future behavior through different emotional, moral, reflexive, and pedagogical dimensions. However, the concept of experientiality allows for the development of a theoretical framework to understand the possibilities contemporary museums hold for mediating war as well as how they generate aesthetic and emotional responses. Experientiality and the simulation of historical atmospheres can be created at authentic battleground locations and in more abstract museum contexts separated from concrete historical events.

It is also evident that the differentiation of primary and secondary experientiality must be discussed on a sliding scale. There is secondary experientiality that is explicitly based on a composite of primary experiences; consequently, empathy and reenactment can also be significant museum techniques to simulate collective perspectives, as exemplified in the Imperial War Museum North, in which voices of children's experiences of different wars create new structural experiences for the visitor. Additionally, there is secondary experientiality when a museum simulates historical structures that can only become experiential when reproduced in historical representation, such as in "The Economy of War in World War II" cabinet on the German armament industry and economy of the Second World War in the Bundeswehr Military History Museum. The cabinet does not merely document the links between the economy, war, and Holocaust; rather, it makes them present, so that the visitor has no doubt about the historical complicity of German society and industry in the Holocaust and the interwovenness of the war effort and Holocaust. The cabinet also contributes to the visitor's general understanding of war and atrocity by letting them experience the interwovenness of the different components that allow war to happen and which sustain it (see also Jaeger 2015b, 238).

The category of experientiality allows us to dissolve this extreme dichotomy between experiential and object-based history museums. It makes it possible to more precisely analyze whether a museum is historical or present- and future-oriented. The four core theoretical elements of this study – restricted experientiality, primary experientiality, secondary experientiality, and transnational memory – do not automatically define which representational techniques a museum, which follows a certain tradition or has a certain political agenda in memory politics, chooses. Therefore, the House of European History might use similar strategies to the Warsaw Rising Museum, the Imperial War Museum North, and the Bundeswehr Military History Museum. However, once one distinguishes between primary and secondary experientiality, it is possible to analyze numerous museum techniques that create experientiality and that do not fall in the trap of the naive mimetic experience model. Instead, exhibitions can perform experientiality in nuanced ways between representing historical knowledge, using the authenticity of artifacts and locations, constructing individual and collective experiences, simulating historical structures, and emotionalizing the visitor on different levels.

To create experientiality, an exhibition must go beyond simply presenting facts and objects. If the historical context is strongly restrictive, this leads the visitor to read every theme within a prescribed narrative or ideological frame. This, in turn, strongly reduces the possibility of integrating the visitors' present perspectives and providing room for their affective, ideological/ethical, and cognitive capacities. The less the visitor is steered toward one ideological or ethical message, and the more that a museum uses networking techniques and creates traces, tensions, and open constellations, the more likely it is that an exhibition will develop the potential for experientiality. The museum must ensure that it provides the basis for clusters and constellations. It needs to go beyond a pre-determined linear path and – at least in addition to a linear structure – set up thematic and historical clustering throughout its exhibition.

Such networking techniques can be philosophically connected to models of time that highlight simultaneity. From a modernist, progressive perspective, Reinhart Koselleck argues in *Futures Past*, that under the condition of accelerating temporality in modernity, the "space of experience" and the "horizon of expectation" redouble "past and future on one another in an unequal manner" (2004 [1979], 263). Applying Koselleck's metaphor of "sediments of time" (2018 [2000])[25] to twenty-first-century museums, in particular to the Ruhr Museum in Essen, Kerstin Barndt demonstrates how museums today can represent the multi-temporal dimensions of time, a kind of "synchronous multitemporality that relies on a dialectical relation between historical events and anthropologically grounded, repetitive structures" (2010, 138). Wulf Kansteiner has employed the metaphor of a "chronosophic net" that does not operate in a chronological or linear way, but rather multidimensionally, so that Holocaust narratives can deal with their representational challenges between history and memory in the twenty-first century (2013, 23).[26] Although Hans-Ulrich Gumbrecht applies a postmodern temporal concept that seems to be the exact opposite of Koselleck's modernist progressive one, the results with regard to exhibiting the Second World War in

---

25 "Zeitschichten" in German.
26 See also chapter 7.

twenty-first-century museums are surprisingly similar. Gumbrecht argues for a new chronotype, a "broad present" (Gumbrecht 2014). There is no entrance or exit to this ever increasing broad present. According to Gumbrecht, the chronotype is rooted in the immediate aftermath of the Second World War, but is only fully at work in the early twenty-first century (2013). Following Gumbrecht's model would negate the effort of many action and progress-oriented ideas museums, such as the Canadian Museum for Human Rights, or the action-related comparative sections of the United States Holocaust Memorial Museum. In contrast, to exhibit, represent, and narrate the Second World War, the difference is less relevant, since almost all museum exhibitions operate in the constant dialogue between past and present – the latter personified through the museum visitor. If an exhibition develops an active dialogue between past and present, visitors are challenged to become part of the past. They do not enter a 'museum temple,' representing a past that is explicitly kept distant from them. Instead, this process then integrates past and present, memory and history, and exhibitions can develop simultaneities and numerous temporal layers. Visitors who find and interpret such constellations and simultaneities that create the exhibition's experientiality must – to a certain extent – decide for themselves whether these constellations indicate a cultural-historical development and perhaps even progress (Koselleck), or an endless cycle with no substantial change (Gumbrecht).

One example of a temporalized cluster in the museum is the cluster of 'humiliating otherness' in the permanent exhibition of the Topography of Terror in Berlin, analyzed below.[27] The documentation center creates numerous systemic networking effects through clustering and the visualization of aspects such as the spectatorship of crimes, scenes of denunciation, scenes of deportation, and mass scenes in general, that allow a dynamic re-arranging of chapters of the museum by the potential visitor. Similarly, the Imperial War Museum North in Manchester mainly depicts historical topics, yet certain themes such as children and war, or the civil war experience, are interwoven in all dimensions of its permanent exhibition, so that they receive a structural, secondary quality.[28] Networking can happen with thematic concepts, such as war and suffering and with historical themes, such as aerial warfare in the Second World War or the Holocaust. The visitor can find – possibly encouraged through hints by the museum – other paths and constellations. On the one hand, museums can challenge an active visitor to interpret the material instead of passively

---

27 See chapter 5.3.
28 See chapter 5.2.

perceiving it. On the other, they must provide the visitor with enough historical context so that different readings are actually possible. If, for example, the visitor merely sees images of suffering that seem similar, an exhibition lacks the historical specificity for the visitor to make connections between them. The visitor might just take away a general message of the universality of suffering. In other words, a networking technique that balances thematic and conceptual issues with historical specificity is more likely to develop experientiality.

To further understand the variations of representational techniques that create or restrict experientiality and to see details of the variations of the sliding scale between primary and secondary experientiality, a close reading of the semiotic, narrative, and aesthetic performances of time and space that an exhibition can offer the visitor is needed. I examine the variety of temporalized acts in the museum that create or reflect cultural memory of the Second World War in the medium of the historical museum, with a focus on the following theoretical concepts that structure my analysis of the twelve museums under study in chapters three to six: restricted experientiality, primary experientiality, secondary experientiality, and the transnational.

Chapter 3:
Restricted Experientiality

Experientiality plays less of a role if the visitor is primarily a passive observer. To create experientiality, a museum must allow the visitor to act as mediating consciousness within the semiotic space of the museum. Experientiality is especially restricted when visitors see all of a museum's individual objects and voices as part of a greater master narrative or argumentative framework, whether provided by the museum's main mission statement or constantly reinforced through specific exhibition techniques. As discussed above, we can differentiate between restricted experientiality (when museums do not leave visitors room to mediate between museum space and history), primary experientiality (where visitors are placed in a position to experience collective perspectives from the past; there is a mimetic relationship between museum simulations and past experiences), and secondary experientiality (in which visitors can have structural experiences of the past that do not have predecessors in an actual historical world, but instead simulate historical structures). Most exhibitions have components of all three forms of experientiality.

Visitors are doubtless deeply impacted by their previous knowledge, and there is no easy way – barring a substantial, empirical visitor survey – to speculate about what knowledge they have upon entering an exhibition about the Second World War. John H. Falk (2009, 58–65, 81–82) has argued that exhibitions often primarily reinforce the visitor's pre-existing knowledge, rather than completely reshaping their views. If a museum on the Second World War puts forward a very clear message about national identity, it follows that such a strategy uses existing master narratives and myths to reinforce an existing cultural memory among its main (most often national) audience. In this way, the museum takes on the task of forming national identity via the promotion of cultural memory. This task can be accompanied by strong commemorative functions, with regard to either heroes or victims, and can intersect with different historical truth-claims. These can function as historiographical truth-claims, authenticated through historical research. They can also be established through the use of emotional and aesthetic representative techniques that give the visitor the impression of factuality.

This chapter demonstrates how three Second World War museums and exhibitions restrict their potential experientiality through the establishment of master narratives and the reinforcement of existing memory patterns. The Canadian War Museum – a hybrid of a history museum, aiming for historical objectivity and a commemorative memorial museum – establishes a strong linear national

---

OpenAccess. © 2020 Stephan Jaeger, published by De Gruyter. [CC BY-NC-ND] This work is licensed under the Creative Commons Attribution-NonCommercial-NoDerivatives 4.0 License.
https://doi.org/10.1515/9783110664416-007

master narrative that builds Canadian national identity through war. The Warsaw Rising Museum, a hybrid of a memorial, narrative history, and experiential museum, establishes a factual narrative of a specific historical event and its significance for national collective memory; the museum reinforces this by using emotional means to steer the visitor toward its represented version of historical truth. On the one hand, the Imperial War Museum in London, particularly in its permanent exhibition *A Family in Wartime* (that closed in January 2019), simulated the collective British experience of war on the home front; on the other hand, visitors had no opportunity to actively use their consciousness to mediate and diversify the collective experience that it presents. Consequently, the exhibition primarily reaffirmed existing cultural memory and restricted experientiality by enabling the visitor to empathize with a historical collective, instead of allowing for the development of primary experientiality.

3.1 The Canadian War Museum in Ottawa

The Canadian War Museum (CWM) in Ottawa re-opened in a new building designed by Raymond Moriyama on May 8, 2005. The design of the bunker-like building is based on the theme of regeneration: "By fully integrating this theme into the building and landscape architecture through energy-efficient features, the use of recycled materials and a green roof, the museum recognizes the harsh reality of war, yet offers hope that, like the regenerating landscape, Canadians will inherit a future free from conflict."[1] Although the CWM was officially founded in 1942, the roots of this national, publicly funded museum can be traced back to a national collection of military artifacts that have been in the possession of the Canadian federal government since 1880. Today the CWM is part of the Canadian Museum of History Corporation and is attended by about 500.000 visitors a year (Canadian War Museum 2016). It is located on LeBreton Flats, west of Parliament Hill. The Peace Tower of the central parliament building forms an axis with the museum, indicating the interwovenness of memorial culture within the city of Ottawa and the CWM (see also Greenberg 2008). In the years before its opening, the proposed museum generated a number of public controversies, especially regarding the role of the Holocaust in the museum and the depiction of the Air War in Europe.[2]

---

[1] https://www.warmuseum.ca/about/building-features/#tabs, accessed 13 October 2019. See also Moriyama 2006.
[2] See chapters 7 and 8 where these debates will be discussed in detail.

In its 2005 permanent exhibition,[3] the CWM presents the Second World War as a national Canadian endeavor: "The Museum's exhibition galleries and public programs have been designed to emphasize the human experience of war. The Canadian Experience Galleries present the military history of Canada from earliest times to present day and Canada's history of honoring and remembrance. Each gallery highlights defining moments in Canada's military history and the ways in which past events have shaped the nation" (Canadian War Museum 2019).[4] The museum functions as a hybrid of military history and memorial museum, which – in its twenty-first-century version – is strongly shaped by its narrative structure. As a military history museum, it aims for historical objectivity by choosing a partially distant, documentary approach in its depiction of themes, images, and artifacts. As a memorial museum, the CWM mainly holds the potential for primary experientiality by simulating the collective perspectives of Canadian soldiers and, to a lesser extent, Canadians on the home front. The master narrative toward national unity "forged out of diversity" (Rukszto 2008, 751), however, reduces this experientiality. It also steers the Second World War gallery away from creating empathy with Canadian collectives and instead toward causally linking the war with nationhood and national identity.[5] There is constant tension between the goal of historical objectivity and the memory narrative promoting national identity (Ives 2012, 120).

In accordance with its mandate, the CWM exclusively exhibits the war from a Canadian perspective, progressing chronologically in the four "Canadian Experience Galleries," comprising 5,028 square meters.[6] The museum developed the concept of four intertwined principles, each one of which becomes a leading principle in one of the four galleries. Gallery 1 is shaped by geography (conflicts

---

3 For a full genesis of the new museum, the debates about its location, and the public debates around the museum see Hillmer 2010.
4 https://www.warmuseum.ca/about/about-the-museum/#tabs, accessed 13 October 2019.
5 Rukszto (2008, 749) emphasizes the didactic and often moralizing style of the linear master narrative of the exhibition: "Its pedagogy is much more teacherly, offering lessons that are meant to connect the visitor to the past and the future, and to others as members of a national community. This strategic pedagogy is 'moralizing': the images of destruction and death, sacrifice and survival, rebirth and democracy provide lessons in the past so that the future will not be the same, to ensure that it will be better."
6 See the construction fast fact-sheet (Canadian War Museum 2015). The four galleries are supplemented by a Memory Hall that functions as a symbolic chapel to commemorate the fallen, the Regeneration Hall, the Royal Canadian Legion Hall of Honour, displaying the ways of heroically commemorating the deeds of soldiers in all Canadian wars, and the LeBreton Gallery displaying large military equipment. Additionally, the CWM features corridors with a collection of large Canadian war paintings and space for special exhibitions.

around rivers, streams, water);[7] gallery 2 by brutality (the dreadfulness of war); gallery 3 on the Second World War by politics (a national and 'almost' just war); and the post-war gallery that ends in the present is shaped by survival (the nuclear war in the public eye).[8] The key concepts are also introduced to the visitor through conceptual phrases on the walls of the opening rotunda preceding the four galleries. Among these are the conceptual pairs of fear and courage, sacrifice and survival, and brutality and humanity. The beginning of the first gallery defines war as "organized, armed conflict," and states that: "Virtually every human society, past and present, makes war." The introductory wall panel expresses that "war has shaped Canada and Canadians for at least 5,000 years," before showing the material roots of war on the geographical territory that constitutes Canada today. In this way, war becomes an anthropological identifier for the emergence of Canadian society and civilization.

At the end of the second gallery "For Crown and Country: The South African and First World Wars, 1885–1931," the visitor reads and hears, on the one hand, about the heavy losses sustained and Canadian grief. On the other hand, the CWM presents a large panel with an image of the Peace Tower of the Canadian Parliament building entitled "An Unfinished Country." The panel text reads: "Canada emerged from the war proud and victorious, and with a new standing in the world. It was also a grieving and divided country." The motive of independence – the Canadians signing the Treaty of Versailles independently from Britain in 1919 and gaining formal independence by 1931 – frames this national master narrative. Implicitly, war is the CWM's medium for Canadian national identity, sovereignty, and the collective feeling of becoming a nation (see also Ives 2012, 124). In this master narrative, the Second World War is necessary for the completion of the Canadian nation. Consequently, the third gallery of the museum entitled "Forged in Fire: The Second World War, 1931–1945"[9] is introduced

---

[7] For a detailed analysis of the memory strategies used to express the development toward national identity in this gallery see Ives 2012, 126–131. Ives argues that the idea of the national narrative out of conflict of is presented "through the eyes of the dominant English-speaking majority" (131): "If war is ultimately about victory and defeat, the War Museum is about how in Canada the winners have tried to integrate the losers, entwining them as one strand in a *national narrative*, swallowing them whole and then asking them to reflect on their place in a wider story" (126).
[8] I am grateful to Dean Oliver, current Director Research at the Canadian Museum of History and former Director of Research and Exhibitions for explaining the original concept of the CWM to me, in a meeting on June 3, 2015. However, all analysis of the exhibition concept is my own.
[9] I am grateful to Jeff Noakes, current curator for the Second World War gallery for his detailed explanation on the curatorial decisions in a personal guided tour on 29 May 2015.

Fig. 4 Opening section of gallery "Forged in Fire: The Second World War, 1931–1945." Permanent exhibition. Canadian War Museum, Ottawa (Photo: Author, 2015, courtesy of Canadian War Museum).

through a synopsis sentence: "Canada's fight against dictatorships overseas transformed the country and its place in the world." In the last section, visitors encounter a large panel entitled "A Nation Transformed," picking up on the theme of the "unfinished" nation from the second gallery. The panel text reads: "The Second World War was a massive national enterprise, and Canada emerged from the conflict as an economic and international power – united, self-confident, prosperous, and determined to make a difference in the world."[10] The gallery develops chronologically. At the beginning, the exhibition presents the political situation in Canada and marks the emergence of dictatorships in Germany, Italy, and Japan through flags and video footage installations hanging from the ceiling (see fig. 4). The artifact of a Mercedes Benz limousine,

---

[10] This allows Canadian peacekeeping efforts to be highlighted in the fourth gallery "A Violent Peace: The Cold War, Peacekeeping, and Recent Conflicts – 1945 to the Present."

which Hitler used as parade car, entitled "Hitler's Car: A Symbol of Evil"[11] serves as focal point for the visitor and emotionally prepares them for the moral need for a just war (see also Matthews 2013, 279). After this, the exhibition touches on air force training in Canada, threats to Canada by sea, and home front efforts during the war, before following Canadian troops through various wartime engagements: these include Dieppe, the Air War in Europe, the Italian Campaign, D-Day, the liberation of the Netherlands, and the last battles on Germany territory. It closes with the discovery of the concentration camps and homecoming after the war. A minor strand highlights the Canadian involvement in the Pacific, the loss in the Battle of Hong Kong in December 1941, and the history and liberation of Canadian prisoners of war from Japanese internment camps.

The national master narrative of the gallery imparts the message that Canada became an independent and confident nation through war, with the Second World War marking the completion of the process of national independence on the international stage. Consequently, the CWM reflects on the Second World War by exclusively presenting Canadian issues and a Canadian collective perspective. This highlights the political situation in Canada, the home front, and the collective gaze of the Canadian soldiers in a manner similar to the American National World War Two Museum in New Orleans.[12] Unlike the New Orleans WWII Museum, the CWM only briefly addresses other wartime events. At the beginning, the visitor encounters a brief info panel on the German attack on Poland to mark the beginning of the war, supported by an iconic image taken during the Warsaw Siege.[13] In the second section "The Canadian Response," a similar panel briefly describes the Blitzkrieg in a short paragraph; later on in the same section, Dunkirk and the Battle of Britain receive similar brief texts and image panels, which are all centered on understanding the Canadian reaction to these events and the decision to engage internationally. From this point in the museum onwards, the

---

11 See Matthews (2013, 278–282) for the curatorial context of the car. Matthews reflects on the different possible reactions of visitors to the authenticity of the artifact through the frame of war trophies and notes that the "curatorial choices speak of the desire to evoke a particular historical narrative by inviting the projection of phantasy" (279), invoking the aura of Hitler, and through the trophy, the defeat of the Nazis by the Allies.

12 See also chapter 4.1.

13 The CWM does not give exact credits for many of its enlarged wall posters, so that the emotional effect of civilian suffering dominates. This is indicative of a certain style of museums, especially in the Anglophone world, that champions the emotional effect of images over documentation. Newer exhibitions from the last decade, however, usually indicate the source (see also Hawig 2019, 77–80). Another large difference between treating an image as a source vs. for emotionalization, that must be reflected on in all museums in this study, is whether photographs are used in varying sizes and/or enlarged to poster size.

war becomes fully Canadian. Whereas the last rooms in the previous section on the First World War come close to giving the impression that Canada won the war on its own, the effect of the Second World War exhibition is slightly less nationally focused. This is due to the fact that many Canadian actions – as found in the weapon exhibits in the D-Day section – are presented as Allied actions with a Canadian focus. As a result of this Canadian focus, the war in the East is mentioned exactly once, in "The Air War" section on the panel "No. 6 Bomber Group (RCAF) and Its Targets," which states:

> From 1943, most Canadian bomber squadrons in Britain were combined into the all-Canadian No. 6 Group of the RAF's Bomber Command. In conjunction with the Soviet Union's epic struggle in the East, the escalating air offensive in the West opened a 'second front' against Hitler's Germany, proving to many Allied civilians and military personnel that the war was being carried to the enemy.

The visitor learns nothing about "the Soviet Union's epic struggle in the East" or about the German policies of conducting a criminal war in the East. Consequently, the visitor is left to understand the expression 'dictatorships of evil' established at the beginning of the Second World War gallery. The museum's narrative assumes that the visitor already understands the justness of the war, allowing it to focus on a military, nation-based narrative of winning the war for the good of humanity.

Analyzing the CWM's "The Air War" section as well as the public debate surrounding its earlier depiction of Bomber command prior to the museum's opening, can help us understand how the museum's master narrative influences its ability to create experientiality for its visitors. To the right of the section's entry gate, the visitor finds two large info panels with four texts explaining the role of the Air War in the overall war effort, the objectives and successes of the Bomber Command, and the Canadian losses suffered. These panels highlight the disproportionally high Canadian contribution to Bomber Command; the reader cannot doubt that the bombing campaign was costly, effective, and successful, as reflected in the header of the main info panel: "Bombing to Win." Throughout, the section takes an aerial perspective. For example, next to a large screen playing footage of air bombings from above, there is a war painting entitled "Air Raid on San Guisto, Pisa," painted by Flight Lieutenant Johann Alexander Goranson in 1947. Painted with mainly red, orange, and yellow, it illustrates a Canadian air raid on a German airfield in September 1943. The apocalyptic image is illustrated from the vantage point of a plane trailing behind those depicted in the painting. Theoretically, museum visitors could empathize with whoever is out of sight on the ground. However, since they have just read about the strategic necessity of the Air War for the destruction of German

Fig. 5 "The Air War" section with subsections "Terror from Below" and "Bomber Command" in background, gallery "The Second World War: 1931–1945." Permanent exhibition. Canadian War Museum, Ottawa (Photo: Author, 2015, courtesy of Canadian War Museum).

infrastructure, it seems much more likely that this painting will enhance the museum's narrative of the war as just and necessary. The interpretive possibilities this painting holds are diminished, as it is instead positioned to serve as evidence for the narrative argument made by the Second World War gallery.

Another example of how the "Air War" section steers the visitor to exclusively reflect on the Canadian perspective can be found toward the left of the entrance in the subsection "Terror from Below" (see fig. 5). This subsection focuses on how Canadian aircrews encountered German aircraft defense systems and is anchored by the artifact of a German anti-aircraft gun. Two enlarged posters of firing anti-aircraft gun batteries in front of a 188 millimeter flak anti-aircraft gun shape the atmosphere of the exhibit, supplemented by the mannequin of a German anti-aircraft gunner. Illustrated especially in the poster on the left, the flak produces orange clouds that indicate the intimidating and destructive effect it holds. In front of the flak is a damaged wheel of a Halifax bomber. The caption explicitly points out that this object serves as "testament to the effectiveness of German anti-aircraft defences." Showcases in front of the scene display letters discussing the deaths of Canadian airmen, medals commemorating their achievements, and, in particular, the case of George Chequer who died in a bombing attack on Berlin on January 30, 1944. The CWM displays Chequer's final letters to his parents, official documents informing his parents that their son was missing in action, and Chequer's service medals. The header of the subsection, "Terror from Below," subverts the traditional phrase used to describe aerial warfare as 'terror from above.' In this way, the museum creates the impression that the main threat in the Air War came from the defenders and not from the attackers on the offensive. There is of course no doubt that the life expectancy for bomber crews was considerably lower than in other service branches, resulting a high element of risk and fear – however, the CWM avoids any other perspective. Indeed, through the indirect effects it has on the visitor, the museum implies that the suffering and dangers faced by Canadian aircrews were at least comparable to the suffering of civilians on the ground.

A small wall display – about one third of the size of the two air defense posters – can be found on the left wall following the "Terror from Below" subsection (see fig. 5). This display deals with the Air War's effects on the ground. The original text of this panel created one of the biggest public controversies in Canadian museum history, resulting in the CWM eventually softening and lengthening the original text (Bothwell et al. 2008; Dean 2009). The visitor sees a large image of a destroyed German city, with three smaller photographs. The first depicts corpses of civilians; the second, a destroyed train station in Münster, citing the effect of collateral damage; and the third shows an image of Cologne in ruins in May 1942, relating to the first thousand-bomber attack in history.[14] The extensively revised text of approximately 200 words describes the efficiency, development, purpose, and public support of the Allied strategic bombing campaign. Describing the end of the campaign's first half, the panel confidently states: "The attacks blunted Germany's economic and military potential, and drew scarce resources into air defense, damage repair, and the protection of critical industries." The second and final paragraph ends as follows: "Industrial output fell substantially, but not until late in the war. The effectiveness and the morality of bombing heavily-populated areas in war continue to be debated." Thus, the revised text allows the visitor a minor opening that brings up small doubts about the effectiveness of the early campaign and possibly triggers reflection on the strategic bombing of civilians in war. On the whole, however, the visitor is fully immersed in the Cana-

---

14 The photographs remain unchanged after the controversy. The CWM's tendency to make the whole Allied war effort, or even the whole war, centered on Canada, can be seen in the formulation of the caption: "an air-attack by more than 1,000 Canadian and Allied bombers." Of course the majority of bombers used in the attack were not Canadian.

dian perspective, justifying the strategic effects of the Air War. Only one image displays civilian casualties – without any indication of specific historical context – making it so that the visitor cannot experience or understand the perspective from below. One of the most complex themes of the war is therefore simplified to fit within the structure of the national master narrative depicting heroic, sacrificial, and morally justified deeds necessary to save the world. This allows the CWM to tell a mostly unambiguous story of Canadian identity. Primary experientiality is reduced to a narrative argument and it is almost impossible to understand the Canadian war effort in relation to the war's larger picture.

Lastly, it is useful to consider the bomber campaign controversy (Bothwell et al. 2008; Dean 2009, 2013, 332–333) and look at the concrete changes the CWM had to enact in order to appease war veteran interest groups. The original text reads:

> Mass bomber raids against Germany resulted in vast destruction and heavy loss of life. The value and morality of the strategic bomber offensive against Germany remains bitterly contested. The Bomber Command's aim was to crush civilian morale and force Germany to surrender by destroying its cities and industrial installations. Although Bomber Command and American attacks left 600,000 Germans dead, and more than five million homeless, the raids resulted in only small reductions in German war production until late in the war. (see Dean 2009, 4; Bothwell et al. 2008, 376–387)

As in the Japanese-Canadian relocation story discussed below, the original text panel diverged from the national master narrative and allowed for debate – to a certain extent – under the header "An Enduring Controversy." At the same time, even the original text read in isolation risks closing itself to interpretation due to the fact that it depicts the raids as a failure. Of course, if one considers the rest of the gallery, an implicit tension would have arisen, since the positive and necessary purpose of the campaign is described and alluded to in all other text panels and subsections. Furthermore, the original display included three quotations, which would have demonstrated openness and varying viewpoints that were later eliminated as a result of the controversy. The first one was by Air Officer Commander-in-Chief of the Bomber Command Arthur Harris, insisting upon the vital contribution of the campaign in bringing the war to an end; the second quotation was by the liberal public intellectual John Kenneth Galbraith, stating "that while the bombing campaign did not win the war, it helped the ground troops who did" (Dean 2009, 4); The third quotation was from the Canadian airman Flight Lieutenant W.E. Vaughan, who reflected on the consequences of his actions: "more than once I wondered 'how many people will those bombs kill?' However, you couldn't dwell on it. That's the way war is'" (Dean 2009, 4).

What detailed historical critiques like the one from Robert Bothwell, Randall Hansen, and Margaret MacMillan (2008) do not take into account, is that the CWM could have employed war veterans' interpretations of their mission as an opportunity to diversify its narrative. The perspectives of veterans could have been added to the quotations already present, diversifying these voices without making moral judgments about historical truth. These quotations may not have contained confirmed historical knowledge, however, diverse perspectives are crucial in understanding how the Air War is part of Canadian cultural memory. If this had been done, the visitor – who is in no position to decide what the factual impact of the bombings really was – could have understood the dilemma of the controversy. Multiple perspectives within Canadian memory among the Canadian public, veterans, and scholars, would have allowed for the potential of primary experientiality, instead of the continued repetition of a single argument. This could have revealed why, from the perspective convinced of the moral prerogative of a just war, targeting civilians could have appeared to be a justified strategy. Additionally, it could have explained from the perspective of a Canadian member of Bomber Command why they carried out the same heroic, sacrificial job as anybody else in the Allied Forces. At the same time, the visitors would have still been able to see a moral issue that could be answered in various ways, and they might have been uncomfortable with the idea of strategic bombing, which would have been portrayed as at least factually controversial in terms of whether it was necessary and/or shortened the war. This would have also played an important role in helping visitors understand what the Second World War actually means for Canadians, both during the war and in its remembrance since then.

Museums mostly shy away from reflecting on public controversies surrounding their own exhibitions but in an altered display, the very root of the controversy could have been a successful topic for the exhibition. The CWM could have even created a more structural, secondary experientiality, since visitors would have had the opportunity to understand how cultural memory is constructed on a meta-level. However, if one integrates the remainder of the gallery, it becomes clear that its narrative emphasizes Canadian soldiers' hardship, sacrifice, and endurance in a just war (see also Dean 2009, 6). The overall style of the Second World War Gallery is clearly geared toward closure rather than openness. The CWM employs the technique of avoiding open voices that could be read outside of its master narrative, while still insisting on factual historiographical statements. This ironically led to public controversy in one of the few instances where they allowed for openness, or at least a perspective that diverged from the national master narrative. Shifting the display from historical truth and toward cultural memory and diverse perspectives would have opened the display to experientiality and might have avoided – or at least defused – the controversy.

An enlarged handwritten poem entitled *High Flight* by pilot officer John Gillespie Magee Jr. at the end of the "Air War" section can serve as final example for the section's one-sidedness. It celebrates flying and its thrills as modeled on human dreams, and it could have come straight from the myth of Icarus: "Oh! I have slipped the surly bounds of earth / And danced the skies on laughter-silvered wings. / Sunward I've climbed [...]. Where never lark, or even eagle flew / And while with silent lifting mind, I've trod / The high untrespassed sanctity of space / Put out my hand and touched the face of God." The museum's caption describes the success of the poem in capturing "the thrill and awe of flying." The American pilot serving in the RCAF (Royal Canadian Air Force) sent it to his parents several months before being killed in a flight accident. Ending the "Air War" section on this note corresponds to the heroic commemoration of individuals that is part of the "Terror from Below" subsection. It displays how the aerial warfare conquers nature, and the religious words at the end of the poem – "sanctity" and the "face of God" – give the exhibit the feeling that the possible death of the pilot is linked to an almost holy mission. The CWM could have easily contrasted such a poem with a description how the Air War is perceived, namely its tension between the sublimity of the lights in the sky and fear and terror on the ground. Or if that was not possible because of the influence of veterans on public opinion, it could have at least added voices of Canadian airmen who knew about the effects of their mission and expressed doubts about the destruction they wrought on the ground. Even if the CWM remains solely focused on a Canadian collective perspective,[15] it could have diversified the Canadian voices it uses. In doing so, it could have created experientiality, instead of merely purporting a prescribed narrative argument.

There are a few examples where the CWM diversifies its represented perspectives, often in regard to Canadian experiences that have been critically discussed from a contemporary human rights perspective.[16] This can be seen in the museum's representation of Japanese-Canadian wartime internment.[17] Under the

---

15 "The Canadian Experience" subsection is a good example for showing how the CWM overemphasizes the national angle. Except for the information that approximately 25% of all Canadians who died during the Second World War were from the Bomber Command, there is nothing Canadian in the Canadian experience. The risk of the bombing missions, of parachuting and being captured by the enemy would be exactly the same for a British or American crew-member.
16 Another example is the controversy about conscription and fighting overseas briefly indicated in the second section of the gallery. Though there is no evaluation of which position is superior, the opponents of conscription and military engagement overseas quickly disappear in the moral prerogative as narrated.
17 See also in detail Jaeger 2017b, 151–153.

header "Forced Relocation," the visitor finds a two-dimensional poster and print exhibit that is divided into two columns. The visitor approaches the right hand side first. The main image is a photo of a truckload of people about to be relocated. The image is reminiscent of images of the transportation of cattle. Three newspaper title headers make clear that the demands for Japanese-Canadian internment come from different political parties, the government as a whole, and the people. The focus of the explanatory texts is racism and fear-mongering. A quotation by Japanese-Canadian Joy Kogawa reads: "The thousand little traumas of racism that were our little diet [sic]. Being despised. Being snubbed by white Canadians. Being portrayed in newspapers, as ugly, as unwanted, as deceitful, as somehow sub-human." The rest of the display presents five individual portraits, two of Japanese-Canadians in the Canadian military. This achieves an effect of contrast between the contributions of Japanese-Canadians to the war and to society and their ill treatment. Here the CWM diverts from its master narrative. It is the most open subsection in the Second World War gallery, since it allows the visitor to decide whether to compare the treatment of Japanese-Canadians to the Holocaust, or whether examples of Japanese-Canadian soldiers serving late in the war and the official Canadian apology in 1988 allow for reconciliation and closure. Because of this undecided tension allowing for secondary experientiality, the visitor can decide whether this is a historical case whose injustice has been overcome in the present, or whether Canadian society today continues to allow for similar injustices.

Unlike some of the objectives in the joint research strategy from 2013 (8) from the Canadian Museum of Civilization (in December 2013 renamed as Canadian Museum of History) and the CWM (Canadian Museum of Civilization and Canadian War Museum 2013), the focus of the current permanent exhibition is clearly restricted to military history and the Canadian perspective. The relevance of commemoration is not restricted to the three halls – the Hall of Honour, the Regeneration Hall, and the Memorial Hall – but impacts all exhibition galleries. Certainly, the museum's commemorative emphasis would enable it to present themes such as the Air War and the debate over the strategic bombing campaign in a hybrid format. Such a format could encapsulate both factual descriptions, such as how the Air War contributed to victory in the Second World War, and various questions and perceptions about these themes. Furthermore, if the exhibition were to be diversified at times with a more international gaze, it could supplement the visitor's understanding of specific Canadian perspectives. Theme C of the 2013 research strategy "Canada and the World" (14) has the potential to offer this opportunity if it creates instances of Canadian stories within the wider the world, instead of simply maintaining Canada's positive role in wars, conflicts, peace-keeping, and, consequently, a relatively undisputed cultural memory of the Second World War.

Through this research strategy, the two museums highlight the importance of commemorating the 150th anniversary of Confederation alongside the overlapping anniversaries of the First World War (100th) and the Second World War (75th). This actively acknowledges the connections between myth, memory, and the nation: "Using selected commemorations to explore concepts of myth, memory, and nation. These opportunities will focus attention on key events, explore diversity, and interpret difficult subjects" (Canadian Museum of Civilization and Canadian War Museum 2013, 8). The research strategy states goals such as documenting "the evolution of national identity since the 1940s" (Canadian Museum of Civilization and Canadian War Museum 2013, 9). On the one hand, this strategy focusing on commemorative issues furthers the CWM's objectives, which have in turn led to the dominance of an evolutionary national master narrative resulting in argumentative closure. This strategy emphasizes, for example, "Depicting the evolution of Canadian democracy" and "Documenting Canadian efforts in support of global security" (12) as two objectives of its theme C.1 "Compromise and Conflict: Power and Politics." These strategies allow for a more open and diverse approach, which becomes clear from the third objective in this category: "Exploring multiple concepts of political power, influence, and nationalism" (Canadian Museum of Civilization and Canadian War Museum 2013, 11). It is described as follows: "Debates over politics, power, community, and nationhood feature as prominently in Canada's past as in its present. The Museums will present multiple voices and unique perspectives on these, and encourage visitor and public engagement" (Canadian Museum of Civilization and Canadian War Museum 2013, 12).

The permanent exhibition of the CWM in general, and its Second World War gallery in particular, are synthesized to serve an evolutionary master narrative of an independent nation that streamlines almost all voices into a narrative argument. If the exhibition instead left room for multiple perspectives, debates, and questions, it could serve as an example for an open national narrative of war that allows visitors room to reflect and make their own interpretative decisions. In other words, it could have created a hybrid of primary experientiality (following simulated collective gazes) and secondary experientiality, so that visitors could approach historical interpretation from multiple angles. Another goal under C.2 "Compromise and Conflict: Population Movements and Settlements" is entitled "Exploring the impact of war and conflict on population movements" (13). The detailed description reads "War-affected refugees, the internally displaced, and post-war resettlement programs (e. g. Canadian and foreign veterans, war brides, and orphans)." Again, this could clearly diversify the museum's mandate, and even the 2005 exhibition diversifies itself in this direction at the very end of its fourth gallery. However, it remains to be seen how this can be implemented within a strongly Canadian perspective on the Second World War. The exhibit on Japanese-Canadian 'resettlement' is only a fraction of the current exhibition, which shows that the museum's exploration of population movements needs to integrate local perspectives from the European and Pacific theaters of war to a larger extent. Alternatively, the CWM could place more emphasis – similar to the "Examining the Holocaust" gallery in the Canadian Museum for Human Rights – on immigration and refugee movements to Canada (see also Maron and Curle 2018, 429–431), and the impact that Nazi Germany and the war had on these movements.

The new enlarged section "War at Home," opened in early 2015, focuses on the years 1917 and 1918 in Gallery 2. It indicates how the CWM intends to evolve from a military history museum, to a military history museum that encapsulates the stories of civilians in wartime, alongside aspects of general political and cultural history.[18] For example, this section contains exhibits such as "Literature at the Home Front," "War and Music," "The Children's War," and "Families and War," among others. Its second room emphasizes the themes of conscription, including its societal impact leading to riots as well as a subsection on the right to vote and women's rights. The exhibition also highlights individual objects and stories that are not necessarily integrated as examples within a tight narrative, as often seen in the Second World War Gallery. This is exemplified in the exhibit "Shattered Love" on the newlyweds Sarah Robson and Ernest Percival Bartlett. Ernest died in combat in Europe in 1918. Among other objects, a gold pendant with Ernest's picture is displayed, which Sarah kept all her life. Visitors can decide whether they see the tragedy or deep feelings of love in the story. In this way, the display remains open as to whether the story expresses an attitude for or against wartime sacrifice. The texts on display here are more open than in the Second World War gallery: the visitor can interpret the information that voting rights were given to some – wives, daughters, mothers, and sisters of soldiers, while taken away from others – Canadians born in enemy countries. The computer installation "You be the judge," also allows the visitor to decide in four historical cases whether to accept or reject an exemption request from military service.[19] Consequently, the section is a hybrid of primary and secondary ex-

---

[18] I would like to thank the curator of the section, Mélanie Morin-Pelletier, for taking the time to explain its design to me on 27 May 2015.
[19] This connects to the technique of debate wheels that is used in the fourth gallery of the permanent exhibition in which a question about the impact of societal developments is answered

perientiality, allowing for a diverse re-experiencing of varied perspectives from the home front in the latter years of the First World War.

Whereas the CWM represents a closed narrative structure throughout its Second World War gallery, in the final parts of its fourth gallery – wherein the roles of the UN and NATO have become more controversial – the narrative opens up, enabling the visitor to ask questions. The second to last room is a roundel that introduces the post-Cold War period. Highly optimistic quotations by US President George H. Bush from September 11, 1990 and by UN Secretary General Kofi Annan from 1992 on the new free and peaceful world are juxtaposed; this is done through an installation of covers from international news magazines in English and French reporting on the endless on-going violence of war, conflict, and genocide around the world. The center installation "The Savage Wars of Peace" supplies a photo-montage of conflicts around the world (including 9/11), a helicopter from the Canadian Forces, and three video screens displaying footage from these conflicts. From here, the visitor enters the final room, which is made experiential through the presence of leading questions, such as "What is war?," "Who makes history?," "What do you fear?," "What will you do?," etc. Thus, contrary to the museum's narrative of Canadian national identity formation, the visitor is finally confronted with a (international or transnational) problem about warfare, which creates tension with the linear story of the majority of the exhibition – namely which war provides hardship and suffering but is necessary for the greater good. Admittedly, the female child narrator in the Savage War film still seems to admonish the next generation to make the world safer, continuing the linear narrative toward peace (Rukszto 2008, 53). Nevertheless, the end of the exhibition sets up a tension that points to an open future. However, since this is not reconnected to the past, there is the overall expression of a linear model toward an open future, with the past and future remaining weirdly disjointed.

Both examples from the end of the permanent exhibition and the revised "War at Home" sections in the First World War gallery demonstrate that there are ways to open up Canadian history to allow for some interpretation and reflection by the visitor. However, the master narrative the museum puts forward in its representation of the Second World War – that the Canadian nation has grown out of war and conflict – indicates that the meaning of this war is stable and factual. The secure frame between good and evil only allows for a single interpretation, which heavily restricts this section's potential for experientiality. From the Canadian national perspective represented and exhibited in the museum, the

---

through six historical quotations. The visitor can decide how to deal with the proposed answers and standpoints.

Second World War only seems to have one story: evil exists; the righteous can defeat evil through sacrifice and suffering; and the valor of the righteous wins out in the end.

3.2 Warsaw Rising Museum

As a hybrid of a historical museum aiming for historical objectivity and a memorial museum establishing and confirming a narrative of Canadian national identity that strongly depends on commemorative techniques, the format of the Canadian War Museum restricts its experientiality. In contrast, the Warsaw Rising Museum (WRM) is a memorial and narrative history museum (Majewski 2011, 151–152)[20] utilizing strong experiential techniques. It employs close-ups of the historical events and emotionally engages the visitor (Heinemann 2011, 227). In doing so, it reaffirms the present worldview and a narrative of romantic martyrdom put forward by the Warsaw Uprising's position in Polish cultural memory (Szczepanski 2012; Kurz 2007; Żychlińska 2009; Korzeniewski 2016, 112–115) as historical truth.[21] Monika Heinemann (2011, 235) notes how the museum operates with auditory, haptic, visual, and written language effects. Monika Żychlińska and Erica Fontana categorize the museum

> as a ritual site where the interplay between authoritative knowledge, grounded in disciplinary expertise, and enchantment, carefully generated through architectural and aesthetic exhibitionary strategies, takes place. The political dimension of the WRM manifests itself in the power of refiguring traumatic past experiences and reshaping contemporary Polish collective identity, as intended by the museum's originators. (2016, 254)

The museum's strong memorial mission allows visitors to empathize with one specific ideological position and to identify with the historical collective of insurgents and, according to the museum's mandate, almost all Polish people. How-

---

[20] It is also the first example of a new, modern museum style in Poland (Szczepanski 2012, 274; Bogumił et al. 2015, 68–69).
[21] Here one can see the dynamic relationship between communicative and cultural memory. Whereas the WRM employs the voices of participants in the Uprising, its emotionalization techniques are geared toward the reinforcement of cultural memory that goes beyond the voices and interests of the survivors. Consequently, the WRM is strongly engaged in educating school classes on the 'true' memory, and engages in the advancement of the Uprising in popular culture, for example in the production of graphic novels, board games, and reenactment events (Stańczyk 2015, 750; 753–758).

ever, it prevents an active primary experientiality in the form of experiencing empathy for the historical collective.

The WRM was more than twenty years in the planning and opened on July 31, 2004 – one day before the 60th anniversary of the beginning of the Uprising – by then-Warsaw Mayor Lech Kaczyński.[22] It received a record number of 713,000 annual visitors in 2017.[23] It is located in the renovated building of a municipal tram power station in the Wola district where major events of and German atrocities during the Uprising took place. Its 3,000 square meter permanent exhibition is located on four floors (ground floor, mezzanine, first floor, and basement) and displays 800 exhibition items and approximately 1,500 photographs, and numerous films and sound recordings.[24] Its focus is a close-up perspective of the sixty-three day Uprising (August 1 – October 2, 1944), framed by a brief section on the German occupation and the visit by Pope John Paul II in 1978 and his praise for the Uprising. The basement is used for the stand-alone exhibition "Germans in Warsaw" (see fig. 3) and a sewer replica as an experiential station for visitors. A large exhibition hall holding a replica of a B-24 Liberator plane, weapons used in the Uprising, a large film theater; a chapel on the side; a small twenty-four-seat theater featuring a 3D film showing the ruins of destroyed Warsaw in 1945; and a freedom and memorial park surrounding the building complete the ensemble.

As seen in the Canadian War Museum, the WRM develops a clear narrative message on how the Warsaw Uprising mirrors the development of Polish national identity. There has been considerable scholarly discussion on the permanent exhibition of the Warsaw Rising Museum. On the one hand, the museum has been seen as a model for a new narrative museum format that emotionally affects the visitor, following in the footsteps of, among others, the United States Holocaust Memorial Museum in Washington, DC and the House of Terror in Budapest. The WRM has also influenced later Polish history museums, particularly the Museum of the History of Polish Jews in Warsaw (2013–2014) and the Gdańsk Museum of the Second World War (Żychlińska and Fontana 2016, 246). On the other hand, the WRM has been criticized for its lack of historical contextualization that only allows for a positive reading of the Uprising, with tragic, religious, and heroic elements being employed to create a collective Polish perspective. The WRM is a memorial museum that morally and didactically codes

---

22 For a history of museum milestones between 2003 and 2011, see the museum guidebook (Muzeum Powstania Warszawskiego 2011a, 13–45).
23 See the interview by *Poland In English* with the Deputy Director of the Warsaw Rising Museum, Dr. Paweł Ukielski (Ukielski 2018).
24 See also the museum catalog, which gives a detailed insight into many of the artifacts displayed in the museum (Muzeum Powstania Warszawskiego 2011b).

its narrative throughout its exhibition. Its webpage announces: "The Museum is a tribute of Warsaw's residents to those who fought and died for independent Poland and its free capital."[25]

As several researchers have pointed out, this is explicitly marked at the beginning of the exhibition. In the cloakroom, the entrance area, a stand-alone quotation by Jan Stanislaw Jankowski on a bronze plate welcomes the visitor: "We wanted to be free and owe this freedom to nobody." In the following vestibule, the visitor reads an approximately 150-word text under the headline "Memory and History," which highlights its false reception during Communism – before the visitor knows anything about the Uprising. The panel ends with the sentences: "The Home army commanders supposedly used the fighting against the Germans to pursue their own personal goals which conflicted with the goals of the Polish nation. Until the fall of Communism in 1989, the official propaganda portrayed the Warsaw Rising by contrasting the heroic struggle of the insurgents with their irresponsible and cynical commanders." A second panel on "Insurgents in the PRL"[26] describes how insurgents were "convicted in fake trials or even murdered by the communists." The panel describes a certain relief after the Thaw in 1956, yet ends with the decisive statement: "Only the independent Poland they were fighting for in the Warsaw Rising would pay homage to them – to those that lived to see it happen and to those that had died." These three texts frame the narrative of the whole permanent exhibition in three ways: First, the WRM's mission is above all commemorative: to "pay homage." Second, the exhibition functions historically under the assumption of a clear truth-value. The communists distorted and falsified the history of the Uprising, and only after Communism could the true version be told. Third, this true version is connected to the concept of the freedom and self-determination of the Polish nation. This links the Uprising to a linear, progressive narrative from occupation toward freedom. This reflects first the insurgents rebelling against German occupation and second, the new Polish independence won by overcoming the Soviet occupation. This framing effect produces a closed structure of meaning throughout the museum, as will be shown in a more detailed analysis below.

The WRM implies a chronological development of the exhibition, which is highlighted through calendar sheets on the wall indicating each day of the Uprising. Large maps of Warsaw chart the development of the Uprising's different phases. Sections that highlight specific phases of the fighting "W-Hour," "Fighting in August," "The Wola Massacre," "Fighting in September" lead visitors to

---

25 https://www.1944.pl/en, accessed 13 October 2019.
26 The Polish People's Republic, 1947–1989 (in Polish: *Polska Rzeczpospolita Ludowa*, PRL).

experience simulated Polish and insurgent perspectives throughout the exhibition, in both the early parts examining Poland under German occupation and the different phases of the Uprising. In contrast to this, the exhibition also creates thematic sections such as "Food and Water," "Religious Life," "Everyday Life in the Rising," and "Field Post" to highlight specific aspects of the Uprising. It features twenty-three main sections on four floors and over fifty audio guide sections, making it at times confusing to navigate (see also Żychlińska and Fontana 2016, 260). Visitors are immersed in the fighting in a multisensory way through the exhibition's creation of an audioscape (see also de Jong 2018b, 93–98). They constantly encounter the sounds of fighting, original footage, and for example, the stroke of a clock for the W-hour, when the Uprising began. This makes listening to the audio-guide difficult at times, which prevents reflective distance. Instead, this immerses the visitor experientially in the scene of the Uprising where it is hard to gain a clear overview.

The museum first serves a commemorative purpose. Considerable prominence to the memory of those who participated in the Uprising is given throughout the museum, mainly through biographical survey texts, the telephone booths installation at the beginning of the section "The Rising after 60 Years," and audio clips of veterans' memories. The museum begins in the present, confirming the affirmative and nostalgic frame it places around the Uprising (Żychlińska and Fontana 2016, 254–257), which the visitor must accept according to the museum's master narrative. This is reaffirmed by the museum's central memorial installation, the monument of a wall-like cuboid full of bullet holes (see also Heinemann 2011, 228–229; Kurkowska-Budzan 2006, 138). The display panel explains that the monument is located "in the very 'heart'" of the museum, metaphorically alluding to the heart of those who fought, those who perished as well as those who survived: "It is a symbol to the Warsaw Rising and those who participated in it." The multimedia installation combines sounds from the fighting, radio reports, popular songs, and prayers running in 8-minute sequences. The visitor is invited to touch the monument and listen at each bullet hole, which allows for the reliving "of the atmosphere of those days." To further reinforce this recreation of the atmosphere of the past, the monument lists the days of the fighting.[27]

The way in which the Uprising's narrative is framed as a counter narrative to Soviet-Communist distortion and as commemorative nostalgia for recreating the past, shapes the whole exhibition. This fundamental meaning remains unalter-

---

[27] Steffi de Jong reads the monument installation with Alison Landsberg as a form of bodily memory production that confuses the visitor through the conflation of the visitor's heartbeat with the heartbeat of historical participants in the Uprising (2018b, 195–197).

able and unambiguous. Therefore, the museum can maintain a descriptive, documentary style throughout that gives the visitor an impression of a factual overview of numerous topics. This is exemplified in the section "Airdrops" on the top level of the museum: one panel, "Allied Airmen over Warsaw," highlights concrete facts and figures: "Allies make about 200 flights over Warsaw. Polish, British and South African crews take part in the airdrops. Only 525 out of 637 Poles return to their airbases in Italy." Throughout the museum facts, figures, concrete times, and locations are important in giving the visitor the impression that the majority of the exhibition is factual. In the subtext, the visitor finds allusions to heroics, which – through the focus on figures – seem to be factual as well: "133 are shot down. 7 of them [the airmen, SJ] manage to survive. They travel over 2.5 thousand kilometers. They have mostly German occupied areas under their wings." The following panel "Airdrops for Insurgents" highlights the concrete efforts and failure to reach the insurgents, similarly focusing on factual data, especially dates and the amount of supplies dropped in tons. In a factually descriptive tone, the responsibility for this failure is placed on Stalin: "Only 50 tons [out of 230 tons of Allied dropped supplies] fall into insurgents' hands. Until September 10, Stalin does not make Soviet airfields available to allied planes." The two subsequent sentences indicate a causal relationship. The visitor will, in all likelihood, simply attribute the failure to Stalin, rather than reflecting on the open question of whether the airdrops could have been more precise.

The overall section tries to show different sides of the airdrops by displaying enlarged poster-size photographs showing the joy they produce, alongside reflections on their failure. One photo-montage shows, among others, an image of an apparently misplaced container, with an image above it showing insurgents gathering the parachute with a container; and above, the insurgents apparently happily carrying the container with the new supplies (see fig. 6). The text accompanying this photo-montage reads: "The frontline in the fighting city is constantly changing and it is hard to spot it from the air. Every parachute reaching the streets controlled by the insurgents brings joy and it is easy to find volunteers to carry the airdrop containers." On the one hand, this factually documents failure and success. On the other hand, it plays upon the emotion of the success. Several quotations and objects on display support the positive impact of the drops as existentially necessary supplies and moral support. The Polish effort in these Allied deliveries is highlighted. There is no major criticism of the Americans, who made just a single attempt to fly over Warsaw; instead, the exhibition describes the American effort as "impressive – 107 'Flying Fortresses,' 1,100 airmen and 100 tons in containers." This connects to the panel "Stalin's Private Airfields," which describes that Soviet airfields were not made available, preventing the Americans from performing a large airdrop operation over Warsaw. The pan-

Fig. 6 Part of section "Airdrops." Permanent exhibition. Muzeum Powstania Warszawskiego (Warsaw Rising Museum), Warsaw (Photo: Author, 2013, courtesy of Muzeum Powstania Warszawskiego).

el's text quotes the British pilot Stanley Johnson: "If only we could have landed there [on Soviet airfields], we could have taken an additional load ... I could never understand the Russians standing on the other side of Vistula River." The quotations blame the Soviets for denying the Allies use of their airfields and are then expanded toward the claim that the Soviets could have prevented the destruction of Warsaw – a crucial claim for the museum's narrative.[28] That

---

[28] See also Bömelburg et al. 2011, especially Król 2011 for the different perceptions and interpretations of the Uprising; see also Chu 2019, 130–131.

the panel personally identifies Stalin several times as a historical agent reinforces the impression that a different outcome of the Uprising could have been easily achieved. Overall, the WRM's Air Drop section creates the impression that it exclusively presents factually unbiased information. One needs to think explicitly about curatorial strategies, in order to understand the ways in which the subtle techniques employed in this section reaffirm the museum's master narrative. This technique of creating a documentary, factual impression repeats itself throughout the whole museum, which makes it likely that the visitor will buy into the master narrative as well.

Many of the exhibition sections in the WRM have a thematic focus. This means they provide fairly factual information about a specific area of life during the Uprising. They often demonstrate how day-to-day life was organized during the fighting, indirectly supporting the part of the master narrative that suggests the Uprising led to freedom and independence. While demonstrating the functioning of civil and social life, the valor and tragic losses of the individuals participating in that life is simultaneously honored and commemorated. For example, the section "Field Post" features a combination of visuals and objects, including, a large display case mounted on the wall holding dozens of postcards, letters, an original mailbox, and a smaller display case with insurgent postage stamps. Individual biographies, accompanied by portrait photographs and approximately 100–120 word texts introduce the visitor to the Polish people who participated in the Uprising. Objects supplement these biographies, such as the shirt that Bolesław Jan Gepner 'Jasnotek' – a 13-year-old who worked as mailman of the Scout Field Post – wore when he was fatally shot. The more tragically stories about death [29] are presented, the more they are portrayed as an almost religious sacrifice for the Polish cause. Other biographies highlight the skill-set and valor of the Field Post workers. The focus is on the everyday person and not on the leaders, reinforcing the message that all Poles were part of the Uprising. It is significant for the creation of a master narrative that these factual-commemorative narratives remain vague in regard to the Uprising's failures: at best, the insurgents encounter challenges. The visitor never hears whether the mail service connected to areas outside the districts held by insurgents. Nowhere does the exhibition reflect on civilians either inside or outside of the insurgent-held areas of Warsaw who might not have the supported the Uprising, nor does it reflect on the risks the Uprising held for the civilian population.

---

29 See also Heinemann 2011, 231, who notices the frequent use of gravestones, usually by lower-rank insurgents throughout the exhibition.

The WRM enforces the message that starting the Uprising was the right decision in many indirect ways, including its representation of German perpetrators (see also Heinemann 2017, 78–90). They are mainly represented in the basement (see fig. 3), which physically separates the commemoration of Polish heroes from German crimes as well as the violence and cruelty of German atrocities.[30] In this section, there are documentary texts, such as the biographies and fates of many German commanders and numerous facsimiles of German orders, among others. These are once again supplemented by a setting that steers the visitor's emotions in a specific direction – here, toward the implied genocide of the citizens of Warsaw. The oppressive atmosphere can make the visitor feel uncomfortable, who has hardly any room to analyze the presented material outside of the museum's good and evil framework. The Germans appear as one collective group, the Poles appear as another, and only Communist Poles are differentiated from all other Poles. The representation of Germans serves the exclusive purpose of providing evidence for the evil that the Uprising has the potential to defeat. To gain a better understanding of how this works, it is useful to look at a small side room in the permanent exhibition, located on the second floor in the final part of the exhibition and entitled "German Units." The room is void of any documentary information, except for the introductory text panel outside of the room describing the structure of the German forces and a chest of drawers with movable cases with biographical information on four German political and military leaders. The visitor enters a shrine-like squared room (Heinemann 2017, 82), with wall-sized, enlarged photographs on all sides. The four posters depict Hans Frank, Govenor of Generalgouvernement, residing in Wawel Castle with his wife and children; Wola insurgents who had to face veteran troops from the division Hermann Göring; a prison execution in Radogoszcz, near Łódź in 1942; and German soldiers on parade, honoring Hitler after capturing Warsaw in 1939. Furthermore, there are small objects throughout the room, such as an SS bronze cross with a sword that was pierced by an insurgent's bullet during the Uprising. The centerpiece of the room is a small table-like display case, containing the open diary of the 8-year-old Jerzy Arct, who experienced the Warsaw Uprising in the district of Sadyba and wandered through the destroyed city afterwards. None of the photographs on display in this room are related to

---

30 The stand-alone exhibition in the basement "Germans in Warsaw" was only opened on June 21, 2007 (Heinemann 2017, 79). For an analysis of this section see also Heinemann 2017, 84–90. Heinemann (2017, 89) notes some nuances that allow for a differentiated reading of the Germans, but also emphasizes that the section is dominated by a dehumanized, abstract depiction of the German enemy; for the depiction of the enemy in the WRM see also Bogumił et al. 2015, 141–143, who point out that human traits of the enemy are absent in the museum's depictions.

the Warsaw Uprising. Instead, they showcase the normality of the perpetrators, the strong resistance against superior forces and war crimes, and reinforce the impression of the German soldiers' collective obedience and facelessness. The objects are all related to the Uprising and at least partially demonstrate the symbolic power of resistance. This display is fully emotive and holds the potential to manipulate the visitor into supporting the heroic deeds of the insurgents. The presence of the child's diary further supports this emotional message. The brutality of the Germans is pinpointed in the pictures of the Frank family and the Wola Massacre, since the visitor already knows about the family's criminality and the events of the Massacre. Thus, this room, which relies fully on affect, leads the visitor toward empathizing with the collective group of insurgents and all victims of the Germans. The strength of the WRM is that it often underlines its narrative message in an affective and emotional manner without overtly spelling it out. Therefore, it avoids explicitly moralizing good and evil, although its narrative is based on this dichotomy.

The exhibition's technique of appearing simultaneously factual and commemorative is also visible in the only section that clearly reports on a controversy or debate. On the one hand, the text on the panel "Views on the Rising" seems quite differentiated: "The Warsaw Rising stirs up extreme emotions, from more or less factual criticism to glorification." An audio station provides eight positions from "decision-makers and participants in the Rising, historians and communist propagandists." In reality, there are the voices of two communists and six insurgents of different rank, so that besides the already rejected Communist view (see also Szczepanski 2012, 277), their opinions only differ regarding details, rather than their interpretations of the Uprising as such. Nevertheless, this station allows the visitor to think about the validity of different positions. However, the panel concludes by stating that the majority of insurgents are part of an emotional community: "Openly biased and unjust are opinions voiced by the Communists, such as Wanda Odolska, the leading propagandist of the Polish Radio. In the opinion of most insurgents the outbreak of the Rising was a necessity and they do not regret their decision to join in the fighting."

Further panels and objects completely undermine any possibility for openness in the audio station, as they continue in the clear black-and-white pattern established at the beginning of the exhibition. A panel entitled "Feud over the Rising" recreates the simple dichotomy of distorted memory under Communism versus free discussion after 1989: "After 1989 the Rising could be freely discussed also in Poland and continuous presence of this debate in the public life proves that the Poles are still tackling their history [sic]." The museum itself does not take an explicit position, as also seen in the implicit affective strategy it employs to represent the Germans. Nor does it encourage an open interpretation. Instead, the visitor who experiences the master narrative of the museum is led to believe that the museum provides the possibility of free debate, after the Communist era of distortion of historical truth, and allows for a fair and differentiated position in the exhibition. Therefore, most visitors, as the success of the exhibition shows (Żychlińska and Fontana 2016, 262–263), will – in all likelihood – draw the exact conclusions to which the WRM directs them. The factual tone throughout the WRM lures the visitor into feeling like debate is reflected in the exhibition. After all, the Uprising itself is marked as the road to Polish freedom, so that alternative interpretations of the Uprising seem unlikely for the visitor of this exhibition. Gaining freedom implies the possibility of stating the truth and establishing facts – in other words, closing a debate instead of leaving it open.

This is also evident in the remainder of the section, entitled "The Big Three."[31] It emphasizes Stalin's propagandistic use of the Uprising[32] and how the Big Three sacrificed Poland in their negotiations over the post-war distribution of power. This section also argues that the Allied Press failed to recognize the Uprising as a major contribution to the Allied cause: the tone of its texts clearly implies that the Uprising was a major contribution, which is confirmed through several quotations. For example, the diplomat George Kennan, deputy chief of the US mission in Moscow during the Warsaw Uprising, is quoted, presumably long after the Uprising and without any contextualization: "I wish that instead of mumbling words of official optimism we had had the judgment and the good taste to bow our heads in silence before the tragedy of a people who have been our allies, whom we have helped to save from our enemies and whom we cannot save from our friends." The WRM uses quotations as Keenan's strategically; similarly, they integrate US President's Ronald Reagan's words at the 40th anniversary of the Warsaw Uprising: "It is right that we pay tribute to those who sacrificed all for independence and freedom." The changes in Poland in the 1980s consequently allow for the collapse of the Communist myth, that the People's Army was the main insurgent force fighting the Germans. Thus, there is no doubt that the post-1989 era allowed for the recognition of the Warsaw Uprising and an open discussion about Polish identity. The WRM uses this to establish an implicit connection between the desire for freedom in the Warsaw Uprising and the freedom gained in 1989. Counterarguments against the Uprising there-

---

31 Referring to Winston Churchill, Harry S. Truman, and Joseph Stalin.
32 Stalin is the ultimate enemy and symbol of evil in the master narrative of the WRM, since he prevented the success of the Uprising and started the suppression of its 'true' narrative.

fore hardly play a role;[33] the amendment of Communist distortions is used as a platform to correct history and establish historical facts and truth. In the earlier section on the Polish Lublin government, the museum corrected the numbers of Communist People's Army soldiers and Home Army soldiers that participated in the Uprising to demonstrate "Communist 'facts.'"

The WRM's permanent exhibition does not have a strong temporal and progressive focus; it is instead built on the dichotomy between the Communists' distortion of truth and dishonoring of the insurgents on the one hand and freedom and factual truth as well as the commemoration of the insurgents' heroic and sacrificial deeds on the other. It simply connects the Uprising with independent Poland post-1989. Instead of futurity, the permanent exhibition's master narrative suggests a nostalgic reestablishment of the same Polish national freedom that was recognized by the insurgents during the Uprising. For example, the last section on the second floor and the end of the permanent exhibition talks about the Vatican and the Warsaw Uprising. It emphasizes two blessings given to the Uprising, the first of which was performed by Pope Pius XII on September 14, 1944, during the Uprising, who pointed out the Polish right to independence. This connects to a video and text panel highlighting how the first Polish Pope, John Paul II, lauded "the exceptional role of the Warsaw Rising in the history of Poland" during his first papal pilgrimage to Poland in June 1979. The last section of the audio guide concludes that the time has come to recognize the historical truth about the Uprising and foreshadows the universal freedom and 'correct' interpretation of the Uprising post-1989: "The time of truth was approaching. This was the time of the next generation." The museum is successful in producing "a sense of nostalgia and personal identification with the participants of the Rising" in its Polish visitors (Żychlińska and Fontana 2016, 262). Visitor analysis has shown the success of the WRM's use of technology (Żychlińska and Fontana 2016, 261). If the goal is to produce a specific historical truth based on cultural memory in the present, the WRM succeeds in doing just that as a memorial site: "a sense of continuity between past and present" (Żychlińska and Fontana 2016, 261) is established for many visitors.

The difference in temporality is also evident in comparison to the Canadian War Museum, in which the exhibition establishes its master narrative of a progressive development toward the Canadian nation and its positive role in the world. The WRM reinforces its master narrative by establishing a staged impres-

---

[33] For example, the exhibition does not mention the controversy in Poland about whether the Uprising was really necessary and useful or whether it was a senseless sacrifice. It avoids any meta-reflection on how the memory or myth of the Warsaw Uprising's impact came into being (For details see Chu 2019, 133–135; Bömelburg et al. 2011, especially Król 2011).

sion of factuality, while extensively fostering visitors' empathy with the insurgents and developing feelings of nostalgia for the past. The museum's skillful use of pseudo-factuality and emotion in its staging of memory as history stands in strong contrast to the argumentative-documentary style of the Canadian museum. Master narratives can be created in war and history museums through numerous techniques. Whether their contents are national, European, universal, heroic, or victim-oriented remains open. This can also be seen in the following chapter on the Imperial War Museum in London. There is no need to challenge other narratives, like in the WRM, or reinterpret existing cultural memory to allow a master narrative to emerge, as found in the Canadian War Museum.

3.3 The Imperial War Museum in London

The main branch of the Imperial War Museum in London (IWML) receives approximately one million visitors a year.[34] It will not present a major Second World War exhibition before 2021, when both the Second World War and Holocaust Galleries are due to be completely redeveloped.[35] Because of this, the discussion of the museum in this book is relatively short.[36] The first phase of "Transforming IWM London," completed in 2014, focuses completely on the First World War and its centenary years. This has led to the opening of the new "First World War Galleries" (see also Jaeger 2017b, 169–172) and a redesigned atrium displaying seven exhibits of one or two objects, entitled "Witnesses of War."[37] Its section "Turning Points 1934–1945," on the first gallery level surrounding the open atrium, presents different themes of the Second World War in

---

[34] Imperial War Museum 2016–2017; the IWM's newer annual reports do not list individual visitor numbers per branch; overall the IWM and its five branches had an attendance of 2.688 million visitors in 2018–2019 (Imperial War Museum 2018–2019, 15).
[35] See the IWM's website (https://www.iwm.org.uk/history/new-gallery-concepts-for-iwms-future-revealed, accessed 13 October 2019). "The second phase of Transforming IWM London (TIWML) has continued with the developed designs being approved for the Second World War and Holocaust Galleries," which will be probably delivered in 2021 (Imperial War Museum 2018–21; see also Imperial War Museum 2019–2024, 7–8, and Imperial War Museum 2018–2019, 11). The current stand-alone *Holocaust Exhibition* from 2000 will be briefly discussed in chapter 7 below.
[36] For the history of the institution and its flagship museum in London (Lambeth), see Cundy 2015.
[37] See chapter 8 below for a discussion of the display of the V1 bomb and V2 rockets as part of the exhibitions. Other 'witnesses' relating to the Second World War are a Supermarine Spitfire plane and a Soviet T34 tank.

eight chapters using artifacts. This section seems like a stand-in to cover the war until the 2021 redevelopment is completed; it is too fragmentary to provide a full storyline and interpretation of the war, or to allow visitors to develop their own interpretations.[38] Nevertheless, the IWML has always been an important model for restricted primary experientiality.[39] Similarly to the Canadian War Museum, the IWML's official message describes its approach as an educational history museum, interested in creating a documentary and open "authentic historical experience" (Bardgett 1998, 32).[40] Cundy (2015, 262–265) has shown how the IWM developed its educational function separately from a commemorative mission. However, this section demonstrates that the IWML still reinforces memory narratives as its primary effect.

One of the museum's objectives during its re-development in 1989–1990 was to immerse visitors in experiences that allow them both to have empathy with the past and to produce constructed yet suggestively real experiences of the past. In particular, this relates to the former Trench Experience (1990) concerning the First World War and the Blitz Experience (1989) concerning the Second World War.[41] Since the first phase of "Transforming IWM London," both of these experiences are gone, much to the chagrin of many visitors – if one follows online blogs.[42] The Blitz Experience contained a stage set with different scenes,

---

38 Its section "Bombers" is briefly discussed in chapter 8 below.
39 The Imperial War Museum's Churchill War Rooms (formerly Cabinet War Rooms) follows a similar concept. This branch is highly based on the authenticity of place, which is intentionally reconstructed through diorama scenes with mannequins and original objects. The IWM is working to make its exhibitions more interactive and includes voices of other people who worked together with Churchill in the Cabinet War Rooms (Imperial War Museum 2016–2017, 8). Yet it does not change its objective to simulate historical authenticity: "Walk in the footsteps of Churchill and glimpse what life would have been like during the tense days and nights of the Second World War. See where Churchill and his War Cabinet met and step back in time in the Map Room, which has remained exactly as it was left on the day the lights were switched off in 1945" (https://www.iwm.org.uk/events/cabinet-war-rooms, accessed 13 October 2019). The Churchill exhibition (Churchill Museum) itself is considerably more dynamic and the way that it simulates a secondary form of experientiality is worth analyzing.
40 This comment relates to the planning for the stand-alone *Holocaust Exhibition* in the IWML, but is indicative of the institution's general approach (see also Cundy 2015).
41 See also Noakes 2004; Schoder 2014, 73–74; Arnold-de Simine 2013, 33; Phillips 2003, 438. Lucy Noakes notes how the Blitz Experience "privileges notions of community togetherness and national unity over images of fear and destruction" (2004, 431).
42 There is still a trench experience, in the 2014 "First World War Galleries." The visitor walks into a large trench with a fairly soft sound installation of battle and airplane noises; the technical equipment of large objects looms over the trench. Yet the museum does not create a specific scene of attack (or the moments before it, as in the old trench exhibition). The visitor sees

and the visitor had the opportunity to see the silhouette of London in flames, walk through the ruins of a street, and sit in an air-raid shelter. The experience affected all the senses through the shaking of the shelter, sound installations, simulated smoke, darkness, flashing lights, etc. This installation did not facilitate much learning and understanding; its objective was to come as close as possible to 'the real experience.' However, these reconstructions of a trench and an air-war shelter seem to have functioned as a playful trick to attract visitors via entertainment, rather than bringing them closer to experiencing the war and empathizing with historical people.

The Blitz Experience was, at least in part, replaced by the independent exhibition *A Family in Wartime*. This new exhibition was open from April 5, 2012 until January 2019, when it was closed so that the space could be re-developed for the museum's new Second World War galleries. The museum advertised *A Family in Wartime* with the words: "Take a step back in time to the Second World War and experience life on the Home Front in London, through the eyes of the Allpress family. A Family in Wartime, IWM London's new major free family exhibition – will explore the lives of William and Alice Allpress and their ten children and what life in London was like during the war."[43] The Trench and Blitz experiences served to illustrate the different stages of two specific historical moments, immersing visitors in a trench attack, or in the experience of waiting out the bombing respectively. The visitor was "invited to relive a specific moment or milieu from the past" (Phillips 2003, 438), which functioned through engagement and proximity. In contrast, *A Family in Wartime* (Imperial War Museum 2017a, 34–35) allowed the visitor to observe and experience simultaneously. However, despite the potential it held for creating a reflexive understanding of the war through a variation of engagement and detachment, or proximity and distance, it ultimately continued to reinforce wartime myths.

The beginning of the exhibition was located in a narrow corridor with a large wall displaying photographs of the Allpress family, interspersed with three small monitors playing identical footage of the air-raids on London and their effects on the city. All photographs and portraits on display depicted a happy family with faces full of laughter. The introductory panel read: "This exhibition is about the Allpresses, a real family that lived in South London. As for so many others, the

---

photographs of soldiers, a devastated landscape, and the shadowy figures of soldiers moving along on the left wall of the trench. Thus, the visitor is never fully immersed and does not receive any information about what to do with this simulated trench. Its message seems to be the dominance and significance of new technologies that are explained in the following section.

43 IWM London press release February 2012. http://www.iwm.org.uk/sites/default/files/press-release/A_Family_in_Wartime_0.pdf (accessed 13 October 2019).

war changed their lives forever." An enlarged quotation by Eva Allpress, one of the ten children, on the right wall stated: "We were a family that were really close together." In the back of the entrance corridor, the visitor walked toward one poster featuring an enlarged photo of a street with several houses completely reduced to rubble. None of the photographs had a caption or source. Whereas the exhibition never overwhelmed visitors into pretending they were close to real past experiences, it immediately steered them emotionally. The quotation, the many portraits, and the text, suggested a perfect and orderly world that was threatened and then destroyed by the war. Since the Allpresses were pitched as a model of "so many others," the visitor could draw connections to this exemplary everyday experience. On the right hand side of the entrance corridor, the visitor found an Anderson shelter, which they could see either at the beginning or very end of the mostly circular exhibition. The presence of this shelter helped the visitor understand the war's threat to the Allpresses' world. The shelter was large enough to climb into, and once inside, one could hear an audio clip of Betty Allpress speaking about her experiences during the Blitz. A photograph of a destroyed Anderson shelter lying in rubble acted as a backdrop to the physical shelter. This further enhanced the feelings of threat, destruction, and the intrusion of the war into everyday life, created by the exhibition. The surrounding walls at the end of the exhibition showed bombed-out houses and numerous bombshells, intensifying this impression.

In the section following the entrance corridor, the visitor came across a model and digital projection of each room of the Allpresses house in Lambeth (i.e. in fairly close proximity to today's site of the Imperial War Museum). It was here that they were introduced to mini biographies of the family's two parents and ten children. Two of the sons served in the war; three of the daughters performed fire watch duties and worked in the Women's Voluntary Service; and the remaining daughters took on maternal or household roles, meaning they did not have to work directly for the war effort. The museum clearly avoided making the story of any family member particularly heroic – they instead served as examples of the ordinary British citizen, mostly on the home front. The visitor was then presented with period-appropriate interior rooms, a living room and a kitchen, and display cases holding everyday objects sorted by topics such as evacuation, rationing, the Blitz, the Women's Voluntary Service, or the Southern railway (where the father had worked in a skilled job as an engine driver that exempted him from conscription).

The object display cases were often accompanied by the voices of the Allpress children reminiscing about this time. This was exemplified in the section on clothes rationing "Make Do and Mend" (see fig. 7). The section notes that Eva worked at a local draper's shop, which sold fabric and dressmaking material.

Fig. 7 "Make Do and Mend" cabinet. *Family in Wartime* exhibition. Imperial War Museum, London (Photo and © Imperial War Museum).

The display case contained a few dresses and pairs of shoes, but it mainly presented posters such as "Please Knit Now" as well as title pages and illustrations from do-it-yourself manuals. The whole section served an illustrative function for the duty and everyday life of British citizens on the home front; the Allpresses made-do and did a lot of mending. In the middle of the exhibition, there was a quotation by Nellie: "we were all so anxious to stay alive that we just sort of carried on," indicating the sober mood of everybody living through the war. Similarly, two quotations from after the war read: "The war had finished, you just couldn't believe it" (Betty) and "We were lucky enough that we had all our brothers coming back" (Eva). These quotations demonstrated the personal relief and joy felt by most at the end of the war, in stark contrast to the photographs of the destroyed Anderson shelter.

The *Family in Wartime* exhibition was clearly aimed at bringing the visitor a surface-level experience of the war; in doing so, it did not fully allow for an internalization or understanding of the Blitz as a historical experience. The exhibition greatly reduced the complexity of history and gave the visitor the impression that all civilians had an almost identical fate. On a primary emotional level, it was easy to identify with John's frustrations over being evacuated. However, this did not make reference to possible variations on his experience, or help one gain an understanding of the bombings' larger repercussions. How did the Blitz influence lives afterwards? What were some of the wartime traumas suffered by civilians? Instead, the IWML closed with facts and figures charting the impact of the Blitz and hopeful quotations from the Allpress children. Thus, the exhibition was seemingly successful in connecting with older generations who recognized elements of their former houses and lives in those of the archetypical Allpress family. It also succeeded in enticing younger generations and children by allowing them to connect with basic human needs and emotions such as food, clothes, housing, and the importance of family. It is telling that the Allpresses were depicted as so ordinary; in doing so, hardly anything unique about their personal story was expressed. The exhibition balanced an emotionalizing experience with the commemoration of a generation through the simulation of a possible everyday experience. It lacked both the ability to raise questions and the means for distantiation. The visitor was always so close to the war experience that its emotional impact dominated without eliciting any kind of analysis. The visitor received the strong impression that this was the real collective experience of the British people during the Blitz.

Therefore, the IWML – even without their original Blitz Experience – still put forward a restricted primary experience of the past. This restricted primary experience contributed to myth building regarding both the place of the Blitz and the every-day life of the typical British family in wartime in British collective memory today. The 2012 exhibition was certainly marked by a change in tone. It was neither heroic nor sensational; it contributed to the visitor's emotional experience in more subtle ways – as seen in the analysis of its opening corridor.[44] However, because of its reconstructive approach, the visitor could only confirm the exhibition curators' meaning making and storytelling. It both fed into an existing collective imagination and confirmed the predominant communicative and cultural memory, which in turn reinforced the mythical status of British wartime resistance. Here, memory clearly dominated history, without allowing the visitor to take an active role in this process. In this way, the exhibition's potential for experientiality was restricted.

---

44 Without a more comprehensive historical exhibition of the war it is impossible to understand how the IWML is aiming to interpret the Second World War in the second decade of the twenty-first century and beyond.

Chapter 4:
Primary Experientiality

Experientiality can only be discussed as a sliding scale between overlapping layers of restrictive, primary, and secondary experientiality; it is a concept that places visitors in a position to experience perceptions and structures of the past. Their role is combined with the experiences of historical people – usually represented collectively, not individually – in the various structures and atmospheres in which they lived. As seen in the previous chapter, there are different forms and layers of restricted experientiality, whether the restriction stems from a linear master narrative, a clear ideology, or an uncritical affirmation of myth and pre-existing cultural memory. In all cases, an argumentative or ideological structure reduces any individual visitor experience of the past. This is often closely related to lack of distantiation. The three museums discussed in this chapter – the National WWII Museum in New Orleans, the Oskar Schindler Enamel Factory in Kraków, and the Bastogne War Museum – all simulate real historical events and historical situations; they mimetically indicate that members of certain historical groups could have experienced the past as it is presented in the museum. For all three museums, experientiality surpasses mere argument or ideology. The visitor has the opportunity to be immersed in collective perspectives of the past, with the awareness that the museum is creating a simulation or theatrical performance of the past. The New Orleans WWII Museum operates along the border of restricted experientiality, as it immerses the visitor in a singular narrative as if it were the war's only existing reality. At the same time, the museum's strong focus on oral history and historical witness accounts allows the visitor some room to experience the past beyond the mere staging of ideology. The focus is thus less on historical truth, as visitors are steered toward the feeling that they are experiencing a multitude of collective perceptions of the war. Both the Oskar Schindler Factory (OSF) and the Bastogne War Museum (BWM) are more of hybrids between primary and secondary experientiality. The OSF challenges the visitor to become a time traveler in a historical space, in which they can both observe and immerse themselves in the collective perspectives of, for example, Polish and Polish-Jewish citizens of Kraków. During this experience, the visitor is aware of the theatricality of this time-traveling journey. The BWM allows for the visitor to be immersed alongside fictitious composite characters, while mixing this immersive experience with numerous other sources and forms of distantiation.

4.1 The National WWII Museum in New Orleans

The National WWII Museum in New Orleans is a typical American military history museum oriented toward combat and military missions abroad. It functions as a narrative memorial museum that uses a considerable amount of experiential techniques. This is done not in the vein of Williams's idea of commemorating suffering and victimhood (2007), but instead more in the sense that it commemorates war veterans from all branches of the American Forces. Because of its strong mission, one could argue that this museum also belongs in the category of restricted experientiality. At the same time, its strong basis in oral history allows visitors to go beyond a single preconceived narrative. The museum was founded as *D-Day Museum* in 2000. In 2004, it was designated by the United States Congress as America's official National World War II Museum "with the new mission to portray the full American experience in the war, including its ongoing meaning for global freedom."[1] The highly popular museum is funded through admission, memberships, and private fundraising.[2] It caters particularly to war veterans and their families. It focuses almost exclusively on the contribution made by the United States to the Allied victory in the Second World War in both the European and Pacific theaters of war. Its six-part mission statement highlights both the museum's goal of contributing to the "understanding of the history and meaning of America's role in World War II and its relevance for today and for the future" and the museum's objective to "[b]ecome a place for people to understand and feel America's strengths and values."[3] There is large memorial slab located in front of the Salomon Victory Theater that is indicative of the museum's approach. It tells the story of how New Orleans historian Stephen E. Ambrose conceived of a D-Day museum in New Orleans to narrate the story of American veterans in wake of D-Day. The museum also honors entrepreneur Andrew Higgins, whose New Orleans factories built the landing crafts that were instrumental in delivering Allied forces to shore in Europe and the Pacific

---

1 Text on memorial slab in front of the Salomon Victory Theater on the Battle Barksdale Parade Ground.
2 It generates high visitor numbers – 754,465 in 2018 (National WWII Museum 2018, 5) and is extremely popular on social media. For years, it has been advertised as a top museum in the USA and in the world on tripadvisor.com; in 2017 it reached the amazing status of being the no. 2 museum in the world (https://www.tripadvisor.com/TravelersChoice-Museums-cTop-g1, accessed 25 March 2018, only after the Metropolitan Museum of Art (MET) in New York; in 2018 it fell to an still impressive eighth place worldwide (same site, accessed 13 October 2019).
3 https://www.nationalww2museum.org/about-us/mission-vision-values (accessed 13 October 2019).

islands. Ambrose started an oral history collection of interviews with Second World War veterans, which has been under constant development ever since. It has also become the core of the museum collection and the backbone of its exhibitions and research expertise (see also Barnes and Guise 2013).

On the slab, there is a quotation by Ambrose that reads "At the core, the American soldiers knew the difference between right and wrong, and they didn't want to live in a world in which wrong prevailed, so they fought and won, and we, all of us, living and yet to be born, must be forever profoundly grateful." The founding CEO of the museum Gordon H. 'Nick' Mueller is quoted on the left hand side of the memorial stone as follows: "World War II served as a crucible. All of the human, spiritual, and material resources of our nation were mobilized to defeat authoritarian and racist regimes and to defend freedom. It was a fight to the finish for civilization itself. The American spirit prevailed." This honors the American contribution within a clear moral framework and pre-defines good and evil regarding the American 'good war' (Terkel 1984; Torgovnick 2005, 59) and the myths highlighting D-Day as American self-liberation (Dolski 2014). The New Orleans WWII Museum has developed its own campus, designed by Voorsanger Mathes LLC, which continues to evolve. Eventually, it will offer about 8,500 square meter (92,000 square feet) of exhibition space.[4] The pavilion architecture with skywalks has a fairly futuristic look, reminiscent of military industrial design. Consequently, the buildings' interiors are designed pragmatically for exhibition purposes. In addition to the original building, the Louisiana Memorial Pavilion,[5] the museum has opened the Solomon Victory Theater (2009), the John E. Kushner Restoration Pavilion (2011), the US Freedom Pavilion: The Boeing Center (2012), and the Campaigns of Courage Pavilion (2015).[6] Throughout the different pavilions, the museum uses the technique of repetition to reinforce factual information about battles, campaigns, equipment, and American soldiers in the war. In this way, a visitor who spends enough time in the museum is consistently exposed to slightly varied narratives of the same themes and events. This technique speaks to the visitor' cognitive and affective capacities; it is less about producing new knowledge than about emphasizing

---

[4] http://www.archdaily.com/209361/the-national-world-war-ii-museum-voorsanger-architects, accessed 13 October 2019 (Voorsanger Mathes LLC).
[5] It reopened several of its exhibitions after major renovations in 2017.
[6] See for a comprehensive history of the New Orleans WWII Museum its "Fiscal Year 2017 Annual Report," https://www.nationalww2museum.org/sites/default/files/2018-01/annual-report-2017-resize.pdf, accessed 13 October 2019. See for further information https://www.nationalww2museum.org/visit/museum-campus, accessed 13 October 2019.

and possibly enriching generalized knowledge already familiar to the visitor, while reflecting the American gaze and American cultural memory.[7]

The New Orleans WWII Museum is interested in recapturing the American gaze, while contextualizing it within military history and displaying mostly objects of illustrative quality. For example, in the interactive Dog Tag Experience, computer screens – set-up in six stations – allow the visitor to use a digitally enabled 'dog tag' IDs to connect with an individual witness's narrative of the war. Visitors can also collect objects on their dog tag ID, and computer stations feature excerpts from selected oral eyewitness accounts.[8] Besides its oral history approach,[9] the New Orleans WWII Museum employs two techniques in particular that create primary experientiality: first, it simulates interior and exterior spaces that American soldiers and commanders would have experienced during military campaigns. This can especially be seen in the museum's 2015 building Campaigns of Courage, which houses the "Road to Berlin" and the "Road to Tokyo" and in the scenic settings used in the "Arsenal of Democracy" exhibition.[10] Second, it features several elaborate multimedia installations, which are aimed at allowing the visitor to experience war. The "Road to Berlin" exhibition consists of nine sections, five of which are set as explicitly immersive scenes: in sequence and with the American soldiers, the visitor enters a North-African landscape, surrounding them with desert and rocks, and then moves through ancient Italian buildings and ruins during the Italian campaign. This is followed by a Normandy landscape made up of hedges found in the room on the Northwestern European campaign, a snowy forest in the Battle of the Bulge, and lastly, a destroyed Germany. Similarly, the "Road to Tokyo" exhibition on the upper floor of the pavilion features a jungle on the island of Guadalcanal and an immersive mountainscape of the Himalayas.

---

[7] It will be interesting to see whether the new National Museum of the United States Army in Fort Belvoir, VA, expected to open to the public on June 4, 2020, will tell the same universalized story of the American role in the Second World War as the New Orleans WWII Museum. The new US Army Museum aims to tell the story of its soldiers. It features the "Fighting for the Nation Galleries" (its main space), the "Army and Society Gallery," and a specific section for soldiers' stories. It "will honor United States Soldiers – past, present, and future – and provide an interactive educational experience explaining the Army's role in creating and defending our nation, as well as the Army's social initiatives and contributions for more than 240 years" (https://armyhistory.org/about-the-museum/, accessed 13 October 2019).
[8] In the Boeing Center, the visitor can access many interviews in detail.
[9] The museum's oral history approach is discussed further in chapter 7 on Holocaust representation in war museums.
[10] This includes, among others, a 1942-style home and an immersive Los Alamos environment where the development of the nuclear bomb via the Manhattan Project is documented.

The last room of the "Road to Berlin" exhibition can serve as model for understanding how the New Orleans WWII Museum creates a hybrid out of primary and secondary experientiality. With the exception of the European/Mediterranean Briefing Room and the little documentary D-Day Theater,[11] all of the rooms immerse the visitor in the collective gaze of the American soldier in North Africa and Europe. Immediately after the immersive snowy scene in the Battle of the Bulge, the visitor sees an enlarged poster, featuring the city of Cologne in ruins, recognizable from the looming cathedral and destroyed bridges on the river Rhine. The wall poster is embedded in a stage set with building fragments and a looming fire in front of it. The visitor then enters the small first part of the final section, which has been made to look like the interior of a destroyed room in a residential house. The wooden ceiling has holes; the edges of ceiling, tapestry, and wooden floor look burned. On the tapestry, a quotation by an infantryman reads "One cannot go to war and come back normal." The visitor can decide whether this refers to the discoveries of destruction and concentration camps made by American soldiers, or whether it serves as a warning to the Germans that they should not expect their country to remain normal and deserve to have their country in ruins. Upon entering this section's larger main space, the visitor becomes immersed in an outdoor scene of destroyed Germany, containing large posters of Hamburg and Bremen in ruins on the right hand side and Dresden and Berlin on the left. These posters are mounted between staged remnants of ruins that are seemingly still burning. Shadows of the fire fall on the room's stone floor. At the end of the room is a large film screen with stone benches, which provides the main survey film for the section (see fig. 8).[12] This setting invites the visitor to sit among ruins and watch the film through the gaze of an American soldier. It is narrated in a somber voice, which is occasionally interrupted by quotations from soldiers that are presumably reenacted.

The music and the decisive tone of the narrative voice create some pathos and establish moral values. The events of the film follow the traditional storyline

---

11 D-Day plays a minor role in the "Road to Berlin" exhibition, since the museum features its original exhibition "The D-Day Invasion of Normandy," revised and re-opened in 2017, on the third floor of the Louisiana Pavilion. This exhibition uses similar techniques to the ones in the Campaigns of Courage Pavilion by simulating the gaze of the American soldier landing in Normandy through enlarged photo posters.

12 The standard technique used in the "Road to Berlin" is to have a survey film in each new section that introduces the visitor to the entirety of the topic through the voice of a narrator, alongside historical pictures and footage. In other words, the visitor receives the same information several times: in the survey panel with a brief text and map, in the chronological photo story with brief captions on wall panels, in the survey film, and in the computer stations with oral witnesses, and possibly through the Dog Tag Experience.

Fig. 8 Immersive film theater in ruins, room "Into the German Homeland" in "Road to Berlin" exhibition. The National WWII Museum, New Orleans (Photo: Author, 2017, courtesy of The National WWII Museum).

regarding the last months of the war featuring a destroyed Germany, the Volkssturm, Hitler sacrificing his people, Americans acting as liberators and not conquerors, the discovery of the concentration camps, Dwight D. Eisenhower and George S. Patton in the Ohrdruf concentration camp, the Nazis' ideology and atrocities, the strategic bombing of the German cities, the meeting of Americans and Russians at Torgau, the Battle of Berlin and the city's surrender, Hitler's suicide, and the unconditional surrender at Reims. Strong statements structure the film's frame, exemplified at the beginning: "There can be only one outcome to this war: Germany's unconditional surrender"; and in the closing statement: "Together, these men and women [the American soldiers] will share a bond of pride, courage, sacrifice, forged on the battlefields of Europe and as they fought to free us from the darkest of tyrannies, and restore a sense of hope to the world." The latter corresponds to General Dwight D. Eisenhower's quotation, which the visitor can read upon exiting the gallery: "No other war in history has so definitely lined up the forces of arbitrary oppression and dictatorship against those of human rights and individual liberty."

None of the events narrated in the film or presented through the text panels and objects within the ruins go beyond the knowledge of the typical American soldier. They would have either experienced these events directly – for example, in their fighting the Volkssturm, or the discovery of the camps – or heard about them in the news or through a comrade, as in the case of Hitler's suicide, details of Nazi atrocities, and the final surrender. The visitor, therefore, experiences the collective perspective of the American soldier; the combined representation of all American perspectives together allows the visitor to empathize with their mission, their beliefs, and the challenges they faced. This is constructed primary experientiality, regardless of whether the visitor's historical experience is more likely to resemble American cultural memory today than historical knowledge. Unlike in the Warsaw Rising Museum and the Canadian War Museum, where argument and historical truth restrict strong visitor involvement, the visitor here is necessary as a mediating consciousness to reiterate the collective American gaze. The immersive effect is strongly supported through the computer stations located at the beginning of the section, which are the fifth of the Dog Tag Experience stations.[13] The visitor can also listen to seven oral witnesses and see a list of items that are relevant for the room's theme. All oral histories relate to wartime events, including the breaking of the Siegfried line, the crossing of the Remagen Bridge, a fight with a fanatical member of the Hitler Youth, and an American soldier unsuccessfully trying to save a baby playing with a hand grenade. The latter event is called "The Cost of War." The close-up collective gaze of the American soldier is intensified through these voices: visitors, who take their time, can immerse themselves even more in the possible views and primary experiences of the American soldier.

The moral mission rendered explicitly by film's and Eisenhower's quotations, as cited above, underline this constructed collective gaze. The museum adds historical facts and information here and there, but does not provide historiographical analysis. In this way, the visitor is not provided with any room

---

[13] There are usually two identical computer stations situated next to each other, which still restricts visitor access immensely. Many visitors pass by the stations or wait to collect artifacts on their dog tag card and listen to their dog tag member identity. However, most visitors did not linger at the stations during my five days of museum analysis in May 2017.

to question the museum's moral vision. The exhibition consistently reduces its conclusions down to simple factual statements, such as "The Führer would rather annihilate the very people and nation he professes to love than admit defeat." This sentence downplays the racial ideology of Hitler and the Nazis: it focuses on 'loving one's people' and 'being defeated' instead of analyzing the multiplicity of reasons behind the fanatical defense of Germany at the end of the war. In other words, the museum does nothing to help the visitor understand ideology and historical actions. Consequently, it is more important to show trophies such as porcelain and silverware allegedly belonging to Hitler or other high-ranking Nazi officers in the object vitrines of this section than to give historical context to the ideology and crimes of the Nazi regime. It becomes evident that the New Orleans WWII Museum is much more of a memorial museum (commemorating the moral achievement of a 'good war') than a history museum. Its constructed gaze indicates what an American soldier could have thought and brings together a multiplicity of primary experiences (usually as un-reflected memories) within this collective construct.

A final example from outside the museum can confirm the effectiveness in which the museum immerses twenty-first-century visitors in its historical settings. On the corner of Canal Street and Magazine Street, visitors to New Orleans can find an immersive bus stop.[14] Instead of a poster advertising the museum and one of its major attractions, the front, back, and sides of the bus stop are designed with imagery that reminds visitors of the ruins analyzed above, in the last room of the "Road to Berlin." The back is transparent and displays a poster of the ruins of Cologne featuring the Cologne Cathedral. This makes it seem like passengers waiting at the bus stop or walking/standing behind it are part of the scene (see fig. 9). Thus, the museum foreshadows its primary experientiality through its advertising and indicates the ways in which it bridges past and present.

The second way in which the New Orleans WWII Museum creates experientiality is through its multimedia installations. The *Final Mission: USS Tang Submarine Experience* in the Boeing Pavilion immerses visitors in the last mission of the Tang in the Pacific. After successfully attacking a Japanese convoy in the Formosa Strait on the South China Sea, the Tang is sunk by its own torpedo. Only nine out of eighty-seven men on board survived. The visitors (maximum twenty-seven per experience) are led into the U-boat, and many are asked to perform specific tasks at their stations to navigate through the battle. In reality, most visitors watch the panoramic view of the South China Sea through the ceiling of

---

14 Based on a visit in May 2017.

Fig. 9 Immersive bus stop in the ruins of Cologne. Advertising for The National WWII Museum, Canal Street, New Orleans (Photo: Author, 2017).

the multimedia installation, while these battle contributions remain more of a gimmick.[15] Nobody, despite the explosions at the end, will feel as if they have come close to participating in an actual battle and even less to being in danger (one can check at the end whether the crewmember that one was assigned survived). Thus, USS Tang experience is a mixture of entertainment, storytelling, and the commemoration of a heroic boat and crew.

To understand how multimedia installations contribute to primary experientiality, the *L.W. 'Pete' Kent Train Car Experience* is more interesting. It is located in the entrance hall of the Louisiana Pavilion, set up in 2014. Next to the admission cashiers, visitors can undergo this train car experience in four and a half minutes and enter a Union Pacific train carriage "in the footsteps of new recruits on their way to war."[16] The inscription of the Nebraskan town North Platte on the

---

[15] The area following this performance is mainly geared toward the commemoration of perished submarine crews.
[16] https://www.nationalww2museum.org/visit/museum-campus/louisiana-memorial-pavilion/train-car-experience (accessed 13 October 2019).

cart might indicate the origin of the train as being somewhere in the middle of the country.[17] The visitor is supposed to feel as if they are in an American train station in late 1941. The visitor enters the train carriage and travels toward the war, while images of the train's departure as well as scenes of rural and urban America pass by the windows. The immersion is supplemented by background sounds of the train running. While the multimedia installation simulates the rattling of the train, the museum guard plays the conductor. The visitor sits on train benches and the backrests in front of them contain a small monitor. When the train experience was installed in 2014, the visitor could listen to five stories of ordinary Americans joining the five different US forces service branches, while seeing photo-album-like scenes of each narrative on the small monitors. Since the museum opened its "Campaigns of Courage" Pavilion in 2015, it has started to explain the use of the Dog Tag Experience to the visitors through the small monitors and a loud narrator's voice. This experience interactively connects each visitor with an individual narrative of the war through the use of digitally enabled IDs.[18] The screens mostly explain how the Dog Tag Experience functions and the visitor can choose an identity while traveling on the train. Most visitors seem focused on understanding this procedure, which reduces the immersive nature of the train ride. At the end, everybody leaves the train to fight a just war. The experiential strategy of the museum leads the visitor to identify with one collective American voice: fighting for the 'good.' The visitor, though different from the individual soldiers featured, nonetheless becomes part of the collective journey. This overall perspective is strengthened by a variety of roles and voices that allow the visitor to fully identify with the master narrative of the heroic war to free the world. In contrast, the Dog Tag Experience allows for individual identification or empathy with one specific role.

The museum's multimedia signature piece *Beyond All Boundaries: a 4D Journey through the War that Changed the World* immerses the visitor in a clearly constructed and thereby secondary experiential world of the past. However, it is geared toward understanding and feeling the collective emotions of the primary historical world (see also Jaeger 2017b, 168). The New Orleans WWII Museum allows the viewer to experience what is at stake, while didactically controlling its message that the war was good, both for freedom and humanity, and that it was shaped by courage, sacrifice, and loss. The 4D film produced, directed, and narrated by Tom Hanks opened in the Solomon Victory Theater in 2009. The posters

---

[17] The inscription was adjusted since its introduction in 2014 (based on a visit in May 2017) from Pullman to Union Pacific with the addition of the place inscription.
[18] See also chapter 7 for further discussion of the effects of the Dog Tag Experience regarding the museum's depiction of the Holocaust.

outside of the theater already begin to highlight the pathos and emotional energy of the experience through iconic texts such as "December 7, 1941 – a day that will live in infamy," "Another bulletin, Japan surrenders ... I repeat Japan surrenders," and the slogan "The war that changed the world." The narrative introduces the visitor to the main events of the war from an American perspective with an eight-minute introduction, followed by thirty-six minutes of footage covering Pearl Harbor to VJ-Day. In the pre-theater screening, the visitor is confronted with eight screens simultaneously depicting the same image or corresponding images in sets of two or four. After the show begins, it first displays statistics about the dead from the war's major participating nations, which highlights the message that the Second World War superseded all individual experiences. Following this, narrator Tom Hanks introduces the narrative that an unprepared America wanted to stay out of the war despite threats from the emerging dictatorships in Japan, Germany, and Italy. The visitor is then pictorially immersed in images of America in the 1930s, touching on themes such as the racial and religious discrimination in that era. The film then sequentially introduces the racial ideologies of totalitarian Germany and Japan, various wartime events spanning from the Japanese invasion of China and the early days of the Second World War in Europe, up until the German invasion of the Soviet Union. The picture screens are extremely effective in stirring emotions and creating pictorial impressions. This is exemplified when the viewer sees eight Adolf Hitlers simultaneously giving a speech or is confronted with eight shots of the iconic photograph depicting a child in a newsboy's cap raising his arms in surrender during a roundup of Warsaw Jews. In this way, the viewer is argumentatively and emotionally prepared for the narrative that America needs to act morally and defend freedom around the world.[19]

The movie theater engages four of the visitor's senses: their audio-visual senses through the use of loud noise, music, original voices, flashing lights, etc.; their sense of smell through the deployment of a sudden fog; and their tactile senses through the use of vibrating seats during a number of scenes, such as the dropping of nuclear bombs, or the first American deployment in northwest Africa. Three-dimensional objects such as a watchtower from a German concentration camp appear to grow out of the stage; the visitor seems to be directly involved in the action of flying bombers against Germany and Japan. The voice of

---

19 Interestingly, nowhere does the New Orleans WWII Museum ask what the Americans joining the war only following the Attack on Pearl Harbor means for the moral imperative of fighting against tyranny. Furthermore, the narrative uses the emotional argument that the American mainland was under threat as a supporting reason without ever reflecting on how realistic that assumption is.

Tom Hanks, full of pathos, narrates a series of events, supported by propagandistic voices from governments on both sides and voices from Americans' letters and diaries, particularly those of veterans and two war correspondents. The illusion of simulated reality remains constant throughout. Every line in the show works toward emotionalizing the visitor in 'hot-media style' (McLuhan 1965 [1964], 22–23), with the message that American soldiers "saved humanity from the darkest of futures" via sacrifice and courage with their "blood, tears, and innocence," a "struggle for freedom that took them and the world beyond all boundaries."[20] The film relies on superlatives such as the largest war "in all of human history." The film constantly builds up dramatic tension with statements such as "If D-Day fails, there is no alternative." Several times, the narrator highlights that this was a new kind of war and draws connections to its global scope and the need to develop unimaginable weapons, using documentary voices to support its rhetoric.[21] A moving globe helps the audience to understand the shifts between the different theaters of war and the home front. The war also becomes the vehicle by which racial and gender discrimination in the United States are overcome, particularly on the home front. A woman says: "Let's look this matter of prejudice straight in the eye. Either we are believers in the principles of democracy, or we are a collection of the greatest frauds the world has ever seen." Thus, each obstacle must and will be overcome, which in turn further confirms the master narrative.

The same goes for the description of the enemies who are exclusively racial tyrants: the installation blends out any shades of good and evil. The Eastern Front only comes into play at the end of the war. Hanks's voice briefly mentions the panicking and fleeing of German civilians, before he shifts to justifying the civilian casualties of the Air War.[22] To reflect upon the cost of war, *Beyond all Boundaries* uses some very successful installations, such as when it highlights the human cost of war. The narrator calls the Western Union telegrams "the nation's new currency of grief," which is followed by the reenacted voices of mothers, overlapping as they read the news of their sons' deaths; at the same time images of telegrams are projected onto the stage. The war's human costs touched upon in the show are fit into its narrative: a fighter pilot describes how terrible the Air War against Germany was, but sees it as necessary; the use of nuclear

---

20 This is the concluding line by the narrator.
21 Such vocabulary cries for differentiation or at least comparative contextualization, since the Germans used the same word, particularly concerning their war of annihilation in the East. See also the discussion of the concept of 'total war' in chapter 8.
22 See also chapter 8 for a more a more detailed analysis of the Air War in the New Orleans WWII Museum.

bombs must not be questioned since they saved countless American lives; celebratory American parades and cheering follow. The 4D-visualization manipulates the viewer into forgetting the constructedness of the narrative. The atmosphere of the fighting and of the collective American emotions is authentically staged in a way that can make the viewer believe this constructed narrative represents historical reality. The story of democracy in the United States being somehow unprepared for war is told without nuance. Therefore, it cannot go beyond the war's historical era and consequently cannot represent the war's aftermath or further perspectives on the war.[23] There is no room for different narratives or for visitors to find their own interpretations or to understand the narrative's constructedness. Consequently, the installation can easily overwhelm the senses of many visitors (Jaeger 2017b, 168), making it so that they share in a collective, authentic experience that confirms the political status quo of the show's master narrative. There is no attempt toward "active memory work" (Crane 1997, 63) or a dynamic collaboration between history and memory. Instead, the success of the museum and film[24] is based on emotionalizing the single existing master narrative they present, which reaffirms the moral message of the war and American collective memory.[25] There is no real difference between American wartime propaganda and the twenty-first-century narrator in this museum. In other words, its interpretation of the Second World War is timeless.

Beyond All Boundaries differentiates itself from other installations in this museum by not simply constructing one collective American perspective or drawing connections to a singular oral witness. In the pre-story and at the beginning of *Beyond all Boundaries*, the installation seems to create the collective gaze of the whole American public. It purports a narrative argument through a directly emotionalized pseudo-experience of the war. Afterwards, it shifts to the per-

---

23 As a minor exception, the Dog Tag Experience stations also tell the biographical story before and after the war / legacy for each featured eyewitness.
24 Generally for such techniques of emotionalization see Apor 2014; Thiemeyer 2010a, 224. The current CEO of the museum, Stephen Watson, highlights in a historynet interview how Tom Hanks's name and the idea of a film that gives "a dramatic, broad overview of the war in a very personal and engaging way" has drawn an audience that may not otherwise have come to a military history museum (Swick 2015).
25 However, collective memory cannot simply be ignored. Susan Crane has shown with the example of the Enola Gay exhibition in the Smithsonian's National Air and Space Museum in Washington, DC, how ignoring existing personal memories of powerful interest groups, such as war veterans, can risk the educational goals of historians: "Historically conscious individuals may turn out to be quite interested in the study of historical consciousness, but it will take time and patience on the part of historians and a willingness to engage personal memories in the production of history" (1997, 63).

spective of Americans volunteering collectively to fight in the war, before simulating a soldiers' perspective in the Guadalcanal and northwest Africa. Whereas these perspectives persist throughout, some of the audio-visual installations seem to express different ones. The planes over Germany seem to bomb the viewers (although the viewer is in the three-dimensional cockpit during the firebombing of Tokyo), as if they were German civilians. The sounds and flashes when the concentration camp tower grows out of the ground are more reminiscent of being inside of a concentration camp, rather than discovering the camp as a liberator. The shock of the atomic bomb is experienced directly through a flash and shaking seats. However, because of the strong moral framework, these things do not allow the viewer to consider what is was like to be in a concentration camp or to experience a firestorm. Instead, these elements underline the war's seriousness and the argument that it had to be fought and won at all costs. Consequently, the multimedia installation still produces primary experientiality in the sense that it immerses the visitor into a single narrative of the war, as if it were the only existing reality of wartime. Here, however, the New Orleans WWII Museum is closer to the restricted experientiality produced in the Warsaw Rising Museum, while in most of its other parts the museum allows for primary experientiality through the interplay of collective and individual gazes. In this way, visitors feel like they can immerse themselves in a variety of perspectives, even if the museum's overarching interpretation of the Second World War remains indisputable.

4.2 The Oskar Schindler's Enamel Factory in Kraków

The permanent exhibition *Kraków under Nazi Occupation 1939–1945* in Oskar Schindler's Enamel Factory (*Deutsche Emailwarenfabrik*, OSF) opened on June 10, 2010.[26] It covers 1,600 square meters in twenty-eight sections, over three levels. As in the case of the Warsaw Rising Museum, the OSF can be described as a narrative museum (Heinemann 2015, 260–261). It is mainly a hybrid of a historical and a memorial museum that takes a strong experiential approach to "building up an 'emotional' history of the city" and permitting "certain identification of the visitors with the city" (Bednarek 2011, 37). To generate such emotional engagement, stage designer Michał Urban and theater director Łukasz Czuj created

---

[26] The museum belongs to the historical museums of Krakow (Muzeum Historyczne Miasta Krakowa). In 2013, it received about 270,000 visitors (Kruczek 2015, 51). See also Heinemann (2015, 255–263) for the genesis of the 2010 exhibition. I am grateful to the leading curator, Monika Bednarek for explaining the original concept of the OSF to me, in a meeting on December 11, 2013.

a theatrical set;[27] it makes it seem like the visitor is time traveling through the years and through different scenes within a cinematic narrative (see also Korzeniewski 2016, 120). The exhibition does not give a clear interpretation or ideology of how to read the past, so that the time-traveling visitor can and must make active interpretative decisions about the past space in which they are immersing themselves in. The exhibition mimetically simulates actual historical spaces and experiences and in doing so fulfills the criteria of primary experientiality. However, its dominating tendency toward the theatrical also allows its visitors to distance themselves from primary immersion. Consequently, the exhibition displays signs of a simulated structural past, making it to some extent a hybrid of primary and secondary experientiality.

This museum uses cinematic and theatrical techniques to design its exhibition, which indirectly references Steven Spielberg's Hollywood production *Schindler's List* (2003); it was this film that made the building, the German entrepreneur Oskar Schindler, and the Polish Jews who worked for and were saved by Schindler, famous. The film was partially shot at the actual factory in 1993. Shortly after, it became a site for memory tourism although it remained a functioning electronic equipment factory up until 2005 (Bednarek 2011, 36). The exhibition attempts to represent the six-year Nazi occupation of Kraków from the perspectives of its citizens, while allowing identification with both ethnic Poles and Kraków's Polish-Jewish citizens (Heinemann 2015, 267–271). In her analysis of visitor reactions in the OSF, Małgorzata Bogunia-Borowska also notes the exhibition's technique to trigger personalization and identification with the past: "The subjective engagement of emotions as well as building relations with representatives of the past make visitors more sensitive to individualized stories and to the tragedy of the times in which they lived" (2016, 249). The exhibition offers neither a meta-reflection of its narrative method, nor perspectives from outside the six historical years it represents. The visitor walks through narrow, corridor-like exhibition rooms, each organized according to a theme and generally following the timeline of the war. Consequently, the exhibition's narrative starts in Kraków before the Nazi Occupation and ends with the Red Army's liberation of the city and an epilogue.[28]

---

27 See also the exhibition's website, http://www.mhk.pl/exhibitions/krakow-under-nazi-occupation-1939-1945, accessed 13 October 2019 (Fabryka Emalia Oskara Schindlera).
28 See Bednarek, 2011, 43 for a detailed description of the exhibition structure. Its twenty-eight sections contain twelve basic thematic parts: introduction: Krakow and its residents in the interwar period 1918–1939; the outbreak of the war and the early weeks of German occupation; the 'capital' of the General Gouvernement; terror; everyday life; railway station: wartime migrations, resettlements, displacements, deportations, escapes; the Jews; Oskar Schindler; history of the

This depiction seems in line with Lubomír Doležel's idea of an actual historical world that the museum attempts to reconstruct in a model world (1999). Yet at the same time, the visitor can experience this historical world in a performative way. The narrative uses sound, sight, and architecture to simulate historical experience. The visitor goes, for example, through a dark, narrow, steel and concrete tunnel, wherein the outbreak of the war is represented. This room focuses particularly on the perception of sound. The visitor hears noises of fighting, radio propaganda, and the roar of air-raids. The darkness intensifies the visitor's loss of orientation during the simulated battle. To highlight the authenticity of the narrative, the room displays different pieces of Polish army weaponry in a model field bunker. Regular panels and a computer station supplement these objects in order to fulfill an informational function.

At first glance, the exhibition works with a very similar technique to that of the New Orleans WWII Museum in constructing primary experientiality. As in the "Road to Berlin" and "Road to Tokyo" exhibitions, the Kraków museum creates stage scenes that allow the visitor to empathize with the collective gaze of the citizens of Kraków. Visitors listen to the cries and sounds from prison cells, highlighting the beginning of the deportation and murder of Kraków's Jews; they then enter the central railway station, experience the establishment and destruction of the Kraków Ghetto, and walk through a set of the Płaszów concentration camp. A closer analysis reveals, however, that this collective perspective is less unified than in the New Orleans WWII Museum: the exhibition simulates the collective perspectives of Kraków's ordinary citizens – both Polish and Jewish as a new "We"-community (Heinemann 2017, 252; 2015, 271) – including the Polish soldier, the German occupiers (albeit in a very limited way), the Jewish inhabitants of the city during their deportations and life in the ghetto, the Polish members of the underground, the inmates of Płaszów concentration camp, the Catholic Church, and children and women, among others.[29]

Despite its theatrical setting, which is potentially manipulative of visitor emotions, the OSF also avoids the strong moral coding seen in the New Orleans WWII Museum. Rather, it uses a documentary style, which leaves room for the interpretation of the historical data and artifacts on display – images, objects, voices, and theatrical installation can affect the visitor. Indirectly, this technique still codes the exhibition, as it has a clear-cut black-and-white pattern. Germans,

---

DEF and its workers; the Polish Underground State and its structures in Kraków; the Płaszów camp; the last months of the occupation; and an epilogue: the "Hall of Choices."

29 See also Guichard-Marneur 2018 for a narratological reading of the museum space, even if it seems a stretch to read the museum as an mere expression of Polish victimhood that particularly points to the 'Communist occupation' until 1989.

including the Nazi occupiers, the newcomers to the city, and the ethnic Germans who lived in Kraków before 1939, never function as collective focalizers. Crimes are explicitly perpetrated by means of German agency. The last room entitled "Hall of Choices" is an exception to this rule, although it also clearly codes good and evil, right and wrong. Thus, the museum ends in explicit moral coding, in contrast to the open-experiential style of the rest of the exhibition (see also Heinemann 2015, 275–277; Heinemann 2017, 259–267). The scenes in each room represent spaces in Kraków before and during the occupation. Yet their setting and the exhibits used throughout, particularly photographs, are not as illustrative and functionalized as in New Orleans. The museum's representational techniques allow considerable room for interpretation.

The third difference between these two museums, which produces a different quality of experientiality, can be seen in their simulated theatrical-cinematic effects (see also Heinemann 2015, 259–260). In New Orleans, the visitors move with American soldiers from one battleground to the next, as if they were also soldiers. In Kraków, visitors become a ghostly presence in a historical space, observing the realities of the city. They are not specifically Polish, Jewish, or German, but are immersed in the simulation of a time traveler walking through a film set.[30] The visitor moves through narrow, corridor-like exhibition rooms, each organized according to theme and generally following the timeline of the war. The museum uses calendar sheets and street signs to give visitors an exact orientation of where they are moving in time and space. On the one hand, this forces visitors to move in a linear fashion as if they were watching a film (Jaeger 2015a, 153). On the other hand, the visitor can experience each scene from a cinematic perspective, so that the history of Kraków during the occupation comes to life in a performative way.[31] The exhibition employs a combination of modern museum didactics, technology, and theater-derived techniques. It targets different senses, in order to create a new, clearly poietic world that guides the visitor through this performative experience of the past. It employs sound, sight, and architecture to further simulate historical experiences. In other words, the OSF's exhibition does not simulate a collective perspective, but rather a historical space. Visitor are never under the illusion that they

---

[30] Another museum that fits in this category is the Resistance Museum (Verzetsmuseum) in Amsterdam (1999) that recreates collective experiences and historical spaces during the German occupation. As in the exhibition in the Oskar Schindler Factory, the visitor becomes a kind of time traveler through the conditions of the occupation. Unlike for example the Warsaw Rising Museum, here resistance against occupation is portrayed less heroically.

[31] See also Bal 2008, 26–35, for cinematic metaphors to describe the effects and possibilities of agency by museum visitors.

are truly re-experiencing the past and are always aware that the simulated space is theatrical and consequently distanced from actual events. Therefore, the OSF creates spaces that immerse its visitors in primary experientiality, although its effects are a hybrid of primary and secondary experientiality.

The representation of the beginning of the occupation further demonstrates the exhibition's hybrid experientiality. The visitor enters the hallway of a Kraków apartment house on September 11, 1939 and hears "the hubbub of gossip and conversations etched with fear" (Marszałek and Bednarek 2010, 16). The hallway looks barren, the floor is made of copper stone, and the white-greyish walls look old and dirty. The visitor encounters an old water basin, a stroller, and twenty mailboxes. Four contain envelopes and postcards in Polish and German writing that, for example, tell the inhabitants of the building that their family members have become prisoners of war. Through a wooden door, the visitor moves outside 'into' the *Aleja Mickiewicza*. The copper stone floor transitions into a brighter color, and the visitor encounters a mass of Nazi announcements accompanied by two large red Nazi Swastika flags on the street, which one must sidestep around. The impression that Nazi propaganda is taking over the city of Kraków is re-created through this performance. The visitor experiences the evolution of Nazi orders regulating life in the city. The exhibition alludes to the fact that the visitor is an inhabitant of the city since they seem to come out of the townhouse. The corridor ends with an enlarged photograph of the Nazis hoisting a Swastika flag as symbol for the newly established Generalgouvernement supplemented by real footage. Then, the visitor steps into Kraków's famous Old Market Square and encounters photographs of German soldiers touring Kraków and humiliating Orthodox Jews by shaving their beards.

A quotation by Julian Waga (presumably a Polish citizen, though the exhibition does not contextualize him) further shapes the impression one gets of the mood in Kraków: "What is left of the high-sounding and expressive words about our power [...] and the moment of lightning defeat is immense ... We walk around in a daze, still unable to admit to ourselves that this is the beginning of a catastrophe we have not seen in our history." A large wall poster that acts as the background to the photographs and texts shows a menacing looking German soldier in the foreground with people passing behind him through the street with flags. Thus, visitors are emotionally prepared to take the side of the Polish and Jewish citizens of Kraków and immerse themselves into the oppressive atmosphere of the occupation. The next exhibit, a façade and the front display window of Heinrich Hoffmann's bookstore opening onto the market square, reinforces this notion. The bookstore's display is symbolic for the beginning of the Germanization of Kraków. Next to it is an excerpt of a German radio interview with Heinrich Hoffmann, one of the few German primary voices in the exhibition. Hoffmann describes the liberation of Kraków's *Volksdeutsche* (ethnic Germans) and how they purchased the Führer's portraits: "Now, enabled to purchase the longed-for likeness of the Führer, they finally feel free. We considered it our principal duty to provide these people with such possibility." He also comments on the constant changing of the items and pictures on display "to show the Poles what our Führer is like!" Of course, the museum visitor is in no danger of identifying with Hoffmann's voice. The exhibition does not focalize ethnic Germans; German quotations are either propaganda or horrific quotations by Nazi leaders. At the end of the exhibit, the visitor can see the outside of a tramcar with the sign "Benutzung für Juden verboten" (use forbidden for Jews). Throughout the exhibition, photographs – at times enlarged to poster-size – play a significant role in capturing the historical atmosphere. In the section "City Square 1," as analyzed above, the OSF creates a very specific experiential effect. Throughout the announcement and flag corridor and the market square, the museum simulates the destructive force of the occupiers. Although the museum does not directly interpret the material itself, the moral interpretation of the section is clear.

The exhibition constantly switches between exterior and interior spaces and indicates these transitions through the setting, particularly the flooring. Moving on from the city square, visitors enter a room that is set to replicate Lecture Hall No. 56 in the Collegium Novum of the Jagiellonian University. It is here that they can hear the original German speech made by Gestapo officer Bruno Müller, regarding the arrest of university professors on November 6, 1939. Visitors become witnesses to the infamous 'Sonderaktion Krakau' and can feel the shock of Kraków's citizens. They travel on a timeline through space, i.e. the unfolding of the historical word depends on the visitor's presence. This is performative in the sense that, on the one hand, it references a historical world; on the other hand, it creates a historical space, as if the visitor is traveling through the past.

The exhibition then switches to the outside in the section "Generalgouvernement," in which the exhibition comes closest to creating the perspective of the German occupiers. The calendar sheet makes note of November 7, 1945, the day when governor Hans Frank moved into the Wawel Castle. The room is extremely bright with white background, walls, and ceilings. The floor consists of white tiles with black swastikas, and the visitor circumvents two advertising pillars each displaying an enlarged photograph of life-sized German soldiers marching and saluting (see fig. 10). The sounds of military marches fill the room. Throughout the room, the exhibition stages the feeling that the public side of Kraków is becoming increasingly Germanized. This is communicated though street signs, official cultural events that are symbolized on a third advertising pillar, and a display of the Nazi's architectural plans for redesigning the city. Although a period-appropriate wooden advertising board introduces the

4.2 The Oskar Schindler's Enamel Factory in Kraków — 113

Fig. 10 Section "Generalgouvernement." Permanent exhibition. Fabryka Emalia Oskara Schindlera, Kraków (Photo: Author, 2013, courtesy of Fabryka Emalia Oskara Schindlera).

role of *Volksdeutsche* and contrasts it to that of the superior Germans, neither the perspectives of the Germans nor the *Volksdeutsche* are expressed in the exhibition. Instead, they are presented through photographs and other descriptive materials, while the German individual remains anonymous. At the beginning of the room, the museum stages it to seem like visitors are present at Frank's triumphal inauguration. As they are forced to walk on swastika tiles and must circumvent the pillars of soldiers, the exhibition creates feelings of alienation in the visitor at this foreign intrusion. Whereas museums normally keep a distance from the enemy, here visitors enter in close proximity with the Nazis staging their political power. The theatricality of the approach is cognitively clear to the visitor, and because of this there is no danger of being seduced by the Nazi propaganda. Although the visitor is immersed in the emotional effects of foreign intrusion, the exhibition also offers plenty of room for interpretation. For example, on the wall are two signs in German "Für SS und Polizei verboten" (prohibited for SS and police) and "Für die Wehrmacht verboten" (prohibited for Wehrmacht members), used by some restaurants in Kraków to deny admittance to members of the SS, Gestapo, and Wehrmacht. While these clearly indicate that there was public resistance, their meaning beyond this is open. Was it a common form of resistance? How did the Germans react? Was it sustainable? The signs open up a space for further interpretation of how one can and should live during a period of occupation.

This double technique that uses, on the one hand, clear and partial perspectives affecting the visitor's sympathies and on the other a more open documentary approach, is visible throughout the whole exhibition. As mentioned above,[32] when visitors enter Kraków's famous Old Market Square in 1944, they walk between transparent plexiglass panels, which are spread throughout the room and tell different stories about historical people, representing different types or groups in Kraków during this era (see fig. 11). This has the potential effect of making visitors like they are encountering these people in their roles in Kraków's main market square as well as their everyday life. For example, one plexiglass panel shows four middle-aged women holding hands and smiling. This text describes how these women's husbands were soldiers that were imprisoned, leaving the women to find their own means of survival: "The occupation forced them to alter their behavior. They became self-reliant and resourceful." Although the OSF avoids naming these individuals, the visitor can empathize with their situation and actions. This is in strong contrast to the indoctrination by Swastika flags and marching anonymous masses seen in the sections "City Square I" and "General Gouvernement." Another example of this is the first section charting everyday life during the occupation "1940 – 41." Here, the visitor can enter a tram cart on the Salvator line, which was established exclusively for German use. This means visitors undergoes a degree of empathetic unsettlement, as sitting down on a seat and watching German propaganda films through the windows of the tram places them in the Germans' position.

My last example of how the exhibition creates a hybrid of primary and secondary experientiality is its depiction of the Kraków ghetto. Visitors climb the stairs to the upper floor and the Planty Garden Ring, where they can watch projected German newsreels. From these bright leisurely scenes, the visitor enters a dark corridor of the ghetto. At first it seems like the visitor is seeing the ghetto from the outside before entering it. Integrated in the wall are photographs of its streets and residents as well as quotations from firsthand accounts about life in the ghetto. In between two parts of the Ghetto wall, there are two reconstructed rooms, symbolizing the extremely overpopulated conditions and the fact that strangers were frequently housed together (Marszałek and Bednarek 2010, 30). The interior diorama shows mannequins made completely of white

---

[32] See also chapter 2.2.

Fig. 11 Meeting historical people in transparent plexiglass panels in Kraków's Old Market Square in 1944. Permanent exhibition. Fabryka Emalia Oskara Schindlera, Kraków (Photo: Author, 2013, courtesy of Fabryka Emalia Oskara Schindlera).

plaster, creating a gap between this representation and the people represented. In other words, although this model ghetto imitates the primary experience of the historical one and thereby impacts the visitor emotionally, visitors never lose the feeling that they are time travelers in space who are unsure of whether they have the right to see what they are viewing. The act of looking at this interior scene is more about the feelings of awkwardness created by gazing into somebody's private space than about the reconstruction of that space. This distances visitors and leads them to the meta-reflection about how immersing themselves in the past is cognitively and ethically possible, leading to effects of secondary experientiality.

4.3 The Bastogne War Museum

As seen in the Oskar Schindler Factory, the permanent exhibition in the Bastogne War Museum: Living Memory of the Ardennes (BWM) is a hybrid between primary and secondary experientiality. Both museums employ their local subject matter to create immersive experiences. The BWM, however, establishes considerably more of a historical structure and employs a larger variety of distantiation to counterbalance its immersive and empathetic techniques. The museum opened on March 22, 2014 and is located in a new building,[33] next to the Mardasson Memorial honoring the American liberators. The mission statement places emphasis on historical tourism: "The point is to turn the 'memorial tourism,' of which the memorial fact is less and less present in the collective memory, into a 'history tourism' with a clear civil and educational calling."[34] The fact that the museum is more interested in tourism than in historiographical research is evident. For example, it only uses an English name, even on its French- and Flemish-language websites. The museum's website also still clearly defines it as a memorial museum by attributing the word "memorial center" to the institution on its entry page.[35] For a local museum on the theme of a specific battle located far away from larger population centers, it is quite successful at about 150,000 visitors per year, almost half of which are international.[36] The museum's exhibition relies on numerous audio-visual features, including image collages, enlarged poster-like photographs, video eyewitness accounts, floor and wall design, and display panels that constantly change color. The museum uses original objects, but they are secondary to the exhibition's visual and experiential approach. The anchor points of the permanent exhibition are three scenovisions, three-dimensional theaters where the visitor enters a stage in order to be immersed in the events of the war. The museum was designed and is managed by the Belgian company Tempora. The new building and exhibition was financed by local and regional tourism funds and the European Union.[37] The architecture of the bunker-like building is nestled into its surroundings by the Atelier de l'Arbre d'Or to disorient the visitor, similar to Libeskind's architecture in the Bundes-

---

[33] It replaced the Bastogne Historical Center, which was more of a traditional military history exhibition with weapons and memorabilia commemorating the battle. The Bastogne Historical Center was closed in 2009.
[34] Bastogne War Museum 2014, 11.
[35] https://www.bastognewarmuseum.be/en/home-en/, accessed 13 October 2019.
[36] At least in first two years after opening, see Bastogne War Museum, "Press Release–May 2016," http://www.bastognewarmuseum.be/press-kit.html, accessed 9 August 2018.
[37] Bastogne War Museum 2014, 38.

wehr Military History Museum and in the Imperial War Museum North: "Creating spaces outside their axe [sic], lead-free materials, and the unbalance in the plans constantly create new points of view, which leave the visitor with a feeling of surprise and disorientation."[38]

The BWM has one of the most original approaches in terms of museums representing the Second World War, with its simulation of war experientiality centering on fictitious characters.[39] The permanent exhibition is situated on two levels.[40] The ground floor is structured as follows: it starts with "Before the Battle of Bulge" with the segments "From War to War" (three rooms including the first scenovision), followed by "Belgium in the War" (one room) and "Towards Liberation" (four rooms with the last focusing on the German preparations for the surprise counter attack). In the basement the visitor encounters the "Battle of the Bulge" (about five sections, including two scenovisions[41]) and the aftermath of the Battle of Bulge with four sections covering the Allied victory in Bastogne and in the overall war, Belgium at the end of the war, and an epilogue). The ways in which the BWM frames the 'before' and 'after' the Battle of the Bulge allows it to exhibit a close-up display of the battle, while simultaneously narrating certain national and global layers of the war. Through the audio-guide, visitors automatically hear the narrative voices of four fictitious characters: Émile, a 13-year-old student, Mathilde, a 25-year-old teacher and casual member of the Belgian resistance, Hans, a 21-year-old Wehrmacht Lieutenant, and Robert, a 20-year-old American soldier of the 101st Airborne Division (see fig. 12). All four characters are visualized as figures from a graphic novel; as soon as visitors approach an illustration of the upper part of the characters' face highlighting their eyes on the walls throughout the museum, they can listen to the relevant part of the character's audio story.

The characters are constructed as composites from many eyewitness accounts of the battle from American, German, and civilian perspectives. Despite their cartoon-like construction, the visitor is likely to perceive the characters

---

38 Bastogne War Museum 2014, 15.
39 The Gdańsk Museum of the Second World War exhibits a children's exhibition entitled *Time Travel: the Story of a Family and its Home*, which is centered around three rooms of the family's home that change over the course of the war. The visitor can, however, only hear the story through the audio installation in Polish and the exhibition is specifically designated for children twelve and under, so that the use of fiction is a mere didactic tool that does not influence most museum visitors (for further context, see Machcewicz 2019 [2017], 83–84).
40 For the structure of the exhibition, see also the visitor guide Bastogne War Museum 2016.
41 Since the visitor follows a sequence with the option of skipping the second and third scenovision, what exactly makes up a room is arguable, especially concerning the corridor-like sections.

Fig. 12 Narrative characters "See the War through our Eyes." Permanent exhibition. Bastogne War Museum, Bastogne (Photo: Author, 2016, © Bastogne War Museum).

as real historical figures.[42] In the exhibition's last section depicting the end of the war, the audio tour ends with the story of all four characters – as if they had lived through the Battle of Bulge – and describes their fate afterwards. In this way, each character is given a typical fate that many endured after the war. Robert, whose brother John died in the Pacific, takes over his parent's shop, has three children, but loses his oldest son in Vietnam. "Wars have caused me so much pain." He returns to Bastogne and the Mardasson memorial with the veterans of the 101st Airborne Division. Hans, originally from Frankfurt Oder in the East, relocates to West Germany in order to get involved in politics alongside Chancellor Konrad Adenauer. "I participated in the reconstruction of my country and Europe so that a war within its borders would never again be possible."

The BWM tries to display the characters' inner tensions, such as the tension faced by Robert after the death of his brother between mourning and the heroism

---

42 The museum catalog – unlike the exhibition itself – clearly marks that they are "fictitious witnesses" but notes that they are also "very real all the same" (Bastogne War Museum 2016, 81).

of his own participation in the war. Despite this, the visitor still experiences fairly stereotypical characters. For example, Hans's story confirms the superiority of Western freedom over the East without challenging possible problems in the West, such as the lack of post-war De-Nazification. The emotional attachment that the exhibition fosters between the visitor and these fictitious individuals, who function as composite models representing possible types of people in specific groups, downplays the multiplicity of options and personal reasons behind different behaviors during and after the war.

The visitor listens to these characters from an up-close perspective, mostly as people who directly experienced the battle, encirclement, and bombardment of Bastogne. Sometimes, however, the characters provide larger contexts from a greater narrative distance. This especially holds true on the upper floor of the exhibition and in the first scenovision, which intersperses an overview of the war from 1939 to the eve of D-Day with concrete accounts by all four characters, framed as a fictitious pre-D-Day press conference. Occasionally a separate narrator touches on certain events of the war that the exhibition cannot directly link to the characters. This corresponds to the exhibition's technique of constant variation between proximity and distance. The visitor is often very close to the characters. For example, when Mathilde joins the resistance her disdain for collaborators and enthusiasm for the resistance is evident, as is Émile's contempt for the German occupiers. Yet Mathilde also expresses fear for her family members in the possible case of her arrest, displaying the potential reasoning behind the collaboration of others. Mathilde and occasionally Émile are also responsible for providing a survey of the political situation in Belgium.

An example of a more distant perspective can be found in the second room, "From War to War," in which both Hans and Robert tell the visitor about their parents and the economic challenges they faced in the 1920s and 1930s.[43] Hans's story is particularly interesting; on the one hand, he tells a story that he has heard secondhand, as he was born in 1923 and therefore too young to experience it himself. Thus, everything he reports comes from others and mainly his father, who fits the classical stereotype of a German worker following Hitler. He blames the Allies and especially the Jews, who he claims had been involved in financial speculation, for the economic crisis. Hans concludes that, from the perspective of the ordinary people, Adolf Hitler seemed to be "the only solution" as well as "the only person to defeat Soviet Bolshevism." The story shifts in proximity: it relates to the characters' real experiences and their feelings in concrete

---

[43] In June 2018, two out of three audio signals in room two did not work and were marked as out of order, significantly reducing the effect of the characters' biographical backgrounds.

situations; it also features a further distance when the characters almost seem to be giving a historical overview on the political, military, or economic situation; as well as a middle distance, where the characters narrate one possible story, which simultaneously incorporates the stories and stereotypes of millions of people during this era. Through this narrative style, the BWM is able to display how immersed a particular character is in his surroundings.

Hans reacts to the historical events and cheers when the German army attacks and defeats Poland,[44] and it follows logically that he becomes an officer indoctrinated by Nazi propaganda. At first, he is convinced that the Germans will win the war: "We are going to bomb the English and they will understand our superiority."[45] However, he later becomes disillusioned and merely acts as a responsible officer in the Battle of the Bulge and, following his imprisonment, simply as a decent human being.[46] At the same time, a lot of stereotypes are mentioned in a way that could potentially allow the visitor to believe the same propaganda that influenced Hans. The display walls with photos, document facsimiles, texts, and small horizontal vitrines with illustrative objects on the walls counteract this impression by employing a documentary style. Furthermore, the rise of totalitarian regimes in Europe (Germany, Italy, Soviet Union) and German racism is clearly documented.[47] Despite this, the risk remains, as the exhibition does not explicitly call the Nazi propaganda into question. This can be seen in one of the computer stations, "What would you have done?," in which visitors can click through a slideshow of texts and contextualizing photographs before they have the opportunity to choose one of four questions. This tool further runs the risk of under-contextualizing cause and effect. For example, one slideshow entitled "After the 1914–18 War," documenting the human, economic, and political legacies of war, reads on its last screen: "Right after the First World War, the bruised and exhausted victors are longing for peace." It then asks the question: "Should Germany be pun-

---

[44] In the first scenovision.
[45] First scenovision.
[46] It is important to note that Hans's story is strangely quiet on his personal experiences in the East, although his first deployment occurs in December 1941 at the gates of Moscow. His character has sympathies for Nazism and Hitler, yet when it comes to real war crimes, he falls silent. Of course, one can argue that this is beyond the scope of the museum and would be the task for a fictitious composite character in a German museum.
[47] The BWM always connects world events with local events in Belgium, so that visitors obtain a documentary overview of economic and political developments in Belgium, including the rising Flemish nationalism.

ished?" The visitor receives two options:[48] "Yes, to get compensation, to take revenge, or to serve as a warning." Or: "No, that could lead to the Second World War." This runs the risk that the visitor will view the Treaty of Versailles as the singular, or at least major reason for subsequent historical developments.

The second and third scenovision emotionalize the visitor through a combination of storytelling and images. They overlap in parts with the audio guide, but add important details to the story and create a consistent multiperspectival narrative. The second scenovision, entitled "The Offensive: In the Woods near Bastogne: At the Dawn of 16 December 1944…," can serve as primary example for how the exhibition creates experientiality for the visitor. Visitors sit on tree benches looking at the stage of the Bastogne Forest, which is covered in tree stumps. Machine-guns emerge out of foxholes (see fig. 13). A three-dimensional projection of visual scenes and audio immerses the visitor in the forest. The occasional wafts of fog and the smell of smoke underline this multisensory experience. The sky projected on the ceiling fills with parachutes at one point. The cartoon characters are projected as images on the wall, which breaks the visitor's illusion of reality. The voices contextualize the fighting and shift between closer and farther proximity to the battle. Although the title of the scenovision identifies a specific moment in time as its starting point, it narrates the whole German counterattack and encirclement of Bastogne through the voices of the four characters, up until the United States Third Army of General Patton relieves the 101st Airborne Division on December 26, 1944 (see also Jaeger 2019, 60–61).

The visitor can empathize with all four roles, although Émile's and Mathilde's roles are more prominent in the third scenovision, highlighting the civilian experience. At the beginning of the second scenovision, Hans and Robert's perspectives as soldiers quickly change. For example, Hans reports on the different villages that the Germans conquer while focusing on Bastogne. At the same time, the Americans have received reinforcements. Hans provides an idea of the general situation, describing where the German advance was halted and what areas are still under American control. He then highlights how his men raze every forest they come across. The narration then switches to Robert, who says "We have been digging foxholes all night long; we are ready for them." Explosions start and the visitor is immersed in a battle narrated from the American perspective through Robert's commands. Dramatic music overlaps with the sounds of fighting, and Hans's voice sets in, talking about the lack of success

---

48 Normally, the visitor receives four options. In June 2018, slightly more than four years after opening, only four out of ten of the computer stations with background information and the "What would you have done?" were still working, considerably reducing the impact of this tool.

Fig. 13 Scenovision 2: "The Offensive: In the Woods near Bastogne: At the Dawn of 16 December 1944 ...." Permanent exhibition. Bastogne War Museum, Bastogne (Photo: Author, 2016, © Bastogne War Museum).

and how exhausted his men are after going for two days without real food. This back and forth between the two situations continues, highlighting the human needs of each group while providing an overview of the military situation. This goes on until Robert's group captures Hans. Iconic images, scenery, a multimedia show, and the narrative all work to authenticate each other. The visitor is emotionalized to empathize with all four characters; they are all represented in a reconciliatory way, so that no conflict between them arises. The visitor can identify just as much with Robert as with Hans because of the narrative's emphasis on their human character traits. However, this identification is continuously broken-up (see also Jaeger 2019, 60); first through the constant shift in proximity and distance to the soldiers' 'real' experiences and summaries of the battle and secondly through the multiperspectival shifts between the four characters. The visitor experiences a secondary meta-reality of the whole battle that consistently includes primary forms of identification with the perspectives of specific characters.

This form of representation carries a conciliatory and – to an extent – anti-war message. Consequently, the visitor could potentially lose the ability to critically engage with war crimes and the soldiers' ideology. Hans seems too moral of a character despite being fascinated by Hitler at the age of 16.[49] At the same time, he seems to be a prototypical German soldier. For example, he alludes to the fact that he served on the Eastern Front in Russia, but does not give any insight into what atrocities were perpetrated during the war of annihilation. However, images, interview footage, and text throughout the exhibition interweave the stories of the four characters with war crimes in the Ardennes, Belgium, and across the world as well as with the Holocaust. The museum transcends cheap empathy or simplistic entertainment experiences through a complex structure that combines iconic images, fully-developed narrative perspectives, and an empathetic experience of an authentic, but clearly constructed scene in the woods near Bastogne. This allows the visitor to develop questions about war beyond the goal of empathizing with the soldiers in the forest or with the civilians in bombed-out Bastogne cellars.

In the third scenovision, all four characters, including the prisoner of war Hans, meet in a café owned by Émile's uncle during the night of the bombardment of Bastogne by the Luftwaffe on December 23–24, 1944 (see also Jaeger 2019, 62–63). The visitor is placed to watch and listen, first in the café, then in its basement. On the one hand, this is a very intimate, if slightly unrealistic setting. The civilians share soup with Hans, who mimics playing the cello, while Robert plays his harmonica and Émile plays a waltz on his accordion in the dimly lit basement. The characters start to bond over music and talking. At the end of the scenovision, Émile hears news of his parents' death and Mathilde describes how she teaches a lesson in a post-war classroom near Bastogne by analyzing a German text, which states that the world may never see such a Christmas again: "To snatch a child from his mother, a husband from his wife, a father from his children, is this worthy of a human being? [...] Universal

---

49 As per his descriptions in the first scenovision and room two. However, in room ten following the second scenovision, the visitor receives a partial authentication of Hans's character through a personal video narrative. Paul-Émile Englebert, who had been taken prisoner by the Germans, remembers a two-hour conversation with an unnamed German soldier who was Catholic and around eighteen-years old from the Rhine region. This soldier told Englebert how his mother had said that he must obey, but that the war was unfair and the Germans would lose. She had asked her son to eat enough and dress warmly if needed, but leave the women and girls alone and not bring any souvenirs home. According to Englebert, the German was proud to have kept his promise to his mother. The visitor can clearly recognize some of Hans's biography and human traits in this unnamed German soldier.

fraternity will undeniably rise from the ruins, blood, and death." The scenovision ends with Émile riding his bicycle, accordion on his back, to the sea. It had always been Émile's dream to see the sea and ride there by bicycle with his father, the owner of a bicycle shop. The cartoon-like character Émile becomes a real person in the footage, who is seen by the viewer disappearing on a road into the distance with images of the sea. Even more than in the previous scenovision, the characters are used to reinforce the overarching message of the brutality of war. The BWM brings the everyday experience of war very close to the visitor, who can empathize with the personalized and stereotypical experiences of the different characters.

In order to understand how this primary reality does not completely overtake the visitors' emotions, it is important to further analyze other exhibition techniques in the museum. The museum highlights eyewitness accounts of civilians and soldiers who lived in the region during the war throughout the exhibition on small video screens.[50] For example, the room following the third scenovision charts the aftermath of the battle in the Ardennes, two video screens display the traumas of war through interviews with three survivors who narrowly escaped the mass executions of civilians in Parfondruy and Bande.[51] The eyewitnesses describe in detail how the Germans killed one civilian after another and the viewer sees the witnesses today remembering these war crimes. This whole section is dominated by the sound of funeral music. The second part of the section contains a very bright aisle consisting of seventeen gravestones of people with different nationalities who died during the Battle of the Bulge. Slideshows of photo albums are integrated into their horizontal parts. Behind both sides of the aisle are large mirrors mounted on the wall that reflect the visitor and the graves multiple times over, creating the illusion of a full graveyard landscape and immersing the visitor deeply in the scene. At the end of the opening to the next section is an enlarged photo poster of the provisional American Military Cemetery in Foy-Recogne. This gives the visitor the opportunity to become immersed in the mourning process while walking through the graveyard. In doing so, the BWM counterbalances the stories of German perpetration and mass execution in the same room and allows for a universalized mourning of all victims of war.

Reflecting on the overall strategy of the BWM, the museum avoids the risk of simply recreating an empty form of reconciliation through its two-way approach

---

[50] Often, the interviews were conducted by young people from Bastogne to create "an engaging and often very moving" intergenerational encounter (http://www.bastognewarmuseum.be/press-kit.html, accessed 9 August 2018).
[51] For video testimony in general see de Jong 2018a, especially chapter 4 "Exhibiting: The Witness to History as a Museum Object," 110–180.

of integrating the local and the global. This leads to a constant use of distantiation. The global elements of the first section on the ground floor, including the first scenovision, are interwoven with local Belgian issues and the roles of Mathilde and Émile. The Belgian section on resistance and collaboration goes back and forth between these two sides and the occupiers. After this, the run-through of the later events in the war across the globe, including D-Day, becomes very personal through the exhibition's collective perspective on the liberation of Belgium as well as the punishment of collaborators. Thus, visitors are well prepared for the more local view found in the basement, before they return to the world events, once more accompanied by the voices of the four characters at the end. In contrast to the New Orleans WWII Museum, the BWM thereby creates a balance between personal witness accounts, real and fictitious-composite characters, and a documentary overview of the war.

It is, however, important to note that the global here is not simply depicted through documentary panels and screens. The museum works with visualization techniques such as photo montages and enlarged photographs throughout the exhibition. It creates vanishing points through its photo posters. The very first artifact the museum visitor encounters is a wall collage of fourteen images presented in two rows of seven images, the top row in black and white and the bottom row colored in red. The images are often well-known icons, such as the staged picture of Germans opening a Polish border post on September 1, 1939, or the mushroom cloud after the nuclear bombing of Nagasaki, marking the beginning and the end of the war. Others refer to iconic historical moments, such as the Allied landing in Normandy, fleeing civilians, children in the Warsaw Ghetto, swastikas painted on the baldly-shaven heads of women accused of being collaborators, and piles of corpses and starved prisoners behind barbed wire in liberated concentration camps. All these moments, often with the same images, re-occur later in the exhibition. Thus, the visitor is prepared for the key emotional moments of the war. There is an emphasis on the Allied perspective, whether during their military advance, through civilian suffering, or during the discovery of the camps. This internal commentary effect is similar to the constant repetition in New Orleans; however, the New Orleans WWII Museum multiplies facts and core narratives and never leaves these to the open effects of images.[52]

In the first room, located above a Sherman tank, the visitor finds a slideshow of about twenty photographs that have been digitized to give the illusion of being a moving image. These images, surrounded by key words about the war in French, English, and German, repeat the exhibition's reference to some of

---

52 See also chapter 4.1.

the war's major world events and also include specific images of the Battle of Bulge. Although visitors have not yet read any text about the war, they are already immersed in the core images of the war on both a local and global scale. Thus, the museum does not reconstruct the war through images, but uses images to create experientiality via iconic memory, various perspectives, structural contrasts, and narrative lines. For example, the main focus of the sixth room of the permanent exhibition – before the beginning of the Battle of the Bulge – depicts the road to liberation after D-Day. It presents the liberation of French and mostly Belgian cities from the perspective of the Belgian people. At its very end, the visitor encounters a model of a Willys Jeep that, according to its description, is as "emblematic of the Second World War and as famous as the Coca-Cola bottle." The sidewall of this liberation room ends in a photo of waving Belgians in Antwerp and the film posters for *The Dictator* and *Casablanca*. In the back to the left of the jeep, an enlarged poster photograph of a Willys Jeep from the arrival of American soldiers in Branchon is displayed. Six children with happy, somewhat shy, and excited expressions are riding the jeep; a young girl on the lap of an African-American soldier is holding the wheel. To the right, the smiling boy in the back of the jeep is even further enlarged. The fact that Émile tells the exact same story in the audio guide, about how he is allowed to ride a jeep and receives chewing gum for the first time in his life, intensifies the emotional effect on the visitor. Émile becomes even more real. The exhibition visualizes war here with an emphasis on civilians' happiness surrounding the liberation. The iconic vehicle of the liberator merges with American consumer culture and Belgian youth, displaying the idea of a new beginning accompanied by jazz music. War is not primarily visualized through authentic reconstruction but through capturing and simulating an atmospheric moment. The transfer to the next room, which focuses on the German preparations for their surprise counter attack and the devastation it inflicted on civilians in the Ardennes, who had to once more flee or endure fighting, also begins with a symbolic visualization. If visitors turn around, they will see three posters: the still-smiling boy in the jeep, an enlarged portrait of Hitler, and a large poster of a swastika. The affective contrast could not be larger; it simulates the emotional letdown of the people in Bastogne and the surrounding region when the war starts up again.

The BWM employs an authenticating networking technique by interweaving numerous stories, images, eyewitness accounts, staged constellations, and objects. The reality effect is not simply created through the four fictitious composite characters. Instead, they interact closely with all other parts, sources, and media in the museum. All of these elements authenticate each other, while also diversifying and sometimes counterbalancing the narrative.[53] The museum's factual techniques, however, risk immersing visitors in a way that prevents them from realizing that these characters are constructed, composite perspectives of the war. This is the standard challenge and also potential objective for the museums analyzed in this section, which mainly create primary experientiality. Despite the distantiation techniques that the BWM uses, visitors are immersed in a historical simulation and can lose their reflexive and analytical skills for interpreting history and the many different perspectives it can offer.

---

[53] Several professionals I talked to after their first visit to the museum felt that the four characters were real historical figures.

Chapter 5:
Secondary Experientiality

Experientiality occurs on a sliding scale between its primary and secondary forms. The main purpose of the three forms of experientiality discussed in the previous chapter is the mimetic imitation of past perspectives and experiences. The New Orleans WWII Museum stages experiences in order to bring the visitor close to the collective experience of the American soldier and the American public during the war. It does so while constructing a strong master narrative that is kept partially dynamic through its reliance on a large number of individual voices. The Oskar Schindler Factory allows the visitor to time travel through the space of occupied Kraków and stages numerous collective perspectives – mainly those of the city's Polish and Jewish citizens – in order to simulate past experiences for the visitor. Finally, the Bastogne War Museum imitates actual composite voices, allowing the visitor to empathize with specific perspectives that serve as individual examples for different group perspectives. Due to the fact that the museum counterbalances its staging of primary experientiality with numerous other distantiation techniques, the visitor is able to perceive a past on the verge of secondary experientiality. This means that no equivalent to the staged world and its structures actually exists in the past.

The three museums discussed in this chapter all create simulated potential realities for the visitor that have no potential equivalent in the past. The Bundeswehr Military History Museum in Dresden is the closest to creating secondary experientiality. It creates structural and thematic constellations and networks throughout the permanent exhibition, while maintaining a high degree of historical specificity. The visitor experiences structures in the present and is not tempted to believe that they are re-experiencing past perspectives. The Imperial War Museum North in Manchester also uses an overlap between historical events and thematic structures. However, it comes much closer to imitating perspectives of the past since it primarily relies on individual historical voices and stories in order to develop its structures. Unlike the three museums discussed in the previous chapter, visitors are not steered by the illusion that they can take on the past perspective of individuals or groups; nor do they act as time travelers through (scenographically staged) space. Instead, the visitor can have structural experiences of the past. Even in cases where the museum stages a historical perspective, such as that of the British collective on the home front, it is clear that the visitor does not re-experience a singular possible perspective of an ordinary British civilian. Rather, the visitor experiences a structural and thematic composite, a heteroglossia of historical voices, which allows them to participate in a concrete memory community in the present.¹ Finally, the Topography of Terror in Berlin, similarly to the Bundeswehr Military History Museum, creates historical clusters and scenes that did not exist in the past, but instead provide structural possibilities with which to experience historical spaces, themes, and perspectives. It also employs visualization via photographs, which creates an aesthetic effect of emotionalizing the visitor through repetition and montage. Whereas the Manchester museum creates more of a closed form of secondary experientiality, the ones in Dresden and Berlin are very open, allowing visitors to create their own interpretations.

5.1 The Bundeswehr Military History Museum in Dresden

The Bundeswehr Military History Museum (MHM) is a model museum for the creation of historical structures, allowing for the active visitor to potentially explore and experience the possibilities stemming from secondary experientiality. The museum reopened with a new permanent exhibition, designed by H.G. Merz and Holzer Kobler, in a redesigned building on October 15, 2011.² A wedge by architect Daniel Libeskind cuts into the 1897 classicist arsenal building constructed in the Albertstadt military quarter³ and disrupts its complex history in order to

---

[1] On the sliding scale of experientiality, one could argue that the Oskar Schindler Factory and the Imperial War Museum North use similar distantiation techniques to express a multitude of heterogeneous collective perspectives; but whereas the museum in Kraków lures the visitor into feeling present in a space of the past, the museum in Manchester ensures that the visitor feels like they are having a structural memory experience in the present.

[2] The museum had about half a million visitors in the year following the re-opening.

[3] See Pieken 2013, 63–64; Rogg 2012a (2011). See for a more detailed description of the history of the arsenal building and the status of the collection around 2000 Scheerer 2003a, 4–27 (Scheerer 2003b; Kunz 2003; Beßer 2003a; Fleischer 2003). First, the main building housed the Royal Arsenal Collection (Königliche Arsenal-Sammlung) and Royal Saxon Army Museum (Königlich-Sächsische Armee-Museum). From 1923 to 1924, it became the Saxon Army Museum (Sächsische Armeemuseum), before becoming the Army Museum of the Wehrmacht (Heeresmuseum; after 1942 Armeemuseum) under National Socialism from 1938 to 1945. In 1972, the museum reopened as the Army Museum of the GDR, which continued to shape the collection and permanent exhibition until the closure of the permanent exhibition in 2010. Shortly before German reunification in 1990, it was renamed Militärhistorisches Museum der Bundeswehr. I am grateful to Gorch Pieken, former Project Lead (2006–2011) and Research Director (2011–2017) of the MHM for explaining the original concept of the MHM to me, in several meetings and guided tours between 2012 and 2014.

Fig. 14 Front façade of main museum building with Libeskind wedge. Militärhistorisches Museum der Bundeswehr (Bundeswehr Military History Museum), Dresden (Photo: Author, 2012).

fragment and complicate the memory of the past (see fig. 14).[4] On June 14, 1994, the MHM was officially designated the leading museum in the Bundeswehr network, making it Germany's de facto principal army and military history museum.[5] By interweaving military history with political, social, and cultural history

---

[4] Matthias Rogg 2012b (2011), 15–19. See also chapter 8 below for the discussion of the top floor and the wedge regarding the MHM's representation of the Air War. For the detailed planning process, the architectural competition, the architectural concept of Studio Daniel Libeskind, and the interior design concept by HG Merz / Barbara Holzer, see also Beßer 2003b, Studio Daniel Libeskind 2003; HG Merz and Holzer 2003. Cercel has noted that "Libeskind's penetrative architectural reinvention of the museum is an authoritative gesture in itself" (2018, 28) that risks over-symbolizing the deconstructive temple characteristic of the museum and consequently, losing its potential for agonism or critical debate (2018, 16). See also Weiser 2017, 52–55, who interprets Libeskind's architecture as "interrupted chronology," while at best scratching the surface of the rhetoric and representational style of the permanent exhibition.

[5] The MHM is publicly funded through the budget of the German Ministry of Defense. Within the hierarchy of the Bundeswehr, the MHM is supervised by the Center for Military History and Social Sciences of the Bundeswehr in Potsdam (formerly the Military History Research Office, in German: Militärgeschichtliches Forschungsamt, MGFA). For a detailed description of its institu-

as well as with the history of what the French Annales historians have termed *mentalités*, the museum claims to approach military exhibitions in a new way.[6] This method, according to the museum makers, allows for the expression of two distinct models of time: first, evolutionary time, in which violence and force are inherent to human behavior (here they display anthropological consistency across the human species); second, the time of cultural change, in which violence depends on its cultural, historical, and social surroundings (see Pieken 2012 [2011], 22). Hans-Ulrich Thamer notes in his conceptual review of the MHM that it surpasses the concepts of traditional military history museums, which primarily exhibit military artifacts and weapons, by radically exploring how the violence of war can be depicted and reflected in a museum (2012). To fulfill its goal of representing the history and anthropology of violence, the MHM takes a twofold approach: first, it presents the traditional story of German warfare from 1300 to the present as a chronological exhibition in the original arsenal building of about 5,000 square meters. Second, a thematic exhibition in Libeskind's wedge – in German, *Themenparcours*, literally a 'tour' of different themes over about 3,000 square meters of exhibition space – confronts the visitor with the violent effects of war as ideas and themes.[7] To visit the different sections of the chronological exhibition, the visitor must walk through the thematic exhibition in the wedge; the architectural design ensures that the chronological and thematic exhibitions are necessarily intertwined. As the chief museum of the Bundeswehr, the MHM's perspective is clearly German, although this perspective is interspersed throughout the museum with that of a more universal anthropology of violence.[8]

---

tional and organizational structure, see Kraus 2011. See also Rauchensteiner 2011 for the advisory process that took place during the planning of the new building.

6 See the exhibition guide, Pieken and Rogg 2012 (2011), especially Pieken 2012 (2011) and Rogg 2012b (2011). See also the summary of the early development of the museum concept by its first research director in 2004–2005, Siegfried Müller (2006).

7 See also the detailed concept of the expert commission, Konzeptgruppe/Expertenkommission 2003 ("Das Militärhistorische Museum Dresden 2006 [Konzeption])." Cercel et al. argue the anthropological approach of the museum almost equates war with nature (2019, 208), but this seems to underestimate the fact that 'violence' is a much more encompassing concept than war and that the open style of the museum only documents war and violence, but allows the visitor to decide whether there are ways to overcome it. Consequently, the close relationship between nature and war is present in many museums discussed in this study. However, for example, the teleological dimension of the Canadian War Museum (see also chapter 3.1), is nowhere to be found in the MHM.

8 In 2017–2018, with the departure of both director Matthias Rogg (2010–2017) and research director / main curator Gorch Pieken (2006–2017), a debate about the mission of a Bundeswehr

The five floors of Libeskind's wedge house a thematic tour of war and violence spread across twelve sections, starting at the top with the "Dresden View," with "War and Memory" directly below.⁹ Level 2 addresses the relationship between society and violence/war in five sections: "Politics and the Use of Force," "Language and the Military," "Fashion and the Military," "Music and the Military," and "War and Play." Visitors – unless they take the elevator – use the original stairwell of the arsenal building to enter the first and ground floors of the wedge. Level 1 focuses on the mentality of war in the section entitled "The Formation of the Bodies," and on the effects of war in the sections "War and Suffering" and "Animals and the Military." Finally, the ground floor is divided into the sections "Protection and Destruction" and "Technology and the Military"; the latter again emphasizes the links between civil society and war. The wedge also creates six "vertical showcases,"¹⁰ shafts or voids at the intersection of the old arsenal building and the wedge, which are used to display large objects and a number of thematically overlapping installations, such as the shell of a V2 rocket.¹¹

In the wings of the old arsenal building, the MHM houses its chronological exhibition, a history of the German military divided into three temporally distinct sections: "1300–1914" (ground floor west), "1914–1945" (first floor west), and "1945–Present" (first floor east). All three sections of the chronological exhibi-

---

museum emerged. On the one hand, this debate originated in struggles relating to internal quarrels and organizational structures within the institution. On the other, it related to the cost and contents of the MHM's 2018 special exhibition *Gender and Violence: War is for Men – Peace is for Women?* (originally planned for 2017) and the cancelled exhibition *Clash of Future: Myths of the Nations 1914–1945*. Even if the MHM denied any change in its mission, the press debated whether the museum still aimed to be a cultural history museum that should compete with large military history museums and general history museums world-wide, or whether it was aiming for the softer educational mission of its military personnel as seen in more traditional military history museums (see also Richter 2017 and Locke 2017). It remains to be seen how the MHM will develop without Rogg and Pieken. With the exception of the *Gender and Violence* exhibition , which was still curated by Pieken, the museum has only presented a minor exhibition *The Führer Adolf Hitler is Dead: Attempted Assassination and Coup d'État on 20 July 1944* since Pieken left (fall of 2017). This seems meagre for a museum that describes itself as a leading history museum in Europe (https://www.mhmbw.de/dauerausstellung, accessed 13 October 2019). The search for a new research director was ongoing in the fall of 2019. Albeit on a smaller scale than the Second World War Museum in Gdańsk, this debate demonstrates that political and institutional pressures can threaten or possibly change the missions and orientations of war museums.

9 For a detailed description of the thematic tour, see also Pieken 2013, 66–74, and Pieken and Rogg 2012 (2011), 52–113.
10 This is Libeskind's terminology; see also Pieken 2013, 66.
11 See also chapter 8 for further discussion of the V2 installation.

tion are sub-divided into three informational layers: introductory symbolic display cases;[12] display cases for the main chronological exhibition; and in-depth sections or "knowledge chambers," in which structures or topics specific to a historical period are represented (Pieken 2013, 74–81; Pieken and Rogg 2012 [2011], 117–192). Generally, the chronological exhibition uses traditional curatorial techniques, wherein most objects are installed in glass display cases and medium-sized military equipment is set on stages between cases. Survey panels, educational experience stations, media stations, and short tabular biographies complement this approach.[13]

The context of twentieth-century German history, particularly the history of the Third Reich, has led to a museum that is explicitly anti-heroic and extremely wary about creating master narratives or immersing the visitor in pre-conceived experiences of the past. The Second World War is represented throughout the museum; it is relevant to all of the thematic tour's sections as well as of the chronological tour in the "1914–1945" gallery and at the beginning of the "1945–Present" section in particular. The MHM's exhibition is carried by three theoretical anchors, which challenge the visitor, open up interpretative gaps for visitors to fill, and create secondary experientiality: networking, its open documentary style that avoids explicit interpretation, and temporality. Arnold-de Simine reads this as putting visitors outside of their comfort zones (2013, 50). Similarly, Cristian Cercel emphasizes the open-endedness of the MHM (2018, 26–28), which allows it to be read as an "agonistic forum museum" with certain limitations: "Pluriperspectivism and openness to contestation are not fully unfolded" (Cercel 2018, 28). The MHM creates a temporal museum space in which the visitor's present merges with the represented historical past. Visitors are constantly challenged to find their own links between artifacts and make their own interpretive choices regarding how to think about the impact of war. Instead of simulating individual or collective experiences, the MHM generates experientiality by simulating abstract effects of war, whereby "[t]he combination of thematic/abstract concepts and historicity in a temporalized setting offers a way of representing ideas with implications for the future while maintaining their historical specificity" (Jaeger 2015b, 242).

One of the MHM's signature installations can be found in the section "Protection and Destruction," and further illustrates the explicit use of structurally staging violence. The MHM utilizes one of the Libeskind voids to install a

---

[12] For example the fragments of a German *Panzer I* tank symbolizing the beginnings of mobile warfare in the Second World War.
[13] See also chapters 7 and 8 for further details on the contrasting pairs of tabular biographies, spread through the chronological exhibition.

'bomb hail' of fifteen aerial bombs, missiles, and shells of various sizes, positioned as if they are raining down directly on the visitor from the upper floors (see Pieken and Rogg 2012 [2011], 111; see also the book cover). Next to the visitor on the bottom floor, there are seven large protection artifacts, which are arranged in two circles. The 'bomb hail' seems to point at the first circle, which is made from three air raid shelters made for one to three people, simulating the destruction of aerial warfare and the desire for sufficient protection. There is no specific war, event, personal memory, or collective memory simulated through this installation. Instead, the visitor is led to understand and possibly experience the violence and emotions of warfare.[14]

The permanent exhibition of the MHM is a prime example of secondary experientiality. Nowhere does the museum simulate historical perspectives of individuals or collectives or pretend to immerse the visitor in an unmediated past.[15] Neither does it recreate historical scenes or sets. Consequently, if emotional empathy, understood as a prerogative to empathize with victim groups, and pre-designed ideological expectations from the museum become normative, one can easily miss the dynamic potential of the exhibition to create critical reflection.[16] The MHM uses the arrangement of objects, the cross-referencing of sections throughout the museum, art, and architecture to create a complex network of inter-woven objects and data to which the visitor must react, so that they do not become detached from the exhibition. In both the chronological exhibition and the thematic tour, the MHM highlights historical artifacts over narrative.[17]

To understand how the MHM creates secondary experientiality, I will first analyze level two of the Libeskind wedge. Its main message is that war, force, and violence are closely linked to society and civil life. War influences civil life through language, fashion, music, and games, and vice versa. The centerpiece of this floor is the section "Politics and the Use of Force." It reflects upon the use of legitimate and illegitimate force in nineteen double-sided panels with thirty-three display walls, which spread in three directions and in doing so undercut any potential chronological aspect. At first glance the headers of the panels seem

---

14 For the MHM's representation of aerial warfare, see also chapter 8.
15 Barring a couple of the educational stations in the chronological exhibition.
16 This happens in the reading by Heckner 2016, 365–368. Elke Heckner is so intent on arguing that the MHM cannot prevent contemporary right wing developments in the city of Dresden that she misses the political and critical potential of the exhibition and the fact that empathetic understanding and emotional engagement can be produced structurally, not only mimetically. Heckner's methodology would criticize any open documentary museum approach (without a cosmopolitan master narrative) that leaves an active visitor space for ethical interpretation.
17 See Jaeger 2015b, 231–240, for further details. See also Jaeger 2017a, 33–37.

to imply a clear linear progression. The first prong leads the visitor from a display case with a historical publication on the use of force to historical paintings reflecting government rule by military force, the role of rulers and states, and the emergence of the nation-state. The second prong focuses on the degeneration of violence in the two world wars, and the third one is entitled "From Utopia to Reason: Peace as a Goal of Politics." Thus, the structure seems to indicate a progressive development from the law of force, to state control of military force, to degeneration of state power, to peace. To read the exhibition as a linear progression toward peace, however, misses its fairly balanced approach regarding the traditions of war and the military, the advancement of technology, and the pragmatic functions of war – aside from its relative pessimism about the ability of any utopian vision of peace to eliminate violence as such.

For example, the portrait of West German Defense minister Kai Uwe von Hassel, who abandoned the use of military insignia in contrast to former politicians, seems to indicate such a development. At the same time, since every panel is either a painting or an object in a display case, the visitor is invited to perceive the obvious contrasts and use the constellations to find new similarities and differences. For example, the third prong branches off again in two further prongs; in one of these, a panel displays two eighteenth-century allegorical paintings on the subject of good government and on a peace agreement; in the other prong, there is a panel showing the infamous advertising poster of the security firm Blackwater, entitled "The Mission Continues," expressing old and new forms of military life. Thus, the historical development, a narration moving from no rules over state control and state abuse of power and toward reason and peace collapses in two ways. First, the allegories point back to the earlier phase of the Enlightenment, destabilizing the idea of progress: despite Enlightenment ideals of reason and peace, the degeneration of the use of force in the first half of the twentieth century nevertheless occurred. Second, the exhibition maintains some ambiguity regarding forms of military force in relation to who controls them. The visitor is able to perceive that the allegories might express hope more than reality. The question of whether the relationship between politics and force truly evolves on a cultural level, or reappears in similar constellations (albeit in new forms) as an anthropological universal, thus remains unresolved.

The museum's website describes this section as follows: "The visitor moves in a kind of stage setting. Images of power and powerlessness are not simply exhibited but performed as in a play. The stage covers the whole floor and gazes upon the other large theme on this level: the military and society."[18] The MHM chooses a symbolic stage that is – unlike the stage settings in New Orleans and Kraków[19] – abstracted from real history through paintings and objects that require interpretation. The section introduces each new theme with a long paragraph explaining the principle behind it. In the first prong of the section, the visitor finds two very similar, colorful oil paintings indicating destruction, chaos, death, and the effect of state force. The first one, *Self-Destruction*[20] by Gustav Alfred Mueller (1928–1929), points to political self-destruction through violence during the Weimar Republic. The second one, *The Duty of a Citizen – Use of Military Force against Civilians during the Berlin Uprisings in March 1848* by GDR artist Bernard Heisig (1977), indicates how, according to the MHM, demands for freedom and justice are often violently suppressed by state powers. Whereas the museum clearly expresses possible functions of the two artifacts, their implications are left open. Does the GDR painting criticize the GDR regime and its suppression of freedom or does it endorse the GDR's positive interpretation of the 1848 revolution? What should one do when there is violence from all factions, as in the case of the Weimar Republic? The museum provides no moralistic answers. The reflective visitor may become lost in the chaos of a painting in which everyone endorses violence.

The Second World War appears as a topic in the section's second prong. Five of the six panels belong to the section "Dictatorships – The Abuse of Power." The introductory text reads as follows: "Dictatorships abolish the division between the legislative, judicial and executive powers in a state. They use physical violence and mass surveillance to maintain power and achieve political and ideological goals. Dictators arbitrarily decide by whom, against whom and how violence will be used." The text then connects this definition to the role of the military in the First World War and to the rise and consequences of the National Socialist movement. The first panel shows a portrait on each side, with a double portrait on the front of the First World War generals Paul von Hindenburg and Erich Ludendorff who were instrumental in militarizing all of German society and who aimed for a totalization of war. On the back hangs a portrait of the Chief of the Army Command of the Reichswehr from 1930 to 1934, General Kurt G. A. P. Hammerstein-Equord, praised in the accompanying text panel as "the ideal of a conscientious officer" for placing his conscience and faith in democracy above his oath to Hitler. The MHM presents both images with a clear

---

18 https://mhmbw.de/dauerausstellung/themenparcours/politik-und-gewalt, accessed 13 October 2019, translation S.J.
19 See also chapters 4.1 and 4.2.
20 In the original German: *Selbstzerfleischung*.

didactic message, making explicit the moral and symbolic contrast. Simultaneously, this symbolic contrast also requires the visitor to contemplate how it fits in with the broader events represented in the section.

The next panel in the "Abuse of Power" section shows a poster announcing the referendum on the annexation of Austria by the German Reich in 1938, with an image of a large, stern-looking Hitler in the foreground and masses of people giving the Hitler salute in background. On the top right, next to Hitler's head, "Ja!" (Yes) is written in Gothic (Fraktura script), while the bottom reads "Führer wir folgen dir!" (Führer, we follow you!) in slightly smaller script. On the backside is a pair of high boots worn by SA members. Here, the museum conveys several things to the visitor: military power can be abused and partially or totally take over civil society; there are organizations such as the SA, which symbolize such a blurring of the military/violence and the state; and there are also people who believe in democracy and law and who work against the abuse of power.[21] The historically educated visitor might remember that Hitler was elected democratically in Germany and recognize the complexity of how democratic systems are used or abused. If the visitor walks through the panels from the other side, it almost appears as if Hammerstein and Hitler are looking at each other (see fig. 15). Because the symbolic message creates constellations rather than imitating the past, the MHM allows the visitor to engage in questions of when and how democracies should be defended against the abuse of power.

The next double panel shows two paintings: on the front is Franz Eichhorst's painting *German Soldiers and Russian Prisoners in Front of the Ruins of a Church* (1942); and on the back, Wilfried Nagel's painting *Night-Air Raid on a City* (1942). The museum's text argues that Eichhorst, a German war artist supporting the Nazi regime, provides "an idea of the brutality of a war in which people were expelled, deported or killed in order to seize territories as part of a 'conquest to seize new living space in the east.'"[22] The museum contextualizes Nagel's painting simply by highlighting that the Nazis referred to the Allied air raids as "terrorist attacks," after they had threatened to "erase" London earlier in the war. Both pictures clearly indicate the impact of war on civilians and the

---

[21] The description accompanying the panel marks the poster as propaganda, yet does not explain the historical context of the staged referendum after the 'Anschluss.' In other words, the MHM – like many war museums – bases its facts on historical research. However, the visitor primarily learns and develops memory patterns, rather than knowledge for critical historical analysis.

[22] For deeper historical context, the visitor needs to visit the chronology section "War of Annihilation." There, they would also find a computer station (in German only) with in-depth information on all German campaigns and atrocities during the Second World War.

Fig. 15 General Kurt G. A. P. Hammerstein-Equord and Adolf Hitler 'looking at each other.' Permanent exhibition. Militärhistorisches Museum der Bundeswehr (Bundeswehr Military History Museum), Dresden (Photo: Author, 2013, courtesy of Militärhistorisches Museum der Bundeswehr).

causal structure between German bombings of civilians and the Allied Air War against Germany. However, the visitor could still ask why a German war artist such as Eichhorst drew this scene. Does it really show the brutality of war or is this simply the museum's interpretation, originating in the twenty-first century? Paintings immediately create space for interpretation if they are presented as openly as in the MHM. Nagel's painting depicts an old central town square; flashes come from the sky; one church and an adjacent house are on fire; and shadowy people are running over the square. Did Nagel want to express the suffering of German people and the destruction of civil space? Is this a political painting or a realistic one that simply captures an atmosphere? The viewer is given the option to interpret the flashes from the sky as Godly punishment or as sublime spectacle. The painting seems to meld human destruction with nature. Due to the metaphorical scene that this section creates, each station provides considerably more experiential potential than the information panel and the individual captions accompanying the respective images and objects.

The final two panels of the second prong display two paintings and one object.²³ A charred Ideal typewriter from an office in the Führerbunker in the Reich Chancellery is paired with Felix Nussbaum's 1943 painting *Jew at the Window*.²⁴ Nussbaum was killed in Auschwitz in 1944; between 1940 and 1944, he was in hiding in Brussels. The painting shows the upper body of a man with a sad and contemplative facial expression in a patched-up shirt or coat marked by a yellow star. He seems to be in a barren interior room, next to the window. He gazes at the floor, as if the window was not there, which could also be read as defiance toward the situation since the border between interior and exterior is ambiguous. Opposite to Nussbaum's work hangs a painting of a Saxon general from the nineteenth century. Soviet soldiers punctured the canvas with their bayonets, which, according to the museum, was a sign of their victory over the dictatorship and German militarism. The combination of the typewriter and the two paintings is truly haunting. Both the typewriter and the nineteenth-century painting were destroyed through military violence. What did the destruction of the canvas mean for the post-Nazi world? What were war and violence used for at that time? The only non-mutilated object is Nussbaum's painting, yet its creator was murdered. At the same time, based on the quality of artwork and the artist's victimhood, do these objects allow the visitor to empathize with suffering rather than with perpetration? The MHM points out how many orders to deport and kill were probably written on this particular typewriter. Can the typewriter then symbolize justifiable destruction? What does the visitor do with the constellation of typewriter and Nussbaum's painting? One almost feels as if the painter's death sentence was written here, even if there is no evidence of this. From one viewpoint, the typewriter, the damaged canvas, and the painting of the church ruins in the East form one visible, intense ensemble of perpetration. On the other hand, the SA boots and the painting of the bombed-out German city can be viewed in consequent succession, as if the SA boots directly led to the destruction of German cities. Since these are dynamic constellations, the MHM creates considerable potential for interpretation and varied visual and emotional effects.²⁵

---

23 The back wall of the second painting remains empty.
24 The painting has been on loan from the Felix Nussbaum Haus in Osnabrück and has been displayed on and off in the MHM. Since 2018 it has been displayed again in Osnabrück, leaving an empty panel side in the MHM, although the explanation continued to be present in the MHM's audio tour.
25 Because the back-side of the damaged canvas painting is blank, one could only see Nussbaum's *Jew at the Window* in combination with the portrait of Hammerstein-Equord, which demonstrates how carefully the MHM has composed the arrangement and its views. The ultimate suf-

On all sides of the "Politics and the Use of Force" section, the visitor finds thematic display cases on the walls that connect war and society: "Language and the Military," "Fashion and the Military," "Music and the Military," and "War and Play." In "War and Play," the objects presented elucidate how quickly a military society can influence the attitude of younger generations toward war and violence. Toys constantly signify either military role models or the enemy, as highlighted by a Hitler tile game contrasted with the antisemitic picture book *Der Giftpilz* ("the poisonous mushroom").[26] The display also includes toy figurines of Göring and Hitler, a clockwork Mercedes toy car ("the Führer's car,"), and a school timetable reading "German Youths flying in the National Socialist Flyers Corp." An American game of skill required players to 'drop' two 'nuclear bombs' in holes on a map of Japan, i.e. on Hiroshima and Nagasaki. The visitor sees how war and its justifications become socially engrained throughout history.

In "Music and the Military," the visitor finds eleven postcards with lyrics of German military songs from the years 1935 to 1945. One postcard, for example, contains the text and an illustration of Wilhelm Stöppler's song "Bombs on England."[27] The postcard's accompanying caption highlights the importance of war songs as part of military life. Several other songs connect the music directly to the Führer and the soldiers' oath to him. What does this tell the visitor about war in general and about Nazi Germany in particular? Are these songs regular war songs about defeating the enemy (as one finds in all nations), or do they symbolize a dehumanizing system capable of killing innocent civilians? If the visitor has previously looked at the "Abuse of Power" section in "Politics and the Use of Force," they have further material on bombings to connect with "War and Music."[28] Does the guilt for total war lie solely with the Nazi leadership or also with the crews of the Luftwaffe? The museum does not provide easy answers, but this example indicates the beginning of its open networking strategy that creates a secondary experientiality for the visitor. Sections are spread throughout the whole museum that connect the questions of what constitutes legitimate warfare and how the war impacts civilians, using an open documentary style without explicit interpretation. Active visitors are thus constantly challenged to make sense out of the objects and constellations on display.

---

fering through the abuse of power stands for itself or can only be paired with a painting symbolizing democratic principles.

26 A typical artifact in museums illustrating racism in Nazi Germany, also displayed in, among others, the Gdańsk Museum of the Second World War and the Canadian Museum for Human Rights.

27 In German "Bomben auf Engeland."

28 The representation of the Air War in the MHM is further discussed in chapter 8.

Although there is some temporal development, and the section indicates that the use of violence and warfare in politics has changed over time, the impression remains that violence never fully disappears: the courage of individuals as well as (often misused) power and violence remain closely interwoven throughout human history. At the same time, the museum does not provide a clear analytic or ideological answer; visitors must decide on their own whether the structural changes in the relationship between state, power, and war indicate a cultural-historical development or an endless cycle without substantial change. The German history of warfare, though it is the topic of the majority of the pictures, seems to be less specific. The challenge of the thematic tour is that the visitor can get lost easily between the different objects. In other words, it requires an active visitor to engage with its objects and with the many constellations created by the museum's networking technique.

To further understand how these networking processes function, I will take a brief look at the section "War and Suffering" on level 1, and more extensively at the "Memory" section on level 3 of the thematic tour. "War and Suffering" is located between the "1914–1945" and "1945–Present" chronological exhibitions, indicating that suffering and war did not disappear after 1945. The majority of "War and Suffering" is sequestered in a structure, which is a few feet thick and covered in what appears to be textured dark green, grey, and black felt.[29] It is not readily visible while either ascending or descending the main stairs from other floors of the museum, and must be actively sought out.[30] At first glance, the section feels like a mishmash of suffering, pain, and mourning, with little structure to make sense of these elements.[31] Gravestones, identification tags, the skull of a soldier who committed suicide, letters from mourning mothers and from soldiers to their families, diary entries and photo albums about war and genocide, and photographs of genocides, particularly the Holocaust, are all displayed next to each other. The objects range from the Wars of Liberation (the Napoleonic Wars, between 1813 and 1815) to the twenty-first century and the war in Afghanistan. However, no actual chronology is provided. The objects show the rituals of perpetrators and confront the visitor with real human remains in order to express the horror of

---

29 See Johnston-Weiss 2016, 102–112, for a detailed analysis; see also Jaeger, 2015b, 234–235, and Jaeger 2017c, 155–156, for brief discussions of the depiction of artifacts in this section.
30 The visitor must enter the showcase to visit its three subsections: "Death," "Injury," and "Remembrance."
31 The museum catalog, like the text panels in the showcase, give some idea of changes to the concept of death during the history of warfare, for example the increasing casualties among civilians, the discovery of trauma, or advances in medical treatment (Pieken and Rogg 2012 [2011], 94–99).

war. They intermingle representational layers of suffering and death, individual, collective, and state remembrance and mourning, death of and caused by soldiers, standard warfare, and war crimes. It is clear that this section cannot create a story or even a structure by itself. It seems to eliminate all traces of historical specificity and juxtaposes themes that are not easily compatible.

To understand why this leads to a form of structural secondary experientiality, this analysis focuses on objects from the Second World War. Here, it is important to understand that the museum is object-based. This is particularly important in the "War and Suffering" section, which highlights individual objects and differs from the larger display cases in the chronological exhibition and other sections of the thematic tour. Within the narrow showcase, the visitor can open sliding windows of parts of the display cases; the cases were built in this manner out of reverence for the dead and victims, so that visitors must decide for themselves whether they want to see these objects of death and suffering. Thus, visitors encounter only one or two objects at the same time. The first artifact that visitors come across if they enter the cabinet clockwise is a concrete grave marker in the shape of a crucifix, with the inscription "A German Soldier." The MHM's description of the gravestone notes "German Reich, no date." The caption then provides a quotation by the German historian Reinhart Koselleck: "Commemorating the dead is part of human culture. Commemorating the fallen ... is part of political culture." Visitors are drawn into a complex situation, since they do not even know which conflict the object refers to. Should they see commemoration of the war dead as a political act in the same vein as Koselleck? Or honor all soldiers as a universal cultural act? Does the artifact relate to the Second World War, to the First, or to a different conflict? Should one honor German soldiers? Is this particular soldier connected to war crimes? Does the object stand for the infinite number of unknown soldiers in war graves? How important is it that this is a German gravestone?

Moving to the next object, a sandstone gravestone with the double inscription of Alois Gebert and an unknown soldier does not answer these questions. The MHM tells the visitor that private Alois Gebert "was fatally wounded on the first day of the German assault on Crete." If the visitor has already visited the chronological exhibition, they will remember the photographs and artifacts relating to explicit war crimes in Greece and in Crete in particular.[32] Does this make it more likely that the person commemorated here might be a war criminal? Or does the fact that he died on the first day of the assault likely make him an innocent victim? Two other nearby objects are a wooden cross for an un-

---

[32] The complexity of depicting German perpetration is further discussed in chapter 7.

known soldier who died in Narvik, Norway in 1940 and a wooden cross for Corporal Hans Schell from 1945, with a swastika and runes that were used as Nazi symbols for life and death and are still used by right-wing groups today. Visitors can be constantly torn between anthropologically honoring the dead and the historically specific circumstances of these deaths, forcing them to make complex decisions about what death and its commemoration means in this setting.

Following this section, the visitor finds numerous artifacts related to the Second World War. These include a letter from a mother to her son, a Wehrmacht lieutenant, in which she expresses her wish that he will survive the war. However, the son fell before his mother's last letter was actually written, which is clarified by an envelope with the handwritten note "Return to sender: Died for Greater Germany." Other artifacts include a birthday letter from the soldier Hans Stock (who later deserted) to his father, describing the atrocities of the war; a letter from a mourning mother whose son just fell in Sicily, to Hans Stock, her son's best friend; a diary entry by a Wehrmacht soldier describing atrocities in Ukraine; a page from a photo album that shows murdered civilians; two photographs of the pogroms in Lviv; and the destroyed skull of an unknown German soldier in the Second World War who committed suicide by filling his mouth with water and then shooting himself in the mouth (see also Jaeger 2017c, 156). There are no black-and-white answers here about what death and the representation of personal tragedy mean; who would want to argue with the mother who writes to her dead son's friend, "I took out an atlas [to find Palermo where her son, whose remains could not be identified, fell] and shook my head because I have no way of bringing him here"? There is also an unsettling video clip of a disturbed woman seemingly lost in the German countryside, recorded by American forces[33] and a photo of Chancellor Willy Brandt kneeling in front of the Ghetto Heroes Monument in 1970, commemorating the Warsaw Ghetto Uprising. The exact constellations will be different for every visitor, but a deep contemplation of the "War and Suffering" section could create the urge to (re)visit the chronological section about the Second World War in order to gain more historical context. There are tensions between mourning and guilt, fighting as both duty and the perpetration of war crimes, death as a soldier and death as a civilian (specifically targeted victims of atrocities in particular), and the question of whether one can live with committing war atrocities or experiencing war as such. These tensions create experiential structures that only come into being through the museum's staging of constellations and the visitor's reflection on them.

---

33 For the MHM's use of videography, through which the museum expresses traumatic experience through varying types of distantiation, see Johnston-Weiss 2016, 110–112.

One could argue that the many different retellings of war's impact, and particularly those of the Second World War, reflect a constant working through of the war, its losses, and its criminal nature. This is most evident in my third example from the thematic tour, the section "War and Memory," which covers the whole third level of the wedge. Here, the visitor encounters thirty-six library-like display panels that make up more than 1,000 objects that are typical of how, who, and what is present in war remembrance. The section is – with minor exceptions – centered on German wartime experiences. The exhibition avoids telling the visitor how Germans have remembered the Second World War as a whole. Instead, the visitor encounters stories and other forms of remembrance that together show the complexity of collective German war memory. Whether that memory is a sufficient and satisfying way of remembering the Second World War and of working through the past is left to the visitor to decide. The Second World War appears in numerous display cases: for example, the war library of General Hans Oster, who was killed because of his involvement in the attempted assassination of Hitler on July 20, 1944, and of his son General Achim of Oster; pictures from the set and costumes used in the Hollywood production of *Valkyrie* directed by Bryan Singer (2008); posters of sentimental West German Heimat films; a model of the courtroom where parts of the Frankfurt Auschwitz Trial were conducted in 1964 and 1965; a display case on myths of flight and expulsion; dollhouses that reflect the playful reenactment of the home front and the Air War; a poster collage of post-war West German soldier films up to the 1960s, entitled "Good Private, Bad Party Member"; and record covers commemorating the war.

Historical museums often ignore the history of memory, despite the fact that their exhibitions more likely influence the collective and public memory of the war (rather than providing or demonstrating a critical historiographical understanding).[34] However, the richness of different stories seen in the MHM allows it to further intensify secondary experientiality of the war. The visitor is confronted with many questions about appropriate forms of Second World War remembrance and representation. Most the time, a story is only alluded to, meaning that visitors still must draw their own conclusions beyond the general idea provided by the museum. They are challenged to ask whether the interpretations of

---

34 A good example is the German Historical Museum in Berlin. Memory appears in the appropriate sections as historical facts in a specific period. For example, the title of *Der Spiegel* from 1965 illustrates the debate on the issue of the statute of limitation on Nazi crimes in West Germany. Most museums analyzed in this study represent the past from the perspective of current memory paradigms, but unlike the MHM they do not give the visitor the reflective tools to understand how memory functions.

the war they are viewing are accurate, which creates a wide network of connected traces that potentially allow one to deal with remembering the Second World War.

For example, one cabinet entitled "Mass Deaths – the Glorification of Dying" assembles so-called 'hero letters' about fallen Wehrmacht soldiers from the town of Rheda that were sent to their mourning families (see also Jaeger 2019, 66–68). The visitor is led to almost empathize with the mothers and other family members receiving these letters and to an extent relives their trauma. The visitor is also steered to ask, for example, whether these families believed the Nazi propaganda or became truly cynical about the Third Reich. The only answer provided is that the local committee reduced its publication of such hero letters in 1944 and stopped completely in 1945. As part of a secondary experience, the visitor can stitch together the meaning of these facts from the artifacts and stories on which they choose to focus. Visitors who think about suffering, mourning, and trauma will immediately remember the letter from the mother to her son in the section "War and Suffering."[35] They might also draw a connection to the educational station "An Honour for Mom – the Mother's Cross in National Socialism." This section holds an advent calendar in which the visitor can open twenty-four drawers providing information on the role of mothers under National Socialism and which also links together racial ideology, social ostracization, and the National Socialist 'euthanasia' program.

Another cabinet displays 308 propaganda portraits on photo cards of 'flying aces' and other idols (mainly pilots and U-boat captains), showing how the war propaganda in both world wars (but particularly in the Second World War) attempted to single out individual stories and heroes from the modern, anonymous mass army. Standing opposite to this is a cabinet on the myth of the 'Red Baron,' the First World War flying ace Manfred von Richthofen, highlighting how the Richthofen myth was used in Nazi propaganda films to aid in the development of the German Luftwaffe during the early days of the Third Reich.[36] Active visitors can use their imagination to understand what the notification of death, lying between propaganda and personal grief, might have been like. The section "The Formation of Bodies" on level 1 also allows for reflection upon the role of the individual in mass armies. The photographs of 'heroic' U-boat captains correspond to the "Submarine Warfare" cabinet in the Second World War chronological exhibition. There, the visitor encounters everyday snapshots of submarine

---

35 See above.
36 Similarly, two cabinets later, the visitor encounters the myth of Frederick the Great and sees that the creation of myth and heroization also occurred during the First World War and the Weimar Republic.

crew members and is left to wonder how these relate to heroes in propaganda. The topic of propaganda appears throughout the museum, for example in the section "War on Film" in another part of the "Memory" gallery, which shows film clips that range from promoting war to being anti-war, or the contrastive section on First and Second World War propaganda in the chronological exhibition.

The MHM also challenges the definition of heroes in another display case on the opposite side of the hero letters cabinet, entitled "Silent Heroes – Suppressed Memories." This highlights artifacts belonging to Lieutenant Colonel Josef Ritter von Gadolla. Gadolla was the military governor of Gotha who was ordered to defend the town at all costs. Instead, he arranged the city's unconditional surrender to American troops and saved many lives. However, he was first intercepted by SS-men before being imprisoned by the Wehrmacht, court-martialed and ultimately executed one day after the liberation of Gotha.[37] There is a group photograph from April 1945, showing Gadolla together with the officers from the Gotha recruiting office, giving the impression of Gadolla as a responsible officer that cares for his men. There is also a newspaper announcement by Thuringia *Gauleiter* Erich Sauckel with the header "Everything for the National Socialist Reich," which demonstrates the Nazi leadership's efforts to ensure continued military engagement and loyalty. The visitor sees a photograph of the undestroyed Gotha; an excerpt of the military penal code that was used against Gadolla; a reproduction of the official notice of surrender by the city of Gotha on April 4, 1945; all four pages from the transcript of the court-martial trial in which Gadolla was sentenced to death; and a letter by Weimar vicar Leo Schramm to Alma von Gadolla informing her of her husband's death. If visitors decide to read this letter, they will find Gadolla's last words: "I must die, so that Gotha can live."[38] The letter gives an extremely vivid account of Gadolla's last hours. The secondary experientiality, which connects to the section on the last days of the war depicting the Volkssturm in the chronological exhibition, is evident. The display is not only about Gadolla as such, but structurally about the actions of Germans during the last days of the Third Reich and the question of why they are either remembered or forgotten.[39] These exhibits create a structural network linking together institutions, laws, an undestroyed city, the heroic act of one man, his execution,

---

[37] This is a good example of the fact that although the MHM does not have a display case or section that exclusively presents the crimes of the Wehrmacht; its complex role is nevertheless present throughout the museum. See also the discussion of perpetration in chapter 7.
[38] These detailed documents are not always translated, making this experiential effect much stronger if the visitor can read German.
[39] Gadolla was mainly remembered locally in Gotha.

and the ideology and insanity during the last days of war.[40] They connect the theme of heroization to the question of who is considered a hero and by whom.[41]

Finally, the following analysis of the chronological exhibition demonstrates how intertwined all of the museum's different sections and artifacts are.[42] The "Barbarossa" cabinet[43] in the subsection on the war of annihilation against the Soviet Union serves as an excellent example of how the exhibition establishes a specific historicity (the sense of actual history) for the visitor that connects to other sections of the museum. In front of the display case is a computer terminal that plays the 1943 film clip *Fahnenjunker* (officer candidate) on loop, showing a Wehrmacht lesson in which future officers learn that they will fight a *weltanschaulicher Krieg* (a war based on worldview and ideology). This film clip sets the overall tone for the Soviet Union display cabinets in particular and for the Second World War exhibition more generally. It lasts for one minute and nineteen seconds and runs continuously; when the audio is not muted, the scene dominates the soundscape of most of the Second World War section. Several anti-Bolshevist propaganda posters supplement its effect and the reproduction of the decree of the Oberkommando der Wehrmacht on May 13, 1941. The decree states that civilians "in the East" who committed crimes against the Wehrmacht were not to receive a proper trial, whereas Wehrmacht members were exempted from any crimes.[44] Typical of the open style of the exhibition, the decree regarding the killing of civilians is not judged; visitors are instead forced to make their own judgments. The cabinet indicates a weak temporality, developing from the planning and the beginning of Operation Barbarossa, to its military affairs and the mass killings it engendered, mostly through sets of photographs and two pages from a photo album.[45] The first set of photographs reflects the German

---

40 Because the display cases reflect just as much upon techniques of memory as on their contents, the international visitor can easily apply these mostly German memory questions to an international context where the phenomena of heroization, mourning, war trials, consolation, memory economy, reenactment, cinematic representation, etc. are just as important.
41 See also the section "Military Resistance" in the World War chronological exhibition.
42 The chronological exhibition also employs the technique of contrasting biographical tables of different actors in the war and structural displays that contrast the two world wars. These will be explored further in chapters 7 and 8 below.
43 An initial, less detailed analysis of this section can be found in Jaeger 2015a, 235–237.
44 The display case also shows a zf1 periscopic sight for the gunner of a tank to help explain the early German superiority in tank battles. Throughout the chronological exhibition, the MHM displays the development of military technology, never for its own sake, but rather as interwoven with the cultural developments of warfare.
45 See also Hawig 2019, 80–83, for an analysis of the depiction of historical images in the MHM and in the "Barbarossa" cabinet in particular.

viewpoint by showcasing destroyed Russian equipment, the seemingly quick German advancement, and distant views of Leningrad. The photographs aim to present the layers of the campaign as seen from a German, partly propagandistic, perspective. Eventually, the images draw viewers closer to the actual events and effects of the war.

Photographs of exhausted, injured, dead, and mutilated Soviet prisoners of war are displayed, accompanied by a text contextualizing the German murder of Soviet prisoners of war. The cabinet's narrative closes with another set of photographs showing images of genocide from Kiev and Babi Yar. The involvement of the Wehrmacht soldiers and Ukrainian auxiliary police in the massacre is evident in the photographs. Finally, a two-sided page of a photo album showing the hanging of Jews in Zhytomyr by an SS mobile killing unit (*Einsatzgruppe*) is highly contrastive in its selection of pictures: it juxtaposes hanging corpses with beautiful amateur landscape photographs of the surrounding area. The visitor is confronted with different constructed perspectives (the photographs seem to be taken by German soldiers or SS men throughout). The exact relationship between the photos is left open, but the cabinet narrates war scenes from the perspective of 'the eye of the beholder,' varying between proximity and distance and thereby creating the idea of war as all-encompassing.

The visitor gets a historical impression of the Wehrmacht's progress and successes, shifting from destroyed armor at the beginning of the campaign to slaughtered human beings and human catastrophe as a result of the German advance. This arrangement leaves the visitor with no doubt that war and genocide/the Holocaust were inseparable during the Second World War, and that it had been planned by the Nazis from the beginning as a war of worldviews. To an extent, the visitor perceives a narrative – in a spatial rather than strictly chronological sense – of the collective experience of the war for German soldiers, with the photographic gaze making the effects and complexities of the war more immediate and present. At the same time, the "Barbarossa" cabinet is not simply a traditional two-dimensional cabinet that represents one historical episode from a distance, giving the visitor a structural overview of a historical phase and the opportunity to zoom in on specific artifacts or images. Instead, the cabinet interacts with the concepts of ideology, suffering, and atrocities throughout the museum, allowing, for example, the visitor to assign the pieces from the thematic "War and Suffering" section their required historical specificity. Rather than providing an in-depth analysis or even an evaluation of historical events, the MHM presents the events to the visitor so that they can be affected by the representation. This approach enables the visitor to have a structural experience of the museum space. Although this approach runs the risk of not providing enough interpretative guidance, it allows for ideas and history to be represented in close conjunction without implying that history merely exemplifies general statements about different concepts prevalent in war.[46]

To summarize, the MHM creates a museum space that places the visitor into a temporalized situation; the past must still be understood, and it becomes present in light of the museum's representation of its cultural impact on society. This ensures that visitors are forced to reflect on the relationship between violence/war and their own personal attitudes and actions as well as the broader future goals of human society. The museum poietically creates experientiality through the acts of reception, connecting themes, imagination, and interpretation. It does not imitate past reality, but rather the exhibition – in dialogue with the visitor – performs a space of data, stories, and links that characterize the Second World War in a manifold form that integrates all parts of society. The museum plants traces hinting at which themes might be linked with each other. In the end, however, empirical visitors will have to find their own individual paths through the museum. The museum's exhibition is not historical reality to be simulated and experienced, but rather structural aspects of war and violence that maintain historical depth and specificity. Therefore, the MHM, while remaining very artifact-based, transcends the predominantly illustrative character of many object-based museums in producing the potential for secondary experientiality. At the same time, the MHM is constantly on the verge of demanding too much from the visitor who could potentially become lost in its mass of objects. The exhibition clearly works to allow an intense encounter with specific objects that goes beyond their serving as functional examples for a historical argument. It allows to an even greater extent for the use of networking effects from which the active visitor can draw an endless number of connections that create questions and insights about the secondary reality of war.

---

[46] Not all display cases in the chronological exhibition have the same effect as a cabinet in and of itself. However, all allow for constant connections to be made to other parts of the museum. The "Barbarossa" cabinet is particularly dense. Another very dense one is the display case on the Polish campaign, as analyzed in Jaeger 2017a, 36–39. Here, the visitor can discern phases and perspectives of a historical event, which leads to experiencing the attack on Poland as a spatial narrative, a kind of 'living scene.' Documenting historical knowledge and providing arguments transfer to the experientiality of narrative, since the visitor encounters an ensemble of perspectives in the text, images, and objects without being provided with one clear interpretation or linear narrative leading toward an argumentative goal. War destroys Jewish and Catholic life, and technological advancement cannot be seen without invoking the humiliation and murder of Jews. In this display case the museum does not provide answers to questions such as why German soldiers so easily participated in humiliations and killings. Additionally, the visitor is drawn again into a number of other connections throughout the museum.

150 — 5 Secondary Experientiality

Fig. 16 Outside view of Imperial War Museum North, Manchester (Photo: Author, 2018).

5.2 The Imperial War Museum North in Manchester

The Imperial War Museum North (IWMN) in Manchester, which opened its current permanent exhibition in 2002, serves as the second example of secondary experientiality in this book.⁴⁷ At first glance, there appear to be many similarities between the IWMN and the Bundeswehr Military History Museum (MHM), though most of these similarities originate with Daniel Libeskind's architecture (see fig. 16), which creates an effect of asymmetry in both museums.⁴⁸ As with

---

47 The IWMN sees approximate 250,000 visitors a year, which is the lowest number of the five branches of the Imperial War Museum. In 2016–2017, 251,416 people visited the museum (Imperial War Museum 2016–2017, 14). Regarding fostering visitor engagement in the IWMN, see Powell and Kokkranikal 2014.

48 Bagnall and Rowland offer a critical perspective about the limitations of Libeskind's design as a participatory museum (2010, 54–59). Similarly, Greenberg notes that Libeskind's architecture has made the exhibition more cinematic than theatrical: Libeskind's "object-making vision has overwhelmed the experience and has taken precedence over the story and the characters in

5.2 The Imperial War Museum North in Manchester — 151

the MHM, the IWMN combines a chronological approach with numerous thematic displays: six thematic silos, two TimeStacks with rotating trays and thematic objects, the Big Picture multimedia shows, and large display objects on the central axis of the main exhibition space. However, a closer analysis will demonstrate that the IWMN creates considerably less historical specificity in its secondary narrative than the MHM while using more individual historical voices, which suggests a primary form of experience despite its staging as secondary experientiality. In other words, the IWMN functions as a hybrid that constructs new structural, i.e. secondary experiences, while relying on primary voices and experiences.

Entering the main exhibition space of about 3,500 square meters, two panels introduce the visitor to the museum's mission. One instructs the visitor as follows: "Explore and discover how war shapes and changes people's lives." The other points out that the Imperial War Museum has been assembling "a national collection" since 1917: "Since then, it has collected thousands of stories about people's experiences during war and conflict." This indicates that any individual might find an object in the collection to which they can relate. The museum focuses on memory and personal experience, rather than an analysis of historical fact (Bagnall and Rowland 2010, 62). It clearly balances a global mandate with one based on national experiences, which at times strongly shifts toward the British war experience. To understand how secondary experientiality works, when it is based on collective primary experiences, this analysis will first compare the exhibition techniques of the IWMN to those of the Bundeswehr Military History Museum.[49] Therefore, it makes sense to start with the six thematic silos in the permanent exhibition. These consist of interior rooms with two entrances with open ceilings: "Experience of War," "Women and War," "Impressions of War," "Empire, Commonwealth and War," "Science, Technology, and War," and "Legacy of War."

The "Experience of War" silo is introduced with the following text: "In this exhibition a small selection of personal stories have been chosen from the Mu-

---

that story" (2005, 232). Angela Loxham argues after analyzing the concepts of architecture, space, and objects in the museum that the museum is not haptic enough: "At IWM North, the architecture and exhibition space envisioned by Libeskind show promise but staff and object mediation instead allow for the familiar to be powerfully reaffirmed. The affect created is diminished and the reinsertion of familiarity and comfort prevent the need for mental reflection because the habitus of the body is not challenged" (2015, 533). For further details on the IWMN's architecture, see its discussion in chapter 8 on the Air War.

[49] Both museums extensively use artwork to open up the museum experience to the visitor (see chapter 9).

seum's collection to show some of the many ways in which people have experienced war since 1914." The silo focuses particularly on the experiences of prisoners of war, the evacuation of children from British cities, the Kindertransport from Germany to Britain, and recruitment. The stories told here are predominantly British. Except for audio stories under the headers "A Sense of Loss," relating to children's experiences in the Second World War and "Pride," relating to the experience of homosexual experiences in the military, the exhibition uses both large and small display cases arranged around a single story or theme. It briefly contextualizes these stories with factual texts without interpretation; its open style is similar to that of the MHM. For example, the exhibition includes a cluster of exhibits on internment in the Far East from 1941 to 1945; the European theater of war is represented through POWs – Germans in the United Kingdom – and British soldiers in Germany. The visitor sees a coffee pot, letters, postcards, and an apron, among other objects. The visitor is invited to pick an object and think about its implications, such as what it would mean to parents to receive a letter from their son explaining that he had become a POW. A wooden food box, a copy of the Japanese Penal code, and instructions for decoding POW postcards make the visitor consider the reality faced by POWs in the Far East. Unlike in the MHM, handwritten texts are not easy to read and are not transcribed. The museum uses far fewer photographs in the silos than the MHM, running the risk that the objects will merely become illustrative if they are not accompanied by a clear story.[50] Such stories are narrated from an audio station. For example, Ruth Watts was a 15-year-old schoolgirl in Berlin who one morning saw the remains of a British airman, who had been killed the previous night. Such a vivid story can allow visitors to empathize with the storyteller and consider what the impact of such an experience on them would have been.

Despite IWMN's story-rich, open approach that allows for structural constellations, there are two major differences here to the secondary experientiality seen in the MHM. First, the IWMN's focus is on primary experiences that are merged through different museum techniques to create structural experiences and secondary experientiality, whereas the MHM presents a combination of symbolic and structural objects, primary experiences, and photographs (among others), requiring an active visitor to connect possible themes. Secondly, the IWMN's networking effect is significantly diminished. With the exception of the Big Picture Shows, the prisoner of war experience and the children evacuees are barely present in the rest of the museum. In contrast to the MHM, the "Experience of War" section simply seems to add further historical aspects and perspectives

---

50 For the IWMN's use of illustrative images see also Hawig 2019, 85.

of the war, sorted into themes that are not part of the historic timeline on the outer walls of the interior exhibition space. Here, it makes sense to compare the MHM's "War and Memory" section as discussed above to the IWMN's third silo, "Impressions of War," and the sixth one, "Legacy of War," in order to understand the differences in how these museums create secondary experientiality.

The silo "Impressions of War" asks what shapes our impressions. It also highlights the means of war propaganda and the post-war reception of conflicts, particularly in relation to the two world wars and the Falkland War from an exclusively British perspective. It is set up to look like a living room scene with couches, a TV playing wartime news footage, bookcase-like display cases, framed war posters that seem like paintings, and other decorative items. The Second World War is represented on a shelf with war propaganda and in a display case full of games including the title pages of books, comics, a spitfire bottle, and toy soldiers. The panel description explains the fascination that many children have with 'refighting' the war. Since the IWMN does not give the visitor any information about the objects, most visitors will accept the idea of reenacting historical war through play. Visitors are neither asked to envision concrete stories about specific objects, nor will they understand the anthropological impact of war. The question of what playing war means for society and whether it differs from war to war is not asked. There is no reason for the visitor to actively engage with or challenge the display; they merely consume these impressions. This lack of contextualization is also evident in a wall calendar installation about war myths. On the front side, the visitor reads a myth, e.g. "The 'Little Ships' saved the British Army at Dunkirk." On the flipside, the visitor can read the 'reality,' in which 95% of the British and French troops saved were rescued by larger ships and "The 'Little Ships' with their civilian volunteer crews brought back 19,000 Allied troops to Britain in very dangerous conditions." Alongside this fact, the visitor also learns that there is mythmaking in war remembrance, which can be resolved factually without addressing complex memory patterns. Occasionally, there are objects that can trigger the visitor's active imagination. On the coffee table in front of the TV, the visitor was previously able to see an Argentinian magazine with a title page relating to the Falklands War, which indisputably represents then-Prime Minister Margaret Thatcher as a Nazi; she is wearing a German steel helmet with a Swastika, which created some openness about what this picture signaled – historically and today – with regard to the moral implications of different conflicts from various perspectives.[51]

---

51 This observation is based on a visit in August 2013. At my last visit in May 2018, the Thatcher

In the last silo "Legacies of War," the IWMN highlights the injuries occurring in war, the effect of landmines in war zones, forced migration due to and during the war, the re-building of Manchester after the Blitz in the Second World War, remembrance, and the readjustment to civilian life. Stories either have positive or negative outcomes, allowing the visitor to reflect upon the impact of war in general. The silo covers all conflicts in which the United Kingdom has been involved since the First World War. Although the IWMN's presentation is more illustrative and didactic than that of the MHM, the visitor can still develop a wide range of thoughts about the transformation from war to civilian life. The exhibition moves chronologically from war to peacetime. Though visitors obtain a structural experience of the effects of war, they remain directly linked to the perspectives of actual soldiers and wartime collectives.

The museum interweaves a number of interdependent representational strategies to create an experiential space.[52] Besides the silos, the timeline, and the Big Picture Shows discussed below, these include large objects spread throughout the exhibition hall, the architecture including the voids, the uneven floor, light and temperature changes, and two TimeStacks with six rotating trays each.[53] Visitors can call up object clusters from specific historical areas such as the Holocaust or the Blitz, or themes such as "Children's War." The TimeStack trays are mainly illustrative and fairly didactic; they are particularly useful for guides who employ everyday objects in "object-handling sessions," although they also help connect the exhibition to different sections of the museum.[54] Whereas the Bundeswehr Military History Museum (MHM) creates a complex balance of historical and structural displays, the IWMN interweaves historical themes. Its displays rely far more on the stories of individuals than those of collectives and on the thematic topics are arranged in a more chronological sequence. This still creates structural experiences; however, it also highlights individual memory, stories, and the overall idea of the war's cost, rather than anthropological elements of violence.

---

title and two other titles from Argentinian magazines had been removed, leaving exclusively British sources and consequently reducing the openness of the display.

52 The museum points visitors to other areas where they can learn more about certain subject areas found in the silos and TimeStacks.

53 As in other museums, especially seen in the newer exhibitions in the Bundeswehr Military History Museum and the Bastogne War Museum, certain technologies are extremely prone to mechanical failure. In May 2018, neither TimeStack was working, reducing their effect to representing only one topic each.

54 The exception is the Holocaust tray, which connects the displayed objects to four Holocaust survivors, see chapter 7 for further details.

5.2 The Imperial War Museum North in Manchester — 155

To further understand this difference, it is important to analyze the museum's timeline cabinets and displays as well as its core, the Big Picture Shows. The museum's chronologically ordered timeline includes one introductory and five main sections, starting with the First World War and the section on the interwar years, "Between the Wars," and ending with the section "1990–Present: Into a New Century." At first glance, the exhibition's technique here seems similar to that of the MHM. However, a closer analysis by way of an example from the section "1939–1945: Second World War" reveals significant differences. The visitor is confronted with large info panels, six glass display cases full of objects and photographs, smaller object captions, larger posters, and some film footage. The perspective here is documentary from above, fairly neutral, and purely illustrative; even ego-documents as artifacts depicting the voices or stories of individuals merely serve as illustrative placeholders. The motto of the timeline is "Total War," written in large letters on the wall above the exhibits. The introductory text confirms the section's global approach, using a language full of pathos: "Global war brings mass death and destruction. 55 million die on battlefields, in death camps, in their homes. Millions more become refugees. Cities, towns and countryside are devastated. Societies are smattered and nations smashed. The impact of this war is total." The chronological panels consist of one photo, a header, and a brief paragraph; they are also global and written in a factual style. The six display cabinets are structured according to theater of war, with the exception of the concluding genocide display case[55]: "War at Sea," "Land War in Europe," "War Effort" (i.e. home front), "Air Attack," "War in the Desert and Jungle," and "Genocide" (i.e. Holocaust). For example, the cabinet "Land War in Europe," unlike the chronological panels, is exclusively British, as the survey panel reveals. It vaguely mentions losses in 1940, and the D-Day landing is the only concrete event named here. The actual cabinet displays objects such as a leather jerkin, two steel helmets, items of personal equipment (a knife, food powder etc.), a gas mask, a battledress blouse, a letter about D-Day,[56] a Christmas card, a rifle, a light machine gun, a first aid kit, hand grenades, a breakfast kit, and two smaller clusters of items.

Except for the final displays of the cabinet "Land War in Europe," which tell two brief stories, none of the items produce experientiality and no object seems to automatically link to something presented elsewhere in the exhibition. The historical specificity that allows the chronological display cabinets in the

---

[55] See also its detailed analysis in chapter 8.
[56] As is the case throughout the exhibition, there is no transcription of ego documents such as letters or diaries. Therefore, whether the visitor can relate to it depends on whether the caption provides more than an identifier and tells a short story of the document's context.

MHM to stage living spaces of the past does not exist in the IWMN. The items could be from any British land operation in Europe. The ego documents can create a certain experientiality, yet they still fulfill a primarily illustrative function. For example, the "War at Sea" cabinet contains a letter and diary by the First Boy First Class William Crawford who was killed on the battleship HMS Hood during its battle with the Bismarck. Even if museum visitors are very unlikely to decipher the letter or the diary, they might take away the message of the cruelty of war when looking at the telegram informing his mother about the boy's death. This connects to other sections about the cost of war in the exhibition. The museum's "Timeline" only constitutes a small part of the museum, which indicates that the museum universalizes historically specific events to a greater degree than the MHM.

The IWMN's signature piece is the audio-visual Big Picture Show, which runs approximately every hour for six to twenty-two minutes. The interior of the IWMN becomes a 360-degree cinema, with the gallery walls and floors turned into screens with thirty-two audio channels for a multi-sensorial experience (Arnold-de Simine 2013, 114–118). The core shows of the museum are "Children and War," "Weapons of War,"[57] and "War at Home" (see fig. 17). The first two focus on a variety of conflicts between 1914 and the present, whereas the third focuses on the Second World War and the collective British experience. The museum highlighted in an earlier edition of its museum brochure as follows: "Deliberately thought-provoking, the shows encourage debate and discussion about strong and often controversial subjects. The experience envelops the Main Exhibition Space, surrounding visitors in a constantly changing environment of images and sound."[58] The multiple projections of images are reflected and fragmented on the inner walls, especially on the void-like walls of the thematic silos. The museum's description continues on to note that "[t]he award-winning Big Picture is a dramatic and engaging way to see and hear IWM's outstanding collection of photographs, art and sound." The effect of the Big Picture Show on the visitor is integral to understanding secondary experientiality in the museum. The observation of the show is not particularly voluntary; if one is standing in the main exhibition, one is automatically immersed in the show and it becomes

---

[57] Not shown in May 2018, when "Remembrance," "Build the Truce," and "Al-Mutanabbi Street," completed the line-up. In 2019, the IWMN presented two new shows: "Mightier Than War," a show, "exploring the triumph of the human spirit in times of conflict," and "Life on the Line: with footage from Peter Jackson's *They Shall Not Grow Old*," see https://www.iwm.org.uk/events/big-picture-show, accessed 13 October 2019.
[58] Imperial War Museum 2012, 6. The latest guidebook (Imperial War Museum 2017b, 14) uses a more measured description and spends less time on introducing specific Big Picture Shows.

Fig. 17 Scene from the Big Picture Show "Children and War." Permanent exhibition. Imperial War Museum North, Manchester (Photo and © Imperial War Museum).

impossible to see any other parts of the exhibition.[59] The IWMN is certainly the museum building by Daniel Libeskind in which architecture and interior exhibition are the most interwoven,[60] in contrast to the MHM or the Jewish Museum in Berlin, where curators and design companies can use the architectural space more freely to develop their exhibitions.

The original idea was that all visitors would continue to move around the museum to experience many different angles of the show, although visitor research shows that they tend mostly to sit on one of the interior wall benches and watch the show passively (MacLeod et al. 2015, 319–320). For an observer

---

[59] The integrative design of the exhibition space and Big Picture Shows makes it hard to imagine a redesigned permanent exhibition in the same museum space and building. Even more than in other Libeskind museum buildings, such as the MHM or the Jewish Museum Berlin, the exhibition space prescribes the concept. An exhibition from 2002 is becoming increasingly dated and creates problems for curators considering exhibition and design changes. The IWMN has reacted with minor adjustments to displays, changes to art displays (the latest addition is from 2013), and a variation of the Big Picture Shows.

[60] See also the design and visitor analysis by MacLeod et al. 2015, who use the IWMN to show the values of visitor-oriented design-thinking. See also Weiser 2017, 54–55.

who follows the effects through the whole exhibition space, new temporal constellations arise when Big Picture Show images overlap with large objects, such as a steel window section from the ruins of the World Trade Center (after 9/11), a tank, or the large painting of a First World War soldier. The experience is structural since visitors are put in an artificial memory set-up that allows them to perceive sensations and voices from the past, instead of mimetically reproducing one collective perspective. The museum description highlights two forms of experience. On the one hand, the visitor is immersed in "a constantly changing environment of images and sound." On the other, the museum emphasizes that it draws on the extensive archives of the Imperial War Museum to "reveal how war has shaped people's lives" (Imperial War Museum 2012, 4). In other words, corresponding to the other elements the museum employs in its permanent exhibition, the IWMN focuses on the primary experience of individuals. As Arnold-de Simine has analyzed in greater detail (2013, 115–116), the visitor has difficulty dissecting individual voices or even identifying the conflict to which images, voices, and sounds refer. Furthermore, the museum's focus on individual experiences seems at odds with the engaging and dramatic multisensory experience the museum promotes, which produces a secondary experience.

This is even more apparent in the Big Picture Show "Children and War." Multiple war-related noises and a collage of eyewitness voices remembering wartime experiences from their childhood create a distinct impression of what it was like to experience the war. The focus of the first half of the show is on the British home front during the Second World War, supplemented by the accounts of Jewish children who were evacuated from Germany to England through the Kindertransport and had who to endure being perceived as German enemies during the war. A wide variety of material is mostly reenacted in children's voices, interspersed with older people remembering their childhood. The fifteen-minute show is full of different experiences and stories described by these outsiders in Nazi Germany, including them seeing the appeal of the League of German Girls (Bund der Mädel), the children's their early fascination in the first days of the Blitz with hiding in a bunker, the loss of parents in the war, their fear of not being picked by any family during the child evacuation as well as the different forms of military and ideological recruitment and becoming a child soldier. Alternating male and female narrators state at the beginning and end of the show that "Every image, every document, every voice is part of someone's story." This highlights that the authenticity of the material as such counts as an overall secondary multimedia montage. The visitor only retains impressions of particularly striking mini narratives or images.

In the second half of the show, the IWMN switches to the experiences of immigrant children who escaped the conflicts in Bosnia and Rwanda to Great Britain. Since there is no explanation of the historical context in the show itself and memory clearly dominates history, the visitor experiences a choir of voices and images that make up a past reality. This can be very effective in emotionalizing topics that link up to other parts of the exhibition in creating secondary experientiality, whether the Kindertransport or the Blitz. It also generates a certain amount of contrasts, for example, between the use of child soldiers in Africa and British experiences during the Second World War, which often sound comparatively adventurous and exciting. The focus, however, is on emotions related to experiences of war, which are universalized as the experiences of all children during wartime. This is emphasized in the statement made by a child in the show; she says that generals should meet to talk about the future, suggesting the idea of universal peace. The show cannot inform the visitor as to why children are particular targets in war. After all, the children are all innocent, as one child's voice expresses: "All we wanted to is play games and see our friends." The visitor is led to empathize with the idea of a child placed into a war caused by adults through endless close-ups of children's enlarged and multiplied faces that demand eye contact with the visitor.

Unlike the introductory mission statement, which points out that each visitor can find an object or a story to relate to, the IWMN here shifts its focus from objects to a total multisensory immersion to which authentic stories contribute. As Arnold-de Simine concludes, "[t]he museum space is converted into a spectacle and individual visitors, who are usually isolated from each other in their museum experience, are turned into a collective audience and into secondary witnesses" (Arnold-de Simine 2013, 116; see also Greenberg 2005, 231–233). Making the visitor part of a concrete memory community changes the form of secondary experientiality, in comparison to the MHM. The IWMN's distantiation techniques lead the visitor to experience direct empathy with all of the children featured in the show. A cognitive analysis is possible if one examines the sensual input from a distance, but is unlikely that one will immediately be able to perform such an analysis while being immersed in the show. Unlike in the New Orleans WWII Museum, the IWMN does not simulate a direct collective primary experience that references historical reality, but rather a constructed one that simulates all children's experiences of war, all experiences at the home front, or the impact of weapons and their aesthetics as such. Visitors have no possibility to dissect and contextualize the sources of the Big Picture Shows, as there are often no concrete sources for photographs and other visual sources in the exhibition. Therefore, historical sources and objects serve an overall aesthetic purpose that immerses and manipulates the visitor. Whereas in the MHM, visitors are supposed to actively engage with the large amount of material from the different angles presented to them, the IWMN uses its networking strategies in part to unify its material into one passive experience: contradictory to the claims in the museum guidebook (Imperial War Museum 2017b, 14), the museum creates a form of prescribed empathy.[61] Although one can argue that the museum at times sugarcoats the costs of war and follows the British tradition of viewing war as a necessary means toward freedom and democracy, the IWMN also creates an experiential space to understand the impact of war, a hetereoglossia of historical voices that connects war and society in a more abstract and structural sense.

5.3 The Topography of Terror in Berlin

The Topography of Terror Documentation Centre (Topographie des Terrors, ToT) in Berlin opened its third and current permanent exhibition on May 6, 2010, on the ground of the former headquarters of the Secret State Police (Gestapo), the SS, and the Reich Security Main Office on the former Prinz-Albrecht-Straße and Wilhelmstraße. In contemporary Berlin, it stands as a reminder of the National Socialist government quarter, while located only a few minutes away from the Memorial to the Murdered Jews of Europe. It is also located between the tourist attractions Checkpoint Charlie and Potsdamer Platz and features the longest existing segment of the outer Berlin Wall along Niederkirchnerstraße (formerly Prinz-Albrecht-Straße). The documentation center receives an estimated 1.3 million visitors per year, of which approximately 70 percent are international visitors.[62] The institution was established with a temporary exhibition in a provisional pavilion, as part of (West) Berlin's 750th anniversary celebration in 1987.[63] The Foundation of the Topography of Terror was established in 1992, and in 1997, the second exhibition moved into the moat under the remaining piece of the Berlin Wall. It endured two failed architectural competitions and

---

[61] The Big Picture Show "Truce" requires the most active visitors, since they are confronted with five identifiable voices from the conflicts/wars in Sierra Leone, Kosovo, Iraq, Northern Ireland, and El Salvador. The five individuals have very diverse experiences of how truce-building processes worked for them personally, which creates an openness and tension to which the visitor can actively react.

[62] For visitors in 2018 see the ToT's website https://www.topographie.de/en/topography-of-terror/, accessed 13 October 2019. For the international visitors in 2017 see Schulz 2018. Since the ToT does not charge an admission fee and many visitors only visit the outdoor exhibition in the moat, these numbers are estimates.

[63] See for its history, Haß 2012 and Till 2005, especially 63–152. See also the catalog of the first exhibition Rürup 2002 (1987) and Seiter 2017.

has a strong history of activist interventions,[64] marking it as a site of political contention.[65] After the construction of the building by the second competition's winner, the Swiss architect Peter Zumthor, was stopped in 2004,[66] a third architectural competition was won by architect Ursula Wilms and landscape architect Heinz W. Hallmann. The buildings and grounds were then finally completed in 2010 with a far less emotionalizing and more pragmatic building. Its metallic facade is intentionally understated so that visitors can focus on the contents of the exhibitions and the traces of the landscape.[67]

At first glance, the ToT seems to be out place in the list of permanent exhibitions analyzed in this book. It is a documentation center rather than a historical or memorial museum, as discussed above, and its mission seems to avoid strong narratives and immersion at all costs. It almost exclusively uses photographs to visualize war, with minimal audio and video footage. The 800-square meter permanent exhibition displays a soft temporal structure by describing the Nazi's rise to power in section 1, institution of terror in section 2, the terror in the German Reich in section 3, the terror in the occupied countries during the war in section 4, and the aftermath of the war and the post-war trials in section 5. The exhibition is organized structurally into perpetrator groups, victim groups, and victim countries. Because of its mandate to represent the perpetrators that operated from the center of Berlin,[68] it avoids the possibility of empathy with any historical people. There can clearly be no primary experientiality to re-experience, for example through scenes, historical atmospheres, and individual or collective perspectives. However – as will be shown – there are effects of structural empa-

---

64 See in particular Haß 2012; see also Young 1993, 81–90. James E. Young emphasizes the importance of 'contested memory' here, inviting "visitors into a dialogue between themselves and their past" (1993, 190).
65 See also Till 2005, 63–105.
66 See Leoni 2014. Claudio Leoni strongly argues – with reference to psychoanalytic poststructuralist theory – in favor of Zumthor's aesthetics, which he reads as a necessary aesthetic solution to deal with the unrepresentability of the Holocaust: "As a positive negation of the site and its history, Zumthor's building would have created a gap within our realities, a gap where the real could have been conjectured" (2014, 117). This reading demonstrates the differences between an emotional, non-representative architectural approach and a documentary and educational one (which was ultimately chosen) – even if in the latter the ToT reflects on the unrepresentability of the Holocaust through its photographic montages as well.
67 For the development and concept of the final building and the landscape architecture, see Stiftung Topographie des Terrors 2011, 10–16.
68 The executive director of the Foundation Topography of Terror (Stiftung Topographie des Terrors), Andreas Nachama, notes that this focus on perpetrators is possible because of the many other documentation and memorial institutions in Germany and abroad that tell the stories of the victims (2010, 7).

thy that confront the visitor with the collective gazes of this era through photographic montage techniques.[69]

The mission of the ToT is to provide a documentary overview of the perpetrators and their acts of perpetration (Nachama 2010, 7). It conveys "in a concise presentation with carefully chosen examples, fundamental information on the headquarters of the SS and the Gestapo located on this site between 1933 and 1945 and on the crimes initiated by these institutions, their leaders, and personnel, which they perpetrated not just in Germany, but above all in many countries of Europe" (Nachama 2010, 7). The exhibition highlights facts to provide evidence of these historical crimes and elaborates on historical structures, deepened through the use of computer stations and printed document folders containing detailed background information. The photographs[70] displayed on the vertical panels suspended from the ceiling serve an illustrative function, rendering subjects such as different branches of the German police and security operations, different victim groups on German territory, and crimes committed in different occupied countries representable.

However, the ToT employs two primary techniques to create secondary experientiality. First, similarly to the chronological exhibition in the MHM,[71] but exclusively based on photographs and official documents, they create mini clusters of material, living scenes of the 'Volk community,' the Secret State Police (Gestapo), the Security Service (SD), Jews in Reich territory, Forced Laborers and Soviet prisoners of war, and Occupied Poland, among others. These scenes only exist as a secondary experiential museum montage; they poietically produce a visitor experience that only exists within the museum space. The ToT generally separates its pictorial and textual documents (Nachama 2010, 6). The former are float-mounted on panels, whereas textual historical source material is presented through facsimiles on lecterns in front of the panels for easier reading. Interspersed with the photographs on the float panels, contemporary quotations by leaders of the regime are printed in black, and contextualizing quotations by renowned academic historians are printed in orange. The clusters connect with each other through historical and structural themes throughout the permanent exhibition, as also seen in the MHM. The ToT uses an open style that enables visitors to distance themselves from any immediate immersion or empathy with ei-

---

[69] For the empathy created by the ToT see also Johnston-Weiss 2019, 96–98.
[70] All photographs are enlarged facsimiles printed on the exhibition floats and arranged in clusters of different size. They have extensive descriptive and contextualizing captions as well as a bibliographical reference to the source of the photograph.
[71] As seen above in the analysis of the "Barbarossa" cabinet in chapter 5.1.

ther the perpetrators or the victims. The visitor can further intensify the exhibition's networking effect by actively connecting these themes to the ToT's other exhibitions: the 200-square meter open-air exhibition *Berlin 1933–1945: Between Propaganda and Terror*, the fifteen-station tour on the grounds of the ToT,[72] special exhibitions, and a specialist archive. Second, the documentation center creates secondary experientiality through its extreme focus on visualization via photographs, which results in an aesthetic effect that emotionalizes the visitor through repetition and montage (Jaeger 2017b, 175–177).[73] The second networking strategy depends on the visitor consciously or subconsciously making connections that establish an emotional cluster that surpasses documented facts and structures.

The themes that are networked throughout the museum are both structural and historical. As in the MHM, they allow the visitor to go beyond individual events or people, in order to understand systemic structures and provoke questions about the emergent subject matter. The ToT creates systemic networking effects through the clustering and visualization of themes such as the spectatorship of crimes, scenes of humiliation and discrimination – antisemitism in particular – scenes of denunciation and deportation, crowd scenes, crime scenes including shootings and mass atrocities, laughter, and portraits of individuals. The latter themes include group photographs of perpetrators and/or institutions as well as the forced assembly of different victim groups. Furthermore, these themes are historical, with some reaching experientiality within one section in particular, such as the persecution of Jews and the Holocaust, or the events in specific occupied territories such as Poland or the Soviet Union.

To better understand the ToT's networking techniques, I will first analyze the theme of humiliation and spectatorship, followed by the theme of laughter. Afterwards, I will examine the clustering of concrete historical spaces by focusing on the particular example of occupied Poland. In the section "The 'Volk Community,'" the visitor sees two photographs displaying a 19-year-old woman having her head publicly shaved in the market square in Ulm, as a punishment for her relationship with a French prisoner of war (see fig. 18). There is a small image showing the shaving on a podium in the center of the market square, with thousands of spectators surrounding the woman, and a larger close-up photograph of

---

[72] Here, the documentation center also serves as a memorial site that commemorates the victims in the prison cells of the cellar of the Gestapo headquarters, where many political prisoners were tortured and executed. See also Stiftung Topographie des Terrors 2010b.
[73] See Hesse 2002 for the photographs' tension between authenticity and ideological construction. I thank curator researcher Klaus Hesse for his detailed introduction in the curatorial techniques and use of imagery in the Topography of Terror in a meeting on July 6, 2012.

Fig. 18 Part of section "The 'Volk Community.'" Interior permanent exhibition. Topographie des Terrors (Topography of Terror), Berlin (Photo: Author, 2017, courtesy of Topographie des Terrors).

some of the spectators. The second picture depicts eager spectators, mostly smiling and happily watching the scene.[74] Whether the audience was staged to produce photographs for propaganda purposes or not, the visitor comes away with an impression of how the Nazis created their community and that the spectators appeared to attending these events voluntarily. Visitors encounter this type of forced public humiliation throughout the exhibition. In a photo in the very first section, "Terror and 'Coordination,'"[75] a Social Democrat and local councilor is led through the city of Hofgeismar on an ox in May 1933. A large number of spectators, especially young people, flank the procession. Right next to this, the visitor encounters an image of anti-Jewish terror in Duisburg, in which SS force three Jewish men to carry a black-red-gold flag through the city. Many spectators are present and the exhibition ensures that visitors are able to recognize that

---

[74] The caption explains that the photo appeared in the newspaper the *Ulmer Sturm/Ulmer Tageblatt*, with the caption "Thousands of faces expressed mockery and disgust."
[75] "Terror und Gleichschaltung" in German.

these images are representative of everyday life in Nazi Germany, rather than exceptional. The "Forced Laborers" section shows the public shaming of a German woman and Polish man who had a relationship with each other in 1940 and the head shaving of a German woman from Altenburg in 1941; visitors also see a Gestapo man shearing the beard of an arrested Jew in Warsaw in 1939 in the Poland section. In this way, visitors become attuned to how violent spectacles were engrained in the historical reality of Nazi Germany. Aside from these examples of public shaming, spectators are present in images watching the destruction of synagogues, the auctioning off of Jewish property, and mass executions. Here, the visualization of war is performed as an implicit aesthetic montage effect, allowing visitors to realize how public and overt both discrimination and daily terror were. They experience a constructed gaze that exemplifies what could be seen through the eyes of the public and the perpetrators.

For example, a montage depicts various phases and angles of the execution of eleven foreign forced laborers by Gestapo officials in Cologne Ehrenfeld in October 1944. The five photographs first depict a large crowd watching the scene. The largest central picture of the cluster captures the moment directly after the execution. In the forefront of the photograph, visitors see the back or side views of the Gestapo officials. Behind the corpses, spectators leave the scene. Two documents in front of this photomontage allow visitors to dive further into the event's factual context. One document is the testimony of an eyewitness in an investigation by the Cologne public prosecutor's office in 1967, the other an interview protocol with a Gestapo member on his participation in the hanging in 1969. The case against him was dropped since it could not be disproved that he believed that the men had been lawfully sentenced at the time, but it is clear that the legality of the hanging was in doubt. The documents also complicate the perpetrator gaze, which visitors replicate by looking at the photographs. On the one hand, this adds the perspective of West Germany's legal system, and on the other, visitors are directly confronted with both the voice of a possible perpetrator and that of a spectator-bystander. The spectator says that he cannot comment on what the crowd was thinking, since everybody was too afraid to state their opinion openly. There is also no indication of whether people were forced to watch the execution as deterrence or watched voluntarily out of curiosity.[76]

---

[76] Visitors can find the full set of sixteen photographs of the execution in Ehrenfeld of the corresponding computer station "Persecution and Extermination in the German Reich" to the side of section 3. Visitors looking for in-depth material can read a photo story that provides considerable evidence of how ordinary Germans witnessed crimes in Germany, allowing the visitors to feel challenged to reflect on their own observer positions. Similarly the computer station provides picture stories of numerous deportations of Jews, particularly the one in Lörrach in Octo-

The ToT restricts itself to an informational, factual description with the effect that the visitor experiences the reality of spectatorship and of terror in the last days of the regime. Further reflection depends on the visitors' background. International visitors might assume all Gestapo or policemen shown are automatically guilty and simply could not be prosecuted. The brutality and public nature of these examples constructs a public gaze. It challenges the visitor to emotionally react to the picture and to self-reflexively take a stand against the humiliations and atrocities on display. One could react similarly to the German public witnessing of different kinds of discrimination throughout the war and the National Socialist regime.[77] Whereas the museum avoids any opportunity for the visitor to identify or sympathize with perpetrators, the aesthetic effect of the Ehrenfeld cluster and the repetition of numerous scenes of humiliation and spectatorship throughout the exhibition forces visitors to reflect on how they may have behaved in a similar situation. Visitors also become bystanders to these events, emulating the historical spectators. Michaela Dixon has described the tension between experiencing the gaze and reflecting on its subjectivity as textual or explicit focalization. She argues that perpetrator sites such as the ToT use "*explicit* focalisation, [...] in the sense that the identity of the perpetrator focaliser is openly acknowledged and clearly marked, which exposes his/her subjectivity and potentially undermines his/her reliability, thereby mitigating the influence of the perpetrator focaliser on the visitor" (Dixon 2017, 246–247). This does not explain why high profile perpetrators did what they did, but visitors can come close to an experiential feeling of the 'Volk community' and the structures and actions emerging from it. Their contexts differ; however, through repetition visitors can understand how intense this climate of humiliating 'otherness' was. This clearly cannot be attributed to individual perpetrators, but can be experienced instead as a systematic structure. This also demonstrates that those readings of the ToT that argue that its exhibition exclusively assembles facts and documents and lacks a master narrative structure or clear thesis[78] overlook the secondary experientiality the exhibition produces.

---

ber 1940, depicting victims, perpetrators, and observers/spectators. See for further context Nachama and Hesse 2015 (2011).
77 See Springer 2002 for the complex relationship between propaganda and private photography under National Socialism.
78 See for example the otherwise very intelligent reading by Jens Bisky (2010). Bisky argues – correctly – that the ToT at best provides "traces" of the debates in historiography and society about German perpetrators and National Socialism and does not engage with the historiography and remembrance culture of the GDR.

5.3 The Topography of Terror in Berlin — 167

Another networking motif that is predominant throughout the exhibitions is laughter. Bystanders or perpetrators constantly – partly staged for portrait purposes – seem to either enjoy the pain and humiliation of others or seem to love and enjoy life despite the horrors around them. The most iconic photograph in this vein, displayed in almost every Holocaust exhibition opened in the last decade, is a group portrait of laughing SS female auxiliaries and SS men from the Auschwitz concentration camp at the SS retreat Sola-Hütte. It is clustered with three other images of smiling and relaxing SS men in the idyllic mountain retreat, including Auschwitz camp doctor Josef Mengele and Auschwitz commandant Rudolf Höß; all taken in late summer 1944. These images all stem from the so-called 'Höcker album' that was given to the United States Holocaust Memorial Museum in 2007 (Busch et al. 2016). In the section on the Reich SS Leader and Himmler's SS State, there is an undated private group photo of a dozen celebrating *Waffen-SS* members holding beer bottles. Regarding the large number of group photographs in the exhibition, it is important for visitors to understand that, on the one hand, they see staged pictures of smiling Germans working for the Nationalist Socialist system and committing crimes; and on the other hand, they see anonymous victim groups being deported and punished from the perpetrators' perspective. War and atrocities manifest themselves as aesthetic impressions on the visitor and as a cognitive challenge: why do we see photographs of laughter? Is it sadistic enjoyment of violence or a coping mechanism? Or both?

This eerie effect is further intensified in the section on terror in the occupied Soviet Union. One large panel displays a group portrait of nine members of *Einsatzgruppe B* (mobile killing squad B) with three local women working for the Gestapo in its center, presumably taken in late summer 1941. Above the picture, a quotation from an activity report reads "On 7.28.: large scale operation in Russian ghetto in Minsk. 6,000 Jews are taken to the pit. On 7.29.: 3,000 German Jews are taken to the pit. The days that followed were again filled with weapon cleaning and equipment repairs." The ToT stages the contrast between mass killing and everyday routines. The motif of 'laughter' in the middle of one genocidal photo of war crimes after another provokes visitors to reflect upon the possibility of laughing in the face of committing or observing atrocities. A final related picture in the section on occupied France, displays an energetically looking and smiling Reinhard Heydrich at the airport Le Bourget in Paris in May 1942. The string of smiles extends from that of the ordinary citizen and bystander, to those of the groups of men involved in the killings, to that of one of the main perpetrators.

As already indicated above, the ToT also creates clusters similar to the display cases in the chronological exhibition of the Bundeswehr Military History

Fig. 19 Right half of section "Poland: 1939–1945." Interior permanent exhibition. Topographie des Terrors (Topography of Terror), Berlin (Photo: Author, 2017, courtesy of Topographie des Terrors).

Museum. For example, the cluster about terror against the German Jews displays the process of creating and distributing antisemitic propaganda; to the passive observation of burning synagogues and public spectacles such as the burning of furnishings at the marketplace; to a carnival float with a dragon swallowing Jews (as "Judenfresser"); to public deportations. The effect of the increasing violence and exclusion of Jews from German society is again supplemented by numerous document facsimiles, several quotations, an introductory text, and a timeline. The section on German Jews connects to all the other sections of the ToT. This allows the visitor to have an abstract experience of how a group becomes socially ostracized and then annihilated, and how this was – at least passively – accepted by many Germans in the case of the Jews.

The two sections on Poland and the Soviet Union in the fourth chapter of the exhibition on terror in the occupied territories seem to be the culmination of the ToT's experientiality of terror and violence. The Poland section (see fig. 19) demonstrates how the documentation center visualizes the period of terror and occupation through photographs supplemented by contextualizing text elements. In

5.3 The Topography of Terror in Berlin — 169

doing so, it creates a secondary experientiality of how terror functioned in Poland. The section consists of two side-panels, a long panel between them, and two lecterns holding supporting documents. The left panel contains an approximately 250-word text about Hitler's policies to create an Eastern Imperium, the measures taken by Germans to reorganize Polish territory, the persecution and murder of the Polish elite and the Polish Jews, and the Warsaw Uprising. The other two panels contain four historical quotations, three by SS leaders and staff, and a comment by a Wehrmacht General critical of a bestialization of the German police forces. The middle panel begins at the top left with a quotation by the head of the Staff Office of the SS Security Main Office, Walter Rauff:[79] "Of the political leadership in the occupied territories at most 3% remain. These 3% must also be rendered harmless and sent to the concentration camps." An excerpt from Rauff's notes, which factually contextualizes the quotation, is available on the lectern in front of the panel. Here, visitors can understand how German planning of occupying Poland differentiated between the intelligentsia and the "primitive Poles." They also can see the measures to be taken to carry out the stated objective. Next to the quotation, the ToT displays a sequence of three photographs showing the shooting of Polish civilians by a unit of the German Order Police (*Ordnungspolizei*) in Bochnia near Kraków in December 1939. Right below this, there is a shot of Friedrich Wilhelm-Krüger, the Superior SS and Police Leader 'East' in the 'Generalgouvernement,' in conversation with Heinrich Himmler, complemented by a chart of the organizational structure of SS, SD, Security Police, and Order Police in the 'Generalgouvernement.' The exhibition thereby maintains a balance between the individuals who organized and ordered the terror and the men who executed it in practice.

After the depictions of the early killings, particularly of the Polish elite, the next quotation is at the bottom in the very center of the large panel that targets the destruction of the Polish Jews by Governor-General Hans Frank in 1941: "The Führer has promised me that the Generalgouvernement will be completely free of Jews in the foreseeable future. It has also been clearly determined that in future, the Generalgouvernement will be a German region." The panel moves through images of a Gestapo raid; to the public humiliation of Jews by Gestapo men and members of the order police; to aggressive retaliations against partisan killings by Wehrmacht soldiers. On the right hand side, this culminates in the extreme contrast of a bar photo showing a "sociable evening" for Gestapo officials and SS men accompanied by a quotation from the General of the Infantry Wil-

---

[79] The large quotation attributes the origin of the sentences to Heydrich, the caption and the full document available on the lectern to Rauff.

helm Ulex in 1940: "The acts of violence by the police forces, which have increased particularly of late, reveal a quite incomprehensible lack of human and ethical feeling, so that one can speak quite literally of bestialization." Both of these views, the occasional intervention of Wehrmacht officers and the orders that confirm such a brutalization of measures, are supported by documents on the two lecterns.[80] The panel continues with a series of photographs depicting the public execution of Poles for alleged black market activities; an image of the expulsion of Polish people; a quotation by Himmler on the task of "purging all persons of alien race" as "the cardinal ethnic policy" that he faces as Reich SS Leader; and images showing deportations of Jews to the ghettos and their total annihilation in 'Operation Reinhardt.' It ends with two iconic pictures of the Warsaw Ghetto and its destruction after the Uprising, highlighting the perpetrators pictured in the photographs, such as commander-in-chief of both the SS and the police units deployed to destroy the ghetto, Jürgen Stroop.

The Polish section creates a kind of living image of all the terror and its agents through images and original documents. As in the "Operation Barbarossa" display case in the Bundeswehr Military History Museum, it has weak temporality, yet the visualization of war is effective in emotionalizing the visitor. Photography suggests authenticity, even if it is an illusion (e.g. Williams 2007, 73–75). The visitor has no way of escaping terror or its public display and no way to avoid acknowledging the paradoxes of the terror politics in the German Reich and in the occupied territories. This allows for an emotional experience of a constructed past to emerge. There is no real danger of visitors replicating the gaze of perpetrators, since their worldview will be in all likelihood too different to do so. Since there is neither an explicit, overarching message nor a strong narrative, the exhibition relies on an open-documentary approach – the documents and image captions guarantee that the context of the images is clear and authenticated. The political trajectory remains open, although one can assume that through the Topography's montages of constructed-gazes, most visitors are steered toward emotions such as abhorrence and shame as well as to a potential cognitive and moral questioning of the terror. Therefore, the ToT's low narrativity, which clearly highlights image over text, is intriguing. On the

---

80 There are quite a few images that show Wehrmacht soldiers participating in or watching war crimes. However, the focus of the ToT is not on the Wehrmacht, with the effect that at times the distanced and open style of the documentation center can lead to the experiential impression that Wehrmacht soldiers and their leadership were less involved in genocide and war crimes than other Nazi organizations such as the SS and the Gestapo. See also the discussion below of the German-Russian Museum in chapter 6.1 and of Holocaust and Perpetration in chapter 7.

one hand, it avoids the obvious direct emotional manipulations in the structural experiences of the other examples discussed above; on the other, it almost reproduces the alluring and emotionally manipulative ability of photography to suggest an impossible authenticity.[81] Visitors are challenged to align themselves with the gaze of the perpetrators and the ethical challenges of being confronted with this gaze. The ToT's visualization techniques let the visitors experience terror and war crimes structurally as secondary experience.

The fifth and final chapter of the exhibition deals with the end of the war and the post-war era, the trials, and the fact that many perpetrators continued their careers unhindered. It counter-balances and frames the experiential effects of the first four chapters. At the end of the war section, the visitor encounters a photograph of a US army truck full of arrested, suspected National Socialists to be taken to an internment camp in May 1945. An attentive visitor could immediately connect this image, among others, to two photographs with truckloads of people in the first chapter of the exhibition. Section 1.1 contains an image of humiliated prominent Social Democrats under arrest in May 1933; in section 1.3 on the "The 'Volk community'," visitors will have seen a photo of a truckload of SA people proudly displaying the slogan "Volk Community is our Strength." The irony of the repetition of the truck motif highlights the manipulative aspects of photographs and propaganda and allows visitors to interpret such secondary experiential moments regarding the beginning and the end of Nazi Germany. Such repetition can also encourage visitors to reflect upon the use of propaganda in other historical eras and political systems.

---

81 Here, one understands why McLuhan sees photography as an example of hot media (1965 [1964], 22–23; see also chapter 2.1), although museum photography can construct an intricate tension between hot and cool media in emotionalizing its visitors.

Chapter 6:
The Transnational

All the museums analyzed so far operate with a clear national perspective on the Second World War. The museums in New Orleans, Ottawa, London,[1] Berlin (Topography of Terror), Kraków, and Warsaw focus either on a national perspective, or – as in Kraków – on a national space. The museums in Manchester and Bastogne connect the local and national to the global; the museum in Dresden connects the national (and sometimes local) to the anthropological and universal. In contrast, the three transnational exhibitions analyzed in this chapter – the German-Russian Museum, the Gdańsk Museum of the Second World War, and the House of European History – both surpass and partially maintain the national. As seen in the discussion of the previous museums, transnational museums are situated between strong master narratives that restrict experientiality; closed forms of experientiality that steer visitors into cognitively and emotionally accepting pre-conceived historical interpretations, collective perspectives, and structures; and open forms of experientiality that allow for an active visitor to engage in the interpretation of the past. Transnational memory museums highlight collective perspectives: if and when they employ individual accounts, it is to illustrate collective stories and perspectives.

6.1 The German-Russian Museum in Berlin-Karlshorst

The transnational *Deutsch-Russische Museum* (German-Russian Museum, DRM) in Berlin-Karlshorst features perspectives from Germany and the Soviet Union. The DRM continues to be a unique bi-national institution supported by the Federal Republic of Germany and the Russian Federation. Its joint German-Russian advisory board was established in 1994. The DRM also cooperates closely with other military history and history museums in Germany, Russia, Ukraine, and Belarus.[2] The museum is located in a historical villa where, on May 8, 1945, the Ger-

---

[1] The gallery "Turning Points: 1934–1945" in the Imperial War Museum in London (from 2014) adds one section on the war in the East to its primarily British perspectives. The "First World War Galleries" from 2014 have a British focus, but feature considerable global segments as well.
[2] For a more detailed description of the DRM's institutional history and set-up see Clarke and Wóycicka 2019, 81–82. Clarke and Wóycicka argue that the DRM cannot fully realize its "cultural diplomacy potential (...) as a tool of reconciliation," because of "the continuing salience of the

man forces signed their official 'Eastern Front' surrender at the end of the Second World War.³ The first permanent exhibition of the DRM opened in May 1995 (Jahn 2003). On April 24, 2013, it reopened with a redesigned and updated exhibition of about 1,000 square meters.⁴ The current permanent exhibition is presented in ten chapters, most of which are located on the first floor.⁵

As seen in the Bundeswehr Military History Museum (MHM) and in the Topography of Terror, the exhibition uses an open documentary style that leaves considerable room for the visitor to interpret facts, images, and objects. This leads to a secondary experientiality operating more historically toward the simulation of collective perspectives and historical spaces, rather than the simulation of abstract concepts and structures, as seen for example in the MHM. In the case of the DRM, this includes the perspectives of Germany and the Soviet Union. The museum's historical focus leads to the abstract simulation of the impacts of war. Like the exhibitions discussed in the previous chapter, the DRM does not attempt to create the illusion that the past can be 'experienced' as such. Instead, it simulates structural experiences that rely on the constructed collective perspectives of specific groups. These include those of Soviet prisoners of war, those found in the interactions between Germans and civilians in the occupied Soviet Union, or those on the Soviet and German home fronts. Herein lies the DRM's difference to the other museums under discussion, which either express the perspective of a nation and subgroups within a nation, or create a general collective perspective, e.g. the victim or the soldier. In contrast, the DRM establishes a transnational effect, which allows the visitor to reflect on the collective memories of nations and national subgroups. This also provides the visitor with room to interpret and understand the similarities, differences, and

---

memory of war in the national context" (2019, 82). Germany's prototypical cosmopolitan memory regime clashes with the Russian nationalistic one (Clarke and Wóycicka 2019, 88–89).
3 The first museum in the villa was inaugurated in November 1967 for the fiftieth anniversary of the October Revolution as the Museum of Fascist Germany in the Great Patriotic War 1941–1945 (Museum der bedingungslosen Kapitulation des faschistischen Deutschlands im Großen Vaterländischen Krieg 1941–1945).
4 On the ground floor, the DRM displays historic rooms from the surrender including the office used by Marshal Zhukkov, the surrender room, and a diorama depicting the storming of the Reichstag from the Museum of Fascist Germany in the Great Patriotic War 1941–1945. The grounds outside the building remain as they were designed in 1967, with a "Victory Park" including a memorial of a T34 tank on a pedestal and a selection of Red Army tanks and artillery.
5 An installation about the memory of the war can be found on the ground floor. The final room "Conclusion, and the Consequences of War" is located in the basement. It is evident that the exhibition works with limited space. For the structure of the exhibition see also director Jörg Morré's introduction to the museum catalog (2014).

universalities between varied national experiences. This creates the interpretative effect of experientiality that allows the visitor to compare the collective wartime experiences of both nations, whether it be the treatment of enemy soldiers or civilians, the will to survive, forms of resistance, atrocities, political movements, societal advancement, journalism, or forms of remembrance. The DRM uses three major techniques in employing the transnational: tangencies and interactions, parallel themes and structures, and parallel collective perspectives or spaces. The transnational allows for the expression of constellations. In this way, the national – or other elements of collectivity comprising the national – is not diminished or eradicated for the sake of a higher collective, i.e. the transnational. Instead, the comparative approach of the DRM brings out certain qualities of national and group identities and in doing so, expresses the transnational as secondary experientiality. Namely, it enables the visitor to interpret the simultaneity of constellations, perspectives, and spaces.

The first dimension of the transnational approach is to demonstrate the tangencies of and interactions between both sides. These are visible, for example, in the first room on the upper floor of the museum's permanent exhibition. This room is entitled "Germany and the Soviet Union 1914–1941," and creates a temporal structure that adheres to the Soviet perception of the war's duration instead of presenting the beginning of the war as the attack on Poland, as is the norm in German museums. This allows the museum to highlight the Soviet-German relationship. Specific tangencies are represented through text, images, and objects and include the Brest-Litovsk Peace Treaty in early 1918, the covert cooperation between Germany and the Soviet military in the 1920s and early 30s, pro-Soviet communists in Germany, and the Molotov-Ribbentrop Pact and its effects. Other tangencies emerge through the ways in which one side perceives the other; for example, the museum presents documents providing evidence of the early roots of anti-Bolshevist ideology in Nazism, but also within Christian circles.

As a second dimension, the museum employs structural parallels between the two countries in single exhibits or thematic sections. In the second, fairly traditional exhibition room providing a chronology of the war, for example, the visitor finds not only uniforms and weapons from both sides – common in most war and army museums – but also sections with Soviet and German objects. These include sections such as "Injury and Death," "Leisure Time," and "Communicating Home." Unlike in most war museums, this contrastive approach allows the visitor to reflect on the simultaneities expressed by these objects – such as field post letters from soldiers to their mothers in both countries – or differences such in the identification case and tag from both countries. Consequently, visitors have the opportunity to judge for themselves whether individual objects express a national, transnational, or universal concept.

The most significant transnational exhibit in this room is the section on war photography. Here, the DRM emphasizes the importance of contextualizing war photography in three sub-sections: Soviet photojournalist correspondents, German photojournalist correspondents, and German amateur photography.[6] The visitor learns that official Soviet photo correspondents had more freedom in the actual selection of photographs chosen for publication than their German counterparts. The museum clusters its three sections around historical objects, partly belonging to the photographers, and the published photographs of three photographers: Timofey Melnik, Benno Wundshammer, and Wilhelm Meyer. A digital photo album station at the end of the display presents and captions twenty war photographs from each photographer. The museum's transnational approach allows the visitor to understand different dimensions of war photography as well as whether it operated differently according to function (public-private) or nation (Soviet-German). This is, of course, strongly guided by the DRM's selection. The private, amateurs soldier's shots are mainly close-ups as well as scenes from behind the front and post-battle scenes. On the other hand, both official photojournalist correspondents have produced aerial panoramic shots, close distance shots, and scenes shot during the battle. The dead, prisoners, and refugees from the other side are mainly presented during winning advances; similarly, the cost of war among one's own soldiers and population is more likely to be depicted from the perspective of the aftermath of a battle in occupied or liberated territory. Symbols of victory play a major role in the photography from the Soviet side. Images taken from the air by Wundshammer could be read as expression of German technological superiority, as demonstrated by the cover of the military magazine *Signal* entitled "Stukas diving on Stalingrad."[7] Visitors see images of German POWs from the Soviet point of view and vice-versa and must wonder whether they had different or similar fates. The visitor learns about how photography can be used and can thereby reflect upon its functions, possible truths, and distortions. In this way, a structural experience is encouraged in the photography section as well as in the reading of photographs assembled throughout the permanent exhibition.

The contrasting of collective perspectives is the third and most important technique used in the creation of a transnational museum. In rooms 3 and 7, the exhibition addresses the theme of Soviet and German prisoners of war;

---

[6] This sub-section also notes that an equivalent of private photography did not exist on the Soviet side because of stricter regulations and a lack of cameras.
[7] The DRM also presented a special exhibition on Wundshammer as a propaganda photographer from November 2014 to February 2015, allowing visitors to further understand how photographs were produced and functioned as a medium during the Second World War (Kindler 2014).

Fig. 20 Room "Soviet Prisoners of War." Permanent Exhibition. Deutsch-Russisches Museum (German-Russian Museum) Berlin-Karlshorst (Photo: Author, 2013, courtesy of Deutsch-Russisches Museum).

room 4 features Soviet territory under German occupation, while room 9 features the Russian occupation of Germany and Berlin and the final days of the war. Additionally, room 5, entitled "The Soviet Union in War," and room 8, entitled "The War in the East and German Society," both place their focus on the two countries' respective home fronts and civilian populations. The effect of the museum's contrastive technique can be demonstrated through a comparison of the two rooms thematizing prisoners of war. The small darkened room on Soviet prisoners of war features an installation displaying a coat and cap of an unknown Soviet POW with "60%," written in large font – referring to the number of Soviet POWs who died in German captivity (in contrast to 3.6% of West European POWs, see fig. 20).[8] Visitors are prepared for this topic in the section at the end of room 1, where they enter a black cube with dimmed lights, which focuses

---

[8] An earlier, considerably briefer version of analyzing this room was published in Jaeger 2019, 64–65.

on German war planning (see also Jaeger 2017a, 34–35, 2019, 64). The cube combines quotations from Nazi and SS leaders as well as leading Wehrmacht officers. Included here is commentary on the politics they planned to implement in the East and eleven résumés of German leaders, including Hitler, Rosenberg, and Jodl, who were involved in the planning of the invasion of the East. It also contains facsimiles of German policies and directives, propaganda flyers, and a map of grain and livestock supplies to be used to feed the advancing German army. The cube leaves no doubt about German extermination policies and the involvement of the Wehrmacht in their execution. It creates a structural experience by simulating the visitor's entry into the collective mind of the planning of a campaign to destroy the Soviet people.

This secondary experientiality corresponds to the Soviet prisoners of war room, which displays the suffering and fate of Soviet POWs through a variety of themes: planned murders, death marches, camps, forced labor, human experimentation, and collaboration. The museum presents these themes in white font, contrasted against the black walls of the rooms. At the top of each thematic section, the museum provides a section header; at the bottom – as in most rooms in the museum – a narrow strip of captioned black-and-white photographs is located underneath the different display cases. The main space in-between the section headers and photographs contains large quotations from German organizers, occasional small display cases with artifacts and documents, some film footage, and digitally projected photographs. The room is supplemented by the first two audio-visual stations (out of a total of fifteen in the museum) featuring the biographies of certain wartime actors and victims, told in the voice of a third-person narrator. This is supported by a slideshow of images and photographs: in this case, of two Russian prisoners of war. From the German perspective, the visitor learns about the atrocities and crimes perpetrated against Soviet POWs, structurally simulating the different dimensions of these crimes. The introductory panel is located following an introductory survey text supplying facts and numbers; it is entitled "Murder, Countless Deaths, Forced Labor." This panel provides details on the commissar order instructing the Wehrmacht that any Soviet political commissar in the Red Army had to be executed, the killing of other military officers, of soldiers on racial grounds, and of soldiers who were separated from their units. It also informs about the deaths of thousands of prisoners during marches and in camps due to hard labor and malnutrition.

The photo strip at the bottom of this panel leads the visitor from the arrest of Soviet soldiers, to the interview of a political officer, and finally to a photo that was originally entitled "A Jewish Commissar digging his own grave." This sequence of photographs slowly establishes factual evidence of the murders. The subsequent section is called "Deliberate Murders." A quotation by Security Police and SD chief Reinhard Heydrich is the focal point of the panel, supplemented by numerous facsimiles of German killing policies and orders: "In particular, the following groups must be identified: all leading officials of the state and the party, ... all former political commissars in the Red Army, ... the leading people of Soviet business, the Soviet-Russian intelligentsia, all Jews, all people who prove to be revolutionaries or fanatic communists."[9] The supplementary documents add depth and authenticity to the killing policies on display. An example of this is a letter from Ralf Lattmann, Chief of the Army High Command legal department, to the Armed Forces Supreme Command, asking whether political officers at the company level were also to be killed; the museum also includes their affirmative response. The photo strip depicts the arrests of people belonging to different target groups, such as an 'Asian looking' Soviet POW or one with a Jewish star. This allows the visitor to visualize the groups targeted for murder as laid out in the Heydrich quotation. Another photograph shows a captured Soviet female soldier, highlighting how German soldiers loathed and often killed women soldiers on sight. The section then shifts to partisans, death marches and mass deaths in the camps, and forced labor. To counterbalance the perpetrator gaze, two audio-visual stories focus on the survival of a woman and a man in the camps and their life trajectories after the war. In summary, the museum creates a structural reality concerning the fate of Soviet prisoners of war from the perspective of the perpetrators. Structurally, the visitor starts to understand the horrible fate and evidentiality of the crimes committed against these POWs in different phases. Although the DRM presents historical facts and evidence, this room creates a structural impression of today's cultural memory of the war. This leads to the experientiality of German atrocities through all kinds of historical actions and agents.

In contrast, the small room on German prisoners of war – technically the wall of a hallway between two larger rooms – is fashioned around an enlarged poster of German POWs and a large map showing the different internment camps where they were held. These items are supplemented by a photo strip exemplifying activities and living conditions in the camps as well as numerous display cases holding small objects such as maps, documents, and everyday items used by the POWs. The exhibition text underscores the lack of legality concerning the ways in which many prisoners were declared war criminals in rushed trials in 1949, in order to keep their labor in the Soviet Union. However, this text also highlights that most of the POWs were treated in accordance with international

---

9 Translation S.J. The text in the DRM is in German and Russian, whereas the English text contains a shorter abbreviated version, so that for example the quotations are not translated.

law. The exhibition employs a documentary representational style, and the DRM forgoes the possibility of adding audio-visual documents on German prisoners of war. Although this section is made up of only one display wall with two display cases, it is significant for understanding the effect of the museum's consequent transnational approach: it allows the DRM to present historical differences and universalities of POW's suffering on both sides so that the visitor can approach the theme from different angles. The museum renders the point at which the treatment of POWs crosses over in war crimes undeniably clear. On the one hand, visitors can see the hardships faced by German POWs in the Soviet Union, but on the other, realize this treatment is not comparable to the killing and exploitation perpetrated against Soviet POWs by Germany. One could also argue that a transnational approach can also be too narrow, since it does not reflect upon the fate of other POWs and forced laborers in the Soviet Union.

This structural approach of simulating the impact of war is generally cautious in creating empathy. Whereas the DRM tells stories illustrating the fate of Soviet POWs, their voices are not focalized and instead merely reported. Why does the museum avoid giving the victims more of a voice? Furthermore, why does it not create a parallel room from the perspective of Soviet POWs? Clearly, the DRM has limited space in its historical rooms. The museum could have underlined the difficulties found in representing the suffering and stories of these POWs; and it could have related to the fact that these victims had a hard time being recognized in the Soviet Union. The DRM is even more cautious in creating empathy with perpetrators. Their institutional and systemic involvement is clear: the visitor observes events through their collective gaze as in the ToT, however, no discussion about individual responsibility, guilt, and motivations beyond the criminal campaign takes place.

The key question is whether the museum creates a transnational perspective that merges different national perspectives, or whether it simply narrates the perspectives of two different states and their sub-groups. Mostly, the DRM succeeds in doing both. While visitors learn about nation-specific narratives, the museum's transnational approach allows them to develop an understanding that goes beyond traditional national perspectives. This is demonstrated, for example, through the juxtaposition of the two POW rooms. Similarly, room 5 in the exhibition, entitled "The Soviet Union in War," stages the enormous collective will possessed by Soviet citizens in withstanding the Germans, signified by their industrial effort, patriotic propaganda, partisan fighting, and the fight for survival in besieged Leningrad. The visitor is made to understand this further both through the radio address of Foreign Minister Vyacheslav Molotov on June 22, 1941 that greets them in Russian upon entering the room, and through the sound of the metronome beating in Leningrad, which can be heard in the section

Fig. 21 Section "Leningrad." Permanent Exhibition. Deutsch-Russisches Museum (German-Russian Museum) Berlin-Karlshorst (Photo: Author, 2017, courtesy of Deutsch-Russisches Museum).

detailing the siege of Leningrad (see fig. 21). At this point in the museum, visitors will have just emerged from the two perpetration rooms concerning Soviet POWs and German atrocities during the occupation of Soviet territory (see also Jaeger 2017a, 35, 2017c, 154–155). They have therefore already been experientially immersed in questions of survival. Whereas a straightforward section on the Leningrad siege might exclusively capture the suffering of the Russian people and their will to survive, the transnational approach of the DRM contextualizes this historical episode in a way that surpasses its portrayal as an isolated event. Therefore, visitors are steered away from simply lamenting the death, atrocities, and costs of war stemming from the siege: instead, the exhibition creates a secondary experientiality surrounding collective behavior. This transnational approach prevents the simple repetition of Soviet or German wartime propaganda and at the same time allows for genuine simulations of collective perspectives.

In room 8, visitors are greeted by a quotation from Joseph Goebbels and an enlarged poster depicting a woman being instructed on how to use a *Panzerfaust*. This ironically expresses the desperation of the Nazi regime in the final days of the war. It is supported by a scene from the last edition of the *Wochenschau* (German weekly), showing Hitler honoring members of the Hitler Youth and Volkssturm in the garden of the Reich Chancellery. More importantly however, it creates a structure running parallel to that depicting the Soviet will to survive, which the visitor will have already experienced. At the end of the room, the visitor is exposed to the collective fanaticism among the German people continuing to fight, despite Stalingrad, the Air War, and the flight from East Prussia. The visitor is also shown the ways in which the Nazi regime manipulated these feelings among the German populace; the mobilization of the Volkssturm is its last propagandistic step. The first display case highlights how the Nazi regime established the belief that Russians were subhuman, and that additionally there was the need for a war against Stalin. In order to do so, this display employs titles of publications and posters. This helps visitors experience to a point – with reflective distance through contextualizing captions and text panels – how the war of ideology developed and how it led to the fanaticism of at least a portion of the German population at the end of the war. The DRM counter-balances this propaganda effect with two audio stations featuring the voices of resistance fighter Herbert Baum and his group and Meta Klibansky and her family, who were deported and died in Maly Trostinets. A display case, showing a montage of quotations by German citizens who knew about the atrocities in the East, also acts as a counterbalance: it is evident that there was no teleological German fanaticism. As in the room on Russian civil society, the visitor can decide on how different forms of collective will and identity are formed, how propaganda works in creating causes to defend one's country, and how the image of the enemy is constructed.

The last room on the upper floor depicts the liberation of Germany by the Red Army, following a brief interlude on the discovery of Nazi crimes and death camps. It also charts the early months of the Soviet occupation, with a particular focus on Berlin. It is almost completely designed from the Soviet perspective. The rape of German women is represented on a panel entitled "Abuses," dominated by a quotation from the military prosecutors of the 1st Belorussian Army Group reporting the arrest and conviction of a Red Army soldier for the rape of a 15-year-old girl on April 22, 1945. The museum provides an additional explanation, which contextualizes both the rapes and the explicit change in policy that occurred on April 20, 1945, asking for the ceasing of crimes against the German civilian population and their better treatment in order to create a better climate during the occupation. In a small display case that is part of the panel, the visitor finds four handwritten notes about the consequences of the mass rape from the medical records of the Charité in Berlin in 1945, accompanied by a factual contextualization of the evidence detailing what data about the rapes is known and what remains unknown. The visitor can immediately draw a comparison between these displays and those found in room 4 concerning German crimes against Russian civilians during the occupation of Soviet territory. The extent of the parallels between these two rooms is left open to the visitor, although the considerable difference between the German and Soviet perpetration and suffering is evident.[10] In other words, the DRM transnationally creates constellations of crimes, facts, and motives without explicitly judging them. This allows visitors to comprehend national experiences and collective national perspectives structurally, so that a competitive memory framework can potentially be overcome. The visitor can understand the circumstances particular to the national memories presented; however, the poietic staging of transnational constellations also allows for an experientiality that surpasses competition. Indeed, this experientiality adds insight that a national representation, whether commemorative or documentary, could not achieve. Although the DRM represents a historically specific world, it moves beyond this specificity by creating a universal experience through different collective gazes focusing on experiences, structures, and moods. Within the limitations of its political framework (see also Clarke and Wóycicka 2019), the museum simulates total war and supersedes national interests in displaying the repercussions of war, despite being based on the wartime experiences of two opposing states. In other words, it operates transnationally, surpassing the nation state while displaying its continued relevance.

6.2 The Museum of the Second World War in Gdańsk

Whereas the German-Russian Museum is a bi-national museum, whose transnational memory methods allow for the expression of secondary experientiality, the Museum of the Second World War (MIIWŚ) in Gdańsk operates as a hybrid of national and transnational museum that combines a strong master narrative of Polish victimhood and German-Soviet perpetratorship with a secondary experientiality simulating the effects of total war. To understand the MIIWŚ's inherent tension between master narrative, experientiality, and transnational memory, one needs to understand its genesis and the intense and highly politicized memory battles it has generated.[11] The museum was established by the state of Poland in 2008 and opened on March 23, 2017, after an impassioned memory debate. In April 2016, the Polish Ministry of Culture and National Heritage

---

[10] Following the thesis of cultural diplomacy's restrictions in the exhibition (Clarke and Wóycicka 2019) one can certainly argue that the DRM is very cautious in presenting Soviet crimes and perpetration, which reduces the comparative potential of the exhibition considerably.
[11] See also Clarke and Duber (2018, 8) for the intended balance between nationalistic and transnational / comparative narratives.

announced a new administrative structure, in which the museum would be merged with another new museum. This other museum has yet to be constructed, will be located on Gdańsk's Westerplatte peninsula where the Second World War began, and will focus solely on the events in Poland during 1939. Only two weeks after the opening and after a year of court battles, the Polish Ministry of Culture and National Heritage replaced founding director Paweł Machcewicz with government protégé Karol Nawrocki. This was done with the intent of creating a more Polish, heroic, battle-oriented museum and a less civilian-based, transnational museum – and in spite of the protests from Polish and international historians as well as the city of Gdańsk, against the Polish Federal Government's interference.[12] These memory battles center on whether Polish public history should follow a nationalistic-heroic trend of establishing a post-Soviet Polish identity, or whether it should create a transnational pro-European discourse.[13] At the time of writing, the majority of the exhibition remains the one that was designed by the previous director's team.[14] However, this political debate has shown how easily the narrative message of a museum and the ideology behind it can shift according to a change in political leadership, especially if that leadership values memory politics. The original museum can be categorized as a

---

12 For an overview in English see e.g. Donadio and Berendt 2017; Ciobanu 2017; Clarke and Duber 2018, 9–12. For an English discussion of the museum's transnational or global concept see Snyder 2016. Former director Paweł Machcewicz (2019 [2017]) provides the most detailed history of the development of the museum, with focus, of course, on the change of directors, especially 117–227 regarding the 'battle' between the former director and the Polish Ministry of Culture and National Heritage and the governing Law and Justice Party (PiS). For a shorter summary in English see the interview by Etges and Zündorf 2018 and the article by former museum researchers Anna Muller and Daniel Logemann (2017); in German see Logemann and Tomann 2019. For a non-Polish source on the rhetoric of the new museum leadership, see the interview by the German radio station MDR with the new director: "Interview mit dem neuen Chef des Danziger Weltkriegsmuseums, Karol Nawrocki" (MDR 2017).

13 Jörg Hackmann (2018, 595–596) notes that the museum was, from its beginning, a political project; see also Clarke and Duber 2018 and Siddi and Gaweda 2019. The latter argue that "the predominantly national (Polish) agents driving the creation of the museum in fact constrained the transnational focus of the project from its beginnings" (258). They point out that Machcewicz's appointment also contributed to the politicization of the debate around the museum (Siddi and Gaweda 2019, 261).

14 The dozen or so changes that were recognizable during a museum visit in April 2018 are analyzed throughout this chapter and in chapters seven and eight below. Unless specifically noted, this book discusses the original exhibition. See also for the new director's description of these changes Łupak 2017. Because of interference with the copyright of the original museum, its creators are suing the current museum management (*Newsweek Polska* 2018; Logemann and Tomann 2019; Siddi and Gaweda 2019, 267).

transnational narrative history museum, with elements of experiential and ideas museums.[15] The museum planners have pointed out that despite the museum's scenographic design and its considerable use of multimedia technology, authentic artifacts – all from 1939 to 1945 – remain the backbone of the exhibition.[16] The exhibition is divided into three main narrative blocks "The Road to War," "Terror of War," and "The Long Shadow of War," which are then divided into eighteen sections varying between one and eight rooms per section.[17]

Comparing the transnational approaches between the MIIWŚ and the German Russian Museum reveals a similarity in their general chronological presentation.[18] However, the MIIWŚ exhibition works simultaneously as a national and as a transnational museum. It uses two angles that shape the exhibition. On the one hand, it creates constellations about human violence and suffering, particularly of civilians in the Second World War, while also including sections on the everyday-life of soldiers. Military campaigns remain an afterthought for the

---

[15] The museum building is located in the district of former Wiadrownia (Eimermacherhof) that was completely destroyed at the end of war. It was designed by the architectural studio Kwadrat. "The main building is located underground while only a leaning tower, half red brick and half glass, extends above ground. (...) Its glass structure symbolizes the life that won over death, the light of peace that won over the darkness of war, and finally the modern present and future that dominates over the difficult past" (Muller and Logemann 2017, 88; see also fig. 22). The permanent exhibition is presented in about 6,000 square meters on level -3, around 14 meters underground (Machcewicz 2019 [2017], 75). The museum varies the size, height, and light of rooms, which allows for numerous experiential effects that can affect the visitor emotionally: for example, there are chapel-like effects in certain rooms on civilian suffering and the feeling of walking through the underground of an occupied city, whose life is happening above the visitor. The design of the exhibition was developed by Tempora, the same Belgian firm that designed and manages the Bastogne War Museum.
[16] Machcewicz (2019 [2017]), 62; Muller and Logemann 2017, 85–86. Machcewicz describes in detail how the museum's collection of 40,000 artifacts, of which 2,000 are displayed in the permanent exhibition, was established (2019 [2017] 62–75). See also the summary of the permanent exhibition in Heinemann 2017, 458–481.
[17] See Machcewicz, (2019 [2017]), 37–91, for the genesis of the actual exhibition, its objects, and design strategies. See Rafał Wnuk et al. 2016; Machcewicz 2011, 165–171 for the original narrative concept of the exhibition. See also Muller and Logemann 2017, 88–94 for the concept of the exhibition. Joachim von Puttkamer (2017) wrote one of the most extensive reviews describing the actual permanent exhibition from a historian's point of view. He emphasizes the museum's ability to access the past of the war through themes instead of historical events (12). See also the historian's debate between Marcin Kula and Piotr Majewski (2017), who argue about the possibilities and limitations of academic reflection and analysis in a narrative and experiential museum.
[18] See also the reflections on adjusting the exhibition concept from a thematic to a chronological concept so that visitors can more easily orientate themselves (Machcewicz 2019 [2017], 84).

Fig. 22 Outside view of Muzeum II Wojny Światowej (Museum of the Second World War), Gdańsk (Photo: Author, 2017).

museum. These constellations work on the European level, sometimes placing strong emphasis on Central and Eastern Europe, and to a considerably lesser extent, a global level. On the other hand, the museum is clearly nation-based: its dominating perspective is of a Poland caught between the two totalitarian aggressors of Germany and the slightly less extreme Soviet Union.[19] The majority

---

[19] See also Siddi and Gaweda 2019, 264. The first section of the permanent exhibitions also features rooms on fascist Italy and Imperial Japan, however since these totalitarian systems do not affect the Polish story, they remain a by-product of the exhibition concept.

of its museum objects and sources are Polish, which is especially notable in general galleries such as that on Forced Labor.[20] It is important to note that the national perspective – in the original exhibition – is anti-heroic and based mostly on collective suffering, particularly that of civilians. This combination leads to an exhibition that simultaneously relies on master narratives; creates a secondary experientiality that simulates structures of resistance, suffering and violence; and expresses transnational constellations that create questions of whether and how experiences are nation- and group-based, or universal. At the same time, the MIIWŚ is able to employ new angles on the story level that have not yet been displayed or highlighted in Polish or other European museums. The museum's master narrative substructure prevents the exhibition from being as open-ended in meaning as, for example, the MHM. There is a clear message concerning the origins of violence: who caused it, who suffered from it (including German and Soviet civilians), and the fact that war and violence create universal suffering.

The visitor enters the permanent exhibition located 3 floors underground and first reads an approximately 1000-word introductory text entitled "The Greatest Catastrophe in History." Its text contains all the elements that make up the museum. It highlights the human cost and locates the cause for the catastrophe in "the totalitarian regimes of Germany and the Soviet Union." The text goes back and forth between a universal approach outlining how "people paid the highest price for defiance," and highlighting the story of Poland "who found itself in the eye of the storm." Without attribution to any one group, the text concludes by reinforcing the values of freedom, dignity, life, and sacrifice,[21] which together with violence, total war,[22] and suffering form the abstract concepts reinforced throughout the museum. This creates a kind of secondary expe-

---

[20] The transnational parts of the Forced Labor section are exclusively expressed through photographs in slide shows. The MIIWŚ has a complex way of acknowledging the Shoah and the suffering of Jews. For example, aside from the survey panel, Jews or Polish Jews are not explicitly mentioned in section 8.5 on concentration camps. The complex balance of exhibiting the suffering of Jews and of Poles in the museum will further be discussed in chapter 7 below.

[21] "Now, just as then, freedom, dignity and life, for which millions of people made sacrifices in 1939–1945, are universal values."

[22] Former director Machcewicz points out that the museum uses the term 'war of annihilation' instead 'total war,' because the latter is shaped too much by Nazi ideology (2019 [2017], 79–80). Yet this choice demonstrates a clear agency of the aggressor countries, whereas 'total war' as it is used in Mémorial de Caen or in the House of European History for instance allows for a more open forum for comparing suffering in an anthropological form. The MIIWŚ never allows the visitor to forget about historically established agency and consequently, in most sections, it cannot diversify its framework of agency.

rientiality. The visitor then enters section A, "The Road to War," which is comprised of a semicircular, darkened film theater. The introductory film exemplifies the ways in which visitors are drawn into a two-fold narrative, which focuses, on the one hand, on the Polish perspective and, on the other, on a transnational humanist perspective. The film starts with the fragility of the order established through the Treaty of Versailles, the threats placed on democracy, and the drive for expansion as Italian Fascism, Soviet Communism, German Nazism, and Japanese Imperialism threaten newly sovereign countries such as Poland. Whereas the traditional storyline in most European museums views the Treaty of Versailles as the first, or at least an important, step in the development of another world war, the film in this theater provides the prologue to the exhibition's two main arguments. On the one hand, the film shows the world collapsing under the impact of new war technology on soldiers and civilians. On the other hand, the Treaty of Versailles is viewed as a positive force. First, the museum notes that US President Woodrow Wilson adopted the idea of giving people the right to self-determination, which fostered independent nation states. After the end of the First World War, the formation of the Second Polish Republic (and other new states in Central and Eastern Europe) is foregrounded and consequently the treaty is represented largely in a positive light, as a creator of independent nation states: "Poland regained her freedom after over a century of Partitions." The MIIWŚ clearly recognizes frictions between neighboring states. Thus, national independence is not narrated with pathos, but described in a factual way by providing a sequence of historical events.

However, the exhibition also emotionalizes its message. This can be seen in its representation of the Russian threat, in which images are used to emotionally support the narrative message and emotionally supplement the text's factual tone, reinforcing a specific master narrative and Polish national cultural memory (see also Logemann and Tomann 2019). The visitor first sees an agitated Lenin preaching revolution after Russia did not participate in the Versailles Peace talks. The narrator then notes that the Soviets wanted to spread the Revolution to the West, accompanied by images depicting a large group of fighters charging forward with their spears out. The narrator continues: "This plan failed when their Red Army was defeated by the Poles outside Warsaw in 1920. The young Polish state defended its independence." The Polish victory is shown through footage of machine gun fire and airplanes, highlighting Polish technological advancement and civilization versus the archaic Russian troops. The film ends with the looming threat faced by the newly independent Poland from its two largest neighbors, Germany and Soviet Russia, who "dreamed of revenge and the destruction of the Versailles order." The end of the film highlights the dangers of totalitarianism as they unfold in the following sections of the museum, with separate rooms on Italy, the Soviet Union, Germany, and Imperial Japan: "Over Europe loomed the spectre of the next conflict." In summary, the opening film is indicative of the overall museum; it creates perspectives that express the values of Polish resistance, the Polish fight for freedom and survival against two enemies who are fully responsible for the war. It does so while highlighting a system of universal human values.

The MIIWŚ conceptualizes totalitarian societies by employing a predominantly documentary, descriptive style.[23] The visitor learns how totalitarian systems emerged in different societies, especially by example of the Soviet Union and Germany. Emotional displays mainly use the propaganda techniques that the totalitarian systems themselves employed. This is found, for example, in a display in the subsection of the room "Nazism in Germany: Dispensing with Morality for the Sake of Race" entitled "The Master Race and Subhumans," in which numerous pages of a coffee-table book displaying images of 'ideal' beauty are contrasted with propaganda photographs of the mentally ill.[24] Nearby, an electronic book that automatically cycles through its pages also emotionalizes the visitor to the effects of book burnings, when a photograph of a book burning in Berlin turns into pages from books by Erich Kästner and Kurt Tucholsky displayed in burning flames. Tucholsky's *Das Lächeln der Mona Lisa* ("Mona Lisa's Smile") appears in burning red and orange: the visitor can almost empathize with the material object whose destruction is being simulated here.

Similar to the German museums analyzed in this study, the Bastogne War Museum, and the Imperial War Museum North, the MIIWŚ uses documentary techniques that establish historical facts for the visitor. However, these facts are always placed within the narrative framework of totalitarianism creating human suffering in total war, which furthermore identifies Poles as victims with minor exceptions. In one way or another, Poland (and to a lesser extent other nations in Central Eastern Europe) sits in-between totalitarian powers. This is also evident in the experiential installation depicting a main street in Poland in the 1920s after the rooms about Soviet, Italian, and German totalitarianism, and before the one about Japanese totalitarianism. The emotional message of the street locates peaceful, regular life between all the oppressive developments around it: the Polish people seem to dream of traveling as one shop window demonstrates, rather than of war and dominating other groups and nations.

---

[23] Puttkamer (2017, 5) notes that the concept of the totalitarian is not problematized, but introduced as a set value.
[24] See Heinemann 2017, 477–479, for a criticism of the lack of contextualization of graphic images in the MIIWŚ.

Consequently, open documentation without interpretative message is – with some exceptions[25] – a less important method for the museum.

The exhibition always represents texts, images, and objects within the double narrative framework identified above. This master narrative structure becomes symbolically evident in two installation rooms early in the exhibition.[26] The last room of the section "Peace at any Price? Ideological Questions and the Collapse of the Versailles Order in Europe" features one of the most prominent symbolic displays in the museum. As the visitor leaves the area on pre-war Gdańsk, they first see an enlarged portrait of Polish Foreign Minister Józef Beck giving a speech to the Sejm, the lower chamber of the Polish parliament. Audio plays continuously, featuring parts of the speech in which Beck proclaims that Poland will not allow anyone to cut it off from the Baltic Sea against German demands. The text panel accompanying this display ends on the motif of Polish resistance: "This was the first time that the Third Reich's drive to expand encountered resistance […]." Following this, the visitor sees facsimiles of the secret protocol of the Molotov-Ribbentrop Pact from August 23, 1939 and then walks through a narrow hallway, in which three large swastika banners are displayed to the left and nine large rectangular Soviet flags to the right (see fig. 23). On the one hand, this establishes an emotional bond between Poland in its double role as both victim of two totalitarian powers and as first resister fighting for freedom. Like threatened and resisting Poland, the visitor must also walk between the menacing symbols of the two totalitarian regimes. The visitor is dwarfed by the two large installations and placed in the position to empathize with the Polish role of being caught in the middle.[27] On the other hand, however, it is important to understand that the MIIWŚ – unlike the House of Terror in Budapest or the Warsaw Rising Museum – also allows the visitor considerably room for distantiation and reflection in its other rooms. Or, to put it differently, and as will be seen below, it does not fabricate a claim of factuality as seen in Warsaw – at least not in the original exhibition.

---

[25] For example, the original film in the final exhibition rooms and the stories of post-war expulsion and migration are fairly open, see below.

[26] When Machcewicz (2019 [2017], 90–91) argues that his museum follows a forum strategy, whereas the new leadership aims for a temple museum, one should consider that the original exhibition also closes off certain interpretive possibilities. In other sections, especially the transnational ones, it can clearly generate debate and more open-ended interpretations.

[27] The new film in the last room of the permanent exhibition plays on this metaphor by showing two walls apparently crushing the Polish resister in the middle, before the Polish underground state miraculously appears to demonstrate continued Polish resistance (see below for further details).

Fig. 23 Corridor between Nazi Swastikas and Soviet Hammer and Sickle Flags. Permanent Exhibition. Muzeum II Wojny Światowej (Museum of the Second World War), Gdańsk (Photo: Author, 2018).

Wartime atrocities originate in the war's first phase, particularly during the Polish campaign and occupation. For example, in the museum's third section, "War after All," the visitor is confronted with the immediate crimes of the German *Einsatzgruppen*, early in the war, following actions of the Wehrmacht against Polish civilians and the Polish elite: this is done through a scenic installation of suitcases, large poster-photographs, and filmic evidence displayed on a small screen. It speaks to the museum's reflectedness that it also reflects on possible Polish atrocities when it displays a film on the so-called 'Bloody Sunday,' in which German civilians were killed in Bydgoszcz, reflecting on the construction of propaganda and history from both sides. The next room symbolizes the beginning of 'total' warfare in Poland.²⁸ Two rooms later, the visitor encounters the siege of Warsaw in a small cinema, playing an original film by Julien Bryan as it was broadcasted to the USA in 1940. Outside of the cinema, the enlarged photographs of two children are shown, among them the iconic picture of the 10-year-old Kazimiera Mika crying over the dead body of her older sister Anna.²⁹ The short sequence of photographs underneath also depicts, among other things, a photograph of the filmmaker consoling the girl. As exemplified in the Julien Bryan room, the museum establishes a reality of war crimes by creating a strong affective impact on the visitor. This feeds both the museum's master narrative of the totalitarian onslaught against Polish freedom, and its message of universal suffering borne by civilians in total war. The exhibition never loses sight of its master narrative and the historical structure that total warfare was caused by the German and Soviet totalitarian regimes. This holds true for events such as the Air War, German and Soviet massacres of civilians, forced deportations of Polish and other people, flight and expulsion, and post-war deportations.

The museum's master narrative also counterbalances the Western narrative and its focus on specific events and turning points during the war in numerous ways. The museum makers have highlighted this as major justification of the museum's existence: many museums downplay the early phases of the war, so that the core of the Western narrative either focuses on the German war against the Soviet Union or on allied efforts (see also Heinemann 2017, 467). The campaign against Poland and its subsequent occupation is more often than not a mere footnote. The original exhibition of MIIWŚ mentions well-known heroic stories – from the defenses of Westerplatte, the Gdańsk post office and the Hel peninsula, to intelligence efforts in informing the Allies about the crimes in Auschwitz and the development of V1 and V2 rockets, to the success of Polish soldiers at Monte Casino and other Allied campaigns. In doing so, however, it avoids taking a heroic or emphatic tone. Instead, its master narrative works toward underscoring universal values such as freedom, dignity, and life, while allowing for a transnational comparative framework. It is significant that Polish perpetration can be mentioned at all: examples of which include the 'Bloody Sunday' display (mentioned above); the Polish state profiting from the Munich agreement by demanding and receiving the region of Zaolzie from Czechoslovakia; the pogrom in Jedwabne; and minor instances of collaboration with the Germans under occu-

---

28 For details see chapter 8 and the "Prologue."
29 The same image without contextualization is displayed in the Canadian War Museum and as part of a film in the New Orleans WWII Museum.

pation. However, all cases of Polish perpetration are clearly marked as being caused by German or Soviet totalitarianism, so that they do not affect the overall master narrative.[30] Themes such as antisemitism in Poland and Polish perpetration hardly appear in the museum.[31] Even the few examples of Polish perpetration depicted strengthen the museum's clearly assigned concepts of right and wrong.

In addition to the Polish narrative, the concept of total war is the second thematic anchor of the exhibition. The MIIWŚ highlights the suffering of civilians, the destruction of public space, genocide, ethnic cleansing, pogroms, and effects of occupation, resistance, and collaboration throughout the museum. It provides clear arguments that fit its totalitarian master narrative to explain later atrocities. For example, the museum underscores that pogroms against Jews or the ethnic cleansings perpetrated by Ukrainians and Croatians were inspired by the genocides of the Nazi regime. What distinguishes the MIIWŚ is its explicit transnational sections; for instance, the air-war section highlights raids on Spanish, Polish, Dutch, British, Finnish, Yugoslavian, Philippine, and Japanese populations.[32] Former museum researchers and curators Anna Muller and Daniel Logemann highlight the potential the museum offers the visitor to draw conclusions about the mechanisms of violence and racism:

> The museum invites visitors to view and ponder various moments and aspects of war; its intent is not to commemorate the death of the innocent and heroic but to understand the scope and consequences of rabid nationalism, racism, and intolerance. The goal should be to settle or challenge established meanings through dialogue at the intersections of many other discussions: about human nature, national histories, and mechanisms of violence and exclusion. (2017, 92)

The main technique of the museum is to achieve such a dialogue through parallel constellations. Indeed, it creates a unique global memory through the integration of global themes. For this global memory effect, it is relevant that – even if it is only evident in three fairly brief sections – it also mentions Imperial Japan's acts of perpetration and the suffering it has caused. The exhibition also features multimedia computer stations with simulations of maps, and brief chronological

---

30 The memory debates and the success of the PiS (the governing Law and Justice Party) also indicate that the majority of Polish people would not accept a stronger focus on perpetration, so that – as seen from the memory debates in the USA and Canada – too daring of an approach would challenge the overall structure of the exhibition.
31 For the tension between perpetration and victimhood in the Polish memory discourse see also Kurkowska-Budzan 2006, 135.
32 See also chapter 8.

captions depicting all of the war's global theaters. The global structure of the museum allows for rooms on civilian suffering in the Soviet Union, such as in those on prisoners of war, which strongly emphasize the experiences of POWs,[33] and in the room featuring the Siege of Leningrad in the section "Merciless War: Criminal Methods of Conducting War."

On the one hand, the museum's transnational approach means that the visitor can compare similar themes across different nation-states, such as totalitarianism, the suffering during air wars, hunger, collaboration, resistance, terror, ethnic cleansing, and the suffering caused by expulsions and resettlements from numerous countries. The analytical question emerging from this approach is whether it challenges visitors to find differences and variations in violence, or whether the simultaneities between different countries simply flatten different historical experiences toward an overarching and universal message. On the other hand, the exhibition creates simultaneities between different topics of perpetration and suffering. This allows the visitor to reflect on how cultures of violence emerge and what effects they have on numerous victim groups within the framework of total war, with a particular emphasis on the suffering of civilians (see also Muller and Logemann 2017, 92–93).

The most prominent transnational section in the exhibition is section B, entitled "Everyday Life during the War and Occupation: The Biggest Front of the Second World War." This section is arranged in two aisles, with its major part located in the museum's main hallway, which the visitor constantly traverses when going back and forth between the first seven sections. The visitor encounters the final section upon leaving section 9 on the Holocaust and crossing into section 10, "Ethnic Cleansing" and 11 "Resistance." Section B is exclusively based on objects in display cases and tables located in the middle of the hallway, along with integrated monitors displaying historical photographs and brief introductory texts explaining subsections such as food rationing, travel, dress and fashion, love, information, music, work, play, and children. It is also clear that in one way or another, these fields affect all of the occupied nation-states. The visitor is given no opportunity to understand the historical specificities regarding the similarities or differences between conditions in different occupied countries. This section also does not allow the visitor to empathize with concrete individual perspectives. Instead, the strength of the section is to trigger the visitor's imagination and empathy for the universal human condition during wartime occupation.

---

33 Heinemann 2017, 464, points out how depicting new victim groups in the war that were before almost unknown in Poland and in many other countries, breaks new ground.

Unlike the "Everyday Life during the War and Occupation" section, the first room of the seventh section on the German occupation of Europe, "Occupation and Collaboration: German, Soviet and Japanese Systems of Occupation," is very dynamic, in allowing the visitor to compare the situations in different occupied nation-states. Visitors can identify both universal and nation-specific elements in human behavior under occupation. This section discusses the German policies in the occupied territories and the forms and causes of collaboration. In order to do so, it uses a blend of survey texts, display cases, computer stations with slideshows combining texts and photographs; quotations in large letters; enlarged photographs and announcements; and propaganda posters.[34] The slideshows help the visitor understand different dimensions of occupation. Though this section does not challenge the general assumption that there is good victimhood and bad totalitarian regimes, the visitor receives a varied picture of conditions under occupation and of distinct National Socialist policies. In this way, visitors are enabled to draw their own conclusions about how specific actions and attitudes during occupation should be assessed. This is most evident in the section on collaboration. The exhibition gives a differentiated picture of various types of collaboration and explains possible motivations behind the decision to collaborate. The visitor can decide how to evaluate the different examples and forms of collaboration. Is it different if an existing police force collaborates with the occupier? How important is it that collaboration is voluntary? Can one demand that everybody support the resistance? Because the MIIWŚ foregoes a moral assessment, the visitor can develop questions from these exhibits. Since visitors first learn about the various occupation policies in different countries, they can judge whether informing on and denouncing other people is the same in all occupied countries, or whether there are explicit differences on a case-by-case basis.

Because the set-up of the room is fairly open, it creates interpretational opportunities for the visitor. For example, in the section on Polish occupation, the visitor finds a quotation, written in large letters, on the Polish population from Colonel Claus von Stauffenberg: "This population is an unbelievable rabble; there are so many Jews and mixed-bloods. It's a population that only feels well under the whip." The quotation serves as an illustration of German attitudes toward Poland during occupation. Furthermore, an informed visitor can contrast this with any lionization of Stauffenberg regarding the July 1944 assassination attempt on Hitler. Another quotation, this time from French Prime Minister Pierre

---

34 This section creates dynamic constellations with the resistance section later in the exhibition.

Laval in 1942 reads: "I wish for a German victory because, without it, Bolshevism will establish iteself [sic] everywhere. France must not remain passive or indifferent to the enormous sacrifices the Germans are prepared to make to create a Europe in which we must occupy the place we deserve." Whereas visitors know, in light of all the Germans crimes presented throughout the museum, that such an opinion is factually wrong, they can consider whether such a conviction could justify collaboration. The visitor also learns that France had very different occupation conditions to those of Poland, which could explain or at least rationalize the quotation. The transnational approach in the "Occupation and Collaboration" section allows the museum to express elements of universal memory within a historically specific context, while maintaining some historical specificity on the national level. The MIIWŚ exhibits a relatively clear historical framework, Polish cultural memory, and master narrative; however, it also succeeds in diversifying historical arguments without flattening historical specificity, similar to the MHM.

Section 11 is introduced by the sculpture-like presentation of the word "OPÓR" (resistance), which creates an immediate connection to the word "TERROR" that welcomes the visitor to sections 9 and 10 on German and Soviet terror and on the Holocaust. Terror and resistance are thus the conceptual dichotomy anchoring the whole museum. The resistance section is divided into five sub-sections. The first sub-section documents the roles of individual resisters from different countries and commemorates their actions; the second informs the visitor about the Polish Underground state in an experiential setting; the third – mimicking an interior room of a house – is a transnational display of civilian resistance in Europe; the fourth documents the struggles of partisans and other underground operations across multiple nations; the fifth is divided into two parts and charts various uprisings against the Nazi state. Above the entire section, large screens with historical footage and photographs depict life under German occupation above ground. The extremely high ceilings make this installation quite effective. Visitors are put into a situation where they empathize with one specific side, the underground and resistance. This works in particular for the Polish underground state, civilian resistance, and uprisings. A more detailed look at the civilian resistance room demonstrates a new effect created by the museum's transnational approach. The visitor steps onto a floor littered with resistance flyers, caricatures, and symbols. Different sections of the room highlight civil resistance as the power of community, of the individual, and of laughter as well as listening to the BBC as act of resistance. Resistance in seven countries is represented, all of which, except for Czechoslovakia, are located in Western

Europe.³⁵ Unlike in the occupation-collaboration section, the visitor does not obtain a picture of the varying conditions surrounding resistance. Additionally, the objective of the display does not seem to be the simple expression of universal conditions of war. Here, the transnational approach makes an emphatic statement about the possibility and effectiveness of resistance in conditions of wartime occupation. The focus is not on German punishment, which can be found in other sections about terror, war crimes, and the Holocaust. However, visitors might ask themselves how they would have acted in similar situations and whether they would have dared to defy the oppressor. While the room also represents facts on civilian resistance in many countries, the overriding transnational message professes overarching support for such resistance. This has the power to shape and confirm the cultural memory of the nations represented. An affective representational mode dominates over a cognitive one, and consequently, the floor made up of resistance posters and the sound of BBC broadcast experientially unify visitors.³⁶

The part of the museum on uprisings is even more effective regarding the emotional staging of transnational memory. However, this exhibit seems to be bypassed or hardly noticed by many visitors, since it takes considerable time to immerse oneself in the presentation and there is limited space for visitors to linger (see also also Heinemann 2017, 468). The transnational display integrates the uprisings in the Warsaw Ghetto, Warsaw, Paris, Slovakia, and Prague. Only the one in Paris was successful; the Prague Uprising is represented as successful, but ending in disappointment, as the Red Army freed the city and not the Americans. The introductory text highlights the motives behind these insurgencies – national freedom, patriotism, and vengeance.³⁷ Visitors can easily miss the lengthy slideshow display to the right of the entrance, which includes data, photographs, captions, factual events, and statistics concerning all five uprisings.³⁸ The presentation remains, for the most part, neutral and factual. Indeed, the most interesting element is that data from the various uprisings is summar-

---

35 The "London Calling" display also integrates illegally listening to the BBC in Germany and Poland.
36 Machcewicz highlights the intention to create transnational constellations of simultaneously depicted countries, (2019 [2017], 85) without reflecting upon the emotional strategies and effects deployed by the museum.
37 The Warsaw Ghetto Uprising does not seem to be part of the general description. Nevertheless, it serves as a contrast to the other four uprisings, fulfilling an important function in highlighting their conceptual differences.
38 The Warsaw Ghetto Uprising and the Warsaw Uprising are represented with considerably more slides than the other three uprisings.

ized on-screen, allowing the visitor to draw comparisons between them; this incorporates data regarding opposing forces, the length of the different uprisings, their end results, and the losses sustained on both sides, including insurgents, soldiers, and civilians. Theoretically, this allows for fascinating comparisons to be drawn between the different uprisings. It shows, for example, that the Paris Uprising had greater numbers and support due to Allied pressure, in contrast to the Warsaw Uprising, which is factually demonstrated to have lacked support from Stalin and the Russians. These numbers also elucidate the staggering losses suffered during the Warsaw Ghetto Uprising and the differences in civilian casualties between all five uprisings. It takes about twenty-four minutes for all five slideshows to run: most visitors I observed over eight days of analysis did not take the time to watch even one slideshow all the way through, if they noticed the screen at all. However, this remains an excellent example of how a documentary and open transnational presentation can trigger comparative thought. It is left to the visitors to draw conclusions from this factual representation as to the need for the uprisings.

Following the slideshow, the visitor walks through a narrow corridor into a fairly dark space surrounded by fragmented brick walls. Eight wooden boxes, with five functioning as seats and three as display cases, further the impression that one has entered a provisional space. On the right-hand brick wall, film footage and historical photographs (presented in slow-motion) of the five uprisings are shown on a circular loop on two screens, with a running time of approximately thirteen minutes, supplemented by audio recordings of the voices of insurgents and other witnesses. Both screens are modeled to look like small garage doors and reflect back onto the floor in the dark scenery, further disorienting the visitor. The film reduces any documentary distance and instead further creates an empathetic setting for the visitor. The Warsaw Uprising film moves from a justification of the Uprising and the early onset of euphoria stemming from freedom and a new cultural life, to unease when the Soviets abandon their artillery shelling.[39] Afterwards, the film shifts to German crimes, the recital of a prayer, and a reflection upon the Uprising's civilian cost: even for those who do not fight, death appears to be everywhere. Clearly, the idea here is to allow the visitor to empathize with the thoughts of insurgents, for example through the use of phrases such as: "I felt that since I was alive I had a right to fight"; or, when one sees the stern face of a Soviet soldier and Stalin in a split screen with the

---

39 Heinemann (2017, 470) has pointed out that the Warsaw Rising Museum and the MIIWŚ display similar contents, but use very different narrative trajectories. The former depicts the absolute necessity of the Uprising, the latter highlights the total destruction and devastation that it wrought.

text: "They stayed there and watched us die." The final part of the film expresses total agony and despair: "This is hope dying. The Uprising at the agonal stage." The right screen depicts mothers holding their children and then ruins with wooden crosses appear on the left screen with the caption "Behind us Warsaw, all our past and all are [sic] hopes buried in the ruins." The camera then pans to a destroyed Warsaw, and the text states the core sentence also seen in the Warsaw Rising Museum: "We wanted to be free and owe this freedom to ourselves." On the left, footage shows one man hobbling through a total wasteland.

The message is clearly mournful and depicts a feeling of tragedy; neither the idea of the rising nor its failure is represented as heroic. However, the visitor is led to empathize with the perspective of the insurgents and their perception of the Uprising. Somewhere on the border between primary and secondary experientiality, the MIIWŚ simulates a collective perspective of how insurgents could have felt in different situations, in a similar fashion to the Imperial War Museum North. The distance between the visitor and the historic perspectives is so strongly reduced that an analysis of the necessity of specific uprisings is impossible: the visitor relies on the hopes and motives of the insurgents. The montage of the five uprisings in the film presentation and its scenic setting allows for secondary experientiality, since the visitor can understand the possible motives, hopes, and desires of various uprisings, and whether or not they had a chance to succeed. Here, universal concepts such as freedom, dignity, life, and sacrifice, emphasized in the opening panel of the exhibition, emerge as structural concepts staged in the museum. At the same time, the visitor receives no tools to conduct a historiographical analysis about whether a given uprising made sense from a strategic or political perspective. The museum stages national and transnational cultural memories, which the visitor could interpret as historical truth. This section presents the emotional message that under totalitarian occupation, resistance and uprisings always make sense from an emotional and moral point of view. The representations are based on individual memories that have become collective, which is reinforced throughout the exhibition.

To understand this further, it is useful to take a closer look at the brick wall representation of the Warsaw Ghetto Rising. Here, the MIIWŚ mixes a number of voices: some are named as Jewish insurgents and ghetto inhabitants, while others are Polish voices outside the Ghetto walls (see also Heinemann 2017, 469). On the one hand, the visitor is led to understand why resistance and uprisings make sense, even if there is no chance for an uprising to succeed: Icchak Cukierman is quoted as follows: "For our time has come, without hope and with no chance of rescue"; Mordechaj Anielewicz notes that Jewish self-defense "has become a fact" and speaks of the "magnificent heroic struggle of the Jewish fighters"; Marek Edelman reports that it was satisfying to see the Germans show fear. It is then made clear to the visitor how the Germans thrashed the Uprising with gas grenades. The utter destruction they wrought is consistently counterbalanced with the Polish will to resist. The final voice in the recording belongs to Adina Blady Szwajger, who worked in the children's hospital in the Warsaw Ghetto, and highlights the total loss of life and witnesses: "But there is not a single fragment of the wall that separated one third of the city from the rest. There is not a single burnt-out house from the windows of which mothers had thrown their children before jumping out themselves." While this audio plays, the viewer sees images of the completely destroyed ghetto, void of life. The transition to voices outside of the ghetto also highlights the isolation faced by ghetto inhabitants during the Uprising.

The visitor can empathize collectively with both the Jewish people inside the ghetto and the Polish people outside of its walls. The film simulates the devastating loss of hope as well as the symbolic significance behind the Warsaw Ghetto Uprising. Naturally, the visitor cannot empathize directly with somebody experiencing certain death in the hopeless situation within the ghetto, but these installations simulate collective gazes that allow for a structural experience of these uprisings and their motives, hopes, successes, and failures. The transnational memory approach taken here allows the museum to bring the concrete and constructed collective perspectives of each historical event to a meta-level. This, in turn, lets the visitor emotionally experience the different motives behind the uprisings that are shown. This is only possible on a secondary level: in other words, the transnational approach of the MIIWŚ prevents the museum from falling into the trap of suggesting that the primary feelings of insurgents can be re-experienced. But visitors are put into a position to emotionally understand the drive behind the uprisings and why they might be emotionally and symbolically relevant beyond any pragmatic, functional, or strategic reason.

My final example of transnational constellations in this museum relates to flight and expulsion (Mikuska-Tinman and Jaeger 2020). The second room in the sixteenth section "The War is Over" is entitled "Fall of the 'Thousand-Year Reich': German Crimes and Population Flights." Here, death marches from concentration camps, the flight from East Prussia and the sinking of the Wilhelm Gustloff, and rapes perpetrated by the Red Army work as one cluster. The room displays the bell of the Wilhelm Gustloff and provides encyclopedic information on the flight of Germans from East Prussia, using a slideshow to depict the fate of German passenger ships and Russian massacres in the region. Death marches and the plight of Polish or Polish-Jewish women dominate the room's displays. For example, an artistically animated, intentionally blurry narrative video is used to tell the story of a woman who escapes from SS guards, while they shoot at her and her sister as they flee over a frozen lake. A similar computer animation, paired with the voice of a German woman living in Gdańsk who was raped by the Russians, underscores the fact that Germans suffered too. The visitor has, at this point, been exposed to German atrocities and terror in occupied Poland and the Soviet Union in previous parts of the exhibition. Here, the MIIWŚ introduces a very original transnational frame, which both includes the suffering of groups from perpetrator nations and gives individual suffering a voice. One can ask oneself the unanswered question of what German or Soviet suffering means in relation to the suffering of others: from a human point of view, is the suffering of people from perpetrator nations comparable to the one of victim groups? Or, given that the museum maintains a narrative framework that depicts all violence as originating from the policies of totalitarian regimes, is there a difference? The MIIWŚ provides a twofold answer to these questions; on the one hand, the answer lies in the master narrative as discussed: namely, that this German suffering is self-inflicted. On the other hand, the museum expresses a perception of universal suffering that allows for a more open comparison.

This interpretation becomes even clearer in the following section "After the War," with the sub-section "Great Transformation: Migrations and Borders – the Great Powers Assigned Many New Borders." Here, the museum integrates the post-war expulsion of Germans with a wider framework of Central and Eastern European expulsions and population movements. The combination of object-based and experiential narratives through photographs, objects, video interviews, and atmospheric settings, allows some room for interpretation. This section creates a secondary abstract reality in the way in which the collective impact of expulsion on the human being, independent of group identity, can be expressed. This room's design is identical to an earlier room in the section "Terror," entitled "Resettlements, Deportations, Expulsions: Hitler's and Stalin's Social Engineering," with a floor map charting migratory movements and thematic huts symbolizing the homes that people left behind. Therefore, it is once again situated in a clear historical-causal context, which also supports the museum's master narrative structure that assigns concepts of right and wrong.

Nevertheless, this transnational approach allows the visitor to leave the national framework behind and to consider different conditions of hardship. The room itself showcases this transnational technique, displaying three victim groups and their stories in separate huts: Poles who were repatriated from formerly Polish, now Soviet territories in the East, to formerly German, now Polish territories in the West; German post-war expellees from Poland, Czechoslovakia, and Hungary; and Baltic and Ukrainian expellees who had to leave their home and resettle in other parts of the Soviet Union. Visitors are led to simultaneously experience the loss of home and hardship during moments of departure and travel, without losing sight of the historical contexts that led to these population movements (Mikuska-Tinman and Jaeger 2020). Objects allow visitors to reflect upon the comparability between different acts of social ostracization on ethnic grounds and different contexts for the emergence of violence. For example, a badge and armband that Germans were forced to wear during the expulsion mirrors the German treatment of the Jews and other concentration camp inmates (Mikuska-Tinman and Jaeger 2020).

The MIIWŚ is clearly able to maintain its historical specificity, while also creating and simulating structures that overcome historical patterns and preconceived narratives: this allows for various forms of experientiality. The dynamic and provoking challenge for visitors is to reflect upon whether, for example, the aforementioned story of the death marches is comparable to that depicting the rape of German women. This provides the opportunity for a dynamic reflection of memory. The historical framework pertaining to how Germans brought suffering on themselves is presented, as is an examination of the human impact of suffering and atrocities. Although the historical framework of the MIIWŚ is closed,[40] its transnational techniques create continuous openness and challenges for the visitor. Indeed, these techniques act as a form of multidirectional memory, which allow the visitor to consider and compare different agents and victims within a certain thematic framework. This especially occurs in the installations that avoid the universalization of national experiences and instead place historically and nationally specific perspectives in tension with transnational and secondary anthropological insights. In this way, one can see the productive effect of this transnational approach.

The largest case of intrusion by the new museum leadership in the original exhibition can also be seen as a warning of how easily the dynamics of the MIIWŚ can be overwritten. In its original version, the viewer had already walked through a Polish street in ruins directly at war's end, indexing the destruction to the reconstructed street they had seen in the second section. They then encountered a film installation as the final part of the museum, where two screens were split by an iron curtain, showing iconic photographs of historical events that occurred post-1945.[41] Here, the museum connected past and present.[42] When the

---

[40] With the exception of the original final film, discussed in the next paragraph.

[41] David Clarke and Paweł Duber (2018, 7) also discuss how the film implements a version of Polish memory "that attempts to acknowledge both heroism and less admirable episodes in the nation's past." They point to the example that the film "shows the anti-Zionist campaign launched by the communist government of Poland in 1968, which led to 13,000 Polish Jews (around half of the remaining population) applying to emigrate to Israel."

events depicted in the film reached the twenty-first century, the two screens merged[43] and showed the destruction of today's Syria, indirectly asking the visitor the question: Why is this destruction, this human suffering reoccurring? Whether this contemporary conflict has similar origins to the totalitarian ambitions and policies of the Second World War remained open. However, this was one of the first changes made by the new government-endorsed museum administration in October 2017. The new film *The Unconquered* is a fast-moving film, rhetorically efficient and highly manipulative in steering the visitor toward a singular emotional response. In order to do so, the film uses the style of a videogame to tell the story of a Poland that, attacked from two sides, resisted and survived two dictatorships. It displays two identical screens, the one on the left providing English subtitles. A narrator full of pathos, accompanied by a dramatic musical score, tells the story in such a way that nobody can miss the symbolic meaning of the film's images. Its heroic tone, with particular emphasis on military success, does not fit to the rest of the exhibition. Instead, it indicates the lack of interest from the new museum leadership in maintaining the transnational theme or tension that allows the museum to create secondary experientiality. There seems to be no open-ended questions or space for critical analysis for visitors or researchers. The only task would be to find further evidence to support the master narrative of an unconquered Poland full of valor.[44] History is seen exclusively in black-and-white. All Polish people have become a single collective and experientiality is reduced to an emphatic ideological framework.[45]

---

42 See also Machcewicz (2019 [2017], 81–82), who describes how the museum planners changed from an optimistic European end to an ending that integrated images of the conflicts in Ukraine and Syria and of the European migrant crisis.
43 A previous scene shows two identical screens of Steve Jobs presenting the Apple iPhone 3G to the global public in 2008, combining East and West in modern technology and capitalism.
44 It seems only logical that the new still-to-be-built branch of the MIIWŚ at the Westerplatte peninsula seems to be planned as an archeological dig for traces of a heroic and matyrological battle of the Polish soldier. This is at least clearly the message of the special exhibition in the MIIWŚ *Seven Looks at Westerplatte*, as it was presented in a special exhibition in the museum from September 1, 2017 to September 30, 2018. Westerplatte can serve as the historical justification and material evidence of the neo Polish master narrative of a heroic struggle won by an 'unconquered' Poland, since it survived two dictatorships. On September 1, 2019, the MIIWŚ held an official foundation stone laying ceremony for the Museum of Westerplatte and the War of 1939 at the Westerplatte Power Plant building. On site, the museum also (re-)opened an archaeological special exhibition on the same day (https://muzeum1939.pl/en/laying-foundation-stone-museum-westerplatte-and-war-1939/2673.html, accessed 13 October 2019).
45 For further analysis of the new movie, see the Holocaust section 7 below.

6.3 The House of European History in Brussels

Up to a certain point, both the German Russian Museum (DRM) and Gdańsk Museum of the Second World War (MIIWŚ) create transnational memories. Both transnational projects are have been restricted through political interests. Both museums create gazes that examine themes and concepts from the perpetrators perspective, including from civilian suffering, flight and expulsion, pogroms, resistance, freedom, and terror. A concrete sense of national reality is mostly maintained in both museums: the DRM reflects contemporary historical knowledge and national cultural memory, while the MIIWŚ comes close to reenacting the political memory battles of today's Poland. Both museums construct collective perspectives, whether they relate to nations, humanity, or specific groups such as prisoners of war or insurgents fighting occupying powers. Transnational concepts, as seen above, are not automatically linked to a closed or open exhibition format. The DRM and the MIIWŚ both use their transnational set-up to open possibilities for interpretation. Constellations emerge and visitors must decide the degree to which these constellations point to comparability or even universality, and whether or to what degree they indicate historically or structurally distinct situations for different national groups and subgroups. Both the DRM and the MIIWŚ have a strong historical basis that is connected to historical events and also – in the case of the MIIWŚ – a master narrative. This historical basis dominates the abstract and structural secondary experientiality that can be seen in the Topography of Terror and in the Bundeswehr Military History Museum in particular.

How does this transnationalism – which allows for the comparison of multiple group experiences despite a strong historical framework – compare to the presumably ultimate 'transnational' museum that opened in Brussels on May 6, 2017: the House of European History (HEH)? It is located in the completely renovated Eastman Building in Parc Léopold in the 'European district' of Brussels.[46] The institution, funded by the European Parliament, is governed by a Board of Trustees and an Academic Committee made up of university professors and museum experts.[47] The museum's mission underlines that the HEH strives to be a

---

[46] The renovation and contemporary extension of the building was done by Atelier d'architecture Chaix & Morel et associés (France) JSWD Architekten (Germany) and TPF Engineering (Belgium). See also House of European History 2017b; Blandini 2017.
[47] The Board of Trustees is chaired by former President of the European Parliament Hans-Gert Pöttering who initiated the project in his inaugural speech in the European Parliament in 2007. For further data see the info brochure *Facts and Figures* (House of European History 2017b); see

dynamic and open transnational museum. Its permanent exhibition covers approximately 4,000 square meters. Though it is not centered on the Second World War as such, the museum makes "the tragedies of the 20th century" (House of European History 2017b)[48] – the two world wars, the rise of totalitarianisms, and the Holocaust – the core foundations of the European integration process after 1945. Its mission statement points out the fragility of peace and prosperity: "In times of crisis, it is particularly important to develop and sharpen consciousness of cultural heritage and to remember that peaceful cooperation cannot be taken for granted" (House of European History 2017b). This statement clearly connects an understanding of historical processes to their relevance for the present and future. It also seemingly advocates for debate and openness instead of closure[49] and for a diversity of memories in Europe.[50] The HEH asks the crucial question: "Will the House of European History replace national histories?" and emphatically answers that "[t]he House of European History will not be a simple sum of national histories, nor does it seek to replace them. The House of European History will be a reservoir of European memory, containing experiences and interpretations in all their diversity, contrasts and contradictions. Its presentation of history will be complex rather than uniform, more differentiated than homogeneous, critical rather than affirmative, but it will focus on the emergence of the European Community" (House of European History 2017b). In other words, national histories and collective memories are supposed to remain valid, but the HEH seeks to express something 'European' that surpasses any national memory. It is important to note that the concept of collective/cultural memory is extremely prominent in this explanation; at times it seems to completely overshadow history, which is also explicitly expressed by head curator Andrea Mork (2016, 220–221). The question that the HEH's mission statement circumvents is: Does the exhibition express a linear and progressive master narrative, which automatically leads to European integration? Or is it open enough to display tensions between a European narrative, different nation-

---

also Vovk van Gaal and Dupont 2012; Kaiser 2017; Mork and Christodoulou 2018. Taja Vovk van Gaal (2018) gives a detailed summary about the genesis of the museum project.

48 See also the website of the museum, https://historia-europa.ep.eu/en/mission-vision, accessed 13 October 2019.

49 "History, which will give citizens an opportunity to reflect on this historical process and on what it means for the present. Parliament believes that the museum can be a place of debate and understanding about contemporary situations from the perspective of their historical roots and in the light of historical experiences" (House of European History 2017b).

50 "From the outset, the project has been driven by a desire to promote knowledge of Europe's history and to raise awareness of the diversity of memories within Europe in an open and inspiring fashion" (House of European History 2017b).

al narratives, and other narratives, so that visitors can draw their own conclusions?[51] Mork uses the metaphor of a "reservoir of European memory" that contains "experiences and interpretations in all their diversity, contrasts and contradictions" (2016, 221). The former academic project leader and current creative director of the HEH, Taja Vovk van Gaal, and historian-curator Christine Dupont noted in 2012: "The museum is always a 'negotiated reality' [...] and the visitor should be aware of the relativity of the choices. Confrontation with different interpretations of history is also one of the tools that will be used to convey this multifaceted view of European history" (46). However, the promise that the HEH's "presentation of history will be ambivalent rather than homogeneous, critical rather than affirmative" (Mork 2016, 221) can be challenged with a precise analysis of the actual exhibition, which demonstrates how political compromises[52] risk the implementation of an ambitious and dynamic museum project.[53]

---

[51] The question of how European memory and identity can be represented in a museum led to a flood of publications discussing the museum and its political and conceptual genesis before its actual opening (Settele 2015; Hilmar 2016, Kaiser et al. 2014, 114–125, 144–152; Kaiser 2017; Remes 2017), weighing in on the balance between national and European narrative. Weiser – before the opening of the museum – celebrates its potential for "transnational unity" (183) and for entangled memories in a "consciously chosen unity as well as rightful diversity" (2017, 185). Daniel Rosenberg, also without referencing the actual exhibition design, summarizes the project as "a political programme that is more compatible with contemporary challenges facing the continent." He continues that "European integration is thus seen at once as an almost determinist process due to the unified nature of Europe, as well as a complex process due to the diverse and multifaceted nature of Europe" (2018, 33).

[52] Wolfram Kaiser (2017) has provided a precise analysis of the political pressures on the museum and an analysis of "the changing constellation of actors and networks who have sought to influence" the process of the HEH's creation and the narratives of the history of Europe and European integration. See also Huistra et al. 2014. Anastasia Remes (2017, 114–115) also highlights – shortly before the opening of the HEH – the inherent tension between the multiperspectivity and openness that the curatorial team wanted to implement and the actual implementation of narratives in the exhibition that might be close to traditional national history museums. For the political complexities of the museum's genesis see Borodziej 2018. Włodzimierz Borodziej highlights two particular points of contention: the differences between East and West and that Germany's approach to its national past that is far more self-critical than those of most other countries (37).

[53] The early reviews of the permanent exhibitions have been mixed. Krankenhagen (2017) and Kesteloot (2018) have been very positive. The latter even seems to imply that all critical views of the transnational, cosmopolitan approach of the HEH are supporters of a "renationalisation of history" (157). For extremely critical reviews see Lutz 2019, who problematizes the universalization of terror, and Fickers 2018, who emphasizes the HEH's approach to Europe as a problematic history of compromises.

The permanent exhibition of the HEH is strongly object-based, with large vitrines, a number of multimedia installations, large-screen films, and some experiential settings.[54] Its core feature is its lack of text or audio throughout the entire exhibition. Instead, the visitor receives a tablet containing all twenty-four official languages of the European Union, giving introductory descriptions of each panel, providing object credits/brief descriptions and audio for the films as well as deciphering the quotations coming from Boris Micka's art installation *Vortex of History*, which covers five floors in a 25-meter high metal installation.[55] Individual voices hardly appear in the museum.[56]

The Second World War, the Holocaust, the totalitarian systems that led to the war and their atrocities are central to European memory. Consequently, the war is present throughout the exhibition: first in the introductory section on the second floor entitled "Memory and European Heritage" where the museum introduces fourteen principles that could bind the continent together, such as "State Terror" and "Genocide."[57] Afterwards, on the third floor (see fig. 24), the museum begins European history with the political revolutions of the late eighteenth and nineteenth centuries. It then develops through the Industrial Revolution and colonialism (see also Mork 2016, 227). Europe's cultural memory, clearly paramount to 'history' in the HEH, is shaped by optimism about the progress of civilization in the nineteenth century; yet it comes after the abolition of slavery with "new forms of intolerance and racism," which are particularly evident in the exploitation and 'advancement' of civilization in the colonies.[58] The museum's narrative uses the idea of the degeneration of humanism to explain the catastrophe of the First World War. This catastrophe allowed for the development of democratic forms of state in Europe following the war. The sub-narrative here is that after the First World War a battle between young democracies and nation-

---

54 See also the guidebook House of European History 2017a and the edited collection / catalog on the creation of the museum by its staff (Mork and Christodoulou 2018).
55 This results in the strange effect that visitors either are in danger of forgetting about the actual museum space, since reading the tablet becomes paramount, or they perceive the exhibition as strongly object-based and open, since they react sensually to the objects and displays without constantly reading the explanations and captions on the tablet (see also Lutz 2019, 49). In contrast, Krankenhagen (2017, 67) follows the HEH design explanations when praising the tablet, but fails to consider the senses and perceptions of visitors in its space.
56 Exceptions only occur in the later parts of the exhibition, such as in the film on the fall of the Berlin Wall or multicultural experiences in today's Europe.
57 The fourteen principles are in order of presentation: philosophy; democracy; rule of law, omnipresence of Christianity; state terror; the slave trade; colonialism; humanism; the Enlightenment; revolutions; capitalism; Marxism, communism & socialism; the nation state; genocide.
58 In the section "Notions of Progress and Superiority."

FLOOR 3: EUROPE IN RUINS

1. WORLD WAR I
2. TOTALITARIANISM VERSUS DEMOCRACY
3. WORLD WAR II
4. THE HARVEST OF DESTRUCTION

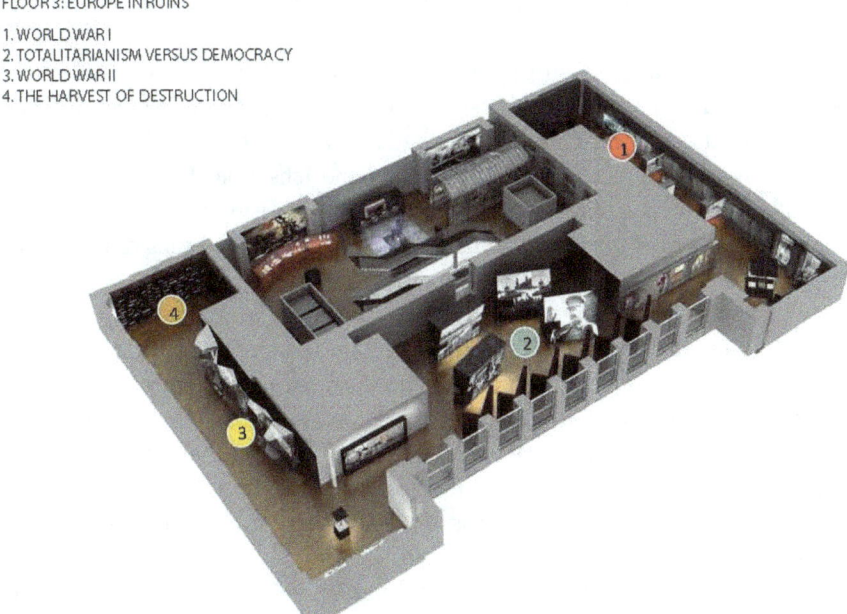

Fig. 24 Floor plan of floor 3 "Europe in Ruins." Permanent Exhibition. House of European History, Brussels (Photo and © House of European History).

alism / totalitarianism evolved. This is highlighted in an installation simultaneously playing films on Soviet and German totalitarianisms in the section "Totalitarianism versus Democracy," supplemented by two large object vitrines each (see also Mork 2018, 159–162). This exhibition creates a differentiated comparison between the National Socialist and the Soviet totalitarian systems by, on the one hand, emphasizing their structural similarities such as leadership, methods of terror, inclusion and exclusion, and mass rallies. It also highlights the supremacy of the collective and the creation of the need to belong. On the other, it examines differences between the systems, such as the different economic systems, the importance of race for the Nazi and class for the Soviet ideology as well as the varieties of terror, e. g. in the Holocaust and Gulag experiences. Unlike in the MIIWŚ, there is no immediate agent – such as Poland – situated between the two totalitarian systems. The last set of images cuts between concentration camp prisoners behind barbed wire and famine victims in the Soviet Union. This has the effect of symbolically connecting the victims of terror under both regimes. If there is a guiding principle to these totalitarianisms, it is the destruction of humanity and the European values named at the beginning of the museum's exhibition.⁵⁹

A small display case on the Spanish Civil War, located directly before the Second World War section, demonstrates the consequences of the two totalitarian systems assessing each other's strengths in a limited arena. The visitor encounters the bronze sculpture *Guernica* by René Iché from 1937, based on his daughter: it depicts a single skeletal young girl expressing terror after the German bombing of her town, symbolizing the most innocent victims of this attack on civilians (Christodoulou 2018, 232). The artwork can affect the visitor as a form of autonomous art, expressing horror (from the perspective of the figure as well as for the observer). The girl's eyes are seemingly empty, her nose is cut off, and her teeth are sticking out. Two distorted shadows of the figure are created on the wall behind it, increasing the statue's horrifying effect. At the same time, the artwork is functionalized in the context of the museum's narrative, as it allows for a transition into the Second World War section, which focuses on the fact that this conflict was a catastrophe for civilian victims on all sides.⁶⁰

The HEH creates a fairly universal Second World War section, which consists of three sections (see also Mork 2018, 162–168). Similarly to the MIIWŚ, its guiding principle – as seen in the survey text on the tablet – is total war that abandoned the distinction between soldiers and civilians. It highlights universal phenomena such as mass execution, deportation, starvation, forced labor, concentration camps, and bombings. The parallels between the brutal effects of National Socialism and Stalinism are mentioned, as is the status of the Holocaust as "an unparalleled event in history" in both "its scale and bureaucratic form." In the first part of this section, the HEH provides factual documentation of main events of the war, from the annexation of Austria, up until May 8/9, 1945. This is done through a timeline of newspaper headlines from different countries in their original languages and layouts, supplemented by historical photographs and maps, displayed on a table. The tablet adds factual information about each event and translates the newspaper headers. This contextualizes the featured events, while giving the visitor a sense of how different national stories were reported. The value of the latter is limited, of course, since the visitor has no further information on whether these newspapers were allowed to report independ-

---

59 For a complete deconstruction of the HEH's totalitarianism, see Lutz 2019.
60 See also the discussion of Iché's sculpture in chapter 9 in comparison to other art work in military history museums.

ently and where they stood politically at the time. Instead they remain a snapshot, in order to provide the visitor with a factual frame.

The second main section covers two walls of a corridor.[61] On the left hand side, the exhibition displays a fairly general film on the Air War across six screens, which shows images of planes, bombs, material destruction, and ruins. Goebbels' declaration of total war can be heard once and the film ends with a flash, following footage of the Enola Gay, indicating that the explosion of the first nuclear bomb on Hiroshima ended the war's destruction. There are almost no humans recognizable in the film; one sees German and Allied planes, though details on what exactly is being shown are impossible to discern. This means that viewers receive a very generalized, de-historicized, exclusively atmospheric and emotionalized message concerning the total destruction wrought during the Air War.[62] Does it indicate that both sides were responsible for the effects of total warfare? Is there guilt in total warfare? The visitor does not receive any data to help them in answering such questions because the HEH uses a transnational technique that often negates the historical specificity of national agency.

The core part of the Second World War section is a large display covering the whole right wall of a corridor, featuring more than 200 artifacts sorted into ten thematic categories: territorial ambitions, mass shootings and massacres, mass expulsions and deportations, starvation, forced labor, concentration camps, the Holocaust, the Air War, collaboration, and resistance (see fig. 25). The objects and photographs mainly function illustratively, but they also create questions about the ways in which they can function together. Every theme is a transnational representation, combining objects from a variety of countries. Some highlight the policies of totalitarian states, i.e. Germany and to a lesser extent the Soviet Union, while the majority of the themes emphasize the civilian victims of total war.

What on the surface seems to hold similarities with the transnational strategy of the Gdańsk Museum of the Second World War (MIIWŚ) in highlighting the human cost of war, it quickly proves to be quite different. With the exception of the minimal contextualization provided on the tablet, the object tableaus lack historical specificity. Whereas the master narrative in the MIIWŚ, the historically specific chronological exhibition in the Bundeswehr Military Museum, the evidentiary structure in the Topography of Terror, and the historical focus in the

---

61 The walls of this section are designed like a shed with a patched-up wood and brick wall, somehow indicating the fragmentary and fragile nature of life during the war.
62 The tablet only lists the copyright holders for all of the footage in the film montage; thus, it does not provide any information on which cities, air-attacks, etc. are represented. Occasionally, visitors might be able to identify specific types of planes or their emblems.

Fig. 25 "World War II" gallery. Permanent Exhibition. House of European History, Brussels (Photo: Author, 2017, courtesy of House of European History).

German Russian Museum and the Imperial War Museum North all use specific historical examples, tell stories, and allow individual voices to be heard, the HEH completely lacks such story-telling. For example, the starvation section works in a very similar way to the every-day life section in Gdańsk. Objects and photographs serve as almost arbitrary token representations of every country: The difference that this exhibition holds to the MIIWŚ, is that this arbitrariness of objects is present across all sections, whether it be the Air War,[63] forced labor, or relocation and deportation sections.

In the latter, for example, the tablet's survey text highlights Soviet and German relocation policies as well as those of German "puppet states." The last sentence also mentions the deportation of Jews. To illustrate this theme, the display case contains seven photographs, eleven documents, and one material object. The photographs show German settlers in the East, Polish people expelled by Germany, Slovenian people presumably expelled from Austria, Jews moving

---

63 See also chapter 8 below.

into the Kaunas ghetto, Serbs expelled from Croatia, civilians expelled from Warsaw after the Uprising and destruction of the city, and Estonians deported to Nargorsk in Russia. Numerous letters from deportees, a list of deportees from Latvia, the identity card from a German 'Volksdeutscher,' a book cover on new German peasantry, and the self-made boots of a Polish deportee to Siberia complete the display. The people and their expressions in the photographs seem to resemble each other, and the letters are simply objects – they are not displayed to be read; the tablet only list captions that identify each object. No image or object is related to a story; one does not seem to distinguish itself from the next. The visitor learns that ethnic expulsions during the war were widespread among totalitarian states and their allies. However, the question of whether they were all of the same value remains (see also also Lutz 2019, 47).

The visitor can return to the two examples of the totalitarian states, Nazi Germany and the Soviet Union, in order to understand some background but overall these transnational objects remain unconnected – unlike in the MIIWŚ – and leave room for interpretation. Nevertheless, the museum does not allow for any networking effects to create secondary experientiality.[64] Instead, the displays express a cultural memory that highlights that many relocations and deportations took place and many people suffered from them. The transnational approach seems to merely confirm that all of Europe was impacted and that all states require a material representation in this display case. At times, the exhibition more clearly differentiates who the perpetrators were; however, the main message of the transnational displays remains that there were many forms of perpetration, suffering, and resistance and that they are all part of the narrative that moves toward a shared European cultural memory. In contrast to the HEH's mission statement, individual national stories are not displayed. There is no real alternative narrative allowing for historical specificity. The visitor is left with a very general emotional effect of total war, particularly as civilian suffering (and to a lesser extent resistance and perpetration) dominates any attempt at intellectual understanding.[65]

The final part of the Second World War section is entitled "The Harvest of Destruction." The visitor enters the darkened end of a corridor and views a space with numbers and stars floating along the walls and ceiling. Eleven display cabinets – like shrines – with dimmed light are visible in the dark. The introductory text on the tablet notes that an estimated 60 million people died in

---

64 With minimal exceptions in the resistance section.
65 One crucial difference from the MIIWŚ is the small number of photographs of casualties. The HEH displays very few corpses, and these only in specific sections like the one on mass killings.

the Second World War, about two thirds of them civilians. It then declares that numbers alone "fail to convey the full extent of the personal tragedies involved or the catastrophic impact of these events on various group of people." Instead, the eleven objects assembled shall "tell the human story behind these events and challenge us all to consider how people come to terms with trauma and loss on such a scale." The goal of creating empathy is overly ambitious, but here the HEH clearly intends to counterbalance the universalizing effects of the previous display. To achieve this, the exhibition displays many forms of suffering through a singular object with an enlarged photograph as background of each display case. One object, for example, is a clothes hanger placed in front of a photograph of mothers, children, and elderly people standing at a set of train tracks, identified as German expellees in Poland. The text references the fate of all civilian migrants during and after the war. The coat hanger belonged to a former inhabitant of the German city of Stettin before it became the Polish city of Szczecin after the war. The visitor is asked to empathize with the fate of the expellee, as with every suffering civilian in this section. This can raise a lot imaginative questions: what can an expellee take – the background photo does not show any luggage – and what part of one's identity is left behind? The clothes hanger seems fairly general, serving as an example for millions of other refugees.

Other exhibits in the "The Harvest of Destruction" section are more personal, such as that of the teddy bear ("Tedis"). The caption of the artifact reads: "This teddy bear – a childhood reminder of happier times before the war – was owned by a young Latvian girl who passed through many of these camps until she eventually arrived in the USA, as one of the 460,000 refugees accepted into the country." The visitor can assume that the teddy bear accompanied the unnamed Latvian girl through the camps and to the United States. It signifies her safer, earlier childhood – life before the camps – and simultaneously the hope for a better future. The teddy bear works to emotionally affect the visitor, prompting them to empathize with the plight of children in war. This iconography of trauma (Arnold de-Simine 2013, 80 – 86; Mikuska-Tinman 2018) allows the visitor to ask existential questions as well as questions connecting past and present. In contrast to the display case previously analyzed, the focus on material objects is here linked to the imagination of the possible worlds of individuals. The photograph behind the teddy bear shows displaced Polish nationals leaving a camp, adding a collective and universalizing dimension to the individual dimension of the stuffed animal. Does the teddy bear therefore symbolically stand for all war refugees?[66]

---

66 A similar universalization of concrete artifacts is achieved in the section's display case on the

Of course, the focus of this section is on empathy and emotion concerning civilian suffering; the materiality of the object and – at times – a concrete story make it possible for the human imagination to grasp this suffering. In this way, it surpasses the general abstraction that dominates the previous section.

Finally, the visitor reads two quotations on the wall at the end of the "Harvest of Destruction" section. The first is by Elie Wiesel from 1986: "... if anything can, it is memory that will save humanity. For me, hope without memory is like memory without hope." The second quotation stems from Winston Churchill in 1946: "There must be ... a blessed act of oblivion. We must all turn our backs upon the horrors of the past. We must look to the future." On the one hand, the visitor can note a tension: should one forget the horrible past or remember it? On the other hand, both quotations demonstrate the idea of temporality that the HEH wants to display. Hope indicates a future. If one reads Churchill's sentence as the oblivion of all atrocities, the HEH's great focus on memory proves him wrong; if it means to leave ideas of revenge, the perception of the enemy, and the different sides of the war behind, it connects to the emerging European memory narrative. One of the building blocks of the new Europe is the human catastrophe of the Second World War.

If one defines the transnational as placing national memories and histories into constellations, as the major definition of the second type of transnationality used in this study does, one could argue that the Second World War section in the HEH does not function transnationally. Although it assembles objects and experiences from many European nations, none of these national narratives and artifacts maintains an autonomous cultural memory. Consequently, there is a clear distinction from the expression of Polish cultural memory seen in the Gdańsk Second World War Museum or the German and Soviet ones found in the German Russian Museum. This second type of transnationality, as discussed above, can overcome the challenge of memory competitions and make transnational memory more than a zero-sum game (Rothberg 2009, 3). Where, then, does the transnational set-up of the HEH lead to instead? To understand its narrative frame, it is important to go back to the fourteen principles of European heritage expressed in its introductory section. In the tablet's survey text, the museum asks: "What binds this continent together?" The three introductory sections defining Europe on the second floor (the entry floor to the permanent exhibition), are the most open parts of the museum. This is because the idea of Europe is mainly presented through artworks and constellations of objects and facts that

---

Air War, where a photograph of people seeking shelter in the London Underground supplements the material object of a portable air-raid siren from Germany.

require the visitor's active interpretation. The fourteen principles or "basic elements" are presented more as something offered to the visitor than as answers to what defines Europe: "Can these be considered distinct hallmarks of European culture? If so, what parts of this European heritage should we preserve, what do we want to change, what should we contest?" Two quotations emphasize the value of memory and the dynamics of defining Europe in this section. First, the Spanish-American philosopher, poet, and humanist George Santayana is quoted: "Those who cannot remember the past are condemned to repeat it" (1905). Second, the French philosopher and theorist Julia Kristeva highlights that the process of constantly defining Europe is an integral part of its existence: "Europe is the only place in the world where identity is not a cult, but a process of questioning" (2013).

The only principle that is directly related to the Second World War and the Holocaust is "Genocide." As with all of the principles, the museum connects two exhibits from the past and present. The topic "Genocide" is marked by a German passport from 1939 marked "Jew," alongside a photograph of a woman wearing a headscarf with a non-Caucasian, i.e., ethnically 'different' woman looking at anti-immigrant graffiti with a swastika in Denmark. Here, the HEH uses the dynamics of transnational and temporal constellations in a very dynamic way. The tablet only gives a minimalistic factual introduction and captions for the exhibits. Aside from this, every one of the fourteen principles receives an approximately one-and-a-half minute audio text, in which the narrator connects the principle to its history and to Europe. These texts always end with an open-ended question for the visitor to further reflect on what the principle truly means for the European past and present. In the case of genocide, the narrator asks: "Could such inhumanity ever take place in Europe again?"[67] Visitors can decide for themselves whether anti-immigrant attitudes in European countries could lead to similar inhumanities or at least represent problematic value systems. Visitors must decide whether the Holocaust is a unique form of genocide or whether they have encountered other comparable 'inhumanities' throughout the exhibition. Here, visitors are challenged to think in comparative and transnational terms from a European or humanist perspective. For the principle of democracy, the narrator asks whether democracy is a fixed part of European heritage.

---

[67] Other questions in this section, even if the objects displayed do not directly refer to the Second World War, ask under the header "state terror": "Can an act of terror ever be justified as a means to an end or is violence of any kind unacceptable?" The "abolition of slavery" principle challenges the visitor on whether slavery is truly abolished or could be still present, while relating its formal abolition to "peaceful activism and self-criticism."

Fig. 26 Section "Memory of the Shoah." Permanent Exhibition. House of European History, Brussels (Photo: Author, 2017, courtesy of House of European History).

These principles of European heritage occur throughout the exhibition, usually without explicit reflections. However, the HEH misses the opportunity to reflect on its open-ended questions again at the end of the exhibition. Unlike the European heritage section, the actual exhibition is far less open. This becomes clear in the memory sections, where the Holocaust and the Second World War re-appear on the fourth and fifth floors of the museum, particularly in the section "Memory of the Shoah" (see fig. 26).[68] This section is comprised of six horizontal vitrines holding objects, each paired with a quotation on the challenges of post-war memories, the silence surrounding complicity, and the emphasis placed on individual national suffering in West Germany, East Germany, Austria, Poland, France, and Ukraine. All of these object arrangements are created to prove the last sentence of the section's introduction: "Today, however, the acknowledgement of this unparalleled crime against humanity is at the core of dis-

---

[68] Chantal Kesteloot argues "the room on the memory of the Shoah is set apart from the main tour, symbolizing its longstanding marginal status" (2018, 156).

cussions about a European memory." In other words, although the HEH tells six varying stories of national Holocaust remembrance, the moment they have reached the present, they are all universalized.

To further understand this process of universalization, the different object display cases need to be juxtaposed with one another. The West German one reads like a slow process of coming to terms with the past, taking place between the 1950s to late 1970s; the East German one reflects upon the fact that Jewish suffering was secondary to that of the communist resistance in the GDR. The Austrian display case highlights the narrative of Austrian victimhood, and that only since the 1980s and the Waldheim affair have the Austrians started to question this narrative of their exclusive victimhood. The Polish and Ukrainian sections emphasize that only after 1990 open memory was possible, contemplating Polish perpetration especially through the display of a copy of Jan T. Gross's *Neighbors* (2001 [2000]), about Polish guilt in the massacre of the Jews in Jedwabne in July 1941. The Polish display case also examines the transformations in post-Soviet memory strategies in the Concentration Camp Museum in Auschwitz and the challenges of recognizing Jews as a specific victim group. The French display expresses how long it took the French to also reflect upon the widespread collaboration and complicity in Vichy France during the Holocaust. The Ukrainian display case is truly puzzling.[69] The majority of objects refer to the Babi-Yar Massacre, whose memory was erased during the Soviet period and then rediscovered after 1990. Yet there is no reflection on the Ukrainian support of German crimes, the memory of the Holodomor, or on possible new memory challenges for an independent Ukraine. No display truly reflects upon the present; it seems that all nations have come together in commemorating the Holocaust today and have all worked through their more problematic pasts. This section is indicative of how political the set-up of HEH really is, even if the curators wanted to prevent this (House of European History 2017b, 4–5). There is no word on memory tensions in Poland today. Nowhere do visitors see how fragile memory actually is (see also Lutz 2019, 46).

Even the artwork that completes the display serves the need to never forget the Holocaust. Ritula Fränkel and her husband Nicholas Morris created the artwork *Jozef's Coat* in 2001. The coat belonged to Rita's father Josef Fränkel, a Holocaust survivor. The artists have incorporated images and written memories into the coat "creating a testament or biographical journey of the father's harrowing wartime experiences." The coat is an impressive artifact; it displays fam-

---

[69] Hilmar describes how the museums planners struggled to integrate Eastern European memories and narratives into the museum's context (2016, 308).

ily and vacation photographs, the Star of David, among other things. Since visitors have no exact way to interpret the photographs and other traces of Josef Fränkel's biography, they feel the mystery of the artwork and its powerful but undecipherable relation to a life between ordinary childhood, family memories, and the horrors of the Holocaust. Yet the section's master narrative makes the presence of this artwork secondary to its pragmatic purpose.[70] Instead of understanding how dynamic Europe and its memory is, with all of its different influences and possible values and principles as the beginning of the exhibition and the quotation by Kristeva suggest, the leading quotation of the section by the historian Tony Judt from 2005 that is paired with the art installation is static: "The recovered memory of Europe's dead Jews has become the very definition and guarantee of the continents [sic] restored humanity." Contextualization overshadows the artwork's individuality. Transnational memory – looking into six national case-studies of Holocaust memory – does not lead to productive constellations and interpretive openness. Instead, all countries finally come together in a universal memory that allows the idea of a humanist Europe to take shape. This clarifies the implicit master narrative of the HEH in regard to the Second World War: total war, the loss of democracy, and the emergence of inhumanity led to civilian suffering. The Holocaust holds a specific status in this memory of suffering. After the war and even more so after the Cold War[71], a European vision comes together. The catastrophes of the Second World War and the Holocaust are stepping-stones to a strong vision of Europe in the present. For a strong Europeanist, this might sound right, yet it shows the risks of representing the Second World War when a transnational, European master narrative simply replaces national master narratives. This museum does not build a European display that encapsulates a multiplicity of voices that also have the ability to contradict each other; it does not show how the European idea can act as an umbrella to negotiate tensions between different nation states; nor does it elude to how easily memories of the Second World War can still become matters of contention in contemporary memory politics. The exhibition's initial approach of holding openly controversial ideas that have shaped a European cultural community in tandem with one another as well as the object-based nature of this exhibition should have invited the visitor to react aesthetically to objects and interpret them in different ways. Instead, the exhibition is clearly disciplined by a linear master narrative toward contemporary European identity.

---

70 See also chapter 9.
71 The European Union appears as mediator in the Cold War at several stages.

On the fifth floor, the visitor discovers the small display "Shared and Divided Memory" that should allow for a dynamic dialogue on European memory. The cube contains four display cases on each side. The survey text highlights the fact that twenty-five years after the collapse of Communism, new memories have emerged and the question "What is Europe?" has received new relevance. One piece of artwork by Yuri Leiderman (Berlin 2005/2015), entitled *The Victims from Khatyn and the Victims from Katyń* ... brings together two massacres: one by the Soviets near Katyń in 1940 and the one by the Nazis when they massacred the population of the Belarusian village of Khatyn/Chatyń in 1943. The artwork is supplemented by a 2005 quotation by writer Jorge Semprún: "One of the most effective ways of moving towards a united Europe ... is ... to pool our hitherto separate memories." One case displays photographs of memorials against the Soviet dictatorship. Some memorials are new; other old Soviet memorials are reinterpreted as counter-memorials. In the end, the whole display, however, only indicates one direction for new memories: the end of Communism leading to a reinterpretation of communist memory politics. The visitor gets the feeling that this is a one-way street; now, all memories can come together.[72] The HEH misses the opportunity to truly show the dynamics of memory battles, particularly in regard to the Second World War and where these can be located in a European context. Instead, there seems to be a linear road to a better, more ethical memory. As in all master narrative-based exhibitions, whether they are national, transnational, or based on other values systems, the visitor is assigned the passive role of observing developments that are represented as true. The HEH runs the risk of being read as a progressive narrative toward freedom and humanity via the medium of the European Union. This master narrative is part of the museum's architecture, which develops from the bottom (second floor) to the top of the building. The reinvention of Europe after the total destruction of the Second World War seems to highlight a constant progress to European unity and freedom, which runs parallel to the development of the European Union.

From the fourth floor onward, the visitor encounters square milestone columns displaying objects and explaining developments in the European integration process after 1945. When a column in the Cold War section explains how the Rome Treaties in 1957 established the European Atomic Energy Community "for the peaceful development of nuclear energy," it remains open as to whether this is simply a fact or specifically selected wording that establishes a master narra-

---

[72] The only area of real memory contention is the display case of symbols of communism, which explicitly reflects on negative and positive memories employed in contemporary Europe in relation to communism.

tive toward a human rights-based and democratic Europe. More clearly, a copy of the European convention of Human Rights in Strasbourg from 1950 fulfills this narrative. The museum notes: "For the first time, individuals could now take a state to court if they felt that their human rights had been violated, an important development to arise out of the experience of state-led terror in the preceding decade." The page on display, citing article 3, supports this: "No one shall be subjected to torture or to inhuman or degrading treatment or punishment." The Second World War is the gateway for this European development of human rights. The master narrative that views Europe and the EU as a guarantor of human rights is made even more clear, as the exhibition highlights the EU's mediating role between the United States and the Soviet Union in the Helsinki Treaty negotiations from 1975: "The European Union succeeded in introducing guarantees on human rights, which became a tool used by dissidents against Communist rule." Whether or not there is an inherent master narrative, the exhibition's objects are often on the verge of being fully functionalized to exemplify a specific historical master narrative. They could also trigger more open visitor reflections on how they fit – or not – into a European narrative, or whether or not they display the diversity of different European nations. The large collection of artwork (in comparison to other history museums)[73] and the large number of quotations speak to a more open transnational approach. Whereas the Tony Judt and Jorge Semprún quotations discussed above point to a restrictive universal memory, on the sixth and final floor, the exhibition presents several highly dialectic quotations that are seemingly more open. The Swiss writer Adolf Muschg, for example, is quoted: "What holds Europe together and what divides it is ... a common memory" (2003). Clearly, the universality of memory is not seen as a one-way road to a unifying memory here. Similarly, the American historian Jay Winter, an expert of memory and the First World War, is quoted in the final installation "Facing the Future" indicating the dynamics and possible tensions of the European integration process: "to understand the integration of Europe, ... you had to understand the disintegration of Europe" (2012). Here, the HEH again highlights the importance of memory without foreclosing its future, as in the quotation by the Ukrainian writer Yuri Andruchovych: "The formula of being human is memory plus hope" (2004). A quotation on the critical spirit "as one of essential tools of Europeans" (1994) by Jacques Le Goff is displayed in the previous section "History, Today and Tomorrow."

However, despite these tendencies toward a more open memory, a negotiation of European identities (see also Mork 2016, 232), and critical memory work,

---

[73] See also chapter 9.

the Second World War and the Holocaust serve as ultimate disasters and become founding myths of contemporary Europe in the permanent exhibition of the HEH (see Leggewie and Lang, 2011; Kaiser et al. 2014, 114, for the concept). Here, different memories of numerous nations become universal through a transnational presentation. Controversies that would complicate the narrative of the Second World War and create inter-European tensions – whether one looks, for example at Hungary and Poland today, or the reception of the German miniseries *Generation War* (*Unsere Mütter, unsere Väter*) in Eastern European countries (Cohen-Pfister 2014) – do not exist, again showing how museums operate within the restraints of political discourses. Although the HEH's permanent exhibition is more dynamic in some parts, this is not the case for its representation of the Second World War. In the end, the visitors have received no means to understand why Second World War memory is still so contentious and why a transnational European discourse allows for varying national memory discourses, while at the same time generating a European universality. Consequently, the museum develops – at least regarding the representation of the Second World War – considerably less secondary experientiality than the German Russian Museum and the Gdańsk Museum of the Second World War. Despite its transnational approach, the HEH seems to return to the concept of restricted experientiality as seen above.

Chapter 7:
The Holocaust and Perpetration in War Museums

The representation of the Holocaust is one of the most significant topics in the analysis of how Second World War museums, and those military and cultural history museums that strongly emphasize the Second World War, combine narrative, memory, and experience to produce restricted, primary, and secondary experientiality. The term 'Holocaust' here will be referred to using the most widely accepted scholarly definition: "The Holocaust was the systematic, bureaucratic, state-sponsored persecution and murder of six million Jews by the Nazi regime and its collaborators."[1] However, this chapter will also show that in war and military history museums, the Holocaust as the systematic murder of Europe's Jews quickly becomes interwoven with other atrocities and genocidal activities carried out by the Nazi regime against various Slavic populations, the Romani people of Europe, the mentally and physically handicapped, Jehovah's Witnesses, black and mixed-race Germans, and homosexuals (see Stone 2010, 2–3). Two decades ago, Holocaust museums and war museums were seemingly different entities with marginal overlap. This has changed in the twenty-first century, allowing Holocaust representations to be used in war museums as a lens for understanding how these museums make the Second World War comprehensible or even experienceable for their visitors. There are two main reasons for this shift: first, the Holocaust, atrocities and genocidal activities – perpetrated by Germany, the Soviet Union, and other totalitarian regimes – and the Second World War are seen as closely interwoven; and second, the merging of history and memory that has been increasingly spearheaded by Holocaust memorial museums has been transferred to representations of the Second World War more generally.

On the whole, there are a number of obvious historical connections that make the Holocaust an important topic in Second World War museums.[2] The perspective of the Western Allies liberating the camps and the subsequent trials have shaped the perception of the 'good' war in the West and established a clear frame of good and evil. In this way, the Holocaust has become an integral part of assessing the war effort. All occupied countries took part, in one way or another, in deportations and in the Holocaust. In the occupied countries of Cen-

---

[1] United States Holocaust Memorial Museum 2019, https://encyclopedia.ushmm.org/content/en/article/introduction-to-the-holocaust. Accessed 13 October 2019.
[2] See also Celinscak 2018, 16 for a survey summary of the Holocaust in Allied war museums.

ᵰ OpenAccess. © 2020 Stephan Jaeger, published by De Gruyter. This work is licensed under the Creative Commons Attribution-NonCommercial-NoDerivatives 4.0 License.
https://doi.org/10.1515/9783110664416-011

tral and Eastern Europe, other victim groups sometimes take priority in narratives of the war, which this study further analyzes through examples taken from recent Polish exhibitions. The Allied countries that remained unoccupied had to react to streams of refugees and reconcile their own values and, in part, their own antisemitism, with their objective of ending the war.

The first significant argument as to why the Holocaust clearly belongs in a contemporary Second World War museum is the concept of the space of violence (Baberowski 2015) or "bloodlands" (Snyder 2010), which connects the war in the East with the events of the Holocaust. As seen particularly in the permanent exhibition of the Bundeswehr Military History Museum in Dresden (MHM), the Holocaust, other atrocities, genocidal objectives, and the war effort are so inter-twined that it is impossible to narrate one story without referencing others. Although the permanent exhibitions opened in the last decade have a clear tendency toward integrating the Holocaust, recent developments in the MHM[3] and in the Second World War Museum in Gdańsk (MIIWŚ)[4] also indicate that such integration might change, whether this is due to a possibly stronger concentration on military forces than on cultural and societal history (MHM), or because the Holocaust has become a sub-theme used to set up other, often national, narratives (MIIWŚ). Holocaust museums mainly represent the persecution and extermination of European Jewry by Nazi Germany and possibly also cover the experiences of other victim groups such as the Sinti and Roma, or the victims of other systematic Nazi killing programs such as the 'euthanasia' program that targeted patients with mental and physical disabilities. In war museums, other Nazi crimes against civilians, the killing of Poles, the deaths of Soviet prisoners of war, Slavs, and political opponents such as Communists and Social Democrats, overlap with the events of the Holocaust. Further exhibitions also represent war crimes and atrocities perpetrated by other powers such as Japan and by the Soviet Union from the Central and Eastern European perspective.

The second compelling justification for interweaving the Holocaust and the Second World War within museum representations is connected to the observation that historical representations of the Second World War in museums today cannot be separated from cultural memory. This can be traced back to the "rapprochement between history and memory in the shadow of the Holocaust" (Assmann 2016 [2006], 32). This shift, in which the clear distinction between history and memory becomes blurry, leads to changes in historical representations. Aleida Assmann identifies three developments that have enhanced history writing

---

3 See also chapter 5.1.
4 See also chapter 6.2.

from the perspective of memory: "the emphasis placed by memory on the aspects of emotion and individual experience; its emphasis on the memorial function of history as a form of remembrance; and the emphasis it places on an ethical orientation" (2016 [2006], 34). All of these developments have been first employed in Holocaust museums' historical representations, particularly in the prototypical United States Holocaust Memorial Museum (USHMM) (Linenthal 2001 [1995]; Luke 2002, 37–64; Hansen-Glucklich 2014; Bernhard-Donals 2016). These developments have since been transferred over to war museums in recent years.

While the representation of the Holocaust has clearly influenced the representation of war, and the Second World War in particular, in museums, there are clear differences between Holocaust and Second World War museums. Furthermore, the Holocaust has become a different global phenomenon than the Second World War (Rothberg 2009). Daniel Levy and Natan Sznaider follow theorists like Max Horkheimer, Theodor W. Adorno, and Hannah Arendt in identifying the Holocaust as a "tragedy of reason or of modernity itself" (2002, 88) that leads – aided by new technology and media in a globalized world – to "a shared consciousness and cosmopolitan memories that span territorial and linguistic borders" (2002, 91). Such a de-territorialization (Levy and Sznaider 2006 [2001], 46–49) is considerably less present in war museums in which national perspectives remain relevant, even when the museum highlights transnational (House of European History) or anthropological (Bundeswehr Military History Museum) themes and perspectives.

Another difference between Holocaust and Second World War museums lies in the discussion about sayability versus unsayability – the challenge in breaking the silence about the Holocaust and the simultaneous need to do so (Lentin 2004b, 2–3). This has channelled into the discussion about the representability and/or unrepresentability of the Holocaust (e.g. Friedländer 1992; Agamben 1999; Reiter 2000; Krankenhagen 2001; Lentin 2004a, Didi-Huberman 2008 [2003]; Frei and Kansteiner 2013). Ronit Lentin argues: "a further crisis in representation is the tension between historical 'facts' and interpretation, or the dilemma of historical relativism versus aesthetic experimentation in the face of the need for 'truth,' on the one hand, and the problems raised by the opaqueness of the events and the opaqueness of language, on the other" (2004b, 3). The question of whether there are immersive representational techniques that allow empathy for victims' suffering, or the mind of a perpetrator to be created is particularly challenging. Any such immersion immediately runs into the criticism that only survivors should be (ethically) entitled to speak about the Holocaust (Lentin 2004b, 2),[5] which leads to the question of generational remembrance (Felman and Laub 1992; Hirsch 1997; LaCapra 2001, 2004). Museums that intend to represent the Holocaust, despite its enormity and incommensurability, which defy materialization, undergo representational and ethical challenges. They need to be aware of "the potential dangers of aesthetic spectacle, preventing victims' voices from being heard" (Carden-Coyne 2011, 168). Consequently, museums are challenged to apply different techniques of distantiation to avoid simplistic immersive techniques. In contrast to Holocaust museums, the explicit representation of trauma in war museums is usually relatively minor (see also Jaeger 2017c). Museums depict the hardship, suffering, and valor of fighting; there is no discussion of secondary trauma. This only shifts when war, atrocities, genocide, the Holocaust, and the suffering of civilians begin to overlap, demonstrating again why this book features chapters on the Holocaust and on the Air War in Europe in order to further understand these connections.

In museum research, the challenges of Holocaust representation have led to a large body of museum scholarship regarding Holocaust commemoration and representation (e.g., Tyndall 2004; Landsberg 2004, 2015; Williams 2007; Lutz 2009; Carden-Coyne 2011; Holtschneider 2011; Hansen-Glucklich 2014; Schoder 2014; Alba 2015; Bernard-Donals 2016; Kleinmann 2017; Bielby and Stevenson Murer 2018; de Jong 2018a; Paver 2018; Reynolds 2018; Sodaro 2018). With minor exceptions (Arnold de Simine 2013; Paver 2018), this scholarship only relates to memorial museums, documentation centers, and exhibitions at memorial sites, sometimes reflecting on the representation and memorialization of other genocides as well (especially Williams 1997; Sodaro 2018). Are the ethical and representational standards for the museums representing the Second World War similar to the ones that have been discussed for Holocaust museums? The institutions in this category that have most often been placed under scholarly analysis include the United States Holocaust Memorial Museum, Yad Vashem – The World Holocaust Remembrance Center with its Holocaust History Museum,

---

[5] Museums have recently started to experiment with hologram technology, which incorporates large sets of data from extensive survivor interviews, allowing the hologram to 'interact' with the visitor, developed in a collaboration between the University of Southern California Institute for Creative Technologies and the University of Southern California Shoah Foundation. The technology aims to replace survivor witnessing beyond the end of living memory. The technology is particularly used and refined in an installation in the Illinois Holocaust Museum and Education Center in Skoke. One of the challenging questions – discussed particularly by Wulf Kansteiner (2017, 320–321) – is whether the hologram is supposed to make the visitor forget about its technology and mediated status, or whether it can also use gaps between it and a real survivor interview to meta-reflect on the mediacy of Holocaust memory and hologram technology.

the Jewish Museum Berlin (Jüdisches Museum Berlin), and *The Holocaust Exhibition* of the Imperial War Museum in London (see Pieper 2006; Williams 2007; Holtschneider 2011; Hansen-Glucklich 2014; Schoder 2014; Alba 2015; Bernard-Donals 2016; Sodaro 2018, 30–57; Donnelly 2019).[6] Additionally, Second World War and military history museums differ strongly from original sites, particularly concentration camp memorial museums, such as those at Auschwitz (see Reynolds 2018, 29–71) and Dachau, sites of deportations like the Kazerne Dossin: Memorial, Museum and Documentation Centre on the Holocaust and Human Rights in Mechelen (2012), and many other historical sites commemorating the victims of the Holocaust, such as the Memorial and Educational Site House of the Wannsee Conference (Gedenk- und Bildungsstätte Haus der Wannseekonferenz) in Berlin. The Information Centre to the Memorial of Murdered Jews in Berlin and the Topography of Terror (ToT) have also been widely discussed (Haß 2002; Till 2005; Pieper 2006). However, these discussions have placed a strong emphasis on the political and institutional history of these sites, and have had less of a focus on the representational techniques used in their actual exhibitions.

The concept of the Holocaust museum is mainly used in reference to commemorative, i.e. memorial museums (Williams 2007), though its relation to documentary and historical museums is variable. All Holocaust museums have a strong emphasis on educational purposes. In her exploration of Holocaust memorial museums, Jennifer Hansen-Glucklich examines different representational techniques in Holocaust memorial museums varying from the illusion of a coherent narrative (United States Holocaust Memorial Museum, USHMM) and ruptures of representation pointing to the unrepresentability of the Holocaust (Jewish Museum Berlin, Yad Vashem). Nevertheless, "all three museums display a similar purpose in their efforts to commemorate unspeakable trauma and to do so in a language that resonates with what is sacred within each of their national

---

[6] Especially the Jewish Museum in Berlin is usually discussed almost exclusively for the architectural concept by Daniel Libeskind and hardly for its exhibition (see e.g. the study by Ionescu 2017).
Another recent example of finding a language for the Holocaust in the museum can be found in the POLIN Museum of the History of Polish Jews (Muzeum Historii Żydów Polskich) in Warsaw, which opened fully in 2014. The museum places visitors into dramatic scenes, through which they experience Jewish history and the Holocaust in particular, in its historical moment of insecurities and historical perceptions (not memories post-1945). For a full explanation of this scenographic and chronothematic concept as a way to represent the Holocaust in the museum, see Kirshenblatt-Gimblett 2015; for a conceptual overview of the permanent exhibition see also Polonsky et al. 2018; for an analysis of the museum's creation of 'social space' see Bogunia-Borowska 2016, 243–252.

and cultural contexts" (Hansen-Glucklich 2014, 217).[7] In contrast to Hansen-Glucklich's orientation toward the past, Michael Bernard-Donals demonstrates in his analysis of USHMM as a memorial space the temporality of museums that integrate the visitor in the interwoven processes of past, present, and future: "the United States Holocaust Memorial Museum does not preserve memory so much as cast memory into the future: at its best, it forces museum visitors to bear witness not to the past but to their involvement in the present, a present both haunted by traces of the past and racing into the future" (2016, 19). Here, history becomes memory.

Understanding the different types and functions of museum exhibitions can help in explaining differences and links between Second World War and military history museums on the one hand, and Holocaust museums, documentation centers, and memorial sites on the other. First is the commemorative function, which commemorates the victims and acts as a reminder of the atrocities that are possible in human society; second is the historical function, serving to understand historical events and processes; third is the educational function – learning from the past for the present and future, including a reflection on how human action and society as a whole can prevent similar genocidal actions. The educational function is closely connected to the comparative function (4) that allows a museum to compare numerous atrocities, which can be performed either through a strong didactic or moral message by the museum makers or in an open style that leaves more interpretative room to the visitor. The authenticity function (5) relates to sites, witness accounts, and artifacts; and the documentary function (6) that reduces the immersive effect because of the unrepresentability of the Holocaust from a victim and a perpetrator perspective. Consequently, the experiential function (7) as a mimetic endeavor must always be subdued: one can neither re-experience the Holocaust, nor does a museum want to allow empathy toward acts of perpetration. At the same time, Holocaust representation in museums can produce empathy (Landsberg 2004, Arnold-de Simine 2013, Johnston-Weiss 2019) and empathetic unsettlement (LaCapra 2001, 2004).[8] Exhibitions can pursue a meta-representational function (8) by reflecting on their own methods of representation and by highlighting the processes of memory

---

[7] Avril Alba argues that analyzing the sacred narratives (of the 'secular museum') in the United States Holocaust Memorial Museum, Yad Vashem, and the Sydney Jewish Museum that the Holocaust "has now also been *eternalized* (….). [T]he mythic scope of the sacred symbols, rituals, archetypes and narratives underscoring the institutions' display and commemoration of the Holocaust 'lifts' the Holocaust from the plane of history and imbues it with the enduring qualities of myth" (2015, 193).
[8] See also chapters 1.3 and 2.2.

that constitute the narratives of the past. With the exception of the historical and documentary functions, the aforementioned functions are more pronounced or differ considerably from those used in most war museums. To further understand the similarities and differences of these representational functions, a precise analysis of how the core museums in this study integrate the Holocaust and other genocides and atrocities in their exhibition is needed.

However, a brief look at the opposite question of how Holocaust museums integrate the Second World War is useful as well. When analyzing the different comprehensive exhibitions,[9] such as the United States Holocaust Memorial Museum (USHMM) or the Imperial War Museum in London (IWML), it is obvious that the Second World War as such plays only a minor role in representing the history of the Holocaust. On the second floor of the USHMM, the war is depicted as a springboard for the start of deportations from the various occupied countries; also, in the final part of the first floor, the museum provides an overview of the downfall of Nazi Germany. Although the Imperial War Museum (IWM) has a mandate for representing wars fought by Britain, its former Empire, and the Commonwealth since the First World War,[10] its *Holocaust Exhibition* (2000) is a stand-alone exhibition. Most visitors will thus perceive the lead-up into fascism as causal explanation for the Holocaust. The redevelopment of the permanent Second World War exhibition and the permanent Holocaust exhibition in the IWML, however, strongly emphasizes the link between the Second World War and the Holocaust. In its 2018–2019 Annual Report, the IWM makes a surprising statement – ignoring all the efforts of war museums across the world analyzed in this chapter – that "the IWM will be the first museum in the world to present the Holocaust within the context of the war" (2018–2019, 11n3). The current IWM Director-General, Diane Lees, notes on the IWM's website: "At the centre of the brutal and barbaric conflict was the state sponsored mass murder of 6 million Jewish men, women and children. This is why we are placing IWM's new Holocaust Galleries at the central chronological fulcrum of our iconic London museum and linking them, architecturally and conceptually, to our new Second World War Galleries."[11] It remains to be seen whether this new strategy will lead to network-

---

9 That do not develop their narrative from a specific site.
10 "IWM was founded in the midst of the First World War with a mission to preserve and tell the stories of all kinds of people, not only from Britain but from the countries of its empire. And we continue to do this work right up to present day conflict, covering 100 years of experience throughout the Commonwealth" (https://www.iwm.org.uk/about, accessed 13 October 2019).
11 https://www.iwm.org.uk/history/new-second-world-war-and-holocaust-gallery-plans-unveiled, accessed 13 October 2019. Lees's quotation could be read with the understanding that the war leads to the Holocaust, providing a linear causal connection rather than networking. Rachel

ing effects between the Second World War and the Holocaust, or whether the idea of a stand-alone gallery dedicated to the Holocaust will prevail and the link between the two galleries will remain mostly rhetorical.[12]

Questions such as the involvement of German soldiers in the crimes of the Holocaust mostly remain a question for German museums. This allows most non-German[13] to present the perpetrators of the Holocaust as a generalized evil collective engendered by evil leaders. Fascism and antisemitism, as well as the events of the Holocaust[14] dominate Holocaust museums and autonomous exhibitions. The only direct connection made to a narrative on the war comes from the liberation perspective.

If we consider all twelve museums analyzed in this study, it is possible to identify five different representational strategies for integrating the Holocaust into war and history museums, which are closely related to the eight functions identified above. First, as mentioned above, there are stand-alone exhibitions such as the one found in the Imperial War Museum in London (see Cooke 2001; Hoskins 2003; Lawson 2003; Bardgett 2004; Holtschneider 2011, 31–44; Schoder 2014, 78–140). While this exhibition can certainly produce different forms of experientiality, it falls outside the scope of this study. Stand-alone sec-

---

Donnelly (2019, 117–120) provides a critical discussion of Holocaust-specific questions and challenges that could influence practical, museological dimensions of the new 2021 exhibition. For example, the IWM is expected to emphasize new perpetrator research and create more space to reflect on second-generation testimony: "Spaces of testimony in the new Galleries will clearly move beyond a largely contemporaneous approach to include multiple narratives and potentially, through co-production with members of the second generation and beyond in Britain, it is hoped visitors will begin to engage with the complexity and legacy of the Holocaust in an innovative way" (Donnelly 2019, 119). Donnelly highlights that new representations need to challenge the idea that the historical knowledge of the Holocaust is "somehow 'fixed' and demonstrate through innovative use of research that multiple interpretations of history can enhance, but also complicate (...) our collective memory and understanding of the Holocaust in the twenty-first century" (2019, 120).

12 The IWM's website notes that a V1 flying bomb will be suspended between the two new galleries, "presenting a striking symbol of how the Holocaust and the Second World War are interconnected." It specifically mentions the British victims killed through the V1 and those who died making these weapons in Nazi Germany, the "thousands of concentration camp prisoners, labouring in the most appalling conditions" (https://www.iwm.org.uk/history/new-second-world-war-and-holocaust-gallery-plans-unveiled, accessed 19 September, 2019). See chapter 8 for a discussion of V2 rocket (and V1 flying bomb) installations in London and Dresden.

13 Or to a lesser extent, non-Austrian museums.

14 Discrimination; failed emigration; destruction of civil structures; deportations; ghettos; Einsatzgruppen killings, presented with focus on genocidal action and not in relation to the war; concentration camps; extermination camps; death marches, liberation of camps; trials, emigration; and remembrance.

tions in which the Holocaust is part of the permanent exhibition can be considered as an alternative within this representational strategy – although they are usually found in a relatively isolated section, as seen, for example, in the Imperial War Museum North.[15] In both cases, the connections these stand-alone sections have to other parts of the museum are fairly minimal. In other words, there are not any forms of experientiality regarding the Second World War, although a different study could easily use this strategy to demonstrate the relevance of the concept of experientiality for networking the perspectives and structures of the Holocaust.[16] In the second and third representational strategies, experientiality is strongly restricted by one-sided perspectives and ideologies. The second representational strategy, the restricted collective perspective, is more typical of classical military history museums. This can be seen in the New Orleans WWII Museum and the Canadian War Museum. Since the Holocaust was neither the focus of the Allied war effort nor part of the soldiers' collective gaze, it only comes into perspective when respective military groups discover and liberate concentration camps. A third representational strategy emerges in the Warsaw Rising Museum. The Holocaust disappears behind the suffering of another group: Polish civilians rebelling against the Germans. The fourth strategy stems from local or thematic restrictions placed on a museum such as in the Oskar Schindler Factory, the Bastogne War Museum, or the German-Russian Museum.[17] All of these institutions find ways to integrate the Holocaust into the fabric of the museum experience. In doing so, the Holocaust takes a minor but significant role in producing different forms of experientiality.

The fifth representational strategy is the most relevant to this study and entails structural networking of the Holocaust. This means the Holocaust – as past events and in terms of its memory – is present in different ways throughout the exhibition, creating secondary experientiality. The war and the Holocaust as well as other atrocities and genocides are so deeply intertwined that they cannot be separated. Versions of this networking strategy can be found in the House of European History, the Gdańsk Museum of the Second World War, the Bundeswehr

---

15 The German Historical Museum (Deutsches Historisches Museum) also presents the Holocaust in a corner section of its 2005 permanent exhibition so that the visitor can easily miss it. It references the destruction of Jews in other parts of the war and post-war period, but remains documentary throughout. This also means that the visitor will not, in all likelihood, experience many networking effects.
16 See also – with a focus on perpetration – the analysis of secondary experientiality in the Topography of Terror in chapter 5.3.
17 Similar to the Warsaw Rising Museum though without its ideological restrictions.

Military History Museum, parts of the Imperial War Museum North, and in the earliest predecessor of these exhibitions, the Mémorial de Caen.[18] After analyzing these five representational strategies, this chapter will contextualize the experiential potential of Holocaust representations in war museums with regard to immersive and emotional exhibition strategies including empathy and consider the use of visual media in the depiction of violence. Finally, this chapter will conclude by discussing perpetrators and acts of perpetration in Second World War and military history museums. Whereas the Holocaust is a significant part of this discussion, to understand how war, the Holocaust, and genocide are interwoven, it is important to consider all kinds of representations concerning perpetrators.[19] These include their depiction as the enemy and as those responsible for the atrocities and crimes committed within their own groups.

An analysis of the stand-alone *Holocaust Exhibition* in London goes beyond the scope of this study. However, the concept of stand-alone sections is relevant in understanding the different options and effects that war and military history museums can produce when representing the Holocaust. With this in mind, the Holocaust section in the permanent exhibition of the Imperial War Museum North (IWMN) serves as a good example. Bagnall and Rowland examine the Holocaust section in the IWMN, as opposed to the ones in the United States Holocaust Memorial Museum and the exhibition on a separate floor of the Imperial War Museum in London: "Representations of the Holocaust in war museums will increasingly figure as scaled-down versions of the exhibitions in spaces that focus more specifically on the event" (2010, 67). Therefore, one cannot compare comprehensive Holocaust exhibitions or autonomous Holocaust museums to representations of the Holocaust in war museums and even less so in cases where museums do not exclusively focus on the Second World War. Bagnall and Rowland describe the Holocaust section in the IWMN as follows: "a sober exhibition rejects the multimedia approach prevalent in the rest of the museum, and deploys minimalist techniques – which are still, of course, a particular form of aesthetics – in a short, but effective, exhibition; one that is for some, '*graphic and almost too personal to look at*'" (2010, 64). Nevertheless, the IWMN chooses an approach that differs from most of the other museums analyzed in this book.

The Holocaust is hardly present in other parts of the exhibition, with the exception of the aforementioned theme Kindertransport, represented in the silo

---

[18] The Topography of Terror could also be mentioned here, but since it is a Holocaust perpetration documentation center, its networking of the Holocaust and war works on a different level (see chapter 5.3).
[19] These include the depiction of the perpetrators as the enemy as well as the atrocities and crimes committed within the same national, cultural, or ethnic group as the perpetrators.

"Experience of War" and the Big Picture Show "Children of War," and a TimeStack tray entitled "Holocaust," in which clusters of objects are represented in relation to the stories of four survivors.[20] In highlighting four stories and objects related to them, it is the least didactic TimeStack tray in the museum, although some items remain merely illustrative. The visitor is presented, for example, with three items related to Vernon Fischer who escaped Germany through the Kindertransport with his mother. Classified as 'enemy aliens,' they were interned for six months in a camp on the Isle of Man, and later Vernon worked in Manchester and survived the Manchester Blitz. The visitor is challenged to interpret the connections between Fischer's Kindertransport suitcase, currency used in an internment camp, and a piece of shrapnel from the Manchester Blitz. How would a child have experienced these different phases? What would it mean to be an enemy of the Germans, persecuted because one was Jewish, and experiencing the Air War, while simultaneously being viewed as a temporary enemy in one's new home? Though the items have an illustrative function, the connections they hold to individuals and their stories have the potential to trigger the visitor's imagination and sense of empathy.

The actual "Genocide" cabinet is located at the lowest point of the museum – the floor slopes down from the permanent exhibition's entrance area (Bagnall and Rowland 2010, 67). In a way, it seems to act as the final continuation of the Second World War timeline before the fourth section, "1945–1990: Cold War," begins, while also being situated in a special spot in the museum. The section contains a 2013 artwork *A Star Shall Stride from Jacob and a Sceptre Bearer Shall Rise* by Chava Rosenzweig and a large display cabinet entitled "Genocide," identical in style to the five previous cabinets in the Second World War section. On the opposite wall, the visitor finds two other artworks relating to the Holocaust: the painting *The Death Cart* by Edith Birkin (1980–1982) and facsimiles of ten 1946-sketches from a thirty-six-sketch series of life in Ravensbrück concentration camp by Violette Rougier Lecoq.[21] The cabinet title "Genocide" provokingly implies that the Holocaust is comparable to other genocidal actions in

---

[20] Because of mechanical failure, it was not accessible in May 2018.
[21] This analysis is based on visits in the IWMN in August 2013 and May 2018. The museum occasionally switches artworks to create different aesthetic effects (however, not since 2013). For example, Bagnall and Rowland (2010, 70–73) base their analysis on stills by Darren Almond's 8 mm film *Oswiecim March 1997*. The spot where Rosenzweig's artwork was presented has also served to present figures from the Second World War, explicitly leaving out figures of those killed in the Holocaust or genocidal actions in the Second World War (Bagnall and Rowland 2010, 66–67).

the Second World War.²² The cabinet itself is very object-oriented, holding the potential to stir the imagination and allowing the visitor think about absences. Unlike the relatively flat Second World War cabinets with almost exclusively illustrative objects, the "Genocide" cabinet works like a spatial arrangement. items displayed are from the Holocaust, depicting the different victim fates that comprised the genocidal action: the visitor sees, among other things, a cluster of sixteen photographs of Jewish people from the Polish village of Frysztak (see Bagnall and Rowland 2010, 75–76, note 32),²³ thirty identity cards for Jewish people living in the Kraków Ghetto from Kraków, currency and other items from the Lodz Ghetto,²⁴ an insulator from an electric barbed wire fence in Auschwitz, and a piece of timber from the destroyed gas chambers and crematoria in Auschwitz-Birkenau. Many items are individualized and attributed to their owners, so that they lead into a story. Upon seeing a photograph and letter of Walter Horwitz to his ex-wife Gretl, the visitor learns that he was a German-Jewish veteran from the First World War who was deported from Hamburg to Minsk in 1941 where he was murdered. This opens up a large array of possible questions. The IWMN does not try to answer them but the visitor emotionally connects to the absurdities and tragedies as well as to moments of resistance that the material items convey. All are contextualized to explain their story or illustrative function. The displayed objects do not fit together, nor are they connected in any narrative sense, but together the spatial arrangement can give the visitor – similar to the Poland cabinet in the Bundeswehr Military History Museum, analyzed above (see also Jaeger 2017a, 36–39) – a structural picture of different pieces of the Holocaust, while surpassing any illustrative or didactic function. Many things remain untold; there is no narrative or interpretation, so that this cabinet is the most open installation in the IWMN, challenging visitors to interpret its meanings for themselves. Its explicit refusal to create a comprehensive overview about the Holocaust strengthens the emotional and imaginative effect of the section.

---

22 Since the museum relates to other genocides in its exhibition, the title seems a bit confusing, since it only relates to the Second World War and the display cabinet restricts itself to the Holocaust.
23 Bagnall and Rowland (2010, 67) read this as "basically a miniature version of the Holocaust Tower of faces [sic]" in the United States Holocaust Memorial Museum (for an analysis of the Tower of Faces, see also Hansen-Glucklich 2014, 91–98). Unlike the Washington museum, the photographs are in a glass cabinet, providing the visitor far more distance to think about the fact that these people were photographed in their regular lives before they became victims of the Holocaust.
24 To understand the full nature of a ghetto or its chronological place in the Holocaust, the visitor needs to possess prior knowledge or educational guidance during their visit.

The artwork further intensifies this effect. For example, Chava Rosenzweig's installation *A Star Shall Stride from Jacob and a Sceptre Bearer Shall Rise* can also challenge visitors to reflect upon their own personal connections to the Holocaust. The rectangular upright-positioned ceramic artwork is held in a glass case and contains a large number of stars of David, "a symbol of pride for Jewish people that was turned into a symbol of humiliation by the Nazis." Each star has been fired in a gas kiln, so that the process affected it "in its own unique way." Thus "[t]he stars invite the viewer to consider how their own families have been uniquely shaped by twentieth century conflict." Separated from the artwork in a small, flat triangular display case that is fitted into the corner, the lowest point of the exhibition space, broken dolls and their body parts represent the impact of the war on children. The artwork first – as the text indicates – speaks to Jewish survivors of the second and third generation. Its deeply religious connotations might lead some visitors to see it as an artwork exclusively for Jewish families. But visitors are also encouraged to go beyond that and feel invited to reflect on their own status as well as the one of their family in the Holocaust, even if one were not Jewish, as bystander, perpetrator, or member of a specific group or nation. The stars fired in a gas kiln turned out very individually. They have a strong material presence of an element or even a symbol of a human who has survived the gas chamber. Thus, Rosenzweig's artwork is a perfect example of how a history museum can include installations that function in a commemorative or in a reflexive way to put the visitor in a mediator position in order to create a structural experiential space. In combination with other forms of commemoration and mourning, the artwork allows for secondary experientiality and for the possibility for self-reflection.

The second strategy of Holocaust representation in a war museum is the restricted collective perspective. In the Canadian War Museum (CWM), the visitor only hears about the Holocaust in the penultimate section of the Second World War gallery. As the visitor approaches the gallery's exit, they pass through a small section of a corridor with display cases on both sides. The cabinet on the left focuses on the Holocaust; the right, on Canadian prisoners of war in Japan (Jaeger 2017c, 149). The Holocaust cabinet is shaped through a quotation by a Flight Lieutenant from the Royal Canadian Air Force saying "Why we fought World War II" pointing to photographs of horror in Bergen-Belsen. By focusing on the spontaneous present reaction of Canadian soldiers at the moment of liberating Bergen-Belsen, the visitor receives the (false) impression that Canada had fought the war to end the Holocaust. Consequently, the Holocaust becomes an argument in a historically progressive narrative that represents Canada's growing self-confidence and national identity and independence originating in war, pointing directly to its subsequent self-understanding as a nation of peace-keepers. The Holocaust functions as a narrative event of the progression of Canadian identity. However, the narrative effect is slightly reduced by two camp uniforms belonging to Hélène Garrigues, who survived the Ravensbrück camp, and to Szlama Zajderman, who survived Auschwitz and the Holocaust, the only member of his family to live.[25] Both objects also partially conceal the photographs of mass corpses in Bergen-Belsen.

It is important to consider here that the Canadian War Museum underwent a large public controversy in relation to the idea of its hosting a separate Holocaust gallery in the second half of the 1990s (Chatterley 2015, 190–192; Moses 2012, 218; Hillmer 2010, 21–23; Celinscak 2018, 18–26). In 1997, the originally planned Jewish war veterans' gallery, was largely transformed into a Holocaust gallery of 6,000 square feet, making it the largest in the entire museum (Chatterley 2015, 191; Celinscak 2018, 21–22). This created an outcry amongst war veterans. The National Council of Veteran Associations in Canada withdrew its support since it did not see any connection between the Holocaust and Canada's military history. Similarly, Jewish groups advocated for a separate Holocaust venue in Canada. Eventually the public debate led to the decision that the CWM would not include a separate Holocaust gallery and the Holocaust story would be told in a separate venue as a stand-alone Holocaust museum. This public debate demonstrates that in a country that sees itself on the right side of a 'good war,' the connection between war and the Holocaust is far less automatic than in European countries. If a museum such as the CWM takes its mandate to inform Canadians of the nation's role in the Second World War literally, it is not surprising that it focalizes the collective view of its soldiers and the general public at the time. The Holocaust did not play a major role in the general public's perception of the war as it was being conducted, and consequently the collective shock of the soldiers liberating concentration camps created the feeling that the horror they saw justified the war effort. However, if a museum represents this collective gaze without further contextualization it inadvertently finds itself complicit with the revisionist narrative that the Holocaust was the reason for Canadian and Allied troops to fight the war. This restricts possibilities for experientiality and differs greatly from most European museums that have opened or revised their Second World War exhibitions within the last two decades.[26]

---

25 The Canadian War Museum added the Zajderman jacket in recent years (post 2012). It is complemented by a small table panel in front of the cabinet telling the story of the family, supported by facsimile photographs and documents. This counterbalances the collective soldier perspective to a certain extent.
26 It is, however, important to point out that the Canadian War Museum has started to change the impression of its 2005 permanent exhibition in recent years. In 2018 alone it featured two

The New Orleans WWII Museum operates in a similar fashion to the Canadian War Museum, with the key difference that the Holocaust is so deeply engrained in the fabric of American collective memory that it seems part of the war whenever it is presented as a fight for freedom and human rights. However, the three virtual maps and tables where the visitor can learn about war events do not mention the Holocaust at all. The large map charting the war's major events in the entry hall of the Louisiana Pavilion above the train station and the virtual map introducing the war in the first room of the "Road to Berlin" exhibition do not allude to the Holocaust or to genocide in general. The interactive Command Central table on the first floor of the Boeing Pavilion is organized by battles and missions. In all three of these installations, the New Orleans WWII Museum proves itself to be a typical, traditional war museum. The museum makes it clear that the Holocaust does not belong in a war museum. Consequently, the visitor hardly hears anything about events on the war's Eastern front, whether in Poland or in the Soviet Union – with the exception of brief references to atrocities and the Holocaust in the chronological timeline.

The museum is restricted to an American collective perspective, similar to the way that the Canadian War Museum restricts its perspective to that of the Canadian collective. The chronological "Road to Berlin" first mentions the Holocaust in the context of the liberation of Auschwitz, located at the beginning of the penultimate room on the Battle of the Bulge. The final room, though much more complex than the one in Ottawa, presents the discovery of the camps by focusing on the Ohrdruf concentration camp[27] through the collective gaze of American soldiers and commanders. What is particularly important, is that it is a total surprise: shades of what was previously known about the Holocaust play no role, making it so that the gaze of American and Allied forces become a universal gaze: "After six years of war, Allied soldiers are certain they have seen the worst of Nazism, but nothing prepares them for what they are about to discover. They stumble upon one concentration camp, then another, and another. These war-weary soldiers and soon the entire world cannot fathom the massive scale of this heinous crime." After providing some data on the atrocities in Nazi Germany, the narrator provides an anecdote: "When a German soldier asks an American GI, why are you fighting, the GI replies, we are fighting to

---

special exhibitions dealing with the Holocaust: *St. Louis – Ship of Fate* and *Canadian Jewish Experience*. Even if both exhibitions were produced by other institutions, their presence demonstrates a change in the museum's objectives and stance on whether the Holocaust should be part of the museum's mission. This change also seems to be related to the adjacent National Holocaust Monument that was unveiled in September 2017.

27 A subcamp of the Buchenwald concentration camp in Thuringia near Gera.

free you from this idea that you are a master race." The museum streamlines the soldier's spontaneous reaction at the horrors they discovered and in doing so points toward Nazi exceptionalism and racism as the reasons for the war.

In six interactive Dog Tag Experience stations,[28] Charlotte Weiss tells her story in the civilian category of the "Road to Berlin." This is comprised of an approximately six-minute narrative, supported by the voice of a male narrator. The very personal, highly emotional story is the only one in the museum that reflects on details of the Holocaust. Weiss charts her "early life," the discrimination and racism she faced, early reports on German atrocities, and her move to the Mateszelka Ghetto in Hungary. She then describes how her family – minus her father – was deported and how Dr. Mengele performed the selection in which her younger brother and her mother were sent to their immediate deaths, while she and her five sisters survived. They were sent to a subcamp of the Natzweiler-Struthof concentration camp in Geislingen. Her story alludes to the fears they faced in the camp and mentions the kindness of two Germans who helped them survive. When they are put on a train they believe they are going to their death, but instead see American soldiers when the train carts open. After the war they find out that their father is still alive – he survived Buchenwald and emigrated to the United States in 1949. The narrator notes that despite all the atrocities that Charlotte Weiss suffered, she still has faith and hope for humanity.

On the one hand, Charlotte Weiss's story seems out of place in the Dog Tag Experience station. All other stories and accounts by oral witnesses employed by the museum are those of soldiers or civilians that accompanied or supported the American forces. Thus, Charlotte Weiss is used as a token witness of the Holocaust. The museum does not contextualize Charlotte Weiss's oral memory further: like in all dog tag stories and all oral witness accounts found on the computer stations in the museum, memory is presented as historical truth. Since most visitors only choose a single Dog Tag Experience, only a fraction of them end up listening to Weiss's story. While this story corresponds to the liberation story and the museum's master narrative, it also clearly goes beyond it in terms of representation depth with regard to the Holocaust. However, if the museum genuinely wanted to integrate the Holocaust as a part of its representation of the war, it should have at least developed a station or section in the "Road to Berlin" exhibition that would allow multiple oral witnesses to speak. The Dog Tag Experiences give an illustrative insight into the different backgrounds, deeds, and experiences of American soldiers. While doing so, the museum

---

[28] See chapter 4.1 for an explanation of this immersive oral history technique in the New Orleans WWII Museum,

also embeds a few Holocaust experience stories within them. For example, Felix Sparks, who led the 3rd Battalion of the 157th Infantry Regiment of the 45th Infantry Division of the US Army, describes entering and liberating Dachau concentration camp. His voice can create a connection for the visitor to the final film in "Road to Berlin"[29] by describing "the ultimate evil of the Nazis" and the emotional reaction to seeing the corpses and people who were barely alive at the moment of liberation and who did not know whether they would be liberated or killed. Sparks' story also creates one of the few experiential tensions in the museum: he mentions how, upon capturing a few remaining SS guards, some US soldiers lost control and shot them before he was able to stop them.

The New Orleans WWII Museum plans to open its final building, the Liberation Pavilion, in 2021. In it, the museum will explore "the closing months of the war and immediate post-war years, concluding with an explanation of links to our lives today."[30] These immersive galleries will seemingly continue the development of the American collective gaze and explore how "the world – and America's place in it – changed after World War II." They will relate to the international tribunals "seeking justice for war crimes" and feature an immersive Anne Frank room (National WWII Museum 2016, 60). The plans for these elements indicate that the construction of a master narrative centering on the American gaze will continue. Furthermore, they also indicate that the message of the war to defeat evil and free the world will include the Holocaust in the post-war construction, despite its lack of presence in the museum's exhibitions before 1945.[31]

In the *Beyond All Boundaries* multimedia show, the Holocaust is introduced when American troops enter Germany. The show then retroactively immerses the audience in giving them the feeling of being in a camp. One hears guards shouting in German as flashlights from the watchtower blind the audience. Narrator Tom Hanks explains the Holocaust with reference to the long outdated and exaggerated number that six million Jews and eleven million people died in the

---

[29] See chapter 4.1.
[30] https://www.nationalww2museum.org/visit/museum-campus/liberation-pavilion, accessed 13 October 2019 (this source references all quotations in this paragraph).
[31] Another way the New Orleans WWII Museum integrates the Holocaust in the museum is through its special exhibitions. Here, the New Orleans WWII Museum clearly identifies the Holocaust as part of its mandate and can represent it in separate venues in the Joe W. and Dorothy D. Brown Foundation Special Exhibit Gallery in Louisiana Pavilion. For example, in 2017, the New Orleans WWII Museum showed the special exhibition *State of Deception: The Power of Nazi Propaganda* and in 2007 it showed *Anne Frank: A History for Today*, both in cooperation with the United States Holocaust Memorial Museum.

camps alone,³² and calls it a "systematic program of organized murder," based on "Hitler's twisted idea of a master race." The voice then switches to a female voice narrating an eyewitness account: she describes how the American troops liberated the camp in Dachau, supplemented by extremely slow, emotionalizing music. In comparison to Spark's voice and personal story in the dog tag section, the individuality of the eyewitness here seems to be subsumed into a pinpointed didactic, moral master narrative. It highlights Dachau as the "first and largest of the Nazi concentration camps."³³ "The minute the two of us entered a [...] barrage of 'Are you Americans?' in about sixteen languages came from the barracks. An affirmative nod caused pandemonium; tattered, emaciated men weeping and yelling 'Long live America' swept through the gate in a mob; those who could not walk limped or crawled." The case may be that this narrative reflects the personal memory or experiences of a single soldier; however, it demonstrates how the museum includes the liberation of the camps as more of a celebration of America than an attempt to understand how this happened and what ordeals prisoners and survivors went through. Since the audience is placed into the perspective of being imprisoned in the camp, it almost seems to be a logical consequence that the show would ask the audience to join in weeping, crawling, and yelling "long live America." That most survivors needed a long time to fully understand that their ordeal was over and to come to terms with the atrocities they experienced is not significant in *Beyond All Boundaries*. The few visitors who have the chance to listen to the voice of Felix Sparks will get a different and considerably more realistic description of the liberation of Dachau. In contrast, *Beyond All Boundaries* shows the core idea behind the museum's retroactive integration of the Holocaust as part of the war without historical or cultural contextualization. Instead, it is enough that the Holocaust is the symbol of ultimate evil, fitting perfectly into the master narrative of the 'good' war guaranteeing freedom in the world. By emotionally overwhelming the visitor, this show restricts any potential for experientiality.

The third strategy for representing the Holocaust in a war museum can be found in the Warsaw Rising Museum (WRM), in which the Holocaust and the identity of the (Polish) Jew almost completely disappear. The victim status of Polish Jews is transferred to all Polish people and particularly to the insurgents of

---

32 For more accurate and methodically reflected estimates, see United States Holocaust Memorial Museum 2019, https://encyclopedia.ushmm.org/content/en/article/documenting-numbers-of-victims-of-the-holocaust-and-nazi-persecution, accessed 13 October 2019.

33 The imprecise claim that Dachau was the largest concentration camp is typical for a film that is so focused on emotionalizing visitors with superlatives and immersing them in a story of good defeating evil that historical accuracy falls by the wayside.

the Warsaw Uprising. This move is particularly important since the WRM has taken major curatorial cues from the United States Holocaust Memorial Museum and from the House of Terror in Budapest (Kurkowska-Budzan 2006, 138). The victim and target of all German atrocities is directly transferred to the insurgents who symbolize all Poles (with the exception of the Communists Poles, who sided with the Soviet Union).[34] The diagram of main events in the museum's entrance vestibule does not mention the Warsaw Ghetto Uprising or any other event related to the Holocaust. In the section dedicated to the German occupation, it is written that: "The Germans established concentration camps where they imprisoned thousands of Poles." In the text's last paragraph, it mentions that Jews were assembled in ghettos and that from December 1941 onwards, Germans carried out the mass murder of Jews. One display wall depicts the ghetto and notes its catastrophic conditions. The text panel ends as follows: "Nonetheless [despite the threat of the death penalty if Poles helped Jews], many brave Poles try to save Jews by offering them food and shelter. Unfortunately, there are others that blackmail Jews or hand them over to the Germans."[35] The exhibition then enters the beginning of the 1944 Warsaw Uprising and any reference to Jewish identity disappears from the exhibition. Since the exhibition highlights religious life, rituals, and values, the visitor obtains the strong impression that all Poles are Catholic. It is only in the later part of the exhibition, in the section "Foreigners with the Insurgent Armband," that the visitor hears about Jewish people again: "Many people of different nationalities decide to fight in the Warsaw Rising alongside the Poles. Jews are the most numerous." The exhibition does not take the idea of Jews fighting in resistance to the Nazis any further. However, it is telling that the WRM follows the tradition of Eastern European historiography regarding the representation of Jews and gentiles in the Holocaust: it differentiates between Poles and Jews when it is important to underscore the collective aid given to the 'real' Polish insurgents, whereas at other opportune points in the exhibition, the Jewish Poles become Polish heroes and martyrs. This is evident in the section "The Death of the City," which features the pianist Władysław Szpilman, who survived in the destruction of Warsaw, as a "Warsaw Robinson." The visitor only incidentally finds out that Szpilman was Jewish because the exhibition mentions that he escaped the Ghetto. The wording remains ambiguous: "After the fall of the Rising, he [Szpilman] shares the fate of the 'Robinsons.'" In other words, it implies that Szpilman was not a Warsaw Robinson himself.

---

34 See also chapter 3.2.
35 See Chu 2019, 133–135, for a more differentiated picture. The MIIWŚ under its new directorship shows similar tendencies as discussed below in this chapter.

In order to hear about the Ghetto Uprising, the visitor must go into the basement to see the stand-alone exhibition "Germans in Warsaw" (see also figure 3). A visitor who reads every line will find a few traces of the Holocaust: one sign indicates that Jews were forbidden in the new German government district; several panels on the biographies of German perpetrators mention their crimes against Jewish people; the Warsaw Ghetto is represented in one photo montage with a map of the ghetto and numerous historical photographs that show the rounding-up of Jews, but in comparison to the museum's representation of the Warsaw Uprising, no atrocities are depicted. The only text is a biographical sketch of the crimes of *SS Brigadeführer* Jürgen Stroop: "From April till [sic] October 1943 he commanded the Warsaw District SS and police; is responsible for the deportation of Jews to the concentration camp in Treblinka and the bloody suppression of the ghetto uprising." In other words, the Ghetto Uprising is an afterthought – one cannot leave it out in its entirety, but here it clearly seems to serve as a springboard for the 'more horrific' atrocities to come. This becomes clear in the second half of the "Germans in Warsaw" exhibition. When the visitor reaches the panel "The Crime of Genocide," there is no doubt that the genocide exclusively relates to German massacres during the Warsaw Uprising in 1944. The Holocaust has been – notwithstanding a few token mentions – written out of history in order to tell the story of the German genocide against the Poles.

The fourth strategy relates to war museums with a more local perspective, which use different networking techniques to integrate the Holocaust into their exhibitions. These include the Bastogne War Museum, the German-Russian Museum, and the Oskar Schindler Factory. In his analysis of Saul Friedländer's *The Years of Extermination: Nazi Germany and the Jews, 1939–1945* (2007), Wulf Kansteiner (2013, 23) has demonstrated how historical writing on the Holocaust can deal with its representational challenges by juggling numerous historical places, peoples, and strands of events to create a chronosophic net that does not operate in a chronologically linear way, but rather multidimensionally. This indicates that networking techniques toward a structural secondary experientiality in the museum are well suited to and necessary for the challenges of representing the Holocaust in the twenty-first century.

My first example of a local museum employing networking techniques, the Bastogne War Museum (BWM), does not represent the Holocaust as an individual theme, with the exception of a systematic summary in a computer station in the penultimate room of the exhibition after the discovery and liberation of the camps. This means that the visitor cannot understand the full historical context of the Holocaust, though it is present in the global and local parts of the museum. The exhibition begins with an image montage featuring iconic photographs and an introductory image slideshow.[36] In the second room, the visitor sees a couple of historical photographs depicting the exclusion of Jews in Fascist German society and the *Reichspogromnacht*. Furthermore, in the first scenovision Mathilde only mentions the round-ups of the Jews in passing. The core room featuring the Holocaust is the fourth devoted to Belgium under German occupation. Photographs show how the discrimination of Jews transferred from Germany to occupied Belgium. One cabinet and a computer station display the topic "Prisoners and Deportees," with a focus on the camp in Breendonk and the Deportations from the Dossin barracks. These deportations included Jews, prisoners of war, and political prisoners. It is clear that the Holocaust was part of Belgian historical reality and that some Belgians were participating as collaborators at the same time that others were resisting the Germans.

In the penultimate room the visitor can see one panel featuring a montage of images entitled "The Jewish Question."[37] This panel provides a survey text that explains some of the Holocaust's historical context, accompanied by supporting images on a computer station. It relies on iconic images of freed inmates from the Buchenwald and Mauthausen camps and masses of corpses from Bergen-Belsen and Ohrdruf. The final room shows a wall panel with photographs of memorials and monuments, among them the Holocaust memorials in Charleroi, Dora, Buchenwald, and Terezin. Clearly, the memories of the Holocaust and the war are intertwined. The BWM functions as an example of a war museum in which there is a no doubt that the war cannot be represented without reference to the Holocaust. To understand the interweaving of the local and global theaters of war and of Holocaust, war, and occupation, the Holocaust must be present throughout. Visitors can decide for themselves, how the suffering of civilians and war atrocities committed by the Germans in the Battle of the Bulge relate to the Holocaust or whether they constitute separate themes.

The German-Russian Museum also connects its focus on the German-Soviet war with the Holocaust throughout the exhibition,[38] without isolating the Holocaust or representing it as a separate theme. From the beginning, the visitor un-

---

[36] The conceptual words framing the wall of the image slideshow include 'Night and Fog,' the Final Solution, Genocide, Night of the Broken Glass, and War Crimes relating to the Holocaust and genocide. See chapter 4.3 above.

[37] The Bastogne War Museum avoids the term 'Holocaust' in its text panels.

[38] The exception is the room "Consequences of War and War Memories" in which the German-Russian Museum seems to run out of space. It has brief display cases on the Nuremberg Trials and on the "Suppression and Reappraisal" of war crimes, but neither the Holocaust nor the concentration camps are mentioned explicitly. The local question of the German-Soviet war seems to become narrower and more traditional here.

derstands the connection between the policies of the war of annihilation and the Nazi's racial policies. The conspiracy theories of 'Jewish Bolshevism' and the consequent genocidal policies are clearly documented: there is no doubt about how they impact wartime policies, first briefly in Poland and then in the Soviet Union. The different victim groups are clearly visible throughout the museum, including Sinti and Roma and psychiatric patients. In the prisoner of war room, the transnational focus highlights camps in the Soviet Union and Germany and places a strong emphasis on forced laborers. The impact of the Holocaust is particularly present in many graphic perpetrator photographs in the room featuring the German occupation of Soviet Territory following the onset of Operation Barbarossa. The visitor is presented with images from the pogroms in Lviv, the humiliation of Jews, numerous mass shootings, scenes from the massacre in Babi Yar, and images and items from the Maly Trostinets extermination camp, among others. The extermination camps on Polish territory are not highlighted due to the museum's Soviet-German focus. The strategy seen here varies from other museums insofar as graphic photographs of victims and corpses are not enlarged; the photographs seem to steer the visitor's gaze more toward the systemic nature of the depicted acts, rather than highlighting iconic images and artifacts of the Holocaust. For a German museum, and even more so, one with transnational German-Russian focus, it is crucial that the war crimes in the East, including the Holocaust, are represented as one overall event that created 'a space of violence.' Similar to other museums that highlight a local theater of war or specific perspectives and weave the Holocaust into their overall representations, the genesis of the Holocaust is only partially or briefly reflected upon.

The Oskar Schindler Factory (OSF)[39] serves as a final example of a museum in which the Holocaust is present throughout the museum while being placed into a local setting. Since the museum is less concentrated on the events of the war than on the events of an occupied city, the decisive choice to represent the Holocaust comes from the decision to present Jewish victims as one clearly identifiable, major collective perspective that experiences the occupation (Heinemann 2015, 267–271). The museum's location in the authentic space of the Oskar-Schindler factory adds another commemorative layer in which the Holocaust is represented. Due to the fact that the OSF stages an experiential space, making the visitor a time traveler who experiences the events of occupied Kraków, the museum must rely on narrative proximity to the historical spaces and events. The exhibition's goal is to see, experience, and understand how the Holocaust unfolded in this specific situation, spanning from pre-war life in Kraków to

---

39 See chapter 4.2 for further details.

the early stages of German occupation. This includes the discrimination and exclusion of Jews from public life, the terror experienced in Gestapo cells, the establishment of the ghetto, and the plundering of Jewish property. The visitor then experiences life in the ghetto, the role played by the Schindler factory and the saving of the Schindler Jews, the ghetto's liquidation, and the Płaszów concentration camp. It is here that the story of Kraków's Jews stops and is mainly taken up in the final room, the "Hall of Choices," and in the studio portraits of former workers in the Oskar Schindler's Enamel Factory. The OSF walks a fine line between ensuring visitors do not believe they can experience the atrocities of the Holocaust as a true primary event and integrating the Holocaust into the overlap between primary and secondary experientiality produced by the museum. However, as seen in Bastogne and in Berlin-Karlshorst, the Holocaust receives its own voice within the local context of the museum. The Polish story of the war cannot be told without the Holocaust, nor can the Holocaust be separated from the war and the Polish story of occupation.

The fifth and most important representational strategy relevant to this study is that of structurally networking the Holocaust. This means that the Holocaust, in its larger historical context, is present in different ways throughout a museum exhibition and complements the experientiality of the Second World War. Since war museums mostly avoid generating direct empathy with the individual or collective perspectives of Holocaust victims and perpetrators, the majority of the networking efforts are toward secondary experientiality and structural experiences. This means that the Second World War and the Holocaust, along with other atrocities and genocides, are so deeply intertwined that they cannot be separated. The Topography of Terror (ToT), House of European History (HEH), the Gdańsk Museum of the Second World War (MIIWŚ), the Bundeswehr Military History Museum (MHM), and the Mémorial de Caen indicate different forms of networking. The Holocaust is present throughout each of these exhibitions. However, a close analysis demonstrates differences in how this networking interweaves the war and the Holocaust and helps to determine whether the persecution and extermination of European Jewry maintains its own status or disappears in the face of other atrocities and civilian suffering.

Though themes like racism, antisemitism, and the Holocaust appear at several spots in the museum, at first glance the Mémorial de Caen seems similar to the Imperial War Museum in London due to its decision to isolate the Holocaust. However, a closer analysis of the current exhibition indicates how closely the genocidal strategies employed in the war and the concept of total warfare are interconnected with the Holocaust. The Holocaust is depicted as a historical event that is closely intertwined with total warfare and other wartime atrocities. The Holocaust and genocide section, entitled "Genocide and Mass Violence – the Extermination of the Jews in Europe," is part of the "World War, Total War" section that charts the development of a European war into a world war. The Holocaust and genocide section is followed by a section discussing the idea of a total war.[40] The former presents important aspects and phases of the Holocaust and the experiences of various victim groups. In doing so, this section employs graphic images of crimes and victims and creates a separate commemorative space entitled "'Face-to-Face' Extermination" in the middle of the gallery in which the voices of survivors can be heard.[41] The difference between this museum and the two branches of the Imperial War Museum is that its focus lies less with the evil of Nazism and its antisemitism / racism (IWML). Neither does it uniquely separate the Holocaust from the war (IWMN). Instead, the Mémorial de Caen's concept of violence shapes its representation of the Holocaust and allows it to be presented as an event that needs to be understood on its own terms on the one hand, but also in close relation to the development of violence during the war on the other. This is evident at the end of the room where two displays are located: "Violence on Part of the Japanese Army" and "Violence and Nazism" explain how violence was at the heart of Nazism and how it affected the German campaigns in Poland and the Soviet Union in particular. These displays also highlight the bombing of cities and civilians as parts of such violence, building a bridge between the atrocities represented in the Holocaust room and the following room reflecting upon the concept and impacts of total war.[42]

Placing the Holocaust in a constellation with total warfare always runs the risk of bringing up questions of comparability. There is also the danger that the Holocaust could be universalized to the point where it becomes part of a generalized scheme of illustrating total war and in which it might lose its individual status – resulting in an exhibition that only generates restricted experientiality.[43]

---

[40] The "World War, Total War" section will be extensively analyzed in the following chapter on the Air War.
[41] The enlarged faces of the survivors who remember the atrocities are combined with large poster walls depicting the overgrown sites of former extermination camps. The pyramid-like glass ceiling of the room opens up to the ground floor above and offers hope for the future.
[42] See also chapter 8.
[43] See Alexander 2009 for the social construction of moral universals explaining how the historical event 'Holocaust' was redefined as a traumatic event for all of humankind with Nazism as the representation of absolute evil: "As the sense that the Holocaust was a unique event in human history crystallized and its moral implications became paradoxically generalized, the tragic trauma-drama became increasingly subject to memorialization" (Alexander 2009, 60). Whereas this memorialization is evident in many Western museums with either a national or a cosmopolitan memory focus, the complication of the Holocaust's reception through recent developments of populisms, antisemitism, and new nationalistic identity policies, casts some

That is not the case in the Mémorial de Caen. However, it is obvious that in the museum's networking of the Holocaust and total war, it walks a fine line in order to maintain the specificity of the Holocaust as a historical event and the individual voices of its victims. As seen above,[44] in the House of European History (HEH), the Holocaust is in danger of being subsumed by an absolute total war concept and as a generalized founding myth of contemporary Europe in the museum's memory sections. The HEH is able to interweave the Holocaust into a long history of violence in Europe, the emergence of totalitarian systems, the atrocities and suffering in a total war context and in totalitarian systems. Yet in doing so, it increasingly runs the risk of eliminating the historical specificity of the Holocaust and other events of the Second World War to establish a new master narrative that centers on extreme suffering in total war as the decisive component leading to European unity.[45]

The Topography of Terror is an obvious exception, due to its status as a documentation center of German perpetration.[46] All phases of the Holocaust are documented throughout: while all victim groups are systematically represented in the third section "Terror, Persecution and Extermination on Reich Territory," in which different sub-sections represent each victim group of German persecution. In the other sections, various victim groups are recognizable. Although the exhibition's perspective is that of German perpetrators, with a strong focus on institution and the 'Volksgemeinschaft,' the visitor is led to understand the Holocaust through the secondary experientiality discussed above.[47] Expressions of antisemitism are present throughout the museum, as has been already mentioned in regard to public shaming. Bystanders watch the destruction of synagogues, the auctioning off of Jewish property, and mass executions. Structural networking creates a strong experientiality concerning the structures of the Holocaust and the different gazes of the perpetrator. Historical specificity is evi-

---

doubt on the exclusivity of Alexander's idea of moral universalism based on "social processes that construct and channel cultural trauma" (2009, 70) at the end of the second decade of the twenty-first century.

44 See chapter 6.3.

45 Occasionally, the House of European History is also historically specific about the special status of the persecution against Jews in Nazi racial ideology, such as in the section on German totalitarianism. Among other items, it displays a copy of the special no. 1 ("Sondernummer 1") entitled "Jewish plans to murder non-Jews revealed ("Jüdischer Mordplan gegen die nichtjüdische Menschheit aufgedeckt"), published in May 1934.

46 For other German and Austrian sites of perpetration see Kleinmann 2017, 2019; for a European comparison between Austria, Hungary, and Italy, see Meyer 2018.

47 See chapter 5.3.

dent in the museum's representation of the events of the Holocaust and how it networks the Holocaust, German perpetration, atrocities, and war.

In the Bundeswehr Military History Museum (MHM), the Holocaust and other genocidal activities during the Second World War are spread around the museum. At first glance, there is only one core display cabinet representing the Holocaust, entitled "The Shoah," in the museum's section on the war of extermination in the East. It displays single shoes from Majdanek concentration camp, arranged on shelves like in a shoe store and mixed between children, women, and men. This can potentially trigger visitor reflections on the background of each shoe, while presenting iconic Holocaust objects re-individualized by their arrangement (Arnold-de Simine 2013, 80–86; Paver 2018, 111–112).[48] The cabinet also displays the text of the poem *Shoes of the Dead*, a survey text, and a map of the camps and population movements during the Holocaust. This is supplemented by a German-language computer station that holds further encyclopedic information on antisemitism and the Holocaust, including photographs and film material.[49]

At second glance, however, the Holocaust is present throughout the museum.[50] This includes the "Economy of War in World War II" cabinet on the armament industry (Jaeger 2015b, 238), the mass murders in Greece in the "Homeland and Hinterland" cabinet; the perpetrator, bystander, and victim biographies throughout the chronological exhibition, and the experience station "Exclusion, Forced Immigration, Murder: Stripping German Jews of their Civil Rights," containing snow-globes depicting scenes of newly enacted racial laws. There are also the in-depth cabinets about "Jewish Fates in the 1930s" (see also Johnston-Weiss 2016, 97–99) and "Resistance in the Arts" during National Socialism.[51] In the sections of the thematic tour, the visitor finds themes related to the Holocaust as well, for example under "Silent Heroes" in the "Memory" sec-

---

[48] Chloe Paver criticizes that the degradation of the shoes which "evokes a powerful sense of physical damage, neglect and dishonouring decay" is not explicitly reflected in the MHM's display (2018, 112).
[49] Here, the visitor has the opportunity to enter an almost encyclopedic archive supplemented with images, footage, and interactive maps. There is, however, only one computer station, exclusively in German. This means the computer station has little to no effect on most visitors. In more than twenty extensive visits to the museum, I have never observed a visitor spending time at the computer station, which would work more effectively as an online museum archive on the museum website.
[50] The cabinet does not merely document the links between the economy, war, and Holocaust, but performs them.
[51] Furthermore, there are several several other historical cabinets such as those about the Poland campaign and the Barbarossa cabinet, as discussed in chapter 5.1.

tion or the pogroms in Lviv in the "War and Suffering" section.⁵² The Holocaust is networked throughout the museum; the MHM takes a documentary approach without explicitly interpreting the networks it creates. This allows for an openness that forces the visitor to interpret the objects, images, and constellations on display for themselves. The Holocaust is clearly not represented in a memorializing mode, nor is it presented as an autonomous topic. Instead, the MHM demonstrates, for example in the "Economy of War in World War II" cabinet, that the Holocaust is closely connected to the war effort and its actors. Eventually the visitor will be led back into the continuities in German history, into challenges of remembering the Holocaust today, and into the human history of violence more generally.

Finally, the networking found in the Museum of the Second World War (MIIWŚ) is complex. At first glance, it is easy to assume that because the museum focuses on civilian suffering, the Holocaust would be overly present throughout. A closer analysis indicates a more subtle dynamic at work. On the one hand, the Holocaust is deeply ingrained in the museum's representation. On the other, there are some places where it seems to either disappear behind Polish suffering, or be held up as a general human form of suffering. This fits with the original mission of the museum. The Holocaust receives a separate large gallery and considerable recognition as a historical event, and additionally is also networked throughout the museum. One can argue whether this networking effect makes the Holocaust more or less prominent as a central theme for the museum. Aside from the dedicated Holocaust section,⁵³ the discrimination of Jews is present in the room on German Nazism; the room on pre-war Danzig/Gdańsk; the room on Hitler's and Stalin's social engineering and the subsequent resettlements and expulsions presented in the terror section; in the section on concentration camps; in the brief section on the liberation of the camps; the "Justice Triumphs" section relating to the post-war trials; and through a Matzevah, a tombstone from a Jewish cemetery in the destroyed road installation near the exhibition's end. The fate of the mentally and physically handicapped under Nazism is present in the room on German Nazism and at the end of the concentration camp room. Sinti and Roma are represented in one computer station at the end of the Auschwitz section. Homosexuals are only mentioned in the introduc-

---

52 See also the Felix Nussbaum painting in the "Politics and the Use of Force" section (see chapter 5.1) or the marking of the parallel between the KZ Mittelbau-Dora, the V2 rocket, and its devastation in London in the "Technology and the Military" and "War and Play" sections (see chapter 8 for a more detailed discussion). The Holocaust is also alluded to in various commissioned artworks (see chapter 9).
53 Here, the visitor, also finds a separate section on the persecution of Sinti and Roma.

tory panel of the concentration camp room. Nevertheless, a careful analysis of the displays indicates that the Holocaust – whether in relation to Jews or to the other main victim groups of Nazi atrocities – and the identities of Jewish victims play a relatively minor role outside of the Holocaust section. The concentration camp rooms in the "Terror" section mainly use the word prisoners or identify victims by name and occasionally as Poles or Jews from other countries. Monika Heinemann reads this as inclusion of Jews and other Polish minorities into the Polish collective (2017, 472).

However, it seems clear that the word 'Poles' is shorthand for non-Jewish Poles and most individualized names refer to non-Jewish Poles.[54] The first room of the "Terror" section is entitled "Terror of the German Occupation: Planned Extermination and Blind Revenge." Its introductory survey text ends with the words: "Polish Jews condemned to total elimination, formed a separate category." This seems to indicate that the section displaying massacres by Germans in villages across Central and Eastern Europe is only concerned with Polish and other gentile victims. More importantly, it seems to signify that the Holocaust can be mainly compartmentalized into a single separate section. In that section, the museum discusses death and extermination camps, which allows the museum to arrange the preceding concentration camp section without highlighting the group identities of most victims unless they are Polish.[55]

In the opening version of the exhibition, the estimates of the number of people killed in the war were listed in millions and categorized by country and soldiers versus civilians. It noted that 0.3 million Polish soldiers and 5.3 million Polish civilians died in the war. Below the table, it read: "The civilian victims included about six million murdered European Jews, of whom three million were Polish citizens." In other words, the original exhibition was careful in differentiating between Polish gentiles and Polish Jews, although it also incorporated all of them as Polish citizens in its numbers. In the new exhibition, a large panel entitled "Casualties Sustained by a Given Country during the Second World War" has replaced the statistical table on a smaller display box. Poland

---

54 This trend has been strongly intensified through the recent additions to the permanent exhibition, such as a cabinet on Maksymilian Maria Kolbe, a Catholic priest, killed in Auschwitz after offering his life for another prisoner. The careful avoidance of most group identifiers in the original exhibition here turns into a celebration of a specific group and Kolbe's Catholic faith.
55 Former museum director Machcewicz reflects exclusively on all victim groups as a "shared fate" (2019 [2017], 87); the partial compartmentalization of the Holocaust seems more of an unintentional side effect of a universalization of civilian victims.

clearly ranks at the top.⁵⁶ Jewish casualties have been merged with Polish casualties so that the number appears higher; there is no way for the visitor to tell how many of the 5.7 million Polish civilian casualties were Jews. In the smaller display box neither the word 'Jewish' nor specific Jewish artifacts appear any longer. Instead, the visitor sees a drawing of Mary holding Jesus made by a Polish concentration camp survivor while receiving treatment for his trauma, among other objects.

The changes made by the new museum team clearly reduce the role of Jewish suffering and replace it in the well-known matyrological narrative of Polish (Catholic) suffering. This consequently reduces any structural experiences of civilian suffering down to mere ideological arguments. For example, at the end of the "Road to Auschwitz" section there is a new display entitled "Poles in the Face of the Holocaust" with a large poster board and a computer. Unlike in other texts and displays in the same section, which acknowledges a degree of complicity on the part of Poles regarding the Holocaust, this new display presents a clear black-and-white narrative. The poster and single story found on the computer station is about the Ulma family, who recently received their own museum.⁵⁷ The text begins "Saving their neighbors cost them their life [sic]." The enlarged poster is a photograph taken by father Józef Ulma, depicting the mother Wiktoria Ulma with her six children and several sheep. In the overall narrative trajectory of the slideshow, it is increasingly made to seem like all Poles formed a single group that had a fully positive attitude toward the country's Jews and were eager to help them – all in the face of Germans implementing the death penalty for everybody aiding or hiding Jews. In regard to the Ulma family the slideshow notes: "Unfortunately, most likely as result of a denunciation, the Germans learned about it [the hiding]." Possible reasons for why good Poles would denounce their fellow Poles are nowhere to be found in this addition to the section. The mostly multifaceted approach of the museum's original exhibition, which differentiated within groups and performed a more complex analysis beyond as-

---

56 The new table is particularly manipulative since the visitor first sees a graph that is more than twice the length of the next one (civilian casualties in the Soviet Union); only upon a closer examination it is revealed that the Soviet percentage was almost as high as the Polish one; if one adds up civilian and military casualties and that the overall number of victims was much higher.
57 https://muzeumulmow.pl/en/, accessed 13 October 2019. The Museum was opened in Markowa on March 17, 2016. Its webpage describes its mission as follows: "The primary goal of the Museum is to show heroic stance of the Poles who helped the Jews during German occupation, risking their own lives and the lives of their families." https://muzeumulmow.pl/en/museum/about-museum/ Accessed 13 October 2019. For a discussion of the museum and its exhibition see Hackmann 2018, 597–600.

signing individuals and events to black-and-white categories has disappeared. Instead, Poles are held up as a collective group with good values. After stating that Polish people are the nationality that has received the most – specifically 6,800 – titles of Righteous among Nations, the slideshow's text continues: "However, it should be remembered that many people who helped Jews during the German occupation remain anonymous." That this holds even truer for Polish people who profited from the plight of the Jews or collaborated with the Germans – whether out of fear of German persecution, out of antisemitism, or for other reasons – is not mentioned. Polish people appear as a collective moral entity.

It is particularly telling that the visitor has to go very deep into the slideshow, specifically to the caption of the third image accompanying the text on the Ulma family, to receive any information about the Jewish family that was killed. The caption accompanying a photo of four men simply states: "The Goldmans, a Jewish family hidden by the Ulma family."[58] Looking at these separate images requires more time than most visitors can invest in the museum. Instead they will in all likelihood stick to the main poster and possibly the survey slides of the computer slideshow. Thus, the impression remains that in contrast to the Jewish family they were hiding, the death of the Polish family was more important – or perhaps even of sole importance. The Jewish victims become anonymous sidekicks to the suffering of the courageous Poles.[59] These kinds of representations lend a feeling of factuality to the ethnic/racial split between gentile

---

[58] For the historical record of the known circumstances surrounding the murder of the Ulma family and the Jewish people they were hiding, see Rozett 2019, 25.

[59] This impression is further reinforced by the fact that the MIIWŚ, at least in April 2018, represents the story of Polish gentile people helping Jews as the core mission of the museum, as stated in the welcoming words of director Karol Nawrocki (2018) in the museum flyer: the visitor will meet "people of the highest standing, such as the first partisan in occupied Europe Major Henryk Dobrzański 'Hubal,' Cavalry Captain Witold Pilecki who volunteered to the Auschwitz German concentration camp, or Irena Sendlerowa who personifies the phenomenon of nearly seven thousand Polish Righteous among the nations." The first display that the visitor saw in April 2018, when entering the museum on level -1 was a display case with several objects entitled "Polish people helping the Jews in the times of German occupation." Next to the cashier desk and entry to the permanent exhibition on level -3, the visitor encountered a poster exhibition with twelve portrait posters with brief captions (ten individuals and two couples/families) detailing Poles helping Jews, among them the Ulma family. Throughout the revised museum, a lopsided narrative is developed, with some specific stories, like the one of the Ulma family, receiving an almost mythic character in their matyrological quality. The 2019–2021 special exhibition of the MIIWŚ, entitled *Fighting and Suffering: Polish Citizens during World War II*, further enhances this matyrological narrative. The MIIWŚ, also unveiled a heroic statue of Witold Pilecki in front of the museum building on September 17, 2019, on the eightieth anniversary of the Soviet invasion of Poland (https://muzeum1939.pl/en, accessed 13 October 2019).

Fig. 27 Section "Poles in the Face of the Holocaust" between "Road to Auschwitz" section (background) and "People like us" installation (foreground). Permanent Exhibition. Muzeum II Wojny Światowej (Museum of the Second World War), Gdańsk (Photo: Author, 2018).

Poles and Polish Jews. Even though the display did not receive much attention from visitors during my two-day visit in April 2018, it is situated at a crucial point between a large iconic poster-sized photograph of the unloading ramps – with remains of the victims in the front and the Birkenau gate in the back – and the "People like us" installation that allows for the commemoration of victims (see fig. 27). Here, visitors walk through rectangular columns displaying portraits of Jewish Holocaust victims.[60] If the visitor stands between the columns

---

[60] The visitor can stop and react to an individual face or take in the overall impression, which –

and turns around to look at the back wall of the portrait room, they can see the Auschwitz gate in the distance and the Ulma family on the side. The Holocaust and German crimes against Polish people seem to have merged, providing the visitor with the possibility of wondering whether all of those portraits truly represent Holocaust victims.

The most extreme transfer of attention from Jewish victimhood during the Holocaust to Polish victimhood can be found in the aforementioned new final film. Early in the film, the narrator says "The Soviets deport Poles in cattle cars to gulags in the East," while a flashing red picture with a train running to the right side, i.e. into the endless East, is shown. This remains the only train metaphor in the film, clearly transferring the image of deportation to Nazi death camps to Soviet perpetration. The Holocaust then appears four times in quick succession, always dependent on Polish heroism and good deeds: Poles help Jews despite the threat of the death penalty, Poles ("we") create resistance movements, "even within the German concentration camps,"[61] and Poles ("we") who are "the first" to alert a dismissive and disbelieving world to the Holocaust. Finally, "Polish Jews fight the Germans in the Warsaw ghetto without even a chance for success," right before the rebirth of the Polish army who, following the image of the underground state rising, fights a successful battle in the Warsaw Uprising. All of the changes that the museum has undergone under the new directorship have employed the same narrative-rhetorical technique: historical facts, such as that there were gentile Poles involved in the resistance in the concentration camps, become universal and all encompassing. Any room for ambiguities or the consideration of other groups with similar achievements disappears into the collective 'we.' Polish Jews seem to be subsumed by Polish gentiles when it comes to overall suffering and the unbroken will of the 'unconquered' Polish people.

In other words, the tendency in the original exhibition toward collectivizing Jewish suffering with Polish suffering – partially to make the museum acceptable to a wider Polish audience – becomes the singular choice for the new muse-

---

if connected to the section's title – seems to indicate that anybody could be persecuted in a specific historical situation. Unlike the installations in the United States Holocaust Memorial Museum or the Imperial War Museum North, the faces are unnamed and from all over the world, which opens up the empathetic possibilities, but also de-contextualizes any historical specificity.

61 Here, the film shows a map entitled "Großdeutschland" (Greater Germany), including all of Poland, with all the larger concentration camps and death camps as part of its territory. This relates to the public discussion around the new Holocaust law in Poland and the law itself that dictates that one can be sued for using the expression 'Polish concentration camps.'

um leadership. In particular, antisemitism outside of Germany and within Poland does not exist in this story; furthermore, the development of Poland into an apparently homogeneous Catholic nation seems logical. Since the war in the museum's interpretation continues until the fall of the iron curtain, it does not seem to matter that the conclusive sentence "We prevail" does not apply to the millions of Polish Jews that did not. Jews are opportunely integrated into a narrative of Polish suffering, neatly separated from the rest of the Poles, or forgotten. Following these changes, any possible experientiality is reduced to a master narrative and ideological argument.

In contrast, the angle of civilian suffering and resistance as well as the transnational constellations found within and beyond sections allows the MIIWŚ to produce a networking effect and secondary experientiality. The Holocaust receives particular attention in its large autonomous section. When considering the museum on the whole, the Holocaust melts into an anthropology of violence perpetrated by totalitarian regimes, in particular Nazi Germany. This does not mean that the original creators of the MIIWŚ argued that the Holocaust was comparable to any other event; it simply means that the understanding of the spaces of violence or bloodlands in the East go beyond depictions of the Holocaust. The MIIWŚ – at least in its original version – includes and concretely depicts the Holocaust as an integral part of the Second World War, while incorporating a universal anthropology of violence and a historical trajectory that represents the suffering of the Polish people and other occupied countries under totalitarian regimes.

Closely connected to the discussion of representability and ethics regarding the depiction of the Holocaust in museums is the use of Holocaust photographs and images of atrocities (see Baer 2002; Prager 2008).[62] Carden-Coyne argues: "Repetition without historical context was seen as producing a Holocaust 'aesthetic' and embroiling historical truth in a 'spectacle of horror.' Voyeurism and dehumanization were seen as the result of such photographs becoming signifiers of reduced meaning and mere depictions that stood in for – rather than explained – the Holocaust" (2011, 172). Photographs of the Holocaust were often taken for propaganda purposes – by perpetrators and by the Allies; any use of perpetrator images in exhibitions runs the risk of directly reproducing the gaze of the perpetrators, so that museums must think of how to contextualize

---

[62] Rachel E. Perry demonstrates the "bifocal" pattern of Holocaust photographs curated in museums, depicting life and death. Whereas documentary photographs are used to provide objective truth, give evidence and allow for the visitor to witness the atrocities (death), "personal photographs act as empathic triggers: to elicit identification and provoke an affective, emotional reaction," pointing to life (2017, 223). See also Holtschneider (2011, 45–78) for a detailed description of the different functions of Holocaust photography in museums.

or rearrange the photographs to avoid the "fragility of empathy" (Dean 2004) and allow for reflections by the museum visitor. To avoid any desensitization via shock value, the visitor must be put in a situation where they can read images and their historical context critically (Carden-Coyne 2011, 172). It is problematic to use photographs of atrocities as historical sources or as simple illustrations of historical facts. The techniques museums employ to deal with this challenge vary. Some provide barriers to watching, such the United States Holocaust Memorial Museum, wherein the viewers only see the footage / the images if they specifically decide to forego the museum's warning and look at the evidence in the container. The "War and Suffering" section in the Bundeswehr Military History Museum gives a warning to the visitor and particularly to children that the section contains human remains, which the museum tries to exhibit in a dignified manner. Museums must be particularly cautious when displaying historical photographs, so that they do not re-objectify victims (Dean 2004, 36–38; Johnston-Weiss 2016, 96–97). In the museums analyzed in this study, one can identify three main functions for displaying images of victims of the Holocaust and other mass atrocities: using iconic images, establishing historical evidence for the audience, and simulating structures of perpetration. These three functions can overlap, and their exact use differs from museum to museum. They can be used in illustrative, emotional, and symbolic ways, and they can reflect the mediality of the image. Distantiation, on a scale between proximity and distance, is an important tool to understand the possible effects of the use of Holocaust and atrocity imagery.

Photographs of atrocities are mostly used sparingly. Their first function is their iconic effect. This is employed throughout museums that represent the Holocaust, but it is particularly common in museums that focus on the discovery and liberation of the concentration camps, such as the Canadian War Museum or the New Orleans WWII Museum. The Bastogne War Museum uses a similar set of iconic images. The well-known liberation images illustrate horror; they emotionally express the historical stage in the war where the Allies felt that the cause of the war was totally justified, while establishing a framework for humanity to overcome such horrors. Especially in newer exhibitions, this use of images relies on the well-known iconography of traumatic events (Arnold de-Simine 2013, 80–86; Mikuska-Tinman 2018). This reduces the shock factor and allows the visitor to reflect in the name of humanity and 'the good war'; in a positive sense it allows for the transfer of the expression 'never again' to the visitor's own present.

The second common function sees graphic images used as evidence. The museum that most aggressively displays images of perpetration, along with those depicting dead and suffering victims is the Museum of the Second

World War in Gdańsk (MIIWŚ). In comparison to the United States Holocaust Memorial Museum – the model for many emotional-mimetic Holocaust and atrocity exhibitions – the MIIWŚ uses a similar amount of pictures showing atrocities and, in general, employs comparable representational techniques in its Holocaust section. The MIIWŚ primarily shows many images of corpses and war crimes for evidence. It is the (original) museum's objective to tell the story of civilian suffering in the Second World War, and in Central and Eastern Europe in particular, within a strong narrative frame (Machcewicz 2016, 7–8). In doing so, it attempts to prove that the responsibility for these atrocities lies with the totalitarian powers and establishes an iconography of death and suffering that relies on visual images that emotionally impact the visitor.[63] In this strategy, the Holocaust becomes part of the evidence of human destruction caused by the war. It clearly receives its own space as an event, yet it is also part of the much wider network of violence stemming from a vast array of German, Soviet, and other crimes committed during the Second World War. The imagery of the sections on German terror in Poland, the section on the killing and death of Soviet prisoners of war, and of the terror section, which includes liquidated villages, is iconographically continued in the Holocaust section.

Whereas different victim groups receive individual attention, including Jewish people in the Holocaust, and their experiences can be understood as separate historical events, the MIIWŚ clearly uses an over-abundance of corpses in the exhibition to bring home an emotional point, while taking the risk of numbing the viewer's experience of seeing so many unnamed corpses: The emotional message of the MIIWŚ highlights the disaster of the war in general human terms and the clearly divided frame concerning the origins of this violence in particular. In comparison, the photographs serving as evidence in the three German museums and the Mémorial de Caen inform the visitor about who committed the crime and about its horror and inhumanity. However, these museums – in contrast to the MIIWŚ – attempt to deepen visitors' understanding of how war and violence – and war and the Holocaust – are interconnected, without emotionally overwhelming them or narrowing their interpretative possibilities through a narrative frame.

---

[63] War and military museums in general, and the ones in North America and Britain in particular, have a tendency to sanitize their exhibitions from depicting too many dead bodies or too much physical mutilation. This goes back to the British and Commonwealth war art tradition, which hardly depicts corpses (Shah 2017, 550, by example of the Canadian War Museum). Shah argues that regarding the display of weapons and data on advanced military technology, "far from removing the element of death and injury technical criteria [can] say a lot about the bloodshed inherent in war" (2017, 563).

If we examine the German museums in this study, the third main function of images of atrocities and violence including the Holocaust becomes clear. Here, the structure of perpetration is particularly emphasized. As seen in the Topography of Terror,[64] visitors are challenged to take on the gaze of the perpetrators and the ethical challenges of doing this, which produces a secondary experientiality of terror and war crimes through visualization. Visual components interact much more strongly with museum objects in the Bundeswehr Military History Museum (MHM). However, when images of atrocities are used, such in the cabinet on "Operation Barbarossa," there is a clear indication that they are part of the perpetrator's perspective on the atrocities. Therefore, Arnold-de Simine's argument that the MHM "clearly wants to shock by showing the horrific psychological and physical wounds inflicted by war" (2013, 77) seems to only capture part of the effects created by the museum's representation of atrocities. The MHM often displays photo albums belonging to German soldiers and emphasizes the presence of German observers and spectators. Similar techniques can be found in the Mémorial de Caen, which shows photographs of the mass killing in Babi Yar as film negatives on an Agfacolor paper. This both highlights that photography is a constructed medium and allows the visitor to follow the gaze of the photographer. As seen in the Bundeswehr Military History Museum or the German-Russian Museum, the Mémorial de Caen also often contextualizes images by (briefly) reflecting on the photographer and on the story behind the photograph. This, at least, provides a starting point for visitors "to learn to *read* images – not just recover their context or believe in them as documents" (Carden-Coyne 2011, 173).

In summary, the analysis of Second World War museums representing the Holocaust leads[65] on the one hand, to restricted experientiality in which the Holocaust is reduced to confirm an ideological statement or master narrative. On the other, it leads to secondary experientiality, wherein the events and structures of the Holocaust become part of structural networking throughout the museum: the visitor can activate these networks to understand the different dimensions of genocide, violence, and the Holocaust, and historical representation and memory. Primary experientiality hardly plays a role, with the exception of soldiers whose collective emotional reactions are depicted during the discovery and liberation of the concentration camps. Bonnell and Simon warn that museums representing difficult knowledge aiming to engage visitors emotionally and elicit empathy have unrealistic expectations of their visitors' attention, depth of

---

64 See chapter 5.3.
65 With the exception of the representational strategy of the completely autonomous exhibition, as exemplified in the Imperial War Museum in London.

involvement, and faculties (2007, 67). In Second World War exhibitions, this challenge in representing the Holocaust seems to be even more evident, since most museums do not have the space to either develop the historical context of antisemitism and the racial ideology in Nazi Germany, or the consequences of the discrimination and persecution of the Jews.

None of the museums under study pretend to be able to immerse the visitor in the victims' perspective on the Holocaust. Immersion only seems possible in a very limited way, as we have seen in the experiential scenes of the Ghetto in Kraków or the Plaszów concentration camp. Yet there is always a strong element of distantiation. The visitor, as a kind of space- and time traveler in the Oskar Schindler Factory, is steered toward distantiation and prevented from merely identifying with somebody else's perspective. Museums, such as the New Orleans WWII Museum or the Canadian War Museum, create immersive collective perspectives from the point of view of the soldiers discovering the concentration camps. The Holocaust cannot become an autonomous event in these institutions, since war museums in the USA and Canada are shaped by the reiteration of the narrative of 'the good war' freeing the world of evil, of which the Holocaust is the ultimate example. In the Warsaw Rising Museum, any Jewish perspective is filtered through those of non-Jewish Poles who observed the crime. In the Bastogne War Museum, the Holocaust becomes part of the museum's fabric, which combines local, national, and global events, while concrete perspectives are restricted to the local level. However, even if there is no immersion with Holocaust victims, museums can create empathy with victims at times – such as in the Topography of Terror (Johnston-Weiss 2019, 97–98). Here, it is particularly important to consider how the object or photograph on display works with techniques of distantiation. Is the visitor put in a generalized situation, such as perceiving a public humiliation through the eyes of a victim? Some museums copy techniques from Holocaust memorial museums, particularly the United States Holocaust Memorial Museum, on a smaller scale. This is done to allow for empathy in the sense that the visitor considers what they might do or would have done in a similar situation. The Holocaust Tower of Faces in Washington is, for example, reproduced in miniature form in Manchester[66] and in the "People like us" installation in Gdańsk.

Immersion can usually only take place in a structural sense, such as in Dresden, where – as seen above[67] – the Holocaust is performed through the mechanisms and connections between industry, the war effort, racist policies, commu-

---

66 See also chapter 5.2 (Bagnall and Rowland 2001, 67).
67 See also chapter 5.1.

nity perception, different forms of memory, and the Holocaust's actual historical events. This kind of structural immersion can also be seen in Berlin-Karlshorst. Alternatively, museums such as the Imperial War Museum North (IWMN), or the Bundeswehr Military History Museum in its display cabinet "Resistance in the Arts," use artwork that allows the visitor to reflect upon how experiences of discrimination, persecution, or imprisonment can be expressed. Artwork can also be used to produce different modes of commemoration, such as in the Rosenzweig artwork in Manchester, while always maintaining or emphasizing a moment of distance between the visitor and the immersive perspective. Ritula Fränkel's and Nicholas Morris's *Jozef's Coat* in Brussels also creates distance between the visitor and Fränkel's father's historical experience in the Holocaust, while fostering an act of commemoration. As seen above,[68] the teleological narrative in the House of European History, namely that Holocaust remembrance is required in order to birth common European values, is primary to the artwork's presence.

If one looks at the representation of perpetration and the perpetrators of the Holocaust in war museums, it quickly becomes clear that these representations can only be discussed by analyzing the ways in which all kinds of atrocities, crimes, and injustices are presented. The last systematic question in this chapter extends the previous discussion about representing perpetration toward the question of how perpetrators and their causes and motivations are displayed in the museums under study.[69] Perpetrators are represented in three different ways in these institutions: first, through the depiction of high-ranked leaders such as Hitler, Himmler, Heydrich, or criminal commanders and officers such as Höß, Mengele, and Stroop. Second, perpetration is depicted through the documentation of criminal acts. Scenes of individual or mass shootings in which the perpetrators and victims are visible point to the perpetrators' participation in crimes. A softer approach is highlighting the role of the bystanders and profiteers of discrimination and crimes to reflect upon the role of society, a technique

---

68 See chapter 6.3.
69 See Linienthal 2001 (1995), 199–210, for the discussion of the boundaries used for representing perpetrators in the development of the concept for the United States Holocaust Memorial Museum (USHMM). Timothy W. Luke notes that the USHMM lacks the ability to depict "[r]eal human complexities" such as "individual acts of resistance as well as personal decisions to accept fascism" (2002, 60). Susanne Luhmann analyzes the "affective economies" of the female guard exhibition at concentration camp memorial site Ravensbrück (Mahn- und Gedenkstätte Ravensbrück), particularly the "ethicality of representing perpetrators" and "anxieties over the kinds of interpretations and identifications" such representations will produce among visitors (2018, 248).

that is particularly prevalent in the Topography of Terror. Third, perpetrators are represented through the focus on criminal collectives, usually the nation-state or the Nazis explicitly – this runs the risk of indicating a difference between the perpetrators and all other Germans.

If one discusses the representation of perpetration and the Holocaust, the question arises of whether war museums – the Topography of Terror as a perpetration museum notwithstanding – are truly interested in the perpetrators or just in the evidence of crimes. The American, Canadian, and British museums minimally discuss the perpetrators of the Holocaust, other atrocities, and war crimes. They name the Nazis or Hitler and possibly some other individual Nazi leaders as the ultimate expression of evil. The Japanese side is similarly represented; once this claim is established, one can focus on the good mission and on commemorating one's own heroes. The evil of the other side appears mostly as a generalized abstraction. In the last room of "Road to Berlin" in the New Orleans WWII Museum, it is Hitler who "flings children and grandfathers into battle." The museum is not interested in understanding the German situation in the war's final days in detail; it is particularly important that ordinary German soldiers surrendered in large numbers to the Allies, implying that they accepted the good cause and the superior American value system and that they saw the Americans as liberators. When the final film discusses the discovery of the concentration camps, it names Nazism, the Germans, and the Nazis as an anonymous collective of perpetrators. The New Orleans WWII Museum displays one info panel with a photograph of murdered American prisoners of war at the Malmedy Massacre in the Battle of the Bulge. It names the 1st SS Panzer Division as a collective perpetrator, but does not go into further details aside from noting that the German brutality often provoked retaliation by outraged Americans. A serious discussion of one's own troops' perpetration of war crimes and atrocities cannot be found in American, Canadian, or British museums. Instances of perpetration in Allied countries, such as the forced relocation and internship during WWII of Japanese Canadians depicted in the Canadian War Museum, name the state, government, or the collective population as the agents of injustice. In the New Orleans WWII Museum, the perpetrator always remains anonymous (e. g. a generic recruitment officer, denying Japanese-Americans or African-Americans a place in the overall community). The British museums similarly abstract German perpetration so that we find the Imperial War Museum North, for example, speaking about the "brutal occupation" by the Germans without going into specifics.

The perpetration of the Holocaust receives the most attention in cases where museums focus on post-war trials, such as the Museum of the Second World War in Gdańsk (MIIWŚ), the Topography of Terror, and to lesser extent the Bundeswehr Military History Museum at the beginning of its "1945–Today" section, and the still-to-be-built Liberation Pavilion in the New Orleans WWII Museum that (presumably) emphasizes on the Nuremberg Trials. The MIIWŚ provides the most detailed exhibition room out of all of the analyzed museums: it distinguishes between trials (justice) and perpetrators who escaped and were never charged by the Allies. Aside from these details, however, the main perpetrators in the MIIWŚ are Hitler, Stalin, other national leaders, and collectives such as the Germans or Soviets.

In the museums that specifically examine countries under occupation, there is a stronger focus on crimes against the local population and on collaboration. In this study, this can be seen in the Bastogne War Museum and in all three Polish museums under analysis. In Bastogne, the museum reflects on collaboration and the excesses taken in punishing collaborators after the war. The House of European History represents collaboration with Nazi Germany as a phenomenon that occurred during the war throughout the whole of occupied Europe. Similar to the Bastogne War Museum, it emphasizes the existential reasons behind collaboration, giving visitors room to make their own moral assessments of this phenomenon. In the same vein, although within a stricter framework, that makes it impossible to identify motives sufficient to justify collaboration, the MIIWŚ dedicates a whole transnational section to the issue.[70] This provides the visitor with the opportunity to use the tool of comparison to make more complex judgments on collaboration.

In almost all of these museums – apart from the Topography of Terror and, to a certain extent, the Bundeswehr Military History Museum – all of the agents of atrocities and war crimes remain anonymous, with the exception of references to certain political leaders and military commanders. On the video screens in the Bastogne War Museum that display the traumas of war in interviews with local survivors of German war crimes during the Battle of the Bulge, the visitor can listen to narratives of these crimes. The actual perpetrators stay anonymous in these narratives, however sometimes the humanity of individual Germans is stressed.[71] Indeed, these agents are always referred to as "a soldier" or "a German officer." The visitor cannot possibly contextualize these crimes in regard to the agency of the perpetrator; nor can they decide whether these atrocities occurred through the individual initiatives of ordinary German soldiers or whether they were acting on orders from superior officers. This is very similar to what happens in the Warsaw Rising Museum: the exhibition "Germans in Warsaw" focuses on crimes against Poles and presents the institutions and leaders of the

---

70 See chapter 6.2.
71 See also chapter 4.3.

German command structure in considerable detail. The visitor is not encouraged to understand how ordinary soldiers participated in these crimes – instead, they receive numerous detailed biographies of criminal commanders and officers. These biographies always first note that the German officer is a war criminal, and then continue to run through his career in the 1930s, his crimes during the Second World War (mainly in the Warsaw Uprising), and end with the post-war war crimes trials. The focus of the section lies more with underscoring the crimes that these people orchestrated than with understanding the spiral of violence. The Oskar Schindler Factory operates in a similar fashion, except that it also explicitly reflects upon the perpetrators of the Holocaust, especially Amon Leopold Göth, the SS-Hauptsturmführer (captain) and commandant of the Kraków-Płaszów concentration camp. The viewer sees photographs of Göth's decadence as he rides a white horse and sunbathes shirtless, while the museum text and eyewitness quotations inform the visitors about the atrocities in the camp.

Most Second World War museums and Second World War sections or galleries in war museums do not focus on perpetrators of the Holocaust or other atrocities beyond well-known political and military leaders, or national and ideological collectives. They present acts of perpetration first and foremost to prove that there were these acts of perpetration and atrocities. The complex German process of working-through the past is not particularly relevant to any museum outside of Germany, with the exception of the House of European History (HEH). In the HEH, the understanding of total war and the Holocaust as universal phenomena of a shared European past dictates conformity to certain memories. In regard to the HEH's representation of the Holocaust, its emphasis is almost exclusively placed on racism and antisemitism, particularly on the racist Nazi ideology. German museums such as the German-Russian Museum or the Bundeswehr Military History Museum (MHM) make clear how the atrocities of the war and the Holocaust were made possible in a structural sense. The German-Russian Museum is, however, more victim-focused, after it establishes the political and military reality of German war policies early on in its exhibition. Despite the fact that there are many quotations and orders given by perpetrators throughout the exhibition, the visitor never has the chance to get close enough to a perpetrator to empathize with him (or her), or to even follow one concrete story. As in the Topography of Terror, the system dominates the individual – however, the documentation center opens enough gaps in its image montages that challenge the visitor to think about individual motivations.

The Bundeswehr Military History Museum depicts perpetrators particularly in the concrete letters and diary entries found in "War and Suffering" as well as in its short tabular biographies spread throughout the chronological exhibition. These are arranged in such a way as to link contrasting pairs of people who lived during the same period, but took divergent routes in the same situation (Pieken 2012 [2011], 23). Tensions between the many tabular biographies of leaders, ordinary people, victims, bystanders, and perpetrators open up room to think about differing life trajectories, and what justifies and changes these paths under certain circumstances. For example, close to the "Economy of War in World War II" cabinet in the chronological exhibition, the MHM contrasts Hitler's architect and armament minister Albert Speer with the Russian forced laborer Ekaterina Nikolaewna Korobzowa, who survived the war but became blind in one eye and was consequently unable to work after returning home to the Soviet Union. Her husband left her after the war because she was seen as traitor, since she had worked for the Germans, and he chose Communist Party membership over his wife. When the visitor reads of her fate and contrasts it with Speer's post-war biography – he was released from prison in 1966 and described himself as an "apolitical technocrat" in his memoirs – the full contrast of suffering and perpetration can be felt by the visitor as a structural experience. How could Speer see himself as basically innocent, while those who were clearly victims had to suffer after the war? The tabular biographies are one of the few installations in any of the museums that lead the visitor to question simplistic black-and-white patterns of good and evil and potentially trigger thoughts concerning shades of grey between the two.

It is here that the biggest representational difference between the Bundeswehr Military History Museum (MHM) and the Gdańsk Museum of the Second World War (MIIWŚ) becomes evident. Whereas the original version of the MIIWŚ mostly places the perpetration of the Holocaust and of all other atrocities in a scheme with clear concepts of right and wrong, the MHM leaves it to the visitor to come to such realizations. This becomes even clearer when one looks at the only concrete story of Polish perpetration featured in the MIIWŚ: the pogrom in the village of Jedwabne on June 10, 1941, in which several hundred Jews were murdered.[72] The text reads: "Poles were persuaded by the Germans, probably following a pre-existing German plan to round up their Jewish neighbours in the market square. They humiliated, beat and killed them there." One object is the facsimile of a 1933 photograph from Jedwabne School, showing Jewish-Polish and gentile Polish children together. The explanatory text names numerous likely and possible victims and highlights one former student that was saved by a Polish woman. The explanation focuses fully on the victims. No Polish perpetra-

---

[72] Jedwabne has become the symbol for Polish perpetration since the publication of Jan Gross's *Neighbors* (2001 [Polish 2000]). See also Orla-Burkowska 2004 and Hackmann 2018, 592–594 for further contextualization of the role of Jedwabne in Polish memory politics.

tors are mentioned by name, nor does the overall display mention the deep divide in Polish society. It is unclear from the exhibition why Polish people might have participated in the pogrom.

However, the Jedwabne exhibit also allows the visitor to empathize with the atrocity's victims and reflect upon their situation: a set of keys to Jewish homes in Jedwabne that was found in a barn where many Jews were burned is one of the most powerful objects in the museum. The museum notes that the keys tell the visitor that the Jews locked their houses and had no idea that they would not be returning. The keys are a strong reminder of how objects can make visitors think and empathize with victims. For example, they might ask themselves how it would have been to go to the market square without knowing that they would never come back. Did they have any foreboding what would happen? Whereas the Jedwabne exhibit fails to allow the visitor understand perpetration beyond a general scheme, the display of keys impressively shows how museums can allow visitors to connect to the past of the Holocaust without objectifying or dehumanizing the victims. In other words, both exhibitions, in Gdańsk and in Dresden, allow for different forms of secondary experientiality.

At the end of the second decade of the twenty-first century, there seems no doubt that the Holocaust belongs in Second World War museums. There is, however, a fine line separating the view that the Holocaust should be represented from a very restricted perspective, for example when it is functionalized for the expression of other war themes, or local, national, or transnational discourses (restricted experientiality), or whether it should be represented so that the visitor can understand the structures connecting the Holocaust to the war, its policies, and other atrocities (secondary experientiality). Because the Holocaust is the most challenging Second World War event in which to immerse a visitor, all museums avoid techniques of immersion that are too aggressive and instead leave visitors at a cognitive distance from individual and collective perspectives. There is no perfect or correct way to represent the Holocaust in a war museum. Some exhibitions raise questions; others foreclose on them. The crucial matter to be determined is how to interweave the Holocaust and the Second World War from the individual perspective of each museum, in such a way that the visitor can understand their interdependence. Here, one can see how the more subtle displays in twenty-first-century war and military history museums need ways of producing secondary experientiality in their representations of the Holocaust, so that the visitor can understand its occurrence without being steered, manipulated, or emotionally overwhelmed into adopting one interpretative or ideological standpoint.

With regard to the representation of perpetrators, museums must continue to explore further approaches that overcome mere stereotypes, allowing the visitor to gain a better understanding of how it is possible to become a perpetrator. Certain approaches, especially those seen in the Mémorial de Caen, the Bundeswehr Military History Museum, the German-Russian Museum, the Topography of Terror, and Gdańsk Museum of the Second World War, offer a variety of displays and techniques devoted to explaining the history of violence structurally. They demonstrate that violence goes beyond the evil of individual perpetrators, yet their techniques of abstraction also run the risk that individual behavior and choices cannot be understood. Overall, the representation of perpetrators in such museums lags behind representations in other media, whether in fictional accounts found in literature and film, or in documentaries, historiographical texts, and biographies.

Chapter 8:
Total War, Air War, and Suffering

This chapter analyzes total war in contemporary Second World War exhibitions by exemplifying representations of aerial warfare during the Second World War.[1] As with the Holocaust in the previous chapter, the Air War offers a thematic and comparative lens to understand the complexities of representing the Second World War in the museum, the tendencies to create master narratives and restrict experientiality in doing so, the question of how museums can simulate primary historical experiences, and the need to find ways of developing secondary experientiality between historical specificity and the anthropological and universal characteristics of aerial warfare. With regard to the question of whether a perpetrator nation (Germany in particular) can and should commemorate its own suffering in the twenty-first century, the Air War is the prime example. The Air War also symbolizes civilian suffering and collective will in many other occupied countries or territories including Poland, the Soviet Union, the Netherlands, France, Serbia, and the Philippines. Great Britain plays a particularly significant role, both as a country where civilians experienced bombing and as the primary Allied nation, together with the USA, responsible for conducting the Air War. Canada is another special case, since its strong support of the British Bomber Command made the Air War one of its prime contributions to the Allied war effort. Finally, there are complex discussions surrounding the Allied bombing of occupied territory to prepare for invasions, exemplified by the American bombing of Normandy in the lead up to D-Day. The Air War is a theme that contains ethical, cognitive, and affective dimensions that can be related to memory politics, to questions of heritage and history, and to anthropological and humanist approaches that emphasize its destruction and call for reconciliation and peace. Consequently, it is an ideal case study for understanding the representational challenges and possibilities of contemporary museum exhibitions. What memorial functions can the Air War serve in exhibitions? Furthermore, how does this specific theme relate to the key concepts of this study – restricted experientiality, primary experientiality, secondary experientiality, and transnational memory?

---

[1] For an overview of memories, narratives, and experiences of the Air War see Wilms and Rasch 2006. The chapter focuses on the representation of aerial warfare in Europe, but considers the depiction of aerial warfare and nuclear bombing in the Asia-Pacific theater of war when it advances the analysis of the exhibitions in question.

OpenAccess. © 2020 Stephan Jaeger, published by De Gruyter. This work is licensed under the Creative Commons Attribution-NonCommercial-NoDerivatives 4.0 License.
https://doi.org/10.1515/9783110664416-012

In museums where the Air War is understood conceptually, it cannot be separated from total war and the suffering of civilians in general. It is seen as part of a war that increasingly encompassed all combatants and civilians and brutalized the war's conduct so that violence without boundaries has come to dominate how the war is perceived. Although it is not one of the main institutions considered by this study, the 'Peace' Mémorial de Caen (opened in 1988), can serve as an excellent example of how a museum can establish a global memory of total war. The third part of its permanent exhibition (revised in 2009–2010)[2] is entitled "World War, Total War." The strongly image- and text-based exhibition displays a stream of escalating violence regarding German warfare in the East, an in-depth section on the Holocaust, and developments and atrocities in the war's Pacific theater.[3] The Mémorial de Caen provides a detailed contextualization of the concept of 'total war,' locating it in "the logic of industrial rationality, of technological weaponry, and the radicalisation of violence," all originating in the First World War. It carefully contextualizes the concept of total war as related to all parties and highlights – next to a depiction of Goebbels's sport stadium speech in which he declared "total war" on February 18, 1943 – how Roosevelt, Churchill, and Stalin used similar rhetoric. A text-heavy panel of more than 200 words defines the concept of total war in detail. Its first paragraph notes that operations spread to all areas of society: "Everything is subordinated to the conduct of the war and its objectives. The whole of society is involved in the conflict and private life is no longer set apart. The foe is demonised without exception, and becomes nothing more than a group of targets that have to be destroyed." Further points emphasize that total war must lead to total victory. Consequently, the conflict "becomes a fight to the death 'for survival,' an ideological war of annihilation with the same characteristics and fanaticism as civil or religious wars." Its provocative thesis that both parties followed these principles of total

---

[2] The museum regularly changes elements of its permanent exhibition.

[3] It is certainly a prime achievement that the Mémorial de Caen emphasized – as early as the late 1980s – the theme of violence beyond national master narratives and collective perspectives of the different parties involved in the war. Displaying the Holocaust and the Second World War as interwoven parts of the same exhibition was another very innovative move on the part of the French museum (see also the discussion of the exhibition in chapter 7 on Holocaust and perpetration). For an analysis of the first permanent exhibition, see Brower 1999. Brower points to the traumatic absences expressed through the museum's scenographic approach, which allows for a working-through of historical trauma: "the Mémorial's museumification points to the traumatic absences of the past by means of banishing their loss. In the Mémorial it is as if the war were yesterday; the absences of the past, absences resulting from the passing of time as well as those inflicted by the violent events of the war, are displaced by its omnipotent media" (1999, 91–92). For a more critical reading of this scenographic approach, see Thiemeyer 2010a, 248–253.

war allows the exhibition to put forth a standpoint of universal suffering. One could certainly argue that its overall presentation demonstrates that both sides conducted the principle of total war differently. However, particularly in reference to the Air War, the concept of total war challenges the perception that there is a categorical difference between the early German or Japanese bombardments of civilians and British and American bombardments solely on the basis of which nation began the bombing.[4] The narrative of the total war section ends with the Air War.

The exhibition panel "Bombing the Cities" explains how the Allies conducted their part in the 'war of annihilation':

> Strategic bombing was the 'anonymous' version of civilian annihilation. The levelling of cities under hundreds of tonnes of bombs, in complete disregard of international agreements, crossed new thresholds in the blind violence of warfare. The atom bombs dropped on Hiroshima and Nagasaki on 6 and 9 August 1945, brought such escalation to a peak.

The next three paragraphs highlight how both sides characterized their bombings as a military necessity. It is clear that the bombings of Guernica, Rotterdam, Coventry, and the Blitz occurred first, yet the museum also bluntly describes Allied aerial warfare. Without further contextualization, the panel's final paragraph challenges the visitor to speculate, from a moral perspective, about why the Allies did not bomb the railroads leading to Auschwitz. The message of the Peace Memorial is clear: bombing campaigns are part of total wars of annihilation on both sides. The images and objects on display show the impact of all bombing campaigns. Within the argument of total war, their interpretations are left fairly open; this can be seen in the description of the stand-out object at the end of the sub-section, a bronze head knocked out of place in a bombing in August 1944, pointing toward Caen's own civilian causalities: "By the end of August, having suffered countless aerial and naval bombardments and endless artillery shelling, Caen, like so many other towns in Lower Normandy, had paid a heavy price for Liberation." The text then lists the human and material losses suffered in the attacks. There is no judgment of the bombings; at the same time, the visitor does not have the opportunity to evaluate the Allies' decision to bomb French towns in preparation for the D-Day Landing and the invasion of Normandy. Consequently, the museum's depiction seemingly lacks con-

---

4 One could certainly argue that the two sides' varying treatment of prisoners of war warrant an exhibition that more clearly states that there were, nevertheless, different methods of conducting war. This becomes indirectly clear, since sub-sections such as "Propaganda" and "Mobilisation" refer to both sides, whereas the sub-section "Deportation" only refers to the German side.

textualization and therefore has the possibility to manipulate the visitor into taking a humanist-pacifist view and condemning all bombings.

The House of European History – as discussed in detail above[5] – uses a similar universalizing technique to that of the Mémorial de Caen. However, it runs the risk that total war and civilian suffering become so all-encompassing that nuances between individual suffering and those responsible could disappear. The civilian is always the victim, and while the Holocaust is clearly highlighted as a special case, the visitor ultimately learns about a universal experience of destruction and civilian cost. Civilian suffering in total war becomes a necessary narrative step toward a better Europe. The visitor does not gain any analytical skills in understanding different causes (and possibilities of agency) for why various groups experience universal suffering, nor are they given reflective tools that could lead to an analysis of permissible means of war. The flash of a nuclear bomb in Hiroshima at the end of its air-war filmic installation[6] presents the nuclear bomb as the ultimate result of total war, but does not allow for any historical contextualization or reflection.[7]

A brief look at the concept of total war and civilian suffering in the Bastogne War Museum indicates similar dangers regarding the universalization of complex historical experiences, particularly in its representation of four fictitious characters. However, the museum avoids simply recreating an empty form of reconciliation through its two-way approach of integrating the local with the global and the development of a hybrid of primary and secondary experientiality.[8] This leads to an intense use of distantiation, making it so that the visitor encounters a variety of perspectives and narrative situations. The museum does not permit circumstances of civilian suffering, such as the Air War, to become fully universalized. The depiction of the Air War is part of a global picture showing the impact of total war, particularly on civilians. However, because the visitor is always thrown back to the local scene of Bastogne, the exhibition maintains its historical specificity. Since the German bombardments of Bastogne play a major role in the museum's narrative, images referencing the Air War's global destruction can function without the exhibition specifically historicizing the reasons behind it. This is evident in the images of Hamburg, Cologne, London, and Hiroshima on display in the penultimate room of the permanent exhibition. The panel "The Human and Material Cost of the War" lists eighteen bombed cities from

---

5 See chapter 6.3.
6 See also chapter 6.3.
7 Provided the visitor actually watches the whole film and attributes the final flash to a nuclear bomb.
8 See chapter 4.3.

Warsaw to Tokyo. It notes: "There is no escaping the terrible shadow it [the Second World War] cast over the entire 20th century." In other words, the Bastogne War Museum can integrate both total war and the Air War in its representation to express a universal message, since it also offers a precise historical local theater of war in which all categories and roles are represented and differentiated. The local aspect, for example, contrasts the experiences of soldiers, civilians, perpetrators, specific victims, resisters, collaborators, and liberators.

To understand the variety of possibilities in representing Second World War as total war, it is useful to briefly compare the Imperial War Museum North, the Gdańsk Museum of the Second World War, and the Bundeswehr Military History Museum. As discussed above, the motto of the Imperial War Museum North (IWMN) is "Explore and discover how war shapes and changes people's lives."[9] On the one hand, "people" includes both combatants and civilians. On the other, it also seems to imply that war is a universal constant with no alternative. The IWMN – similarly to the Canadian War Museum[10] – interprets war as an anthropological constant of human life. Architect Daniel Libeskind explains his structure as follows: "I wanted to create a building that people will find interesting and wish to visit, yet reflects the serious nature of a war museum. I have imagined the globe broken into fragments and taken the pieces to form a building; three shards that together represent conflict on land, in the air and on the water." As discussed above, the museum's architecture programmatically structures the timeline of the Second World War (see fig. 16).[11] The main structure divides the display cabinets into fighting "on land, in the air and on the water."[12] The terms 'total war' and 'global war' overlap. Since the IWMN situates the concept of total war as part of its chronological Second World War timeline, it employs a descriptive historical touch. The exhibition neither provides an explanation of why the world moves into total war, nor does it really tackle this concept. The expression of totality lies mainly in the architecture of the exterior building and that of the interior design, in which the Big Picture Shows are performed. Here, the visitor is steered to experience war in an all-encompassing way: one cannot escape its impact on the senses.

---

9 See also chapter 5.2.
10 Although the Canadian War Museum highlights the topic of peacekeeping in its fourth gallery.
11 See below for the reduction of Libeskind's concept in the actual building in 2018 in which neither the Air Shard, nor the Water Shard were accessible to the public.
12 See Arnold-de Simine 2006, 303–305, for further criticism of equating natural forces and war branches in the Imperial War Museum North.

The Gdańsk Museum of the Second World War (MIIWŚ) is primarily concerned with total war, although it uses the term 'war of annihilation.'[13] In particular, it emphasizes the focus of total war on civilians and the historical effects of emerging violence. Although the museum occasionally highlights the perspective of the soldier, it is a prime model of the "civilianization of the collective memory of war."[14] Unlike the Bastogne War Museum in which perpetrators – mainly Germans and collaborators – are represented but hardly dominate the exhibition, the MIIWŚ represents total war through a clear framework of perpetration and suffering. After the MIIWŚ presents German crimes at the beginning of the war, the next room marks the first explicit use of 'total war' in the permanent exhibition. The beginning of 'total' warfare is symbolized through the display of six enlarged vignette-like photographs of bombed-out Polish cities on a wall, a toy-truck that survived an air-raid, as discussed in the "Prologue" above (see fig. 1), and a sequence of enlarged photographs of Germans shooting Polish prisoners during a massacre near Ciepolów on September 8, 1939. There is a presentation on a computer terminal entitled "Total War," which is then subdivided under two headers: "Terror Bombings" and "Destruction of Polish Cities, Towns and Villages." The MIIWŚ highlights aspects of terror and military experiments during the German air campaign. The exhibition debunks any German efforts to justify the reasons behind city and village bombings as primarily military in nature. Beyond their definition of the terror bombings, the tone of the slide descriptions remains factual; they mention dates and statistics concerning fatalities and the percentage of cities or villages that were destroyed. The end of the description of the bombing of Wielun reads: "Among the bombed buildings was the hospital with clearly marked Red Cross symbol on its roof. In the town there were no Polish military units." In other words, total war requires a perpetrator who leaves traditional rules of warfare behind, and at its root are totalitarian regimes that redefine these rules.[15]

Importantly and in contrast to the House of European History, all overarching reasons for violence disappear in Gdańsk. These include colonialism, the brutalization of warfare and the perception of the enemy in the First World War, and the emergence of totalitarianism in numerous societies, which poses a threat to weak democracies. Specific totalitarian powers are at fault, rather than anything inherent to the development of civilization. The atrocities featured in the introductory film on the First World War seem disconnected from the vio-

---

[13] Machcewicz 2019 (2017), 79–80.
[14] Winter 2019, 254.
[15] See also chapter 6.2.

lence unleashed by the totalitarian systems of Germany and the Soviet Union. The museum does not reflect upon whether the waging of the Air War automatically led to total warfare. For example, in the section "Peace at Every Price," Picasso's *Guernica* painting is briefly mentioned on a computer station. However, aerial warfare carried out before the German attack on Poland is not allowed to impact the narrative, resulting in Guernica and the Legion Condor, which are simply mentioned in passing. This is in contrast to the House of European History, where they become the symbol of humankind's development toward the horrors of total war.[16]

An alternative explanation for the roots of total war can be seen in the anthropological approach of the Bundeswehr Military History Museum (MHM). On the one hand, the MHM introduces the concept of total war in relation to German perpetration and the Air War, similarly to the Gdańsk Museum of the Second World War. On the other hand, the Air War, as one of the ultimate examples of total warfare, seems to be an anthropological phenomenon that expresses violence in human civilization outside of specific historical constellations. The interior section "Dresden View" on the top level of the wedge, features three air-war attacks during the Second World War: the *Luftwaffe* (German Air Force) attack on the Polish city of Wielun on the first day of the war, the Nazi air raid on Rotterdam, and the Allied firebombing of Dresden. This ensures that Dresden's trauma cannot be understood outside of the context of German responsibility for the suffering of civilians in the war at large. The introductory panel reads: "From the outset, war was waged even against civilian populations with extreme brutality, particularly in eastern Europe." The survey panel notes how the war developed into a "war of annihilation based on racial ideology." The concept of total war is introduced in relation to the Air War: "Countless families throughout Europe became homeless. In the Soviet Union alone, 1,700 towns and cities were destroyed." Although the MHM clearly highlights German perpetration, the visitor immediately perceives the exhibition's anthropological approach, which is interested in exposing the effects of aerial warfare as a new weapon on human civilization and violence: "Air forces had seen all-out use for the first time in any war. Aircraft were able to deliver their bombs to almost any location within the warring nations, thus eliminating any separation between front and hinterland. During aerial warfare under total conditions, no difference was made between military and civilian targets." Whereas visitors of the museum in Gdańsk could get the impression that without Hitler and Stalin there would have been no total war, visitors in Dresden, Brussels, or Caen clearly get the feel-

---

16 See chapter 6.3.

ing that the conditions of total war and the effects of aerial warfare would have materialized even in different historical conditions. A clear cause-and-effect model stands against an anthropological explanation of war and violence.

Representations of total war are by no means restricted to museums that highlight the universal human cost of war. The degree to which the concept of total war is important in a museum with a strong master narrative can be seen in a specific installation in the Warsaw Rising Museum.[17] On the side of the "Liberator Hall," there is a little twenty-four-seat theater that features the 3D film *Miasto Ruin* (*The City of Ruins: a 3D Flight over the Ruins of Warsaw in 1945*, installed in 2010).[18] It does not seem to be directly integrated into the chronological course of the exhibition, though the audio guide and museum map indicate that it is supposed to be located at the very end. Since the visitor must pay a surcharge on their admission in order to see it, the spectacle is immediately highlighted as a special event. The six-minute film simulates aerial views of a completely destroyed Warsaw (supported by dramatic instrumental music). It contains hardly any text besides three sentences in subsequent screenshots at the end of film in Polish and English: "On September 1, 1939 Warsaw had 1,300,000 inhabitants." "On August 1, 1944 there was [sic] 900,000." "After the fall of the Warsaw Rising no more than 1,000 people [sic] left in the ruins." After seeing the main exhibition, it is clear that the third statement is not an implicit criticism of the Uprising, but rather an emotional encapsulation of the total destruction of life caused directly by the Germans and indirectly by the lack of Soviet action. There is no room for gaps or interpretation and the visitor can leave the museum with the impression that all inhabitants of Warsaw were sacrificed. The permanent exhibition carefully and purposely erases the difference between insurgents and civilians. As often seen in total war and aerial warfare displays, the focus is on ruins, rubble, and emptiness. Human beings disappear in material loss, or, as is the case here they become mere numbers. *Miasto Ruin* is an example of how an audience can be manipulated into an emotional, universalizing understanding of the cost of total war and how the visitor's potential experientiality can be restricted.

---

17 Museums with a strong master narrative and a restricted perspective toward a victory narrative, such as the New Orleans WWII Museum and the Canadian War Museum, are considerably less likely to highlight the concept of total war. However, there is an exception when they explain the utter destruction of the war regarding the Tokyo fire bombings and the nuclear bombs on Hiroshima and Nagasaki, which will be discussed below in relation to the New Orleans WWII Museum.

18 The visitor receives 3-D glasses at the entrance. The museum also offers regular 2D screenings.

The political debates surrounding both the Enola Gay exhibition in Washington, DC in 1995[19] and the bombing campaign panel in the Canadian War Museum[20] have shown how morally and emotionally loaded the representation of the Air War can be. The latter involved strong objections from war veterans in particular, despite the fact that the exhibition was almost exclusively designed to represent the experience from the air. Similarly, the gallery "The Air War" in the New Orleans WWII Museum's exhibition "Road to Berlin" seems to completely exclude any perspective from the ground. This indicates the limitations of campaign-based perspectives that are unable to grasp the overall impacts of the Air War and total war on civilians. They reduce the Air War to a merely strategic operation. When the visitor encounters a destroyed Germany in the final room of the "Road to Berlin" exhibition, they will in all likelihood mainly associate the destruction and effects of total warfare with the war of annihilation, the Holocaust, and the horrors of warfare in general, rather than with the Air War.[21]

The Imperial War Museums in London and Manchester also avoid the challenge of representing different sides of the Air War. The Imperial War Museum London, which currently lacks a full Second World War exhibition, certainly displays objects, footage, and voices that relate to perspectives from the air and from the ground. However, the "Turning Points 1934–1945" exhibition is so anti-narrative and impressionistic that its fourth section, "Bombers," does not have to provide much interpretation of the Air War. The visitor sees film footage of an air raid against Hamburg, reads quotations from survivors of Hamburg's firestorm in July 1943, sees technical objects from bombers and German air defenses, and hears voices from the cockpit. The quotations by curator Roger Tolson, historian Nigel Steel, and curator Roger Mann[22] emphasize the situation of British air-crews, yet they also reflect upon a model of "contested space," which

---

19 The exhibition's full title was *The Crossroads: The End of World War II, the Atomic Bomb and the Cold War*. See also Crane 1997, as discussed in chapter 4.2 above. See also Kohn 1996; Linenthal 1996; Engelhardt 1996, 240–249; Gieryn 1998. Vera L. Zolberg summarizes the multiple perspectives (curators, official Japanese version, official US American version) to demonstrate how the exhibition functions as a site of remembrance and carrier to express contested and ambiguous meanings of nationhood (1996).
20 See chapter 3.1.
21 The New Orleans WWII Museum focuses more on the effects of bombings when it represents the Tokyo fire bombings and the nuclear bombs. Here, it needs the argument that area bombings of civilians were strategically necessary (see below). The Air War in Europe is presented as surprisingly clean.
22 The Imperial War Museum London uses this innovative technique of providing meta-commentaries on its object arrangement throughout the "Turning Points 1934–1945" section. It replaces any narrative arrangements of the clusters.

was precarious for everybody both in the air and on the ground. This little section exemplifies how an Allied museum could represent the Air War and create the potential for experientiality as a structurally 'contested' space for the visitor, without answering questions of morality. This space in the museum simulates the historically contested space of the Air War.

In British museums in general, the tendency to focus strongly on British collective wartime experiences and the Blitz reverses the North-American representation. The focus is on a fairly sanitized depiction of aerial warfare; the British perspective from the ground during the Blitz remains dominant. An affirmative or critical discussion of the Bomber Command campaigns is thus avoided, corresponding with the British silence on the morality of the bombing campaign following the war.[23] The Imperial War Museum North states in its survey text on the Air War, entitled "Air Attack," that: "Losses among Royal Air Force and United States Army Air Force bomber crews were very heavy. It is debatable whether the bombing of Germany's cities had a decisive impact on its economy or on the morale of the German people." The text highlights that both sides had high costs and the visitor learns about the existence of the debate; however, the museum does not provide further material. Thus, the visitor can return to safer ground when learning about the perception of the aerial warfare during the Blitz in 1940–1941, particularly in the Big Picture Show "War at Home" and in a Time Stack. Only one German city, Cologne, and no German individuals involved in the Air War are mentioned by name.

Considerably more interpretation is given to the Air War in the Gdańsk Museum of the Second World War (MIIWŚ). After establishing the roles of the German and Soviet perpetrators in September 1939, the museum dedicates two smaller rooms of the section "Merciless War" to the Air War. First, the museum grabs the visitor's attention in a small corridor with the simulation of a scene in a British air raid shelter that depicts the universal fear of civilians in the Air War: "Living with bombardments: the threat of bombardments changed the lives of millions." Small display-case 'holes' in front of the shelter exhibit items related to the air defense measures from Britain, Germany, and France. The visitor then enters a small rectangular room with a high ceiling through a steel door. Aside from some additional random artifacts, including bombs, the room is dominated by the images and sounds playing on one large wall high above the heads of the visitors, showing footage and photographs of the Air War. It is immediately clear

---

[23] See e.g. Neillands 2001. For an analysis of recent British memory of Bomber Command in the context of the Royal Air Force Bomber Command Memorial in Green Park, London and the emotional pleasure of remembering the British effort in the bombing campaign today, see Williams 2015.

that the museum has switched from the universal framing of the previous room back to historical analysis, highlighting cause-and-effect. First, the visitor sees the text: "The military actions of the German Third Reich and the Empire of Japan, rejecting all legal and moral constraints, brutalised the actions of all sides in the war." Then, it displays photographs from the bombings in Guernica (04/1937) and Nanjing (12/1937), marking them as "harbingers of terror bombing." This is done before the museum adds that the third totalitarian perpetrator country, the Soviet Union, conducted similar raids in the Winter War against Finland. Thus, the three main totalitarian perpetrator states are established as the first to utilize aerial warfare against civilians. Then the film continues with Warsaw (09/1939), drawing connections with the section on the Polish campaign where the viewer sees footage and images from key air raids against civilians during the war conducted by both sides. Subtitles identify the historical places corresponding to the images shown: Warsaw (09/1939), Helsinki (11/1939), Rotterdam (05/1940), Belgrade (04/1941), Manila (12/1941), Stalingrad (08/1942), London & Coventry (1940–1944), Cologne (1942–1945), Hamburg (07/1943), Dresden (02/1945), and Tokyo (03/1945). The MIIWŚ clearly divides the events; first come German, Japanese, and Soviet air raids, then Allied ones.

Although the film displays a mixture of pictures from the air and ground for all of the air raids it shows – skewed slightly toward the material destruction and human suffering on the ground – the MIIWŚ manipulates the viewer into accepting its narrative frame. This is obvious from the film's textual frame, which moves from the brutalization of the war through the early air raids by the totalitarian states to a highly didactic final screen, which reads: "The bombing of cities became an element of the 'total war' proclaimed and implemented by the Germans. But soon they were themselves to learn the destructive power of aerial bombardment when the Allies came to the conclusion that the war could be won thanks to massive bombings of German cities." Unlike virtually every museum in the Western world, nowhere in the MIIWŚ is there any indication of the debate about whether and how the Air War shortened the war and whether it was a necessary means to victory. Only after this does the exhibition return to a final universal message: "The greatest victims of these air raids were the civilians who actually suffered the greatest losses." Whereas the museum didactically indicates who is responsible for total war with regards to the Air War, it is even more interesting that the chosen images support the idea that the totalitarian regimes caused unlimited destruction in contrast to the Allied forces, who are depicted as reacting in self-defense or justified revenge.

Nuances disappear as the visitor is not given space to interpret history outside the given narrative and didactic framework.[24] The final campaign – attributed to the perpetrating totalitarian states – is London and Coventry (1940–1944). The viewer sees images of Churchill in the destroyed cathedral in Coventry, a sober-looking girl with an English flag (presumably indicating the morale of the British people), several images and footage of V1 and V2 bombs, and collective images of adults and children dealing with the impact of the air raids. The images then shift to British wartime production, displaying endless rows of bombs and line-ups of bomber planes. The viewer sees a Polish member of the RAF writing the message "From the people of Warsaw to Berlin" on a bomb, before looking into the faces of two confident Polish RAF officers. In other words, the viewer follows images displaying the wartime spirit of avenging Warsaw and other Polish cities. The skillful staging of images and text makes it almost impossible for viewers to distance themselves from the visualized narrative in order to question its ideology. The first bombed German city represented in the film is Cologne, with its cathedral standing in the midst of ruins. The viewer then sees a portrait of Hitler in flames, before a German woman in front of the cathedral looks sidelong into the camera, as if ashamed. Destruction is bound to Hitler and the German people who followed him; the museum thus indicates that this suffering is different from that caused by German and Japanese bombing campaigns. Similarly, the famous and iconic image by Richard Peter, taken in September 1945, transfers to a double screen; this image depicts the statue of a hunched figure on the tower of the City Hall, implying a look of suffering and pain, pointing a hand downwards to a devastated Dresden after the firebombing. The second image shows a close-up shot of a skull on a Nazi uniform with the Swastika clearly visible. Suffering and perpetration cannot be separated: the historical master narrative will always dominate any universal form of suffering in the MIIWŚ. The images' composition makes it impossible for the viewer to simply empathize with the suffering of German or Japanese civilians.

The depiction of aerial warfare in Gdańsk is a good example of how the exhibition surpasses a documentary factual presentation and steers the visitor to a specific interpretation of historical events. Historical context trumps universality, as is also clear in the other rooms that display information on the Air War and the strategic bomber campaign. This holds especially true for the computer stations in the sections "The Terror of War" and "Allies on the Attack," which rep-

---

[24] The additional computer station with slideshows on German, Japanese, Soviet, and Allied bombings provides supplementary factual depth to some of the bombings mentioned in the film; its tone and didactic message are the same.

resent the events of the first and the second half of the war with simulated digital maps and encyclopedic captions. On the one hand, this allows for a clearly positive and heroic representation of Polish efforts in the Battle of Britain and the Allied bombing campaign. On the other, it demonstrates that there can only be one correct interpretation of history.[25] Once the frame of totalitarian perpetration has been accepted, there is no room for possible perpetration or wrongdoing if one is on the right side of history. In other words, unlike in the museum's depiction of themes such as collaboration, resistance, and flight and expulsion, the depiction of the Air War in the MIIWŚ does not maintain its transnational approach. In this way, the balance between a historically specific framework and comparative openness is lost here, restricting the experientiality for the visitor more than in other sections of the museum.

Architectural space and the Air War connect in numerous ways in the museums under study. The two buildings – the Imperial War Museum North and the Bundeswehr Military History Museum – partially or fully designed by Daniel Libeskind are particularly interesting in this regard. In the Imperial War Museum North, one of the three shards representing the fragmented world, the Air Shard, leads the visitor into a semi-open tower. This conflates interior and exterior space, as the visitor steps onto a viewing platform that allows them a partial view of the gentrified Salford quays, the location of Manchester's shipping canal and docks during the war. The area also hosts Manchester United's Old Trafford soccer stadium, which was damaged during the German air raids in December 1940. The architecture allows a fairly harmless insight into the museum's surroundings and their role in the Second World War. The visitor also sees the city's transformation into today's modern Manchester. In May 2018, the Air Shard was completely closed off to the public and had disappeared from the museum maps.[26] The visitor can easily get lost in the spectacle of projections and

---

25 After noting the number of civilian dead in Germany in "Allies on the Attack," the museum states: "The Allies were responding to the ruthless methods of air warfare initiated by Nazi Germany. // The destruction of factories and rail lines, and the need to build shelters, anti-aircraft artillery and a radar network presented a significant burden for the German war industry. This helped the Allies to win the war." The MIIWŚ fully buys into the rhetoric of total warfare; no distantiation is possible. Consequently, the firebombing of Tokyo does not even have to be justified in the section's computer simulated maps. Laconically, the text states: "Heavy bombers based on the Marianas began area bombing of Japanese cities. Hundreds of thousands of civilians died." In similarly simplified fashion, the MIIWŚ subscribes to the use of nuclear bombs in its simulated map station. Its purpose – unquestioned – is "to force Japan to surrender and to demonstrate the power of the United States."
26 This was due to the fact that the elevator was non-operational, which created accessibility restrictions. Most of the Water Shard was not accessible to the public either. The museum

corners, tilted floors and walls – all of which creates the overwhelming notion of being lost in various sensations during wartime.[27] This can relate to the Air War, yet it is mainly a general metaphor for how war attacks the human senses.

In contrast to the Imperial War Museum North, Libeskind's architecture in the Bundeswehr Military History Museum is connected much more explicitly to the Air War. The wedge, a massive, five-story 14,500-ton wedge of glass, concrete, and steel, cuts into the former arsenal's classical order.[28] Architecturally, Libeskind's wedge symbolizes the traumatic effects of war in general and the Air War in particular. The tip of the wedge points toward the triangulation of the area where the firebombing of Dresden first began, "creating a space for reflection." Visitors can enter the tip of the wedge on the fourth floor, exiting the interior of the museum through a glass door, which opens up to view of Dresden's reconstructed cityscape, obstructed through tilted slabs. This obstruction reminds the visitor of traumatic destruction and asserts that the healing and reconciliation process of trauma can never be complete.

Inside the wedge, the Bundeswehr Military History Museum (MHM), similar to Libeskind's extension to the Jewish Museum Berlin, creates voids that complicate the viewing of particularly large objects. This will be seen in the subsequent analysis of documentary techniques of the V2 rocket in the Imperial War Museum in London (IWML) and in the MHM. The IWML re-opened its reconstructed atrium in July 2014. Whereas the previous atrium was considerably smaller and clattered with large objects, the new atrium only displays seven exhibits of one or two objects in its "Witnesses of War" exhibition. All exhibits are supplemented by one computer station with a slideshow on loop that provide further data on the objects. They consist of historical photographs, brief captions, some footage, and graphics.[29] One exhibit is a cluster of a V2 rocket and a V1 flying bomb (see fig. 28). The slideshow, entitled "German Long-range Weapons," emphasizes British targets, provides technical data and figures on victims of V weapons based in London and particularly Lambeth. One slide reads: "During the Second World War, the museum was damaged 41 times, including from these V1 and V2 attacks." The visitor sees a sketch of the museum building

---

café had been moved to the ground floor and the upper level of the Water Shard space was used for private functions. Consequently, the Libeskind architectural concept of Earth, Air, and Water shards became limited to the Earth Shard and the permanent exhibition where the Big Picture Shows take place.

27 See chapter 5.2.

28 https://libeskind.com/work/military-history-museum/ accessed 13 October 2019.

29 Since there is only one small display screen per exhibit, the majority of visitors will only see the large objects but not the slideshow, or at least only a random fraction of its slides.

Fig. 28 Atrium and "Witnesses of War" exhibition. In center, installation of V2 rocket and V1 flying bomb. Imperial War Museum, London (Photo and © Imperial War Museum).

with a little red square and the caption "YOU ARE HERE." The map of the attacks then extends to the museum's surroundings in Lambeth, followed by photographs of the damage. In the second half of the slide show, the visitor sees images of the appalling conditions in the concentration camp Mittelbau-Dora where the V2 was partially produced. The visitor is pointed to *The Holocaust Exhibition* on the fourth floor, where a uniform worn by Jan Imich, a survivor of the V-weapon production, is displayed. The museum then juxtaposes Wernher von Braun's post-war work on rocket development in America (influential, among other things, for the moon landing) with his knowledge of the conditions of Mittelbau-Dora. It notes: "A generation after his V2s had terrorised cities across Europe, von Braun became a national hero in the United States."[30] The slide show closes with the words "His legacy, and those of the rockets he designed, is deeply ambiguous."

Whereas the visitor can admire the shape of the V2 in the atrium in London, Libeskind's architecture prevents this in Dresden. Here, its shell is presented in

---

[30] The New Orleans WWII Museum does not mention the role of von Braun at all, avoiding the discussion of his ambiguous legacy.

such a way that it can never be fully seen as a complete object.³¹ The V2 spans the three floors from "Technology and the Military" at the bottom up to "Animals and the Military" and "War and Play." It is arranged in a symbolic spatial cluster. Next to it, in the "Technology and the Military" section, the viewer learns about the history and working conditions in Mittelbau-Dora at a computer station.³² For example, an improvised ear protection plug focalizes the agony of the forced laborers working in the mine-shafts, but also their will to live despite their atrocious circumstances. Next to the V2, hanging high in the air, the visitor sees the manned space capsule Sojus 29, used by the East-German astronaut Sigmund Jähn and a Soviet crew to return to earth in 1978. The proximity of these two objects initially seems to highlight the contrast between their military use (V2) and civilian research (Sojus 29). However, they have a far more complex relationship, as indicated by the last sentence of the survey panel: "East German leaders celebrated the first German space flight as proof of the superiority of socialism over capitalism." In other words, the simplistic contrast of the military and civilian usage of rockets is immediately differentiated by their political and propagandistic usage by both sides in the Cold War. This technique is typical of how the MHM avoids black-and-white depictions in its exhibition.

Whereas the IWML emphasizes that the military development of the V2 also allowed for civil advancement, the MHM stresses that the civil trajectory of rockets is mirrored by further military intensification through its selection of objects and survey texts: it links the post-war development of intercontinental rockets to that of nuclear war heads. The visitor is always challenged to consider all sides of technological development. Behind the shadow of the V2 and underneath the Sojus 29, the MHM projects an art film by Klaus vom Bruch und Manuela Günther showing passages from Galileo's monologue in Bertolt Brecht's third version of *Life of Galileo* (*Leben des Galilei*). The play was created in 1955 in the wake of the Manhattan project, highlighting the risks of acquiring new knowledge: "Our knowledge has become a frightening burden" (see fig. 29). Finally, the V2 rocket creates a constellation with a dollhouse owned by Faith Eaton of Clifton Gardens No 16, London, which is part of the "War and Play" section two floors above. Faith's dolls have gas masks and the house features an Anderson shelter in its garden. It clearly symbolizes the effect of aerial warfare on civilian life and

---

31 To take a picture of the whole V2, one must basically lie flat on the floor and take the photograph vertically upwards.
32 As always in the MHM, the detailed encyclopedic media station is only available in German. It describes the technology and history of the V2 using text, images, and footage, including facts about the production sites and working conditions as well as about its impact.

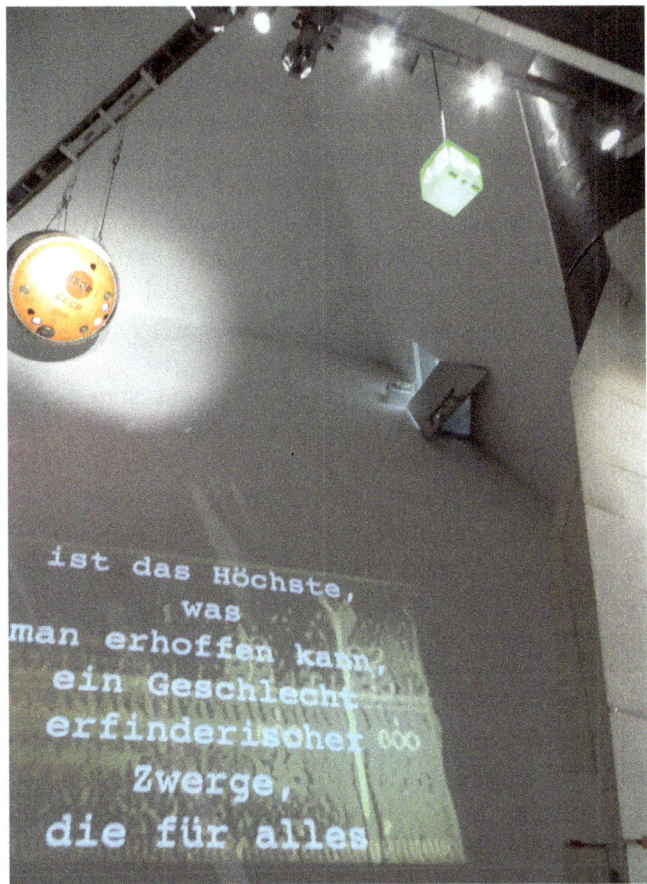

Fig. 29 Cluster of V2 rocket, dollhouse, Sojus 29, and art installation *Galilei's Monologue*. Permanent Exhibition. Militärhistorisches Museum der Bundeswehr (Bundeswehr Military History Museum), Dresden (Photo: Author, 2014, courtesy of Militärhistorisches Museum der Bundeswehr).

the everyday reality of living under the threat of the V2 – which would certainly not be withstood by an Anderson shelter.

Whereas the IWML merely states that von Braun's story is deeply ambiguous, the MHM performs this ambiguity. The visitor is forced to decide what to do with the Sojus capsule, the dollhouse, and the information on Mittelbau-Dora in regard to the art installation. The IWML's more documentary approach also highlights the ambiguity and different aspects of V2 production, but its representation remains strictly war-related. The visitor has two possibilities to empathize with the historical situation. First, the installation's slide show emphasizes the fact that the visitor is on the actual ground where V1 bombs and V2 rockets hit; it involves the visitor directly by reflecting upon the close proximity between the rocket's destruction and their current position. Second, the display of the full objects and technical data in the slide show allows visitors to simply admire technological progress while the aura of the objects remains intact. The relatively simple ambiguity with which von Braun's role is represented comes close to implying that he was merely a victim of circumstance. In contrast, the MHM forecloses the possibility of any aura of the object of the V2 through its broken spatial set-up. The spatial ensemble in the MHM makes the V2 part of the complex meanings behind an unstoppable rocket within and beyond war for civilians, forced laborers, scientists, and humankind as such.

Throughout the museum, the MHM uses its networking approach to encourage visitors to interpret data for themselves. At first glance, however, its Second World War chronology appears to be similar to the clustering of diverse topics seen in the "Turning Point" exhibition in the IWML. The MHM's cabinets "The Battle of Britain" and "Total War – Bombing War" create spatial ensembles of objects and images that incorporate perspectives from all sides. However, the representation goes beyond the explanation and contextualization of objects. Both artworks and tensions between objects and clusters, challenge the visitor to interpret the spatial arrangement of objects beyond their informative value and illustrative function as types of historical people, artifacts, and events. What does one do, for example, with Paul Eickmeier's pencil sketch *Explosions [Bang]*[33] showing about ten – presumably female – people sitting hunched on boxes? The visitor is forced into an aesthetic reaction; due to the fact that in other parts of the museum, the MHM highlights German perpetration in the Air War, the visitor can almost accept the pictures as a gruesome anthropological fact for any human experiencing aerial warfare helplessly from the ground.

Even more ambiguous is the museum's use of tabular biographies.[34] Before the display case on the Battle of Britain, the MHM presents two biographies: the first is that of Johannes Steinhoff, a fighter pilot with 176 aerial victories in the Second World War. He was involved in efforts to remove Göring from office for incompetence, suffered severe burns late in the war, and made a career in the Bundeswehr and NATO after the war. Following his retirement he became a member of the Supervisory Board of the Dornier Company. Next to this biography is the much briefer one of British bomber pilot Michael Giles Homer. Homer was transferred from Bomber Command to Fighter Command in the Bat-

---

33 *Einschläge [Es bumst!]*.
34 See also also chapter 7.

Fig. 30 Cabinets "Battle of Britain" and "Luftwaffe Personnel." Permanent exhibition. Militärhistorisches Museum der Bundeswehr (Bundeswehr Military History Museum), Dresden (Photo: Author, 2013, courtesy of Militärhistorisches Museum der Bundeswehr).

tle of Britain and fell in September 1940. The visitor can ask endless questions about either biography. What would have happened if Homer had been alive when the Royal Air Force started its strategic bombing campaign? Was Steinhoff merely a fighter pilot doing his job? Did they want to remove Göring purely for military or also for ideological reasons? What did Steinhoff do when he was a fighter pilot in Russia? How did he support the bombing of civilians? The contrast between the two biographical tables intensifies the possible questions. Rather than answering some of these questions, the MHM employs a representational technique that, through gaps such as these, forces the visitor to reflect upon possibilities and open questions.

Similarly, the visitor encounters two clusters of different biographies in the display case on the Luftwaffe staff in the Second World War (see fig. 30). On the one hand, there are photographs and documents telling the story of Lieutenant pilot Klaus-Dieter Bambauer who died while flying over the Atlantic shortly after becoming a pilot in September 1943. Bambauer seems to serve as an example of a German pilot who began to enthusiastically engage with the Nazi military during his time in the Hitler Youth. The MHM contrasts this presumably every-day story to that of Fritz Lübbert, half-Jewish and a flying ace in the 'Red Baron's (Manfred von Richthofen's) fighter wing in the First World War. After the war, Lübbert attended veteran's meetings together with Reichsmarshall Hermann Göring. When threatened with deportation by the Gestapo in 1944, Lübbert used his connections to Göring's aide-de-camp Karl Bodenschatz to avoid them, but to survive he had to accept sterilization. "After the war, Lübbert helped some Air Force officers who had helped him." The MHM displays a cluster of objects that includes a photo of Bodenschatz, Lübbert and Göring at a veterans' meeting in 1936 and the receipt for Lübbert's sterilization surgery in 1944. It presents Gestapo documents summoning Lübbert and a letter from Lübbert asking Bodenschatz for help. Bambauer's and Lübbert's stories are connected through the display of a coat that was worn by Göring. On the one hand, these stories humanize Air War participants without reducing the criminal nature of the Air War, symbolized by Göring's coat. They indicate the enthusiasm for the Nazi ideology, but also display the complexities of many biographies. Was Lübbert a hero, a profiteer, or a victim? What about his continued relationship with Nazis after the war? The visitor is steered toward a story without a moralistic message. With the exception of Göring, the visitor will in all likelihood hesitate to make moral judgments pertaining to any of the men whose stories are represented.

One of the crucial questions regarding representations of the Air War in the museum is how graphic or clean their images and stories should be (see also Watson 2017). Do images of corpses limit the intellectual capacities of the visitor through shock? Can and should they produce empathy with the victims? Would that allow for an understanding of the historical context surrounding the cause of the Air War? The analysis undertaken in this study demonstrates a clear trend: when museums use photographs to highlight the damage caused by the Air War, they almost exclusively show *material* destruction. This trend seems to be independent of the general approach of the museums under study. Whereas contemporary Second World War museums clearly disagree about how to deal with images of victims taken by perpetrators,[35] human suffering caused by the Air War is hardly represented.[36] When it is, it is clearly instrumentalized. There are two instances of this in the Bundeswehr Military History Museum (MHM). First, on the top floor, the visitor encounters an image depicting the cremation of bodies on Dresden's Altmarkt in the days after the bombing, expressing the ultimate horror

---

[35] See also the discussion in chapter 7.
[36] Sheila Watson notes "that photographs of the dead in the bombing wars that marked the Second World War are rare in museums in Britain and Germany" (2017, 76). However, she does not discuss the Bundeswehr Military History Museum.

of a firestorm. In the bombing war cabinet in the chronological exhibition, the MHM displays three small photographs of piles of corpses from people who suffocated from lack of oxygen and inhalation of toxic gases and fumes in Dresden's basements. The photographs seem to have been chosen not for their shock value, but rather to document an important fact of the firestorm.

Similarly, as seen in the discussions and public debate surrounding its "Air War" section[37] the Canadian War Museum shows one image of civilian corpses in its display of the strategic bombing campaign. It is entitled "Civilian Casualties" and its subtext reads: "Images like this one fuelled the post-war debate over the bomber offensive." The museum needs the image to make the visitor understand the reasons for the debate in the first place. In museums where there is no mention of debate, air-war victims can only be displayed if they belong to the 'right' victim group, as is the case in the Gdańsk Museum of the Second World War's exhibition (MIIWŚ). It represents some images of air-war victims, although exclusively in the context of German attacks on Polish cities or the Allied bombing of Japanese cities. Whereas the MHM displays photographs as originals or as reproductions in their original size, the MIIWŚ uses enlarged posters to emotionalize the visitor. Only once the historical message of the responsibility of the totalitarian powers for all 'terror' in the Air War has been established can a more universal approach to victimhood emerge. However, it remains the case that most museums do not display photographs of war victims. This reduces both the possible shock effects and the issue of comparing different types of victims and victimhood. It also runs the risk of sanitizing the Air War.

It is useful to take another look at the New Orleans WWII Museum in order to understand the subtle balance between producing emotional shock and fitting the bombing campaigns into a master narrative. As seen in the analysis of the multimedia show *Beyond All Boundaries* above,[38] the New Orleans WWII Museum utilizes a clear master narrative. The museum clearly marks the escalation in the bombing of Japanese mainland cities as strategic and inevitable, focusing on the firebombing of Tokyo and the two nuclear bombs dropped on Hiroshima and Nagasaki. In particular, this can be seen in the final room of the "Road to Tokyo" exhibition, entitled "Downfall: Endgame against Japan." Here, a timeline presents the nuclear bombing as the only possible strategy to end the war and save American lives, following the textbook approach in post-war American cultural memory (see e.g. Leahy and Dechow 2006; Engelhardt 1996). As we have

---

37 See chapter 3.1.
38 See chapter 4.2.

seen elsewhere in the museum, there is no room to discuss whether other strategies could have been used to end the war.[39] Additionally, the New Orleans WWII Museum emotionally prepares the visitor throughout the "Road to Tokyo" exhibition for the impossibility of a Japanese surrender by highlighting the fact that all Japanese soldiers and civilians were willing to fight to their absolute death. The timeline in the last room starts off with an entry for March 1945 with the factual description that: "The Japanese government declares all males aged 15 to 60 and all females aged 17 to 40 combatants, ending the effective distinction between combatants and noncombatants." The exhibition thus creates a subtext for total war: the Allied forces are no longer risking the death of 'civilians,' thereby retroactively justifying the bombing campaign. Following this, the New Orleans WWII Museum notes that in June 1945, Japanese leaders were resolved to continue the war despite their knowledge that "this will result in mass starvation of the Japanese people in 1946." Again, this declaration is represented as an undisputed fact and supports the chain of arguments that the atomic bombs were the sole and justified means of ending the war.

Later, in the entry for August 9 following the bombing of Nagasaki, the caption notes "The bombing and Soviet invasion compel Japanese leaders to consider terms of surrender for the first time." Interestingly, the visitor is led to believe that the Soviet Union declared war on Japan and entered Japanese-occupied Manchuria only *after* the drop of the second atomic bomb, since the entry is situated underneath the Nagasaki entry. Afterwards, apparently as a consequence of the second nuclear bomb, the Japanese offer a conditional surrender – a strategy that is only abandoned on August 15, 1945. The timeline and its factualized style exemplifies the New Orleans WWII Museum's technique of creating a one-sided narrative that places all responsibility for destruction on the Japanese leaders. This is justified by the museum's statement that the Americans dropped leaflets over Japanese cities to warn them of their relentless strategic bombing campaigns. The visitor does not receive the opportunity to consider different military or diplomatic options. For example, there is no discussion of whether unconditional surrender was really needed to end the war.[40] The viewer receives the historically problematic impression that the Japanese never considered how they could end the war before both nuclear bombs were dropped. There is no room for reflection on whether the second nuclear bomb, dropped three days after the first, was really necessary. Therefore, the room "Downfall" becomes a

---

39 It is obviously not possible in this book to resolve historical debates; rather, the question is whether ambiguities in historical interpretation are taken up by museums or whether museums close gaps to represent a streamlined narrative.
40 For a divergent view see e.g. Hasegawa 2007.

prime example of how a museum can use techniques of factualization to reinforce existing master narratives.

The room "Downfall" also creates a visual effect. The room is dominated by one large screen placed over the exit and six large posters. Four enlarged aerial photographs, hanging on the upper halves of the wall above the display cases and exhibits, show the detonation of bombs and the destruction of the Japanese cities Osaka, Tokyo, Omura, and Toyama. Two wall-size pictures depict the total destruction of Hiroshima and Nagasaki. Only the film over the exit features people; accompanied by monotonous instrumental music, it displays pictures of the loading and dropping of both atomic bombs. After depicting the rubble of a destroyed city, the visitor sees dead bodies and distressed people affected by the atomic blasts for the first time. Despite its human element, the film could still be read as a reinforcement of the master narrative, since its first depictions of death and pain are followed by the second atomic bomb. This might suggest – in the wake of everything the visitor has read before – that the Japanese did not act to prevent a second wave of such pain. This results in a very strong emotional message. The museum shifts from its military narrative (representing the collective perspective of the American soldier during the campaign) to a humanist perspective. It is painful to look directly into the faces and eyes of these tormented people.

One scene in the film taken after the dropping of the second atomic bomb depicts a woman walking away from the viewer into a total wasteland of tree stumps and ruins. This is strongly reminiscent of an image from the original final film in the Gdańsk Museum of the Second World War, in which a cyclist moves through the ruins of today's Syria – except in this case he is moving toward the viewer. Even if the narratives of these two museums differ greatly, here in the moment of utter destruction wrought through war, the humanist emotional message is identical in New Orleans and Gdańsk. Ironically, the new film in the MIIWŚ indicates how easily a divisive, nationalist, and militaristic ideology can replace humanist messages like these.[41] The film in the New Orleans WWII Museum ends with a written quotation from US Secretary of War Henry L. Stimson: "War has grown steadily more barbarous, more destructive, more debased. / Now with the release of atomic energy, man's ability to destroy himself is nearly complete." On the surface, the museum displays a clear tension between humanism and wartime pragmatism, which is made evident by the juxtaposition of Stimson's quotation with one by General Douglas MacArthur. Macarthur's quotation comes from an address delivered at the Japanese Surrender Ceremony,

---

41 See chapter 6.2.

which took place on the USS Missouri on September 2, 1945 and is displayed on the right hand wall, next to the film screen. Here, MacArthur expresses his "earnest hope" that the "blood and carnage of the past" leads "to a better world," one "dedicated to the dignity of man and the fulfillment of his most cherished wish for freedom, tolerance, and justice." In analyzing this display, it becomes clear that the integration of the firebombing's necessity and of the use of atomic bombs into the exhibition through the use of factualizing rhetoric allows the museum to transition into a more humanitarian argument. Although on the surface, Stimson and MacArthur's quotations seem to clash, upon closer analysis they in fact supplement each other. The destruction wrought by atomic bombs is presented as necessary for saving the world; only after their detonation can humankind come to its senses and seek "freedom, tolerance and justice." As always, contentious issues represented by the museum can be integrated into the American master narrative. The oral witnesses at the computer station in the "Downfall" room speak out against the mass killings of civilians and report on their scruples about using nuclear bombs, yet they all ultimately accept that this sacrifice was needed for the 'good' of the world.

A brief comparison to other representations of Hiroshima and Nagasaki in non-American museums analyzed in this study indicates two trends. First, there is a trend toward brief factual representation that follows the American master narrative that the surrender was a direct result of the bombing – sometimes as facts, sometimes as a causal connection – as exemplified in the Canadian War Museum, the Imperial War Museum North, and the Bastogne War Museum. The second trend is in museums such as the House of European History and the Bundeswehr Military History Museum, which highlight the human element of universal destruction. The Gdańsk Museum of the Second World War also highlights the effects of the bombs on civilians, though it foregoes the discussion of whether the atomic bombs were necessary – the bombings are simply represented as an American decision. Overall, no exhibition analyzed in this book allows the visitor to understand the historical context surrounding the decision to use nuclear bombs. No American or Japanese primary sources are displayed.

An analysis of the representation of the Air War in museum exhibitions consistently leads back to the question of whether the Air War is presented as a (necessary) narrative sequence, or whether the visitor can react to gaps and is asked – explicitly or implicitly – to interpret material and constellations. Here we can see the tension between master narrative-dominated exhibitions and exhibitions that produce different forms of secondary experientiality. Additionally, modern museum makers around the world avoid producing primary experiences of the Air War. Experiential basement or air raid shelter installations appear to be a technique of the past.⁴² The Air War in all its variations seems to be too contentious for museums to simulate actual historical experience. Consequently, the Air War can either be fitted into a closed national narrative or a universal master narrative, or it can be integrated into displays containing more open constellations.⁴³

Finally, the question remains: what happens if a museum explicitly asks the visitor to make a choice? The Bastogne War Museum allows for such a situation at the end of each of its computer slideshows. In the section directly preceding the Battle of the Bulge, the museum places the visitor in the following scenario in the slideshow "The Boffin's War": "Should Hiroshima and Nagasaki have been bombed?" The visitor has four options to choose from: "A: YES, to end the war." "B: YES, to save the lives of US servicemen on the Pacific front." "C: NO, nuclear warfare is inhumane as it destroys civilian populations." And finally, "D: NO, science should serve the advancement of humankind, not its destruction." As is always the case in these scenarios, the visitor must live with over-simplification. The visitor only receives a relatively small amount of data before making their decision.⁴⁴ More important is the fact that the Bastogne War Museum makes the visitor aware of the contradictory reasons for the bombing and the possibility that there is possibly not just one correct or true answer; thus, the quizzes fulfill an important meta-function that leads to a reflection on historical truth.

The New Orleans WWII Museum's Boeing Pavilion contains an exhibit entitled "What would you do?" From sixteen computer terminals on the ground floor, the viewer follows five scenarios on one of two large wall screens.⁴⁵ All five scenarios develop a historical case through a montage of images and a narrator's voice that forces the visitor to make an either-or decision while taking on a specific role. All scenarios are connected to real historical cases and a specific commander, journalist, or volunteer who had to make that decision in real life. The scenarios ask, for example, whether an American journalist should endanger his life by staying in Germany to report on an upcoming Nazi Rally in Nuremburg in 1933 or if an African-American man should try to enlist for a second

---

42 See also chapter 2.2.

43 This connects to the Holocaust representations discussed in the previous chapter, which clearly disallow primary experientiality, though different layers of empathy and emotion are possible.

44 A snapshot on June 4, 2018 noted that out of 10,394 visitors 44% chose answer A, 18% B, 25% C, and 13% D.

45 Each scenario is between three and three-and-a-half minutes. However, since the exhibition screens switch between the shows "Arsenal of Democracy," "My Gal Sal," and "What would you do?" with no clear timetable provided, whether the visitor might be around when the quizzes start is left to chance. Since there are no further instructions on the quizzes, besides the actual films, it is more than likely that most visitors will miss the installation.

time after his voluntary enlistment was denied on the basis of racial discrimination. The decision relevant to aerial warfare relates to the preparations behind D-Day. The visitor is asked to empathize with the position of President Franklin D. Roosevelt and is presented with two options. Option A. is to bomb urban rail yards; option B. is to bomb only roads and rail bridges. The bombing of urban rail yards would "knock out Hitler's ability to rush reinforcements into Normandy." However, the visitor is also offered another possibility: "would you call off the bombing of urban rail yards and bomb only roads and rail bridges, saving the lives of civilians," "the very people you want to liberate?" The visitor also hears that Supreme Allied Commander General Dwight D. Eisenhower was in favor of the bombings, whereas British Prime Minister Winston Churchill was against them. After the vote, visitors see the results from the current session and the past year, before they are informed: "Here's what really happened." The bombing campaign against urban railroads was carried out as planned; the invasion took priority; and at least 12,000 civilians were killed in France and Belgium. "But [it] was an effective military strategy. Allied bombers inflicted devastating damage to the rail system, preventing Germany from moving massive reinforcements into Normandy. The Allies took heavy casualties on the beaches, but the invasion [...] turned the tide of the war in Western Europe." The narrator highlights that despite the bombing the Allies were welcomed and celebrated "as liberating heroes by the French and Belgian populations." The narrator closes with how the American President had to weigh "military objectives against deadly consequences for civilians." The difference between this set-up and the Bastogne War Museum is clear. In the New Orleans WWII Museum, the challenge is to find the didactically correct answer. There is no real open historical debate. From the exhibition's perspective, what happened historically was the correct military decision in each of the cases it presents. The visitor learns that there was a conflict but certainly not that there could still be different interpretations of its circumstances and outcomes. An 'either-or' quiz manipulates the visitor into believing that there is a single right answer. Therefore, aerial warfare seems less contentious, as the truly omniscient narrator always has the correct answer.[46]

In conclusion, representations of the Air War tend toward either a factual and documentary approach or highlight the chronological development of the war with a focus on the initial aggressors. No museum comes close to creating

---

[46] Interestingly, in the snapshot results from May 22, 2017, the visitor votes were close to being evenly split over the course of the year. 56% would have bombed the rail yards, 44% would not have.

primary experientiality that allows a structural re-experiencing of the events in the Air War.[47] Even the museums that do create gaps and openness avoid explicitly reflecting upon political, military, and individual choices. At least in the Mémorial de Caen, the Bundeswehr Military History Museum, the Bastogne War Museum, and, in part, the House of European History, the visitor has a choice of narratives and encounters tensions between historically specific events and anthropological as well as structural constellations. This eventually allows for the development of some secondary experientiality. To an extent, even the Gdańsk Museum of the Second World War and the New Orleans WWII Museum offer the choice between historical responsibility and a humanist message. In both of these cases, however, the master narrative provides a strong frame that shapes all interpretations and restricts experientiality.

No Second World War museum analyzed in this study really reflects on the cultural history of aerial warfare. The early bombings of civilians – the British in Iraq in the 1920s or the Italians in Ethiopia in the 1930s – are totally absent.[48] This means that representations of aerial warfare are always situated between Guernica in April 1937 and Hiroshima and Nagasaki in August 1945. This makes it easier to highlight the historical context of the Second World War and the aggressor roles of totalitarian regimes, such as in the Gdańsk Museum of the Second World War. The expression 'terror bombing' is sometimes used, but only in reference to German, Soviet, and Japanese forces. German museums, such as the Bundeswehr Military History Museum, strive to avoid the charge of de-historicizing the historical causality of the Air War. Consequently, they cannot reflect upon the pre-Nazi history of aerial warfare. The Allied museums under study also want to commemorate their heroes – whether bomber pilots or heroic civilians. Only the House of European History had the possibility of presenting the earlier part of aerial warfare. However, a full-scale narrative that allowed the visitor freedom to decide whether the strategic area bombing in the Second World War were similar to earlier or later bombing campaigns would have threatened the master narrative of European unity and freedom. Therefore, it is not surprising that exhibiting the Air War is one of the most morally, politically, and representationally restricted topics in contemporary Second World War museums.

---

47 One could argue that both Imperial War Museums in London and Manchester allow for a certain primary experientiality but their main tendencies are to restrict experientiality such as in the *Family in Wartime* exhibition in London (see chapter 3.3), or simulate secondary structures as in Manchester (see chapter 5.2).
48 See e.g. Lindqvist 2001 [2000], 44–74.

Chapter 9:
Art in Second World War Museums

The last chapter of this study deals with the use of art in historical Second World War exhibitions in today's museums. Analyzing history museums' use of art provides the perfect lens for understanding how museums can restrict or produce experientiality for their visitors. Artworks – such as sculptures, paintings, or drawings – are functionalized as additional historical sources. As such, they can provide introspective opportunities for understanding primary experiences and can allow for critical and reflexive thinking. Art is present in the form of paintings and sculptures, and more indirectly in the architecture and scenography of interior museum spaces in all of the museums analyzed. However, only a few museums trust artwork as an autonomous medium that allows the visitor to form aesthetic judgments outside the narrative, ideological, or historical framework provided by the museum. The aesthetic potential of art can be explained using Immanuel Kant's theory of the four possible aesthetic reflective judgments: the agreeable, the beautiful, the sublime, and the good. The two subjective universal judgments of the beautiful and the sublime, which Kant developed in his *Critique of Judgement* (*Kritik der Urteilskraft*), help us understand how the visitor can use artworks for further reflection, contemplation, and critical interpretation of history, without either falling into merely subjective statements or being bound to a predestined ethical imperative. Kant notes:

> The beautiful coincides with the sublime in that both please for themselves. And further in that both presuppose neither a judgment of sense nor a logically determining judgment, but a judgment of reflection: consequently the satisfaction does not depend on a sensation, like that in the agreeable, nor on a determinate concept, like the satisfaction in the good; but it is nevertheless still related to concepts, although it is indeterminate which, hence the satisfaction is connected to the mere presentation or to the faculty for that, through which the faculty of presentation or the imagination is considered, in the case of a given intuition, to be in accord with the *faculty of concepts* of the understanding or of reason, as promoting the latter (Kant 2000 [1790], 128).[1]

Obviously, historical events in war go beyond Kant's concept of the beautiful and sublime. Knowledge presented in a museum will never reach the autonomous and self-referential status that a piece of artwork that pleases or overwhelms the recipient aesthetically can achieve. Nevertheless, Kant's tracing of a concept

---

[1] 5: 244. Beginning of § 23. "Transition from the faculty for judging the beautiful to that for judging the sublime."

OpenAccess. © 2020 Stephan Jaeger, published by De Gruyter. This work is licensed under the Creative Commons Attribution-NonCommercial-NoDerivatives 4.0 License.
https://doi.org/10.1515/9783110664416-013

of reflection that brings together the indeterminate of imagination and the understanding of reason helps us reflect upon how artwork in history museums contributes to the development of experientiality by creating spaces for the visitor's perception, contemplation, and interpretation.[2]

There are also drawings and paintings of the Holocaust in almost every war and Holocaust memorial museum. The victim-authored, mimetic language in a history museum still offers some of art's resistance, or in Theodor W. Adorno's words from *Aesthetic Theory* (*Ästhetische Theorie*), some of the tension and gaps between the empirical thing and the spirit of the artwork (Adorno 1997 [1970], 277). These allow art to be an adequate language for the unspeakable experience of extreme violence in history. Unlike Kant's focus on the perception of the subject, Adorno locates art's truth content in the internal dynamics of the art object and in its socio-historical context. He emphasizes that all artworks are enigmas that express "the duality of being determinate and indeterminate" (Adorno 1997 [1970], 124) and sees the dialectical process of artwork between their experience and their "enigmaticalness" (Adorno 1997 [1970], 125). Consequently, works of art resist their mimetic explanation; they cannot be fully utilized for an illustrative purpose or as part of a closed narrative structure.

A historical museum normally uses artwork for a pragmatic purpose, reducing its aesthetic truth content by treating art as a merely cognitive argument, ignoring its enigmaticalness. Most visitors are probably less likely to engage in the autonomous or self-referential quality of artwork if it fulfills either a narrative or illustrative function. However, if a war or history museum uses autonomous artwork, it invites or challenges the visitor to explore its inherent meanings and ambiguities. These works are connected to the exhibition space around them; they might be marked through a primary symbolic interpretation provided by the museum or the artist. However, they also draw the visitor into a one-on-one communication with the artwork. Since the violence of war, atrocities, and suffering offers plenty of challenges to which there is hardly one answer, artwork relating to war, violence – and the Second War in particular – offer the visitor the potential to interact with the past, which is even more relevant with the looming end of living memory that requires the activation of the visitor's imaginative perception capabilities.

Most exhibitions analyzed – with the exception of the Bundeswehr Military History Museum, the Imperial War Museum North, and the House of European

---

[2] For the role of Kant's aesthetics in the development of the exhibition concept for the Bundeswehr Military History Museum and an artifact's potential for unearthing multiple layers of history in the process of reception see also Müller 2006, 758.

History – do not use autonomous artwork. One only occasionally finds paintings and portraits illustrating a theme or depicting a person in a typical wartime scenario. In these cases, war paintings supplement other visual media, particularly photography, posters, and film. The Canadian War Museum (CWM) – in addition to the Imperial War Museum as the institution with the largest collection of war paintings – serves as an excellent example of how war paintings can supplement a museum exhibition about the Second World War through the use of painting as a mimetic medium to mediate experiences of the past (see also Thiemeyer 2010a, 283–290). The museum presents its art collection as a witness that will endure after the end of (human) living memory: "As it does, the Canadian War Museum's war art collections of 13,000 works increasingly provide a link to the conflicts from the perspective of those who witnessed them. While, to a certain extent, the paintings act as illustration, they also convey the feelings of the participants in the conflicts. This, perhaps, is their most important legacy" (Brandon 2019). The Canadian War Records of the Second World War (1939–45) contains over 5,000 small paintings. "There are no huge memorial compositions focusing on destruction, tragedy, and misery. Instead, the somewhat depersonalized emphasis […] is on the locations, events, machinery, and personnel of Canada's war on all fronts" (Brandon 2019).

In a history exhibition, paintings are usually integrated into the overall narratives and typically illustrate or supplement a theme. For example, in the section about the Battle of the Atlantic, the CWM exhibits the painting *Corvette Bridge*. The description first explains that corvettes were unsuited to the rough conditions of the Atlantic. It then provides an interpretation: "This painting by Donald MacKay captures the discomfort of command on an open bridge in bad weather." Therefore, the painting and the postures and emotions of the three men on the bridge offer no further questions to the visitor. They confirm and intensify the argument about how the war was experienced by the Canadian soldier. In the D-Day / Normandy section, the visitor encounters Eric Altwinckle's painting *Invasion Pattern Normandy*, which "depicts a Canadian Mustang in action." The description highlights the invasion stripes that made the aircraft recognizable to other Allied aircraft. The painting shows the aircraft itself from above, its bombs, some landing crafts, and a beach beneath it. Again, war art here is merely illustrative.

If and when interpretation is needed, the CWM provides one explicit interpretation. This can be seen in the next section, where the visitor comes across Orville Fisher's painting entitled *Scheldt Crossing*, depicting the campaign in the Netherlands. According to the CWM, the painting "captures the dismal weather that dogged Canadians during the campaign." On the one hand, this supports the general narrative of Canadian valor and hardship. On the other, the painting itself is ambiguous; the Canadian soldiers are barely visible at the top of the transport vehicle. The painting could just as easily be read as a metaphor for man and machine, wherein the former becomes the latter. However, because the museum treats all artworks as historical sources that supplement arguments, such an openness of interpretation is not encouraged. Art is supplementary and maintains a documentary function, as opposed to a self-referential one.[3]

The more playful arrangement found in the chronology gallery in the Bundeswehr Military History Museum (MHM) serves as an exception to paintings that function as illustration of a story, theme, or argument. Here the museum creates a meta-representational display that reflects upon the evolution and function of war and battle painting as an artistic genre. It uses two large walls in its "1300–1914" and "1914–1945" galleries, respectively, to depict the artwork of the time.[4] The section on Second World War battle paintings is entitled "The End of Battle Painting? The Two World Wars in German Painting until 1945–46." The paragraph about the Second World War reflects upon Nazi Cultural Policy, war painting in propagandas companies, and the persecution of 'degenerate' art. The MHM also mentions the decline of the medium in comparison to photography and cinema in the age of the world wars. Ten paintings on the wall were painted during the Second World War. They include: propaganda portraits; pictures depicting technological strength, such as a charging U-boat or an advancing tank; and images of the German army supporting local refugees from the Red Army, destroyed Soviet tanks, and Soviet prisoners of war. Whereas the MHM contextualizes most images – i.e. paintings are used to illustrate certain arguments – their setting invites the visitor to ask further questions. For example, the 1944 painting *Vor dem Angriff* (Before the Attack) by Werner Höll depicts three soldiers moving forward with stern facial expressions: the leader looks on determinedly with a machine gun in hand. The description provides context concerning Höll's career as a painter in the style of new objectivity (*Neue Sachlichkeit*) before becoming a Nazi propaganda painter. It also states that Höll resumed abstract painting after 1945. Placing the artwork in its historical context allows

---

[3] At times, museums like the Canadian War Museum and the Imperial War Museum in London in particular, hold war art exhibitions as such. Here, the visitor has the potential to understand the range and expressional possibilities of the medium, which can develop a certain autonomy beyond the museum's explanations and display structures.

[4] The MHM uses paintings as historical sources throughout the chronological exhibition as well. As seen, for example, in the analysis of the "Politics and the Use of Force" section above (see chapter 5.1), the spatial arrangement often allows the artwork to surpass a merely illustrative function.

for open questions. The viewer can wonder whether the stern faces of the soldiers only express support for the war, think about the careers of various artists in the National Socialist era, and what choices they were faced with. Again, the MHM's networking technique can intensify the experientiality of the visit if the visitor connects this section to the near-by sections "Resistance in the Arts" or "Politics and the Use of Force."[5] Of course, if one compares the curation of war art from the Second World War in Britain, Canada, and Germany, it is evident that the German perpetrator perspective requires a more contextualized and reflexive approach.

Aside from the use of war art, the visitor can most often find artwork in historical museums that want to either express trauma or mediate authenticity through witnessing. Museums present numerous sketches and paintings as personal expressions of suffering.[6] These paintings can be created during wartime (as direct expressions of experience) or after the fact, as seen in the sketch series of life in Ravensbrück concentration camp by Violette Rougier Lecoq, displayed in the Imperial War Museum North (IWMN). Similarly, the IWMN shows five facsimiles of linocut prints by Helmuth Weissenborn from 1941, depicting post-war bomb sites across London, such as Holland Park, Oxford Street, and a suburban church. Weissenborn was a German veteran of the First World War, who – as a Social Democrat married to a Jewish woman – escaped Nazi Germany in 1939. Whereas these prints have a clear documentary function of illustrating the effects of the Blitz, the separate hanging of the paintings allows visitors to reflect upon their own perception: on what the paintings express, how authentic or beautified they are, and if and how they can empathize with Weissenborn's gaze. Considering his personal background, what might he have thought while capturing the destruction caused by Germans? On the opposite side of a narrow aisle, between two interior walls of voids, the IWMN displays the 1940 oil painting *A House Collapsing on Two Firemen* by Leonard Henry Rosoman. This painting functions in a similar way: on the one hand, the image is documentary, and on the other, the visitor is challenged to re-imagine the scene, whether as the firemen on which the house is collapsing and who will in all likelihood die, or more likely as an observer of the gruesome scene. The painting's documentary function is secondary to its emotional function.

As seen in the above analysis of Holocaust and genocide artwork in the House of European History, museums have the choice between on the one hand, integrating art into a pragmatic narrative – as partially seen in the case

---

5 See chapter 5.1.
6 See also chapters 7 and 8.

of Ritula Fränkel's and Nicholas Morris's *Jozef's Coat* and even more so in Yuri Leiderman Khatyn/Katyń's artwork.[7] On the other hand, as demonstrated above, Chava Rosenzweig's installation *A Star Shall Stride from Jacob and a Sceptre Bearer Shall Rise* in the Imperial War Museum North functions as an artwork that challenges the visitor to explore a personal connection to the Holocaust without fulfilling illustrative, pragmatic, or documentary functions.[8] Similarly, the Nussbaum painting in the Bundeswehr Military History Museum[9] supersedes a documentary purpose, partially as autonomous artwork, partially because of the constellations with other artifacts that it opens up within the museum space.

As Rosenzweig's artwork demonstrates, autonomous art in historical museum exhibitions explicitly challenges observers to situate themselves to interact with it. Similarly, visitors can reflect upon their own position in Ingo Günther's art installation *The Hiroshima Thank-You Instrument* found in the "Protection and Destruction" section of the Bundeswehr Military History Museum's thematic tour (MHM). A strobe light illuminates a darkened space at regular intervals. The visitor's silhouette, whether accidentally captured or deliberately posed, is temporarily frozen on a wall covered with phosphorescent paint until erased by the next flash.[10] Arnold-de Simine argues that the installation is based on constant repetition and resembles trauma rather than memory in its reenactment and repetition of horrific events. However, she also recognizes that the art installation inspires "playful encounters rather than sober reflection" (2013, 73). In other words, the visitor might be more interested in the original shadow effects than connecting them to the traumatic nature of the event. As the audio guide explains, art and the violence of the nuclear bomb separate human beings from their shadows, allowing visitors to question their own position when their shadow is forcibly and violently separated from their person.[11]

---

7 See chapter 6.3.
8 See chapter 5.2.
9 See chapter 5.1.
10 Günther originally created *The Hiroshima Thank-You Instrument* for the Hiroshima City Museum of Contemporary Art in 1995. It was adjusted for the space in the Libeskind wedge in 2011.
11 This chapter primarily highlights art installations that refer to the Second World War. Museums, such as the MHM, that are interested in violence as a structural phenomenon often exhibit commissioned artworks that have a more symbolic character that does not refer to specific conflicts. For example, upon entering the wedge on the ground floor, the visitor encounters the installation *Love and Hate* by Charles Sandison from 2005. The words 'love' and 'hate,' relating to anthropological feelings, are repeated thousands of times on the walls of the wedge. They seem to be in a never-ending fight, generating each other. Neither concept can disappear completely. The audio guide explains that visitors are supposed to become part of the installation with their feelings – love and hate – toward war and violence. Whether this succeeds is unclear; the art-

The most ambiguous artwork in the MHM, which (partially) reflects upon the Second World War, is Klaus vom Bruch's video installation *Capriccio*, which was specifically commissioned for the MHM's "Protection and Destruction" section of the thematic tour in 2011.[12] As the title indicates, it is a fantastic game, free of rules, that blurs time and space. The film is centered on a dragoon vase from China from before 1717 that was given – among other pieces of porcelain – to the Polish Electorate and King Augustus II by the Prussian King Frederick William I in exchange for 600 spare (enslaved) cavalryman. Two men wearing uniforms from Baroque Dresden perform scenes around a curtain, which – according to the museum audio guide – are intertextually reminiscent of paintings such as Raphael's *Sistine Madonna* and Johannes Vermeer's *Girl Reading a Letter at an Open Window*, both acquired by August III for Dresden in the mid-eighteenth century.[13] At times, they carry the vase, inspect it, or put the lid on it; at times, the vase explodes in the fore- or background. The second layer of the film is footage from the Allied preparation of the Dresden bombing in February 1945. The vase – a symbol of Baroque Dresden – becomes the target and is destroyed multiple times. An analysis of the film's opening reveals the dynamics of artwork in relation to interpretations of the Second World War. First, the viewer sees four Mustang aircrafts emerging from the curtain, presumably flying to Dresden. The two soldiers – one riding on the other, possibly indicating a power relationship – then enter the scene and draw the curtain over the Mustangs. The next shot depicts both soldiers in a reflective pose sitting and lying on the ground; one is playing with the open dragoon vase. In the background, a damaged Red-Cross flag and a destroyed castle are shown, before a brief shot of knights riding horses and carrying swastika flags is shown. Then the curtain is completely drawn, before the soldiers open it to reveal an airfield. In the following scenes, the destruction (and reconstruction) of the dragoon vase becomes the pre-dominant theme of the installation.

What does the artwork tell the visitor about the destruction of Dresden? Violence clearly preceded the bombing, as indicated by the swastika knights and the selling of enslaved soldiers to obtain the vase. Was Dresden a legitimate target? The Red-Cross symbol could be a strong argument against the bombing, but

---

work is also a typical example of art with a strong symbolic message that forecloses further interpretation in similar ways to the illustrative and functionalized art discussed above.

12 Vom Bruch served as art curator for the permanent exhibition for artwork, both his own and that of six other artists, which were specifically commissioned for the thematic tour in the Libeskind wedge (Altmann 2012).

13 For the visitor to find such intertextual links, it is presumably crucial to listen to the audio guide.

also a cover-up of Dresden's military past. The whole set-up feels very much staged, alluding to the illusions of theater. The soldiers and the knights seem to reenact older scenes, so that the viewer is consistently challenged to differentiate between theatrical play and historical reality. This is enhanced through the metaphor of the curtain. Is it possible to simply open and close the past? To see the destruction of Dresden's beauty? The film playfully ironizes such gestures, while displaying the interwoven dynamic between high culture and violence. While this symbolic meaning is evident, the viewer must decide what play they want to see. What violence can be justified and in which circumstances? The fact that the museum exhibits a dragoon vase, acquired on loan from the *Porzellansammlung* by the Staatliche *Kunstsammlungen*, in its "1300 – 1914" chronological section supplements the effect of vom Bruch's installation in challenging the visitor to reflect on the vase's presence in a military history museum.

The curtain also alludes to Libeskind's wedge. Whereas from the tip of the wedge on the top floor, the visitor can see an obstructed view of Dresden's reconstructed cityscape as if looking through a semi-open blind, in vom Bruch's artwork, the curtain can be fully opened or closed. The viewer is eventually confronted, however, with a similar ambiguity regarding how to connect Baroque Dresden and the Dresden of the Second World War and how to connect culture and war. The visitor has the best view of the artwork from the staircases of the old arsenal building, and *Capriccio* therefore also reflects the tension between the old Arsenal building – erected in the 1870s and used as museum during the Third Reich and the GDR – and Libeskind's deconstructing wedge. Increasingly, the relationship between violence and Dresden's past, between victimhood and perpetration, and between its cultural heritage and destruction allows for secondary experientiality that connects the artwork with the museum's architecture, the permanent exhibition, and Dresden's cityscape.[14]

---

14 Other self-reflexive commissioned artworks include several installations that anchor the third level "Memory" in the wedge. Nancy Davenport's *Der Koyote* (*The Coyote*) shows an awkward male protagonist on the construction site of the museum experimenting with explosives and weapons. He consistently fails in his violent ambitions, and the violence turns against him – without any indication that he learns from his failures – creating humorous incidents in the tradition of the American cartoon series *Coyote and Roadrunner*. What one should do with this artwork is left completely open. Is it a critique of all forms of violence? A meta-commentary on the need of the MHM to be a dynamic institution in order to prosper? Does it force visitors to reflect upon their own enjoyment of violence in the comic tradition? Or is it just entertainment? How do visitors accept that artwork in a military history museum can tell them something about violence and make them think about their own attitude toward violence and its consumption.

Regarding the idea of deconstructing the monumentality of war as well as the unquestioned affirmative monumentality of Dresden's cultural past, one of arts' effects manifests where the commissioned artworks, Libeskind's architecture, and the spatial patterns of the exhibition meet. As seen in the air-war chapter above, the deconstruction of the V2's aura relies on the cooperation between the art installation of Klaus vom Bruch's und Manuela Günther' *Galileo's Monologue*, Libeskind's voids, the interior design, and curated spatial connotations between objects.[15] The effect of the artwork – sometimes stronger, sometimes less intense – is a constant interaction between play, symbolic meanings, gaps, and ambiguities.[16] These works of art – similar to the Imperial War Museum North and the House of European History[17] – mainly offer a playful, multifaceted, or symbolic reflection; whether or how to interact with the artwork, re-

---

Similarly, Martha Colburn's film installation *Triumph of the Wild I&II* (2008) forces visitors to situate their own perception in confrontation with the artwork. On the one hand, there is a clear symbolic message that is explained in the audio guide: humans become animals, hunters become the hunted, and vice versa. In flashbacks, the film attempts to simulate the post-traumatic stress disorder of American soldiers who fought in the Iraq and Afghanistan wars. On the other hand, viewers must decide whether they invest emotionally in the images to become – to a certain extent – part of this experience. At the same time, the visitor is challenged to connect the artwork to other forms of expressions of trauma in the permanent exhibition to make sense of an encounter with artwork in this space.

15 See chapter 8.

16 Another artwork that the visitor cannot decipher in its historical context, but relates the Libeskind building with the visitor experience of war and violence, can be found in the section "The Formation of the Body." The sound installation *Mass Block* by Carsten Nicolai was also specifically commissioned for one of the museum's voids. The visitor experiences "[a] collage of original sounds from theaters of war and propaganda" that "forms the acoustic sphere that associates with modern music." The sounds and vibrations become a physical experience for the visitor entering a kind of tunnel on a grid, which reveals a deep void underneath. This can raise questions about one's own position in regard to the sounds and formations of war. It seems like an abstract form of empathy, in which the visitor can connect to the possibility or impossibility of feeling violence and war in a museum. One possible historical contextualization is given by the diorama installation, by Jens Najewitz and Maik Rohde, of people, animals, and vehicles that were part of a military division in the First World War. The viewer can feel as if they have become part of the 13th Bavarian Infantry Division in February 1918, which was comprised of about 13,000 people, 3,000 horses and 26 field artillery guns. The last sentence of the description notes that every two days, 16,000 soldiers died in the First World War, so if the viewer follows the link between the two installations, the unease produced by Nicolai's artwork will increase.

17 The majority of freestanding artworks in the House of European History appear in its very first section "The Myth of Europa" as a representation of the idea and myth of Europe/Europa, i.e. in a very symbolic way. Artists try to capture the essence of Europe through art in multifaceted ways, leaving considerable room for interpreting the artwork on its own.

garding aesthetic and ethical judgments on a cognitive, emotional, imaginative, or ethical level, is left up to each visitor.[18]

Between February 8 and April 10, 2018, the MHM displayed another work of art in the open space in the wedge, between the sections "Technology and the Military" and "Protection and Destruction": a bronze statue entitled *Chor der Überlebenden* (Choir of Survivors) by Dresden artist Helmut Heinze, who experienced the bombing of Dresden as a 13-year-old. The actual statue was donated to Coventry Cathedral and unveiled as part of the celebrations surrounding the fiftieth anniversary of the cathedral's rebuilding in 2012. Seven column-like figures stretched to the sky as a single group, like a choir of witnesses, expressing de-

---

18 Artwork has a strong symbolic, but also thought-provoking, value when it establishes constellations and associations in an exhibition between objects, interior, and exterior spaces. The MHM's 2018 special exhibition *Gender and Violence: War is for Men – Peace is for Women?* was accompanied by the exhibition *Targeted Interventions* that displayed seven art objects (six exterior works located around two sides of the building, on the building, and in the interior). On the one hand, the majority of this artwork served a symbolic function and none of it explicitly expressed anything about a specific historical period. They all were meant to challenge the visitor's perception of war and violence in an anthropological sense. On the other hand, upon closer inspection, the visitor could find many resonances with the museum's architecture, interior design, and artifacts from the permanent exhibition. At least four artworks referred to bombs and rockets, some blandly provocative like Morten Traavik's *Honest John*, a short range rocket capable of carrying nuclear warheads covered by condoms, while others were more dynamic, such as Birgit Dieker's *Crazy Daisy*, a rocket made out of mutilated female mannequin bodies. The museum's text panel explicitly related Dieker's artwork to the history of the V2 and to the habit of American Second World War pilots of decorating their planes with pin-up girls. But the visitor could find constellations to the formation section in the thematic tour, the mutilated bodies from the "War and Suffering" section, or the displayed corpses after the air attacks on Dresden in the "1918–1945" chronological and "Dresden View" sections (see chapter 8). Similarly, the shape of eight lipstick colored rockets or grenades in Sylvie Fleurie's *First Spaceship on Venus* in the wedge in the "Protection and Destruction" section even created a direct 'viewing axis' with the 'bomb hail' installation in the permanent exhibition. The extent to which the visitor felt inspired to draw conclusions from this remains open. Lastly, the Guerilla Girls created a large poster *The Estrogen Bomb* on the side façade of the museum building: "pink bomb heads towards Earth for the Museum of Military History of the Bundeswehr." The text on the billboard-like artwork requested a world without homophobia, inequality, etc. Visitors could think of Davenport's *The Coyote,* since this time the museum was targeted with a different bomb. However, they could have also linked the artwork to the game of skill, *Nuclear Bombs on Japan,* displayed in the "War and Play" section, or to the many installations referring to bombs. Must bombs destroy society or could they change it? If a bomb hit the MHM, would it have any impact on the rest of the world? Visitors who wanted to engage with artwork could therefore challenge their own perceptions.

struction and hope simultaneously.[19] The visitor could clearly emotionally connect to the bodily gestures seen in the statue and support the message of reconciliation. Furthermore, the relationship between Coventry and Dresden, which have been official partner cities since 1959, seemed to have surpassed any violence caused by the war. Nevertheless, even more than Iché's *Guernica* sculpture in the House of European History, a narrative framework tamed the symbolic gesture of the artwork. The exhibition presented a singular interpretation: the Air War is in the past. Instead of analyzing its multifaceted relations to the present, including the continuance of violence, the museum encompassed the Air War's significance in one symbolic gesture. Of course, one could argue that the MHM's overall set-up, including the exhibition of vom Bruch's nearby *Capriccio*, complicated such a reading. However, Heinze's bronze sculpture was presented as an artwork with an aura of its own – prior to Walter Benjamin's shift, in the age of mechanical reproducibility, to constant simulations of aura (2008 [1935]). There were no connections through which the visitor could easily associate this artwork with other parts of the exhibition or the building's architecture. This had the effect of intensifying the stated symbolism of the artwork and discouraging alternate interpretations. Although it was located in the Libeskind wedge, it could just as easily have been placed anywhere else within the museum. Placed inside the wedge, it had the effect of simplifying or contradicting the staged, broken, and complex gaze from the top of the wedge's platform. In Heinze's artwork, the sky is unambiguously open.[20]

If one reflects on art in history museums, it is very noticeable that, with the exception of the Bastogne War Museum, none of the museums uses fiction (in literature or film) as a documentary source. Fiction is used – particularly in the Bundeswehr Military History Museum – to express the function of different memory media and to represent war after the fact, but not to support the simulation of historical reality. Even the four fictitious characters in the Bastogne War Museum[21] do not create a fictional world, since they establish the factually illustrative claim of documenting the potentially real consciousness and perspectives of an American soldier, a German soldier, and Belgian civilians. They are created to document possible historical experiences. Their constructed nature stemming from numerous eyewitness accounts underlines this referential function. There-

---

19 Surprisingly, the text explaining the artwork was only in German. This neither fit with the MHM's general bilingual presentation style nor the message of the artwork expressing reconciliation between Dresden and Coventry.
20 Another form of artwork in the MHM that functions more symbolically can be seen in educational stations.
21 See chapter 4.3.

fore, the visitor most likely never feels that these characters are part of a fictional story; they are a medium to express collective perceptions of history. Consequently, they do not violate the pact of truthfulness (Doležel 2010, 36) between museum and visitor. A historical museum that uses a fictional representation to enhance its simulation of history – whether of its own creation, or whether it stages a fictional scene from a film or literary text – has yet to be created. This would most likely require an experiential style, which would allow the visitor to empathize with fictitious characters. However, fiction could be used in a style that employs a higher degree of distantiation if the visitor was provided with the opportunity to choose between different roles in fictional scenarios. Such a tool would be more likely employed didactically, similar to the hypothetical scenarios – "What to do?" – found in the New Orleans WWII Museum. Nonetheless, fiction and possible creative demands on the visitor could add to the imaginative possibilities of understanding history and its limitations and choices of interpretation.

Fiction in film and prose does not seem to work in representing war history. Despite this, the Imperial War Museum North (IWMN), in addition to its visual artwork, uses poetry by 'writer-in-residence' Mario Petrucci as an artistic intervention. Petrucci comments in particular on objects that are personified in poems and speak to the visitor with their own fictionalized voices. Originally, this collection of poems about personified objects included a poem from the point of view of a T-34/85 tank.[22] When it was on display, the museum's description highlighted the object's use in the Second World War by briefly mentioning that T-34s were in active service until the 1990s. The poem brought the artifact's background and destructive power to life, noting how boys, women, and old men produced it "deep in Russian forest" (5). Then the poem expressed a warning from the point of view of the personified tank: "For Germans I was / the can opener from Hell." (16–17). The poem ended by relating to the active duty of the tank "not so very long ago" with the line "My motto? You're dust" (20).

---

[22] The tank – still on display in August 2013 – was replaced by a British Second World War infantry support tank, the Matilda II, as seen on a visit in May 2018. Consequently, Petrucci's poem disappeared without a replacement. Generally, the IWMN does not seem to have a continuous program for their "Reactions: Artist Interventions at the IWMN." There was no new artwork displayed in the permanent exhibition between 2013 and 2018. However, the museum continues to display three poems by Petrucci: a reflective poem on the meaning(s) of friend and fiend; a poem from the perspective of a First World War artillery field gun; and a poem about the AV-8a Harrier combat aircraft. It also exhibits a poem by Simon Armitage about the feelings surrounding 9/11 (see also Bagnall and Rowland 2010, 59–64, for the "playful discombobulation" and creation of aesthetic contemplation through artwork, and the installation of the Harrier jet in the context of Libeskind's architecture in the IWMN in particular).

The visitor was invited to consider the meaning of certain lines beyond their literal interpretation. How did the poem portray the destructive power of the tank? Was this power acceptable since the tank was used against the Germans? How and in which conflicts was the tank used more recently? The visitor could combine the appearance of the artifact with the poem, which created numerous affective, ethical, and cognitive allusions. Petrucci's poem – as staged in the museum – opened up possibilities for further reflection without being limited by a pragmatic museum narrative.

Even though the AV-8a Harrier was not flying in the Second World War, but rather in the 1970s and 1980s, Petrucci's Harrier poem challenges visitors to imagine themselves in a city being attacked from the air by using the point of view of the plane. This creates many allusions to the Second World War and the Blitz, as represented elsewhere in the IWMN. The plane threatens that it "can […] see you in the City" (6–7) and that "I'll remove you from your teacup / and not spill it" (8–9).[23] The visitor is forced into an emotional dialogue with the object through the poem. Whether the poem, in the safe atmosphere of the museum, creates fear, laughter, or cognitive insights to the threats from the air aimed at civilians remains open. It certainly forces visitors who come across it to think and react for themselves and engage further with the display.

Artwork and poetry (i.e. mainly non-narrative media) – if staged in a dialogue with the contents of exhibitions, museum spaces, and exhibition's representational strategies – allows museums to engage the visitor in reflexive situations. It is perfectly suited to trigger debate or agonistic memory, in which the visitor is drawn into structural networking to understand abstract concepts such as violence and historical structures. The visitor can learn about the complexity of simulating the past. Visitors – if they are willing to engage with art – can be drawn out of the comfort zone of easily digestible historical information or straightforward narrative to reflect upon the general consequences of warfare. Historical context can feed autonomous works of art; however, they more often also imply more general messages about suffering and violence as well as the human impact of war. In particular, museums that are reluctant to use artwork integrate historical works of art as expressions of suffering and trauma, such as

---

[23] The Harrier and the poem also form a unit of reflection with Gerry Judah's sculpture *The Crusader* (2010), which hangs on the wall to the right of the exhibition's entrance. It is a network of war-damaged buildings in the shape of a plane, so that the viewer immediately connects it to the nearby 'real' Harrier artifact. The artist is quoted as saying that his sculpture "explores the violence of conflict against a perceived righteousness of purpose. The beauty of the sculpture contrasts with the darkness of the subject matter." The visitor must decide how to address these contrasts.

experiences in concentration camps or the rapes of Asian women forced to serve as sex slaves for Japanese soldiers. If the meaning of the artwork and its contextual setting in the museum is not pre-determined, museums can supplement historical representation with a more abstract reflective potential. This can draw visitors into situations of war and violence without implying cheap empathy as an alleged copy of historical reality. The constructive nature of art, poetry, and – even if it is under-used – fiction, creates friction with the understanding of history. This means that it is perfectly suited to supplement the cognitive understanding of the past by triggering the visitors' imagination, which allows them to develop reflective perceptions and meaning-making skills. Museums – as a medium that creates spaces that are filled by visitors' perceptions and decisions – are ideally suited both to integrate art and history in order to widen the emotional, ethical, cognitive, and aesthetic insights of their visitors and to develop experientiality.[24]

---

24 Sharon Macdonald takes a considerably more critical and cautious view to the use of conceptual art as part of exhibiting difficult heritage and perpetration, by example of an artwork installation on the Nazi Party Rallying Grounds (2008, 110–115). Although there are limitations to the use of unguided or ambiguous art in war museums when exhibiting violence and perpetration, its meta-representational function of evoking critical thinking is undoubtedly significant.

Conclusion

The concept of experientiality helps us to understand how museums create potential actualities of the past for their visitors. It allows for a structural understanding of the potential an exhibition space holds for the possible or 'ideal' visitor as an anthropomorphic experiencer; one that is neither reduced to the mere intentions of its curators, architects, and interior designers nor to the empirical reactions observed or recorded from actual, onsite visitors. The concept also proves useful in developing a method to read the specific medium of the 'history museum.' Whereas recipients – the reader of fictional books or the viewer of fictional films – can imagine themselves empathetically into another fictional world, the history museum first maintains its referential function toward the past. It upholds the pact of truthfulness with its visitors, even when using art, poetry, or fictitious composite characters, as seen above. Second, the visitor always remains as a physical entity in the museum and therefore in present space. While the visitor never experiences the past as such, she or he becomes the consciousness that constitutes the narrative of the past and allows for the development of experientiality. Due to the natural relationship between the represented past and the visitor's experience, museum makers can construct spaces that try to limit visitor's freedom of experience or that direct them to affirm a specific narrative or ideological path. These factualization techniques clearly reduce experientiality and can be seen in virtually all Second World War museums. This is true, however, to a widely varying extent.

Experientiality offers a wide range of understandings in terms of how museums explicitly and indirectly construct realities and how they react to existing cultural memory. This concept can be used to exclusively examine what realities museums create when they decide on how an exhibition should be structured. These decisions include: the balance between, on the one hand, a historical or chronological clustering, and, on the other, a thematic or structural clustering and an exhibition's relationship between historical specificity and anthropological universalization. The latter could also relate to a social justice approach, which can speak to visitors in the present, even if they do not have a direct relation to the Second World War. As this study has shown, the discussion of the representational possibilities of war museums with regard to perpetration and different forms of suffering and victimhood is in its infancy. Specific historical topics such as flight, expulsion, and emigration in relation to the Second World War have just recently moved into scholarly focus (Mikuska-Tinman 2018). How museums depict and narrativize collaboration is another historical topic for further exploration. The exploration of other themes such as the representation of the enemy (Bogumił et al. 2015), of motherhood, children, games and toys, or of cultural forms like mourning and remembering would produce in-depth understanding of the experientiality of Second World War museums. Media-based analyses – such as those on video testimony and sound recently published by de Jong (2018a; 2018b); the museum object (Paver 2018); or on general immersion techniques – could further explore the concept of experientiality in order to understand how exhibitions allow for distantiation, for openness and closure, and how they manipulate the visitor into specific didactic, ideological, or ethical beliefs. Most of all, scholars can analyze how the medium of the history museum does and can reflect upon the remembrance of the Second World War and allow for the questioning of existing cultural memory, or whether they remain focused on the historical past as such and therefore on hiding from the visitor the fact that all museum representations of the past are products of their present.

The theoretical comprehension of experientiality in and of itself is probably insufficient for museum professionals to understand the effects of the exhibitions they design. In a practical sense, experientiality studies could be combined with empirical visitor studies in order to understand the frames to which the majority of visitors of an institution react. This could also help weigh the likelihood of whether certain exhibitions will be able to steer visitors toward deep contemplation, self-reflection, critical thinking, and learning beyond their pre-established patterns of cultural memory surrounding the Second World War. Empirical visitor studies could provide insight into how active a visitor can be, if and when a visitor feels lost in too many choices, and how much guidance, narrative, and structure is needed. It can also prove whether visitors notice the factualization techniques museums use in their attempt to manipulate visitors toward specific reactions and interpretations. However, empirical visitor studies is not capable of dissecting the narrative, semiotic, aesthetic, and critical potential of an exhibition. In contrast, the concept of experientiality, in combination with concepts such as historical distance, empathetic unsettlement, multidirectional memory, agonistic memory, and difficult knowledge, can achieve such an analysis.

As contentious as the Second World War is in memory politics, many museums – such as those in Brussels, London, New Orleans, Ottawa, and Warsaw – create the impression museum representation of the Second World War is about representing and understanding a factual reality. On the historical level, experientiality allows for openness; exhibitions can demonstrate that there are different interpretations of or perspectives on the past. On the level of remembrance, experientiality provides opportunities for the explicit understanding that decisions about how to represent the Second World War – as an anthropological understanding of violence, a negative foundation myth toward human rights and justice, or a story essential to the development of a national identity – are always part of the construction of group memories.

The chapters on the presentation of the Holocaust and of perpetration in war museums and on total war and the Air War have shown the limitations of contemporary museums in creating openness, self-reflexivity, and experientiality in dealing with topics that are part of intense memory battles. The permanent exhibition of the House of European History in Brussels is the best example of this observation. The museum makers have been unable to integrate the tensions inherent to current cultural memory politics into their wider exhibition. Consequently, the exhibition does not have much to offer to visitors who believe whole-heartedly in a specific national perspective. In contrast, cosmopolitan visitors will likely feel reassured by the openness of contemporary social justice values as represented by the museum and might only question whether this development can really be as closely connected with the emergence of the idea of Europe and the institution of the European Union as the museum suggests. Most museums are careful to adhere to the cultural memory of their main target audience – in which cultural diversity can be included – and their dominant political discourses. Taking this into consideration, it is not surprising that the House of European History has not been able to find a suitable approach to address tensions among and within their twenty-eight member states.

How can exhibition makers circumvent political and institutional pressures? One way around this challenge is through international partnerships and collaboration between scholars and museum professionals. Although funded by national and multinational institutions, academic projects can maintain a more self-reflexive approach and follow standards of academic freedom, since they are less dependent on visitor numbers.[1] An example of this is the special exhibition *Feeling War* (*Der Gefühlte Krieg*) that displayed, staged, and simulated emotions related to war, particularly the First World War. It was exhibited between 2014 and 2015 in the Museum for European Culture (Museum Europäischer Kulturen) in Berlin-Dahlem and was a cooperative project between the museum and the Max Planck Institute for Human Development (Bildungsforschung) in Berlin. The exhibition was comprised of numerous installations representing grief, mourning, and commemoration of the dead. Visitors had to work through structural experiences of fear, loss, grief, and mourning, which arguably was as close to a simulation of structural trauma as a museum space can get, unless the

---

[1] This relates more likely to special exhibitions than to permanent exhibitions, which are considerably more restricted by political, societal, and institutional pressures.

visitor transfers a museum representation into a personal story (Jaeger 2017c, 158–159; Redlin and Neuland-Kizerow 2014).

Another exhibition that allowed for active visitor reflections was *Diversity Destroyed: Berlin 1933–1938–1945* (*Zerstörte Vielfalt*). It was exhibited in Berlin from January to November 2013 and was put on by the German Historical Museum in cooperation with Cultural Projects Berlin (see also van Dülmen et al. 2013).[2] The exhibition brought together more than forty projects from museums, private associations, and initiatives that dealt with the history of Berlin under National Socialism through exhibitions, temporary art projects, theater performances, readings, film projects, and audio guides.[3] It transformed the city of Berlin into an exhibition space that created historical traces and gaps, confronted the visitor with memories of the Nazi past, and connected the past to the position of the visitor in the present. For example, in Berlin *U-Bahn* (underground) stations, the visitor encountered large advertising posters with slogans such as "You are not allowed to live here any longer."[4] These slogans were accompanied by historical context in much smaller print, available to any viewer drawn into reflecting upon their historical meaning. A tension between historical and contemporary meaning thus arose. Around the city, citizens and tourists encountered typical Berlin advertising pillars that introduced diverse people from the past who experienced discrimination in Nazi Germany. Throughout the German Historical Museum itself, a reflexive layer was added, which allowed the visitor to rethink the role of the arsenal building (*Zeughaus*) – today's museum building – and its exhibition functions during National Socialism and today. This therefore enabled the visitor to reflect upon the purpose of a museum representing history and war.

Another academically inspired exhibition was *War. Power. Meaning: War and Violence in European Memory* (*Krieg. Macht. Sinn: Krieg und Gewalt in der europäischen Erinnerung*). This exhibition took place in the Ruhr Museum in Essen, from November 12, 2018 to June 10, 2019, as part of the EU-funded project UNREST (Unsettling Remembrance and Social Cohesion in Transnational Europe; see Berger et al. 2019; Cento Bull et al. 2019, 620).[5] The exhibition, which focused on the German visitor, was explicitly designed to put agonistic memory into mu-

---

2 Kulturprojekte Berlin.
3 https://www.dhm.de/archiv/ausstellungen/zerstoerte-vielfalt/en/, accessed 13 October 2019.
4 "Du darfst hier nicht mehr leben."
5 I am particularly grateful to Emma Mikuska-Tinman who worked together with me on analyzing the exhibition in spring 2019, to Wulf Kansteiner for a discussion about the exhibition design, and to Cristian Cercel for giving Mikuska-Tinman an individual guided tour of the exhibition on May 28, 2019.

seum practice as an alternative to cosmopolitan and antagonistic approaches to memory.[6] The museum venue – both spatially and in the collaboration between internal museum and external agonistic memory researchers – restricted what the exhibition designers could experiment with.[7] Similar to the Bundeswehr Military History Museum, *War. Power. Sense* avoided a strongly didactic perspective, allowing visitors to operate as an experiencing consciousness and to form their own interpretations of the exhibition. In particular, they were challenged to situate themselves between quotations, documents, and objects that saw 'sense' in war and those that were opposed to it. For example, the subsection "Dresden," as part of the aerial warfare section "Fire Falling from the Sky," displays a photograph showing fans of the FC St. Pauli soccer club, provoking the fans of the FC Dynamo Dresden – who are presumed to be right-wing – with banners whose translation read "Your Grandparents already burned for Dresden: Against the myth of German victimhood." Next to it, the exhibition showed a photograph of right-wing extremists marching through Dresden, with a banner expressing that "[t]he Bombing Holocaust cannot be negated."[8] Visitors could recognize the controversies and different positions; in other words they could understand that the same historical event can be utilized differently by different agents of memory. Nevertheless, it is arguable as to whether these contrasts would have moved visitors to reflect upon and possibly change the attitudes they held toward Dresden, the myth of victimhood, and aerial warfare prior to their museum visit. The exhibition did not simulate the genesis of positions toward aerial warfare or how the myth of victimhood came into existence. Extreme positions from the left or right are most likely to leave the visitor in a distant observer position, instead of challenging visitors to see themselves acting within these memory patterns. However, the following subsection entitled "Humanitarian Interventions," with references to the German use of aerial warfare in Kosovo and Afghanistan since the 1990s, also allowed an active visitor to reevaluate whether one can or should condemn aerial warfare. The exhibition implicitly led the visitor toward an anti-war stance that also managed to undercut right-wing arguments sur-

---

[6] Museum director Heinrich Theodor Grütter expresses a certain caution in the preface to the museum catalog while reflecting upon whether the exhibition successfully reflects agonistic principles: "at least some elements" of the exhibition might achieve this (Grütter 2019, 24). Stefan Berger and Wulf Kansteiner emphasize agonistic moments achieved through "pitch[ing] divergent, easily identifiable remembrance strategies against each other," for example through quotations (2019, 33).

[7] For example, the exhibition only displayed the survey texts in English and German, whereas its object captions and explanations were exclusively displayed in German.

[8] In the German original: "Der Bombenholocaust lässt sich nicht widerlegen!"

rounding how the memory of the Second World War and German suffering could be read. It attempted to enable visitors to differentiate between various kinds of victimhood, and it avoided making equivalences between German suffering and that of Jewish Holocaust victims. Instead of presenting a singular collective memory or experience, it attempted to express – and in some cases succeeded in expressing – a multiperspectivity of German experiences.

In summary, the exhibition required an active visitor working together with structural constellations, in order to understand how the German memory of war in the twentieth and twenty-first centuries functions. How would a German, Polish, Hungarian, Ukrainian, or Russian nationalist react to such an exhibition? Would they really start to think critically about their own ways of remembering? There is a strong possibility that visitors would have become disoriented in the exhibition's unguided representation, in a similar fashion to the Bundeswehr Military History Museum. This is due to the fact they were unsure about what they should learn from the exhibition and unable to read the different memory constellations without a guide.

Experientiality is crucial for researchers analyzing the structures and potential cognitive, aesthetic, ethical, and emotional effects of history and war exhibitions. This is because it reveals how museums can maintain a balance between the integration of educational or ethical goals in understanding the past, while at the same time allowing for reflection upon the function of war remembrance. Without narrative structure, visitors might be confused by too many semiotic possibilities. Without historical contextualization, visitors cannot obtain the tools needed to question narratives and historical judgments. They end up simply confirming the status quo of their existing cultural memory and pre-existing knowledge. Without techniques of immersion through empathy with individual or collective perspectives, or through structural simulation, visitors might remain at a great distance from the past, which does not allow for empathetic unsettlement, the learning of difficult knowledge, and a questioning of their own positions. Visitors might just read the exhibition for passive information, irrelevant of how it relates to their own positions, aside for the fact that they are German (or that they belong to a particular group). It then becomes easy for the German visitor to empathize, for instance, with German resistance groups, or to separate oneself from the majority of Germans who silently supported the Nazi regime.

To reference a current example: only if visitors can question the construction of history and memory from multiple angles, can they understand the logic – in the context of how the history of Second World War memory relates to the contemporary political situation – behind why German Chancellor Angela Merkel was invited to the Western Allies' commemoration celebration of the seventy-fifth anniversary of the D-Day landing in Normandy on June 6, 2019, while Russian President Vladimir Putin was not. A museum that produces experientiality could allow the visitor to understand the construction of the Western Allies' master narrative and myth that D-Day (alone) began the liberation of Europe. A museum could do so by contrasting D-Day to the war in Eastern Europe and the role of the Soviet advancement, and the role of the USSR in Communist Central and Eastern Europe during the Cold War.[9] Only if an exhibition puts the visitor in the experiencer position, so that the experience and possibilities of thinking and acting in the past and the present collide at certain points, the visitor can understand not only how historical facts, but also how experiences and memories, are constructed. Since the museum visitor can never completely take on the role of a historical character or collective, experientiality is crucial for dissecting the different techniques that museums offer their visitors in cognitively and emotionally connecting with the Second World War from their unique positions between past and present. Visitors can learn that the meaning of the past is not stable, but rather constantly reconstructed.

If the memory of the Second World War is fairly static, in cases such as North American memory, a museum does not have to deconstruct its own cultural memory. Instead, it could lead its visitors toward understanding the memory narrative's relevance. If visitors are given the potential to diversify this narrative by integrating themselves and their contemporary society in the museum experience, the museum can open up different experiential possibilities without risking scandal, by making factual statements that contradict memorial myths (as happened, for example, during the debate surrounding the Enola Gay exhibition in Washington, D.C. in 1995). Visitors might still prefer the master narratives that have already shaped their cultural memory, but exhibitions could at least offer ways to understand the genesis and reasons behind different positions, narratives, and cultural memories.[10] With the approaching end of living memory of the Second World War, it is only under these circumstances – wherein the visitor understands the constructedness of memory and cultural narratives – that we can truly consider the different options available to us to understand and narrate the past. Visitors could receive the tools to connect past and present as well as to critically reflect upon the possibilities of how individuals and society can react in situations of totalitarianism, war, violence, and genocide. This can be done in

---

[9] In its "The Liberation of Belgium" section, the Bastogne War Museum offers one of the few attempts in Western museums to explicitly ask the visitor whether the war in the East is sufficiently represented in Western memory of the war.
[10] See the discussion on the debate about the Bomber Command depiction in the "Air War" section in the Canadian War Museum in chapter 3.1.

such a way that they can truly 'transcend boundaries' in the present without giving up the specificity of the past.

Bibliography

Adorno, Theodor W. *Aesthetic Theory*. Ed. Gretel Adorno and Rolf Tiedemann. Trans. and ed. Robert Hullot-Kentor. Minneapolis: U of Minnesota P, 1997 [German 1970].
Agamben, Giorgio. *Remnants of Auschwitz: The Witness and the Archive*. Trans. Daniel Heller-Roazen. New York: Zone Books, 1999 [Italian 1998]. Homo sacer 3.
Agnew, Vanessa. "Introduction: What is Reenactment?" *Criticism* 46.3 (2004): 327–339.
Agnew, Vanessa. "History's Affective Turn: Historical Reenactment and Its Work in the Present." *Rethinking History* 11.3 (2007): 299–312.
101st Airborne Museum Le Mess, Bastogne. Website. http://www.101airbornemuseumbastogne.com/. Accessed 13 October 2019.
Airborne Museum Hartenstein. Website. https://www.airbornemuseum.nl/en/home. Accessed 13 October 2019.
Alba, Avril. *The Holocaust Memorial Museum: Sacred Secular Space*. Basingstoke: Palgrave Macmillan, 2015. The Holocaust and its Contexts.
Alexander, Jeffrey C. "The Social Construction of Moral Universals." *Remembering the Holocaust: A Debate*. By Jeffrey C. Alexander with commentaries by Martin Jay, Bernhard Giesen, Michael Rothberg, Robert Manne, Nathan Glazer, Elihu Katz, and Ruth Katz. Oxford: Oxford UP, 2009. 3–102.
Allen, Matthew. "Ghostly Remains and Converging Memories: Yūshūkan and the Australian War Memorial Exhibit the Pacific War." *Asian Studies Review* 39.3 (2015): 430–446.
Allen, Matthew, and Rumi Sakamoto. "War and Peace: War Memories and Museums in Japan." *History Compass* 11/12 (2013): 1047–1058.
Altmann, Susanne. "Militärhistorisches Museum Dresden: Kunst statt Militaria," *Art: Das Kunstmagazin* 6 January 2012. http://www.art-magazin.de/kunst/47904/militaerhistorisches_museum_dresden/. Accessed 20. April 2013.
Apor, Péter. "An Epistemology of the Spectacle? Arcane Knowledge, Memory and Evidence in the Budapest House of Terror." *Rethinking History* 18.3 (2014): 328–344.
Apsel, Joyce. *Introducing Peace Museums*. London: Routledge, 2016. Routledge Research in Museum Studies.
Arnold-de Simine, Silke. "Memory Cultures: The Imperial War Museum North and W.G. Sebald's *Natural History of Destruction*." *Bombs Away: Representing the Air War over Europe and Japan*. Ed. Wilfried Wilms and William Rasch. Amsterdam: Rodopi, 2006. 295–311. Amsterdamer Beiträge zur neueren Germanistik 60.
Arnold-de Simine, Silke. *Mediating Memory in the Museum: Trauma, Empathy, and Nostalgia*. Basingstoke: Palgrave Macmillan, 2013. Palgrave Macmillan Memory Studies.
Arnold-de Simine, Silke. "The Ruin as Memorial – The Memorial as Ruin." *Performance Research* 20.3 (2015): 94–102.
Assmann, Aleida. *Geschichte im Gedächtnis: Von der individuellen Erfahrung zur öffentlichen Inszenierung*. Munich: Beck, 2007.
Assmann, Aleida. *Shadows of Trauma: Memory and the Politics of Postwar Identity*. Trans. Sarah Clift. New York: Fordham UP, 2016 [German 2006].
Assmann Jan. *Das kulturelle Gedächtnis: Schrift, Erinnerung und politische Identität in frühen Hochkulturen*. Munich: Beck, 1992.
Baberowski, Jörg. *Räume der Gewalt*. Frankfurt/M.: Fischer, 2015.
Baer, Ulrich. *Spectral Evidence: The Photography of Trauma*. Cambridge, MA: MIT P, 2002.

Bagnall, Gaynor, and Antony Rowland. "The Imperial War Museum North: A Twenty-First Century Museum?" *The Future of Memory*. Ed. Richard Crownshaw, Jane Kilby, and Antony Rowland. New York: Berghahn, 2010. 51–76.
Bal, Mieke. *Double Exposures: The Subject of Cultural Analysis*. New York: Routledge, 1996.
Bal, Mieke. "Exhibition as Film." *(Re)visualizing National History: Museums and National Identities in Europe in the New Millennium*. Ed. Robin Ostow. Toronto: U of Toronto P, 2008. 15–43. German and European Studies.
Bardgett, Suzanne. "The Genesis and Development of the Imperial War Museum's Holocaust Exhibition Project." *Journal of Holocaust Education* 7.3 (1998): 28–37.
Bardgett, Suzanne. "The Depiction of the Holocaust at the Imperial War Museum since 1961." *The Journal of Israeli History* 23.l (2004): 146–156.
Barndt, Kerstin. "Layers of Time: Industrial Ruins and Exhibitionary Spaces." *PMLA* 125.1 (2010): 134–141.
Barnes, Lindsey, and Kim Guise. "World War Words: The Creation of a World War II-Specific Vocabulary for the Oral History Collection at The National WWII Museum." *Oral History Review* 40.1 (2013): 126–134.
Barthes, Roland. "The Discourse of History." *Comparative Criticism. A Yearbook* (1981): 7–20 [French 1967].
Bastogne War Museum. "Presentation Bastogne War Museum." 2014. http://www.bastogne warmuseum.be/photo/pagecontent/239/bwm_english_version.pdf, accessed 9 August 2018.
Bastogne War Museum. *Bastogne War Museum: Living Memory of the Ardennes – Visitor Guide*. Ed. Elie Barnavi, Henri Dupuis, and Adrien Roselar. Bastogne: Bastogne War Museum/tempora, 2016.
Bastogne War Museum. Website. https://www.bastognewarmuseum.be/en/home-en/. Accessed 13 October 2019.
Baudrillard, Jean. *Simulacra and Simulation*. Trans. Sheila Faria Glaser. Ann Arbor, MI: U of Michigan P, 1994 [French 1981].
Becker, Jean-Jacques. "The Origins of the Historial." *The Collections of the Historial of the Great War*. Ed. Caroline Fontaine, Annette Becker, Stéphane Audoin-Rouzeaui, and Marie-Pascale Prévost-Bault. Paris: Somogy Art Publisher, 2008. 30–33.
Bedford, Leslie. *The Art of Museum Exhibitions: How Story and Imagination Create Aesthetic Experiences*. Walnut Creek: Left Coast P, 2014.
Bednarek, Monika. "Kraków under Nazi Occupation 1939–1945: The Concept behind the Exhibition." *Kraków under Nazi Occupation 1939–1945*. Ed. Monika Bednarek, Edyta Gawron, Grzegorz Jeżowski, Barbara Zbroja, and Katarzyna Zimmerer. Trans. Michal Szymonik. Kraków: Muzeum Historyczne Miasta Krakowa, 2011. 36–55.
Beil, Christine. *Der ausgestellte Krieg: Präsentationen des Ersten Weltkriegs 1914–1939*. Tübingen: Tübinger Vereinigung. für Volkskunde, 2004. Untersuchungen des Ludwig-Uhland-Instituts der Universität Tübingen 97.
Benjamin, Walter. "The Work of Art in the Age of its Technological Reproducibility: Second Version." [1935] Trans. Edmund Jephcott and Harry Zohn. *The Work of Art in the Age of its Technological Reproducibility, and Other Writings on Media*. Ed. Michael W. Jennings, Brigid Doherty, and Thomas Y. Levin. Cambridge, MA: Belknap P of Harvard UP, 2008. 9–55.

Beier-de Haan, Rosmarie. *Erinnerte Geschichte – Inszenierte Geschichte*. Frankfurt/M.: Suhrkamp, 2005. Edition Zweite Moderne.

Beier-de Haan, Rosmarie. "Re-staging Histories and Identities." Trans. Allison Brown. *A Companion to Museum Studies*. Ed. Sharon Macdonald. New York: Blackwell, 2006. 186–197. Blackwell Companions in Cultural Studies 12.

Berger, Stefan. "Remembering the Second World War in Western Europe, 1945–2005." *A European Memory? Contested Histories and Politics of Remembrance*. Ed. Małgorzata Pakier and Bo Stråth. New York: Berghahn, 2010. 119–136. Studies in Contemporary European History 6.

Berger, Stefan, Heinrich Theodor Grütter, and Wulf Kansteiner, eds. *Krieg. Macht. Sinn: Krieg und Gewalt in der europäischen Erinnerung / War and Violence in European Memory – Katalogbuch zur Ausstellung des Ruhr Museums auf Zollverein 11. November 2018 bis 10. Juni 2019*. Essen: Klartext, 2019.

Berger, Stefan, and Wulf Kansteiner. "Antagonistische, kosmopolitische und agonale Erinnerungen an Krieg / Antagonistic, Cosmopolitan and Agonistic Memories of War." *Krieg. Macht. Sinn: Krieg und Gewalt in der europäischen Erinnerung / War and Violence in European Memory – Katalogbuch zur Ausstellung des Ruhr Museums auf Zollverein 11. November 2018 bis 10. Juni 2019*. Ed. Stefan Berger, Heinrich Theodor Grütter, and Wulf Kansteiner. Essen: Klartext, 2019. 17–35.

Berkhofer Jr., Robert F. *Beyond the Great Story: History as Text and Discourse*. Cambridge, MA: Belknap P of Harvard UP, 1995.

Bernard-Donals, Michael. *Figures of Memory: The Rhetoric of Displacement at the United States Holocaust Memorial Museum*. Albany: State U of New York P, 2016.

Beßer, Klaus Udo. "Das Arsenal-Hauptgebäude." *Arsenal und Museum: Vergangenheit, Gegenwart, Zukunft*. Ed. Thomas Eugen Scheerer. Dresden: Militärhistorisches Museum der Bundeswehr, 2003a. 17–20. Militärhistorisches Museum der Bundeswehr 5.

Beßer, Klaus Udo. "Vorarbeit, Ausschreibung, Entscheidung zum Arsenal-Hauptgebäude." *Arsenal und Museum: Vergangenheit, Gegenwart, Zukunft*. Ed. Thomas Eugen Scheerer. Dresden: Militärhistorisches Museum der Bundeswehr, 2003b. 45–47. Militärhistorisches Museum der Bundeswehr 5.

Bielby, Clare, and Jeffrey Stevenson Murer, eds. *Perpetrating Selves: Doing Violence, Performing Identity*. Cham: Palgrave Macmillan, 2018.

Bisky, Jens. "Topographie des Terrors: Zentrale der Niedertracht." *Süddeutsche Zeitung* 7 May 2010. https://www.sueddeutsche.de/kultur/topographie-des-terrors-zentrale-der-nieder tracht-1.939927. Accessed 13 October 2019.

Blandini, Lucio, Martin Groß, and Werner Sobek. "Das Haus der Europäischen Geschichte in Brüssel." *ce/papers* 1.1 (2017): 41–49.

Bogumił, Zuzanna, Joanna Wawrzyniak, Tim Buchen, Christian Ganzer, and Maria Senina. *The Enemy on Display: The Second World War in Eastern European Museums*. New York: Berghahn, 2015. Museums and Collections 7.

Bogunia-Borowska, Małgorzata. "The Museum as a Space of Social Relations: Oskar Schindler's Enamel Factory Museum in Cracow and POLIN Museum of the History of Polish Jews in Warsaw." *Monitoring of Public Opinion: Economic and Social Changes* 135 (2016): 233–255.

Bömelburg, Hans-Jürgen, Eugeniusz Cezary Król, and Michael Thomae, eds. *Der Warschauer Aufstand 1944: Ereignis und Wahrnehmung in Polen und Deutschland*. Paderborn: Schöningh, 2011.
Bonnell, Jennifer, and Roger I. Simon. "'Difficult' Exhibitions and Intimate Encounters." *Museum and Society* 5.2 (2007): 65–85.
Borodziej, Włodzimierz. "The Academic Committee of the House of European History: Personal Impressions and Memories, 2009–2017." *Creating the House of European History*. Ed. Andrea Mork and Perikles Christodoulou. Luxembourg: Publications Office of the European Union, 2018. 32–38.
Bothwell, Robert, Randall Hansen, and Margaret MacMillan. "Controversy, Commemoration, and Capitulation: The Canadian War Museum and Bomber Command." *Queen's Quarterly* 115.3 (2008): 367–387.
Brandon, Laura. "Canada's War Art – Dispatches: Backgrounds in Canadian Military History." https://www.warmuseum.ca/learn/dispatches/canadas-war-art/#tabs. Accessed 13 October 2019.
Bragança, Manuel, and Peter D. Tame, eds. *The Long Aftermath: Cultural Legacies of Europe at War, 1936–2016*. New York: Berghahn, 2016. Studies in Contemporary European History 17.
Britzman, Deborah P. "If the Story Cannot End: Deferred Action, Ambivalence, and Difficult Knowledge." *Between Hope and Despair: Pedagogy and the Remembrance of Historical Trauma*. Ed. Roger I. Simon, Sharon Rosenberg, and Claudia Eppert. Lanham, MD: Rowman & Littlefield, 2000. 27–57.
Brower, Benjamin Claude. "The Preserving Machine: The 'New' Museum and Working through Trauma – the Musee Memorial pour la Paix of Caen." *History & Memory* 11.1 (1999): 77–103.
Busby, Karen, Adam Muller, and Andrew Woolford, eds. *The Idea of a Human Rights Museum*. Winnipeg: U of Manitoba P, 2015. Human Rights and Social Justice Ser. 1.
Busch, Christophe, Stefan Hördler, and Robert Jan van Pelt, eds. *Das Höcker-Album: Auschwitz durch die Linse der SS*. Darmstadt: Zabern, 2016.
Buschmann, Heike. "Geschichten im Raum: Erzähltheorie als Museumsanalyse." *Museumsanalyse: Methoden und Konturen eines neuen Forschungsfeldes*. Ed. Joachim Baur. Bielefeld: Transcript, 2010. 149–170. Kultur- und Museumsmanagement.
Canadian Museum of Civilization and Canadian War Museum. Research Strategy. 15 July 2013. https://www.historymuseum.ca/wp-content/uploads/2015/09/research-strategy.pdf. Accessed 13 October 2019.
Canadian War Museum. Fact-sheet 2015. https://www.warmuseum.ca/wp-content/uploads/2015/10/construction-e.pdf. Accessed 13 October 2019.
Canadian War Museum. "Annual Report 2015–2016: Your Country. Your History. Your Museum." https://www.warmuseum.ca/wp-content/uploads/2016/08/annual-report-2015-16.pdf. Accessed 13 October 2019.
Canadian War Museum. Website. https://www.warmuseum.ca. Accessed 13 October 2019.
Carden-Coyne, Ana. "The Ethics of Representation in Holocaust Museums." *Writing the Holocaust*. Ed. Jean-Marc Dreyfus and Daniel Langton. London: Bloomsbury Academic, 2011. 167–184.
Caracciolo, Marco. *The Experientiality of Narrative: An Enactivist Approach*. Berlin: de Gruyter, 2014. Narratologia 43.

Celinscak, Mark. "The Holocaust and the Canadian War Museum Controversy." *Canadian Jewish Studies / Études juives canadiennes* 26 (2018): 12–30.
Cento Bull, Anna, Hans Lauge Hansen, Wulf Kansteiner, and Nina Parish. "War Museums as Agonistic Spaces: Possibilities, Opportunities and Constraints." *International Journal of Heritage Studies* 25.6 (2019): 611–625.
Cento Bull, Anna, and Hans Lauge Hansen. "On Agonistic Memory." *Memory Studies* 9.4 (2016): 390–404.
Cercel, Cristian. "The Military History Museum in Dresden: Between Forum and Temple." *History & Memory* 30.1 (2018): 3–39.
Cercel, Cristian, Nina Parish, and Eleanor Rowley. "War in the Museum: The Historial of the Great War in Péronne and the Military History Museum in Dresden." *Journal of War & Culture Studies* 12.2 (2019): 194–214.
Chatterley, Catherine D. "Canada's Struggle with Holocaust Memorialization: The War Museum Controversy, Ethnic Identity Politics, and the Canadian Museum for Human Rights." *Holocaust and Genocide Studies* 29.2 (2015): 189–211.
Chirot, Daniel, Gi-Wook Shin, and Daniel Sneider, eds. *Confronting Memories of World War II:* Seattle: U of Washington P, 2014. European and Asian Legacies.
Christodoulou, Perikles. "In Quest of Objects." *Creating the House of European History*. Ed. Andrea Mork and Perikles Christodoulou. Luxembourg: Publications Office of the European Union, 2018. 229–233.
Chu, Winson. "'Warschau erhebt sich': The 1944 Warsaw Uprising and the Nationalization of European Identity in the Berlin Republic." *Views of Violence: Representing the Second World War in German and European Museums and Memorials*. Ed. Jörg Echternkamp and Stephan Jaeger. New York: Berghahn, 2019. 129–148. Spektrum: Publications from the German Studies Association 19.
Clarke, David, and Paweł Duber. "Polish Cultural Diplomacy and Historical Memory: The Case of the Museum of the Second World War in Gdańsk." *International Journal of Politics, Culture, and Society*, 5 September 2018. 1–18. https://doi.org/10.1007/s10767-018-9294-x.
Clarke, David, and Zofia Wóycicka. "Cultural Diplomacy in the War Museum: The Case of the German-Russian Museum Berlin-Karlshorst." *History & Memory* 31.2 (2019): 78–116.
Ciobanu, Claudia. "Poland's WWII Museum under Political Bombardment: In Gdańsk, the Battle for Country's Future is Waged in the Past." *politico.eu*, 15 May 2017, updated 17 May 2017. https://www.politico.eu/article/polands-wwii-museum-under-political-bombardment/. Acccessed 10 August 2018.
Cohen-Pfister, Laurel. "Claiming the Second World War and Its Lost Generation: *Unsere Mütter, unsere Väter* and the Politics of Emotion." *Representations of War Experiences from the Eighteenth Century to the Present*. Ed. Stephan Jaeger and Susanne Vees-Gulani. Spec. Issue of *Seminar: A Journal of Germanic Studies* 50.1 (2014): 104–123.
Cooke, Steven. "'Your Story Too?' The New Holocaust Exhibition at the Imperial War Museum." *Remembering for the Future: The Holocaust in an Age of Genocide*. Vol. 3: Memory. Ed. John K. Roth and Elisabeth Maxwell. Basingstoke: Palgrave, 2001: 590–606.
Crane, Susan. "Memory, History and Distortion in the Museum." *History and Theory* 36.4 (1997): 44–63.

Cundy, Alys. "Thresholds of Memory: Representing Function through Space and Object at the Imperial War Museum." *Museum History Journal* 8.2 (2015): 247–268.
Dean, Carolyn J. *The Fragility of Empathy after the Holocaust*. Ithaca, NY: Cornell UP, 2004.
Dean, David. "Museums as Conflict Zones: The Canadian War Museum and Bomber Command." *Museum and Society* 7.1 (2009): 1–15.
Dean, David. "Museums as Sites for Historical Understanding, Peace, and Social Justice: Views from Canada." *Peace and Conflict: Journal of Peace Psychology* 19.4 (2013): 325–337.
Denton, Kirk A. *Exhibiting the Past: Historical Memory and the Politics of Museums in Postsocialist China*. Honolulu: U of Hawai'i P, 2014.
Deutsch-Russisches Museum Berlin-Karlshorst. *German Russian Museum Berlin Karlshorst: Catalogue of the Permanent Exhibition*. Berlin: Deutsch-Russisches Museum Berlin-Karlshorst, 2014.
Deutsches Historisches Museum. "Diversity Destroyed: Berlin 1933–1938." https://www.dhm.de/archiv/ausstellungen/zerstoerte-vielfalt/en. Accessed 13 October 2019.
Didi-Huberman, Georges. *Images in Spite of All: Four Photographs from Auschwitz*. Chicago: U of Chicago P, 2008 [2003].
Dixon, Michaela. "The Unreliable Perpetrator: Negotiating Narrative Perspective at Museums of the Third Reich and the GDR." *German Life and Letters* 70.2 (2017): 241–261.
Doležel, Lubomír. "Fictional and Historical Narrative: Meeting the Postmodern Challenge." *Narratologies: New Perspectives on Narrative Analysis*. Ed. David Herman. Columbus, OH: Ohio State UP, 1999. 247–273. Theory and Interpretation of Narrative Ser. 8.
Doležel, Lubomír. *Possible Worlds of Fiction and History: The Postmodern Stage*. Baltimore, MD: Johns Hopkins UP, 2010.
Dolski, Michael R. "'Portal of Liberation': D-Day Myth as American Self-Affirmation." *D-Day in History and Memory: The Normandy Landings in International Remembrance and Commemoration*. Ed. Michael R. Dolski, Sam Edwards, and John Buckley. Denton, TX: U of North Texas P, 2014. 43–84.
Donadio, Rachel, and Joanna Berendt. "Poland's the Second World War Museum is Imperiled." *The New York Times* 24 January 2017. https://www.nytimes.com/2017/01/24/arts/design/polands-world-war-ii-museum-is-imperiled.html. Accessed 13 October 2019.
Donnelly, Rachel. "Imperial War Museums: Reflecting and Shaping Holocaust Memory." *Remembering the Holocaust in Educational Settings*. Ed. Andy Pearce. London: Routledge, 2019. 107–121. Remembering the Modern World.
Dotzler, Bernard J. "Simulation." *Ästhetische Grundbegriffe: Historisches Wörterbuch in sieben Bänden*. Ed. Karlheinz Barck, Martin Fontius, Dieter Schlenstedt, Burkhart Steinwachs, and Friedrich Wolfzettel. Vol. 5. Stuttgart: Metzler, 2010 [2003]. 509–533.
Dülmen, Moritz van, Wolf Kühnelt, and Bjoern Weigel, eds. *Zerstörte Vielfalt / Diversity Destroyed: Berlin 1933–1938–1945 – Eine Stadt erinnert sich / A City Remembers*. Berlin: Kulturprojekte Berlin, 2013.
Echternkamp, Jörg and Stefan Martens, eds. *Experience and Memory: The Second World War in Europe*. New York: Berghahn 2010 [German 2007]. Studies in Contemporary European History 7.
Echternkamp, Jörg, and Stephan Jaeger, eds. *Views of Violence: Representing the Second World War in German and European Museums and Memorials*. New York: Berghahn, 2019a. Spektrum: Publications from the German Studies Association 19.

Echternkamp, Jörg, and Stephan Jaeger. "Introduction: Representing the Second World War in European Museums and Memorials." *Views of Violence: Representing the Second World War in German and European Museums and Memorials*. Ed. Jörg Echternkamp and Stephan Jaeger. New York: Berghahn, 2019b. 1–23. Spektrum: Publications from the German Studies Association 19.

Engelhardt, Tom. "The Victors and the Vanquished." *History Wars: The Enola Gay and other Battles for the American Past*. Ed. Edward T. Linenthal and Tom Engelhardt. New York: Metropolitan Books, 1996. 210–249.

Erll, Astrid. "Wars We Have Seen: Literature as a Medium of Collective Memory in the 'Age of Extremes'." *Memories and Representations of War: The Case of World War I and World War II*. Ed. Elena Lamberti and Vita Fortunati. Amsterdam: Rodopi, 2009. 27–43. Textxet: Studies in Comparative Literature 58.

Erll, Astrid. "Cultural Memory Studies: An Introduction." *A Companion to Cultural Memory Studies*. Ed. Astrid Erll and Ansgar Nünning. Berlin: de Gruyter, 2010. 1–15.

Erll, Astrid. "Travelling Memory." *Parallax* 17.4 (2011): 4–18.

Erll, Astrid, and Ann Rigney. "Introduction: Cultural Memory and its Dynamics." *Mediation, Remediation, and the Dynamics of Cultural Memory*. Ed. Astrid Erll and Ann Rigney: Berlin: de Gruyter, 2009. 1–11. Media and Cultural Memory 10.

Etges, Andreas, and Irmgard Zündorf. "[Interview with Paweł Machcewicz)]: History and Politics and the Politics of History – Poland and Its Museums of Contemporary History." *International Public History* 1.1 (2018); DOI: https://doi.org/10.1515/iph-2018–0006.

Fabryka Emalia Oskara Schindlera. Website. http://www.mhk.pl/exhibitions/krakow-under-nazi-occupation-1939-1945. Accessed 13 October 2019.

Failler, Angela, and Roger I. Simon. "Curatorial Practice and Learning from Difficult Knowledge." *The Idea of a Human Rights Museum*. Ed. Karen Busby, Adam Muller, and Andrew Woolford. Winnipeg: U of Manitoba P, 2015. 165–179. Human Rights and Social Justice Ser. 1.

Falk, John H. *Identity and the Museum Visitor Experience*. Walnut Creek, CA: Left Coast P; 2009.

Falk, John H, and Lynn D. Dierking. *The Museum Experience Revisited*. Walnut Creek, CA: Left Coast P, 2012.

Fehr, Michael. "Art – Museum – Utopia: Five Themes on an Epistemological Construction Site." *Thinking Utopia: Steps into Other Worlds*. Ed. Jörn Rüsen, Michael Fehr, and Thomas W. Rieger. New York: Berghahn, 2005. 169–173.

Fehr, Michael: "Zur Konstruktion von Geschichte mit dem Museum – fünf Thesen." *Die Magie der Geschichte: Geschichtskultur und Museum*. Ed. Martina Padberg and Martin Schmidt. Bielefeld: Transcript, 2010. 39–51.

Feindt, Gregor, Felix Krawatzek, Daniela Mehler, Friedeman Pestel, and Rieke Trimçev. "Entangled Memory: Toward a Third Wave in Memory Studies." *History and Theory* 53.1 (2014): 24–44.

Felman, Shoshana, and Dori Laub. *Testimony: Crises of Witnessing in Literature, Psychoanalysis and History*. New York: Routledge, 1992.

Fernández-Maya, Tatiana: "Agonistic Memory: Introducing a Dialogic Way of Remembrance in a Museum Environment." *KULT_online* 58 (2019). https://doi.org/10.22029/ko.2019.261. Accessed 13 October 2019.

Fickers, Andreas. "Kompromissgeschichte, serviert auf dem 'Tablet': Das Haus der europäischen Geschichte in Brüssel." *Zeithistorische Forschungen/Studies in Contemporary History* 15 (2018): 173–183.
Finney, Patrick. "Politics and Technologies of Authenticity: The Second World War at the Close of Living Memory." *Rethinking History* 21.2 (2017): 154–170.
Flacke, Monika, ed. *Mythen der Nationen: 1945 – Arena der Erinnerungen: Eine Ausstellung des Deutschen Historischen Museums – Begleitbände zur Ausstellung 2. Oktober 2004 bis 27. Februar 2005 – Ausstellungshalle von I. M. Pei*. 2 vols. Berlin: Deutsches Historisches Museum / Mainz: Zabern, 2004.
Fleischer, Wolfgang. "Die Magazine des Militärhistorischen Museums Dresden an der Schwelle zum 21. Jahrhundert: Ein Sachbericht." *Arsenal und Museum: Vergangenheit, Gegenwart, Zukunft*. Ed. Thomas Eugen Scheerer. Dresden: Militärhistorisches Museum der Bundeswehr, 2003. 21–27. Militärhistorisches Museum der Bundeswehr 5.
Fludernik, Monika. *Towards a 'Natural' Narratology*. London: Routledge, 1996.
Fludernik, Monika. "Fiction vs. Non-Fiction: Narratological Differentiations." *Erzählen und Erzähltheorie im 20. Jahrhundert: Festschrift für Wilhelm Füger*. Ed. Jörg Helbig. Heidelberg: Winter, 2001. 85–103. Anglistische Forschungen 294.
Fludernik, Monika. "Experience, Experientiality, and Historical Narrative: A View from Narratology." *Erfahrung und Geschichte: Historische Sinnbildung im Pränarrativen*. Ed. Thiemo Breyer and Daniel Creutz. Berlin: de Gruyter, 2010. 40–72. Narratologia 23.
François, Etienne. "Meistererzählungen und Dammbrüche: Die Erinnerung an den Zweiten Weltkrieg zwischen Nationalisierung und Universalisierung." *Mythen der Nationen: 1945 – Arena der Erinnerungen: Eine Ausstellung des Deutschen Historischen Museums – Begleitbände zur Ausstellung 2. Oktober 2004 bis 27. Februar 2005 – Ausstellungshalle von I. M. Pei*. Ed. Monika Flacke. Vol. 1. Berlin: Deutsches Historisches Museum / Mainz: Zabern, 2004. 13–28.
Frei, Norbert, and Wulf Kansteiner, eds. *Den Holocaust erzählen? Historiographie zwischen wissenschaftlicher Empirie und narrativer Kreativität*. Göttingen: Wallstein, 2013. Vorträge und Kolloquien: Jena-Center Geschichte des 20. Jahrhunderts 11.
Friedländer, Saul, ed. *Probing the Limits of Representation: Nazism and the 'Final Solution.'* Cambridge, MA: Harvard UP, 1992.
Fulda, Daniel. "'Selective' History: Why and How 'History' Depends on Readerly Narrativization with the *Wehrmacht* Exhibition as an Example." *Narratology beyond Literary Criticism*. Ed. Jan Christoph Meister. Berlin: de Gruyter, 2005. 173–194. Narratologia 6.
Gable, Eric. "How We Study History Museums: or, Cultural Studies at Monticello." *New Museum Theory and Practice: an Introduction*. Ed. Janet Marstine. Malden, MA: Blackwell, 2005. 109–128.
Gable, Eric. "Ethnographie: Das Museum als Feld." *Museumsanalyse: Methoden und Konturen eines neuen Forschungsfeldes*. Ed. Joachim Baur. Bielefeld: Transcript, 2010. 95–119. Kultur- und Museumsmanagement.
Geertz, Clifford. "Thick Description: Toward an Interpretative Theory of Culture." *The Interpretation of Cultures: Selected Essays*. By Clifford Geertz. Foreword Robert Darnton. New York: Basic Books, 2017 [1973]. 3–33.

Gieryn, Thomas F. "Science, Enola Gay and History Wars at the Smithsonian." *The Politics of Display: Museums, Science, Culture.* Ed. Sharon Macdonald. New York: Routledge, 1998. 197–228.

Greenberg, Reesa. "Constructing the Canadian War Museum / Constructing the Landscape of Canadian Identity." *(Re)visualizing National History: Museums and National Identities in Europe in the New Millennium.* Ed. Robin Ostow. Toronto: U of Toronto P, 2008. 183–199. German and European Studies.

Greenberg, Stephen. "The Vital Museum." *Reshaping Museum Space.* Ed. Suzanne MacLeod. London: Routledge, 2005. 226–237. Museum Meanings.

Grethlein, Jonas. "Experientiality and 'Narrative Reference,' with Thanks to Thucydides." *History and Theory* 49.3 (2010): 315–335.

Gross, Jan. T. *Neighbors: The Destruction of the Jewish Community in Jedwabne, Poland.* Princeton, NJ: Princeton UP, 2001 [Polish 2000].

Grütter, Heinrich Theodor. "Die Präsentation der Vergangenheit: Zur Darstellung von Geschichte in historischen Museen und Ausstellungen." *Historische Faszination: Geschichtskultur heute.* Ed. Klaus Füssmann. Cologne: Böhlau, 1994. 174–187.

Grütter, Heinrich Theodor. "Vorwort / Preface." *Krieg. Macht. Sinn: Krieg und Gewalt in der europäischen Erinnerung / War and Violence in European Memory – Katalogbuch zur Ausstellung des Ruhr Museums auf Zollverein 11. November 2018 bis 10. Juni 2019.* Ed. Stefan Berger, Heinrich Theodor Grütter, and Wulf Kansteiner. Essen: Klartext, 2019. 11–15.

Guichard-Marneur, Maud. "Forgetting Communism, Remembering World War II? The Case of the Permanent Exhibition of the Schindler Factory Museum, Krakow, Poland." *International Journal of Heritage Studies* 24.8 (2018): 811–827.

Gumbrecht, Hans Ulrich. *After 1945: Latency as Origin of the Present.* Stanford, CA: Stanford UP, 2013.

Gumbrecht, Hans Ulrich. *Our Broad Present: Time and Contemporary Culture.* New York: Columbia UP, 2014. Insurrections: Critical Studies in Religion, Politics, and Culture.

Hackmann, Jörg. "Defending the 'Good Name' of the Polish Nation: Politics of History as a Battlefield in Poland, 2015–18." *Journal of Genocide Research* 20.4 (2018): 587–606.

Halbwachs, Maurice. *On Collective Memory.* Ed. Lewis A. Coser. Chicago: U of Chicago P, 1992 [French 1925]. The Heritage of Sociology.

Hansen-Glucklich, Jennifer. *Holocaust Memory Reframed: Museums and the Challenges of Representation.* New Jersey: Rutgers UP, 2014.

Hasegawa, Tsuyoshi. "The Atomic Bombs and the Soviet Invasion: What Drove Japan's Decision to Surrender?" *The Asia-Pacific Journal* 5.8 (2007): 1–31.

Haß, Matthias. *Das Aktive Museum und die Topographie des Terrors.* Berlin: Hentrich & Hentrich, 2012. Stiftung Topographie des Terrors: Notizen 4.

Hatch, Walter. "Bloody Memories: Affect and Effect of World War II Museums in China and Japan." *Peace & Change* 39.3 (2014): 366–394.

Hawig, Jana. "Exhibiting Images of War: The Use of Historic Media in the Bundeswehr Military History Museum (Dresden) and the Imperial War Museum North (Manchester)." *Views of Violence: Representing the Second World War in German and European Museums and Memorials.* Ed. Jörg Echternkamp and Stephan Jaeger. New York: Berghahn, 2019. 75–91. Spektrum: Publications from the German Studies Association 19.

Heckner, Elke. "Fascism and Its Afterlife in Architecture: Towards a Revaluation of Affect." *Museum & Society* 14.3 (2016): 363–381.
Heinemann, Monika. "Emotionalisierungsstrategien in historischen Austellungen am Beispiel ausgewählter Warschauer Museen." *Medien zwischen Fiction-Making und Realitätsanspruch: Konstruktionen historischer Erinnerungen*. Ed. Monika Heinemann, Hannah Maischein, Monika Flacke, Peter Haslinger, and Martin Schulze Wessel. Munich: Oldenbourg, 2011. 213–236. Veröffentlichungen des Collegium Carolinum 121.
Heinemann, Monika. "Die 'Emaillewarenfabrik Oskar Schindlers': Die neue Dauerausstellung vor dem Hintergrund der Musealisierung des Zweiten Weltkriegs seit den 1980er Jahren." *Krieg im Museum: Präsentationen des Zweiten Weltkriegs in Museen und Gedenkstätten des östlichen Europas*. Ed. Ekaterina Makhotina, Ekaterina Keding, Włodzimierz Borodziej, Étienne François, and Martin Schulze Wessel. Göttingen: Vandenhoeck & Ruprecht, 2015. 255–284. Veröffentlichungen des Collegium Carolinum 131.
Heinemann, Monika. *Krieg und Kriegserinnerung im Museum: Der Zweite Weltkrieg in polnischen historischen Ausstellungen seit den 1980er-Jahren*. Göttingen: Vandenhoek & Ruprecht, 2017. Schnittstellen: Studien zum östlichen und südöstlichen Europa 5.
Hervouet, Sébastien, Luc Braeuer, and Marc Braeuer. *1.500 musées, 1939–1945: guide Europe = Unique European military guide book: World War II*. Batz-sur-Mer: Éditions Le Grand Blockhaus, 2016.
Hesse, Klaus. "Die Bilder lesen: Interpretationen fotografischer Quellen zur Deportation der deutschen Juden." *Vor aller Augen: Fotodokumente des nationalsozialistischen Terrors in der Provinz*. Ed. Klaus Hesse and Philipp Springer. Essen: Klartext, 2002. 185–211.
HG Merz, and Barbara Holzer. "Die Ausstellung im Arsenal-Hauptgebäude (Konzeption)." *Arsenal und Museum: Vergangenheit, Gegenwart, Zukunft*. Ed. Thomas Eugen Scheerer. Dresden: Militärhistorisches Museum der Bundeswehr, 2003a. 52–60. Militärhistorisches Museum der Bundeswehr 5.
Hillmer, Norman: "The Canadian War Museum and the Military Identity of an Unmilitary People." *Canadian Military History* 19.3 (2010): 19–26.
Hilmar, Till. "Narrating Unity at the European Union's New History Museum: A Cultural-Process Approach to the Study of Collective Memory." *European Journal of Sociology* 57.2 (2016): 297–329.
Hinz, Hans-Martin, ed. *Der Krieg und seine Museen*. Frankfurt/M.: Campus, 1997.
Hirsch, Marianne. *Family Frames: Photography, Narrative, and Postmemory*. Cambridge, MA.: Harvard UP, 1997.
Hoffmann, Detlef. "'Authentische Orte': Zur Konjunktur eines problematischen Begriffs in der Gedenkstättenarbeit." *GedenkstättenRundbrief* 110 (2002): 3–17.
Holtschneider, K. Hannah. *The Holocaust and Representations of Jews: History and Identity in the Museum*. London: Routledge, 2011. Routledge Jewish Studies.
Hooper Green, Eilean. "Studying Visitors." *A Companion to Museum Studies*. Ed. Sharon Macdonald. New York: Blackwell, 2006. 362–376. Blackwell Companions in Cultural Studies 12.
Hoskins, Andrew. "Signs of the Holocaust: Exhibiting Memory in a Mediated Age." *Media, Culture & Society* 25.1 (2003): 7–22.
House of European History. *Guidebook: Permanent Exhibition*. Luxembourg: Publications Office of the European Union, 2017a.

House of European History. *Info Brochure in English: Facts and Figures.* 2017b.
House of European History. Website. https://www.historia-europa.ep.eu/. Accessed 13 October 2019.
Huistra, Pieter, Marijn Molema, and Daniel Wirt. "Political Values in a European Museum." *Journal of Contemporary European Research* 10.1 (2014): 124–136.
Huyssen, Andreas. *Present Pasts: Urban Palimpsests and the Politics of Memory.* Stanford, CA: Stanford UP, 2003. Cultural Memory in the Present.
Imperial War Museum. *Imperial War Museum North: Guidebook.* London: Imperial War Museum, 2012.
Imperial War Museum. *Imperial War Museum London: Guidebook.* London: Imperial War Museum, 5th ed., 2017a.
Imperial War Museum. *Imperial War Museum North: Guidebook.* London: Imperial War Museum, 3rd. ed., 2017b.
Imperial War Museum. "IWM Patrons Annual Review 2016–2017." https://www.iwm.org.uk/sites/default/files/documents/iwm_patrons_annual_review_2016-2017.pdf. Accessed 13 October 2019.
Imperial War Museum. "Annual Report and Accounts 2018–19." https://www.iwm.org.uk/sites/default/files/files/2019-07/Annual%20Report%20and%20Accounts%202018-2019.pdf. Accessed 13 October 2019.
Imperial War Museum. Website. https://www.iwm.org.uk/. Accessed 13 October 2019.
Imperial War Museum. "Corporate Plan 2018–21." https://www.iwm.org.uk/file-download/download/public/3618. Accessed 13 October 2019.
Imperial War Museum. "Corporate Plan 2019–24." https://www.iwm.org.uk/file-download/download/public/9202. Accessed 13 October 2019.
Ionescu, Arleen. *The Memorial Ethics of Libeskind's Berlin Jewish Museum.* London: Palgrave Macmillan, 2017. The Holocaust and its Contexts.
Iser, Wolfgang. *The Act of Reading: a Theory of Aesthetic Response.* Baltimore, MD: Johns Hopkins UP, 1978 [German 1976].
Iser, Wolfgang. *The Fictive and the Imaginary: Charting Literary Anthropology.* Baltimore, MD: Johns Hopkins UP, 1993 [German 1991].
Ives, Andrew. "Museography and Narratives of Nation-Building: Deconstructing the Canadian War Museum." *Cercles* 24 (2012): 118–131.
Jacob, George. "Overcoming Illiteracy in Idea-Driven Museums: A Curatorial Conundrum." *The Idea of a Human Rights Museum.* Ed. Karen Busby, Adam Muller, and Andrew Woolford. Winnipeg: U of Manitoba P, 2015. 247–261. Human Rights and Social Justice Ser. 1.
Jackson, Anthony, and Jenny Kidd, eds. *Performing Heritage: Research, Practice and Innovation in Museum Theatre and Live Interpretation.* Manchester: Manchester UP, 2011a.
Jackson, Anthony, and Jenny Kidd. "Introduction." *Performing Heritage: Research, Practice and Innovation in Museum Theatre and Live Interpretation.* Ed. Anthony Jackson and Jenny Kidd. Manchester: Manchester UP, 2011b. 1–8.
Jaeger, Stephan. "Multiperspektivisches Erzählen in der Geschichtsschreibung des ausgehenden 20. Jahrhunderts: Wissenschaftliche Inszenierungen von Geschichte zwischen Roman und Wirklichkeit." *Multiperspektivisches Erzählen: Zur Theorie und Geschichte der Perspektivenstruktur im englischen Roman des 18. bis 20. Jahrhunderts.*

Ed. Vera Nünning and Ansgar Nünning. Trier: Wissenschaftlicher Verlag Trier, 2000. 323–346.
Jaeger, Stephan. "Erzählen im historiographischen Diskurs." *Wirklichkeitserzählungen: Felder, Formen und Funktionen nicht-literarischen Erzählens*. Ed. Christian Klein and Matías Martínez. Stuttgart: Metzler, 2009. 110–135.
Jaeger, Stephan. "Poietic Worlds and Experientiality in Historiographic Narrative." *Towards a Historiographic Narratology*. Ed. Julia Nitz and Sandra Harbert Petrulionis. Spec. issue of *SPIEL* (Siegener Periodicum zur Internationalen Empirischen Literaturwissenschaft) 30.1 (2011): 29–50.
Jaeger, Stephan. "Historical Museum Meets Docu-Drama: The Recipient's Experiential Involvement in the Second World War." *Exhibiting the German Past: Museums, Film, Musealization*. Ed. Peter M. McIsaac and Gabriele Mueller. Toronto: U of Toronto P, 2015a. 138–157.
Jaeger, Stephan. "Temporalizing History toward the Future: Representing Violence and Human Rights Violations in the Military History Museum in Dresden." *The Idea of a Human Rights Museum*. Ed. Karen Busby, Adam Muller, and Andrew Woolford. Winnipeg: U of Manitoba P, 2015b. 229–246. Human Rights and Social Justice Ser. 1.
Jaeger, Stephan. "Between the National and the Transnational: European Memories of World War II in the Twenty-First-Century Museum in Germany and Poland." *The Changing Place of Europe in Global Memory Cultures: Usable Pasts and Futures*. Ed. Christina Kraenzle and Maria Mayr. Basingstoke, 2017a. 23–47. Palgrave Macmillan Memory Studies.
Jaeger, Stephan. "Visualization of War in the Museum: Experiential Spaces, Emotions, and Memory Politics." *Visualizing War: Emotions, Technologies, Communities*. Ed. Anders Engberg-Pedersen and Kathrin Maurer. London: Routledge, 2017b. 165–181. Routledge Advances in Art and Visual Studies Ser.
Jaeger, Stephan. "The Second World War and Trauma in the Museum: Canadian and German Depictions in the 21st Century." *Wor(l)ds of Trauma: Canadian and German Perspectives*. Ed. Wolfgang Klooß. Münster: Waxmann, 2017c. 145–163. Diversity / Diversité / Diversität 3: Publications of the International Research Training Group (IRTG) Diversity (Trier/Montreal/Saarbrücken).
Jaeger, Stephan. "The Experientiality of the Second World War in the 21st-Century European Museum (Normandy, the Ardennes, Germany)." *Views of Violence. Representing the Second World War in Museums and Memorials*. Ed. Jörg Echternkamp and Stephan Jaeger. New York: Berghahn, 2019. 52–74. Spektrum: Publications from the German Studies Association 19.
Jahn, Peter. "Gemeinsam an den Schrecken erinnern: Das Deutsch-Russische Museum Berlin-Karlshorst." *Museumskunde* 68.1 (2003): 30–36.
Jarausch, Konrad H. "Reflections on Transnational History." 20 Jan. 2006. http://h-net.msu.edu/cgi-bin/logbrowse.pl?trx=vx&list=h-german&month=0601&week=c&msg=LPkNHirCm1xgSZQKHOGRXQ&user=&pw=. Accessed 13 October 2019.
Johnston-Weiss, Erin. *Empathy and Distanciation: An Examination of Holocaust Video- and Photography in the Topography of Terror, the German Military History Museum and the Canadian Museum for Human Rights*. MA Thesis U of Manitoba, 2016. http://hdl.handle.net/1993/31672.
Johnston-Weiss, Erin. "In the Eye of the Beholder: Gaze and Distance through Photographic Collage in the Topography of Terror and the Canadian Museum for Human Rights." *Views*

of Violence: Representing the Second World War in German and European Museums and Memorials. Ed. Jörg Echternkamp and Stephan Jaeger. New York: Berghahn, 2019. 92–108. Spektrum: Publications from the German Studies Association 19.
Jong, Steffi de. *The Witness as Object: Video Testimony in Memorial Museums.* New York: Berghahn, 2018a. Museums and Collections 10.
Jong, Steffi de. "Sentimental Education. Sound and Silence at History Museums." *Museum & Society* 16.1 (2018b): 88–106.
Kaiser, Wolf. "Bildungsarbeit in Gedenkstätten für die Opfer des Nationalsozialismus." *GedenkstättenRundbrief* 100.4 (2001): 105–111.
Kaiser, Wolfram. "Limits of Cultural Engineering: Actors and Narratives in the European Parliament's House of European History Project." *Journal of Common Market Studies* 55.3 (2017): 518–534.
Kaiser, Wolfram, Stefan Krankenhagen, and Kerstin Poehl. *Exhibiting Europe in Museums: Transnational Networks, Collections, Narratives and Representations.* New York: Berghahn, 2014. Museums and Collections 6.
Kansteiner, Wulf. "Gefühlte Wahrheit und ästhetischer Relativismus: Über die Annäherung von Holocaust-Geschichtsschreibung und Geschichtstheorie." *Den Holocaust erzählen? Historiographie zwischen wissenschaftlicher Empirie und narrativer Kreativität.* Ed. Norbert Frei and Wulf Kansteiner. Göttingen: Wallstein 2013. 12–50. Vorträge und Kolloquien: Jena-Center Geschichte des 20. Jahrhunderts 11.
Kansteiner, Wulf. "Transnational Holocaust Memory, Digital Culture and the End of Reception Studies." *The Twentieth Century in European Memory: Transcultural Mediation and Reception.* Ed. Tea Sindbæk Andersen and Barbara Törnquist-Plewa. Leiden: Brill: 2017. 305–343. European Studies 34.
Kant, Immanuel. *Critique of the Power of Judgment.* Ed. Paul Guyer. Trans. Paul Guyer and Eric Matthews. Cambridge: Cambridge UP, 2000 [German 1790].
Kavanagh, Gaynor. *Museums and the First World War: A Social History.* London: Bloomsbury Academic, 1994.
Kesteloot, Chantal. "Exhibiting European History in the Museum: The House of European History." *BMGN – Low Countries Historical Review* 133–134 (2018): 149–161.
Kidd, Jenny. "Introduction: Challenging History in the Museum." *Challenging History in the Museum: International Perspectives.* Ed. Jenny Kidd, Sam Cairns, Alex Drago, Amy Ryall, and Miranda Stearn. Farnham, Surrey: Ashgate, 2014. 1–17.
Kirchberg, Volker. "Besucherforschung in Museen: Evaluation von Ausstellungen." *Museumsanalyse: Methoden und Konturen eines neuen Forschungsfeldes.* Ed. Joachim Baur. Bielefeld: Transcript, 2010. 171–184. Kultur- und Museumsmanagement.
Kimura, Maki. *Unfolding the 'Comfort Women' Debates: Modernity, Violence, Women's Voices.* London: Palgrave Macmillan, 2016. Genders and Sexualities in History.
Kindler, Sebastian: "Benno Wundshammer: Vom Sportreporter zum Propagandafotografen der Wehrmacht." *Propagandafotograf im Zweiten Weltkrieg: Benno Wundshammer.* Ed. Deutsch-Russisches Museum Berlin-Karlshorst. Berlin: Links, 2014. 32–49.
Kirshenblatt-Gimblett, Barbara. *Destination Culture: Tourism, Museums, Heritage.* Berkeley, CA: U of California P, 1998.
Kirshenblatt-Gimblett, Barbara. "A Theatre of History: 12 Principles." *TDR: The Drama Review* 59.3 (2015): 49–59.

Kjeldbæk, Esben, ed. *The Power of the Object: Museums and World War II*. Edinburgh: MuseumsEtc, 2009.
Kleinmann, Sarah. *Nationalsozialistische Täterinnen und Täter in Ausstellungen: Eine Analyse in Deutschland und Österreich*. Tübingen: Tübinger Vereinigung für Volkskunde, 2017. Ludwig-Uhland-Institut für Empirische Kulturwissenschaft: Untersuchungen 120.
Kleinmann, Sarah. "The Challenging Representation of National Socialist Perpetrators in Exhibitions: Two Examples from Austria and Germany." *Views of Violence: Representing the Second World War in German and European Museums and Memorials*. Ed. Jörg Echternkamp and Stephan Jaeger. New York: Berghahn, 2019. 109–128. Spektrum: Publications from the German Studies Association 19.
Kohn, Richard H. "History at Risk: The Case of the Enola Gay." *History Wars: The Enola Gay and other Battles for the American Past*. Ed. Edward T. Linenthal and Tom Engelhardt. New York: Metropolitan Books, 1996. 140–170.
Konzeptgruppe/Expertenkommission. "Das Militärhistorische Museum Dresden 2006 (Konzeption)." *Arsenal und Museum: Vergangenheit, Gegenwart, Zukunft*. Ed. Thomas Eugen Scheerer. Dresden: Militärhistorisches Museum der Bundeswehr, 2003. 28–44. Ser. Militärhistorisches Museum der Bundeswehr 5.
Korff, Gottfried. "Ausstellungsgegenstand Geschichte." *Interesse an der Geschichte*. Ed. Frank Niess. Frankfurt/M.: Campus, 1989. 65–76.
Korff, Gottfried. "Reflections on the Museum." Trans. John Bendix and Regina Bendix. *CulturalBrokerage: Forms of Intellectual Practice in Society*. Spec. issue of *Journal of Folklore Research* 36.2/3 (1999): 267–270.
Korzeniewski, Bartosz. "Das veränderte Bild des Zweiten Weltkriegs in polnischen Museen." *Der Zweite Weltkrieg im polnischen und deutschen kulturellen Gedächtnis: Siebzig Jahre danach (1945–2015)*. Ed. Jerzy Kałążny, Amelia Korzeniewska, and Bartosz Korzeniewski. Frankfurt/M.: Lang, 2016. 107–142. Posener Beiträge zur Germanistik 36.
Koselleck, Reinhart. *Futures Past: On the Semantics of Historical Time*. Trans. Keith Tribe. New York: Columbia UP, 2004 [German 1979; English 1985].
Koselleck, Reinhart. *Sediments of Time: on Possible Histories*. Ed. and trans. Sean Franzel and Stefan-Ludwig Hoffmann. Stanford, CA: Stanford UP, 2018 [German 2000]. Cultural Memory in the Present.
Krankenhagen, Stefan. *Auschwitz darstellen: Ästhetische Positionen zwischen Adorno, Spielberg und Walser*. Cologne: Böhlau, 2001. Beiträge zur Geschichtskultur 23.
Krankenhagen, Stefan. "Exhibiting Europe: The Development of European Narratives in Museums, Collections, and Exhibitions." *Culture Unbound* 3 (2011): 269–278.
Krankenhagen, Stefan. "Gegründet 2017 als House of European History." *Merkur: Deutsche Zeitschrift für europäisches Denken* 71.820 (2017): 64–70.
Kraus, Herbert. "Die Organisation der Neukonzeption des Militärhistorischen Museums der Bundeswehr." *Militärhistorisches Museum der Bundeswehr: Ausstellung und Architektur*. Ed. Gorch Pieken and Matthias Rogg. Dresden: Sandstein, 2011. 40–47.
Król, Eugeniusz Cezary. "Perzeptionen des Aufstands in Polen." *Der Warschauer Aufstand 1944: Ereignis und Wahrnehmung in Polen und Deutschland*. Ed. Hans-Jürgen Bömelburg, Eugeniusz Cezary Król, and Michael Thomae. Paderborn: Schöningh, 2011. 171–191.
Kruczek, Zygmunt. "Analysis of Visitor Attendance at Polish Tourism Attractions." *Tourism* 25.1 (2015): 47–56.

Kula, Marcin, and Piotr Majewski. "Muzeum II Wojny Światowej: Dwugłos / Museum of the Second World War: Two Stances." *Muzealnictwo* 58.1 (2017): 102–108.

Kunz. Manfred. "Ein Stück von Sachsens Glanz: Das Arsenal in der Dresdner Albertstadt." *Arsenal und Museum: Vergangenheit, Gegenwart, Zukunft.* Ed. Thomas Eugen Scheerer. Dresden: Militärhistorisches Museum der Bundeswehr, 2003. 5–16. Militärhistorisches Museum der Bundeswehr 5.

Kurilo, Olga, ed. *Der Zweite Weltkrieg im Museum: Kontinuität und Wandel.* Berlin: Avinus, 2007.

Kurkowska-Budzan, Marta. "The Warsaw Rising Museum: Polish Identity and Memory of World War II." *Martor, revue d'anthropologie du Musée du Paysan Roumain* 11 (2006): 133–141.

Kurz, Iwona. "Przepisywanie pamięci: przypadek Muzeum Powstania Warszawskiego." [Rewriting of Memory: The Case of the Warsaw Rising Museum]. *Kultura Współczesna* 3.53 (2007): 150–162.

LaCapra, Dominick. *Writing History, Writing Trauma.* Baltimore, MD: Johns Hopkins UP, 2001. Parallax.

LaCapra, Dominick. *History in Transit: Experience, Identity, Critical Theory.* Ithaca, NY: Cornell UP, 2004.

LaCapra, Dominick. "Trauma, History, Memory, Identity: What Remains?" *History and Theory* 55.3 (2016): 375–400.

Landsberg, Alison. *Prosthetic Memory: The Transformation of American Remembrance in the Age of Mass Culture.* New York: Columbia UP, 2004.

Landsberg, Alison. *Engaging the Past: Mass Culture and the Production of Historical Knowledge.* New York: Columbia UP, 2015.

Lawson, Tom. "Ideology in a Museum of Memory: A Review of the Holocaust Exhibition at the Imperial War Museum." *Totalitarian Movements and Political Religions* 4.2 (2003): 173–183.

Leahy, Anna, and Douglas Dechow. "Keep 'Em Flying High: How American Air Museums Create and Foster Themes of the World War II Air War." *Bombs Away: Representing the Air War over Europe and Japan.* Ed. Wilfried Wilms and William Rasch. Amsterdam: Rodopi, 2006. 313–326. Amsterdamer Beiträge zur neueren Germanistik 60.

Lee, Jooyoun. "Yasukuni and Hiroshima in Clash? War and Peace Museums in Contemporary Japan." *Pacific Focus* 33.1 (2018): 5–33.

Leggewie, Claus, and Anne Lang. *Der Kampf um die europäische Erinnerung: Ein Schlachtfeld wird besichtigt.* Munich: Beck, 2011.

Lehrer, Erica, Cynthia E. Milton, and Monica Patterson, eds. *Curating Difficult Knowledge: Violent Pasts in Public Places.* Basingstoke: Palgrave Macmillan, 2011. Palgrave Macmillan Memory Studies.

Lehrer, Erica, and Cynthia E. Milton. "Introduction: Witnesses to Witnessing." *Curating Difficult Knowledge: Violent Pasts in Public Places.* Ed. Erica Lehrer, Cynthia E. Milton, and Monica Patterson. Basingstoke: Palgrave Macmillan 2011. 1–19. Palgrave Macmillan Memory Studies.

Lentin, Ronit, ed. *Re-presenting the Shoah for the Twenty-First Century.* New York: Berghahn, 2004a.

Lentin, Ronit. "Introduction: Postmemory, Unsayability and the Return of the Auschwitz Code." *Re-presenting the Shoah for the Twenty-First Century*. Ed. Ronit Lentin. New York: Berghahn, 2004b. 1–24.
Leoni, Claudio. "Peter Zumthor's 'Topography of Terror'." *Architectural Research Quarterly* 18 (2014): 110–122.
Levy, Daniel, and Natan Sznaider. "Memory Unbound: The Holocaust and the Formation of Cosmopolitan Memory." *European Journal of Social Theory* 5 (2002): 87–106.
Levy, Daniel, and Natan Sznaider. *The Holocaust and Memory in the Global Age*. Trans. Assenka Oksiloff. Philadelphia: Temple UP, 2006 [German 2001].
Lindqvist, Sven: *A History of Bombing*. Trans. by Linda Haverty Rugg. New York: The New P 2001 [Swedish 2000].
Linenthal, Edward T. "Anatomy of a Controversy." *History Wars: The Enola Gay and other Battles for the American Past*. Ed. Edward T. Linenthal and Tom Engelhardt. New York: Metropolitan Books, 1996. 9–62.
Linenthal, Edward T. *Preserving Memory: The Struggle to Create America's Holocaust Museum*. New York: Columbia UP, 2001 [1995].
Lippert, Julia. "A 'Natural Reading' Reading of Historiographical Texts. George III at Kew." *Narratology in the Age of Cross-Disciplinary Narrative Research*. Ed. Sandra Heinen and Roy Sommer. Berlin: de Gruyter, 2009. 228–243. Narratologia 20.
Lippert, Julia, *Ein kognitives Lesemodell historio(bio)graphischer Texte: Georg III. – Rezeption und Konstruktion in den britischen Medien (1990–2006)*. Trier: Wissenschaftlicher Verlag Trier, 2010. WVT-Handbücher und Studien zur Medienkulturwissenschaft 4.
Locke, Stefan. "Militärhistorisches Museum: Kleinkrieg um Kondome." *Frankfurter Allgemeine Zeitung* 20 December 2017, https://www.faz.net/aktuell/politik/inland/militaerhistorisches-museum-sagt-teuerste-ausstellung-seiner-geschichte-ab-15344550.html. Accessed 13 October 2019.
Logemann, Daniel, and Juliane Tomann. "Gerichte statt Geschichte? Das Museum des Zweiten Weltkrieges in Gdańsk." *Zeithistorische Forschungen/Studies in Contemporary History* 16.1 (2019): http://www.zeithistorische-forschungen.de/1-2019/id=5685. Accessed 13 October 2019.
Loxham, Angela. "Shaped by Familiarity: Memory, Space and Materiality at Imperial War Museum North." *Museum & Society* 13.4 (2015): 522–538.
Lübbe, Hermann. *Der Fortschritt und das Museum: Über den Grund unseres Vergnügens an historischen Gegenständen*. London: Institute of Germanic Studies, U of London, 1982.
Lübbe, Hermann. *Schrumpft die Gegenwart? Über die veränderte Gegenwart von Zukunft und Vergangenheit*. Luzern: Hans-Erni-Stiftung, 2000. Panta rhei 23.
Luhmann, Susanne. "Managing Perpetrator Affect: The Female Guard Exhibition at Ravensbrück." *Perpetrating Selves Perpetrating Selves: Doing Violence, Performing Identity*. Ed. Clare Bielby and Jeffrey Stevenson Murer. Cham: Palgrave Macmillan, 2018. 246–269.
Luke, Timothy W. *Museum Politics: Power Plays at the Exhibition*. Minneapolis: U of Minnesota P, 2002.
Łupak, Sebastian. "Dyrektor Nawrocki: 12 zmian w wystawie stałej MIIWŚ – Były dyrektor Machcewicz: Będzie pozew sądowy!" [Director Nawrocki: 12 changes in the permanent exhibition of the MIIWŚ – Former Director Machcewicz: There will be a lawsuit!], 30

October 2017. www.Gdańsk.pl. https://www.Gdańsk.pl/wiadomosci/MIIWS-12-zmian-wys tawy-stalej-do-grudnia-W-2achce018-kolejne,a,92411. Accessed 13 October 2019.
Lutz, Thomas. *Zwischen Vermittlungsanspruch und emotionaler Wahrnehmung: Die Gestaltung neuer Dauerausstellungen in Gedenkstätten für NS-Opfer in Deutschland und deren Bildungsanspruch*. Diss. TU Berlin 2009.
Lutz, Thomas. "Das Haus der Europäischen Geschichte in Brüssel oder reicht die Totalitarismustheorie zur Erklärung der europäischen Geschichte?" *Politisches Lernen* 1–2 (2019): 45–51.
Lynch, Bernadette. "Reflective Debate, Radical Transparency and Trust in the Museum." *Museum Management and Curatorship* 28.1 (2013): 1–13.
Macdonald, Sharon, ed. *The Politics of Display: Museums, Science, Culture*. New York: Routledge, 1998.
Macdonald, Sharon. *Difficult Heritage: Negotiating the Nazi Past in Nuremberg and Beyond*. New York: Routledge, 2008.
Macdonald, Sharon. *Memorylands: Heritage and Identity in Europe* Today. London: Routledge, 2013.
Macdonald, Sharon, and Gordon Fyfe, eds. *Theorizing Museums: Representing Identity and Diversity in a Changing World*. Oxford: Blackwell, 1996. Sociological Review Monograph Ser. 43.
Machcewicz, Paweł. "Das Museum des Zweiten Weltkriegs in Danzig." *Erinnern an den Zweiten Weltkrieg: Mahnmale und Museen in Mittel- und Osteuropa*. Ed. Stefan Troebst and Johanna Wolf. Leipzig: Leipziger Universitätsverlag, 2011. 161–172. Schriften des Europäischen Netzwerks Erinnerung und Solidarität 2.
Machcewicz, Paweł. "Why Do We Need the Museum of the Second World War?" *Museum of the Second World War: Catalogue of the Permanent Exhibition*. Ed. Rafał Wnuk, Paweł Machcewicz, Oliwia Galka-Olejko, and Łukasz Jasinski: Gdańsk: Muzeum II Wojny Światowej, 2016. 7–13.
Machcewicz, Paweł. *The War That Never Ends: The Museum of the Second World War in Gdańsk*. Berlin: De Gruyter Oldenbourg, 2019 [Polish 2017]. Public History in International Perspective 2.
MacLeod, Suzanne. "Rethinking Museum Architecture: Towards a Site-Specific History of Production and Use." *Reshaping Museum Space*. Ed. Suzanne MacLeod. London: Routledge, 2005. 9–25. Museum Meanings.
MacLeod, Suzanne, Jocelyn Dodd, and Tom Duncan. "New Museum Design Cultures: Harnessing the Potential of Design and 'Design Thinking' in Museums." *Museum Management and Curatorship* 30.4 (2015): 314–341.
Majewski, Piotr M. "Die Musealisierung des Zweiten Weltkrieges in Polen." *Erinnern an den Zweiten Weltkrieg: Mahnmale und Museen in Mittel- und Osteuropa*. Ed. Stefan Troebst and Johanna Wolf. Leipzig: Leipziger Universitätsverlag, 2011. 151–158. Schriften des Europäischen Netzwerks Erinnerung und Solidarität 2.
Makhotina, Ekaterina, Ekaterina Keding, Włodzimierz Borodziej, Étienne François, and Martin Schulze Wessel, eds. *Krieg im Museum: Präsentationen des Zweiten Weltkriegs in Museen und Gedenkstätten des östlichen Europas*. Göttingen: Vandenhoeck & Ruprecht, 2015. Veröffentlichungen des Collegium Carolinum 131.
Makhotina, Ekaterina, and Martin Schulze Wessel: "Neue Konfliktlinien in den Erinnerungen an den Zweiten Weltkrieg im östlichen Europa: Zur Einleitung." *Krieg im Museum:*

Präsentationen des Zweiten Weltkriegs in Museen und Gedenkstätten des östlichen Europas. Ed. Ekaterina Makhotina, Ekaterina Keding, Włodzimierz Borodziej, Étienne François, and Martin Schulze Wessel. Göttingen: Vandenhoeck & Ruprecht, 2015. 1–14. Veröffentlichungen des Collegium Carolinum 131.

Makhotina, Ekaterina. *Erinnerungen an den Krieg – Krieg der Erinnerungen: Litauen und der Zweite Weltkrieg*. Göttingen: Vandenhoeck & Ruprecht, 2017. Schnittstellen 4.

Maron, Jeremy, and Clint Curle. "Balancing the Particular and the Universal: Examining the Holocaust in the Canadian Museum for Human Rights." *Holocaust Studies* 24.4 (2018): 418–444.

Marszałek, Anna, and Monika Bednarek. *Oskar Schindler's Enamel Factory. Guidebook*. Kraków: Muzeum Historyczne Miasta Krakowa, 2010.

Matthews, Sara. "'The Trophies of their Wars': Affect and Encounter at the Canadian War Museum." *Museum Management and Curatorship* 28.3 (2013): 272–287.

McLuhan, Marshall. *Understanding Media: The Extensions of Man*. New York: McGraw-Hill Book Company, 1965 [1964].

MDR. "Interview mit dem neuen Chef des Danziger Weltkriegsmuseums, Karol Nawrocki." MDR, 6 June 2017, https://www.mdr.de/heute-im-osten/weltkriegsmuseum-danzig-106.html. Accessed 10 August 2018.

Meyer, Birga. "Identifying with Mass Murderers? Representing Male Perpetrators in Museum Exhibitions of the Holocaust." *Perpetrating Selves Perpetrating Selves: Doing Violence, Performing Identity*. Ed. Clare Bielby and Jeffrey Stevenson Murer. Cham: Palgrave Macmillan, 2018. 223–245.

Mikuska-Tinman, Emma. *Mediating Memory through Materiality: Trauma Iconography of Flight and Expulsion in the 21st-Century Museum*. MA Thesis U of Manitoba, 2018. Web. http://hdl.handle.net/1993/33568.

Mikuska-Tinman, Emma, and Stephan Jaeger. "The World War Two Refugee in the 21st Century Museum between Nationalism, Transnationalism, and Human Rights." *From Far and Wide: German Studies in Canada*. Ed. Nikola von Merveldt and Andrea Speltz in collaboration with Gaby Pailer. Spec. Issue of *Jahrbuch für Internationale Germanistik*, expected 2020.

Militärhistorisches Museum der Bundeswehr. Website. http://www.mhmbw.de. Accessed 13 October 2019.

Moriyama, Raymond. *In Search of a Soul: Designing and Realizing the New Canadian War Museum*. Vancouver: Douglas & McIntyre, 2006.

Mork, Andrea. "Constructing the House of European History." *European Commemoration: Locating World War I*. Ed. Edgar Wolfrum, Odila Triebel, Cord Arendes, Angela Siebold, and Joana Duyster Borredà. Stuttgart: ifa Edition Culture and Foreign Policy, 2016. 218–232.

Mork, Andrea. "The Narrative." *Creating the House of European History*. Ed. Andrea Mork and Perikles Christodoulou. Luxembourg: Publications Office of the European Union, 2018. 129–224.

Mork, Andrea, and Perikles Christodoulou, eds. *Creating the House of European History*. Luxembourg: Publications Office of the European Union, 2018.

Morré, Jörg. "Introduction." *German Russian Museum Berlin Karlshorst: Catalogue of the Permanent Exhibition*. Berlin: Deutsch-Russisches Museum Berlin-Karlshorst, 2014, 10–12.

Moses, A. Dirk. "The Canadian Museum for Human Rights: The 'Uniqueness of the Holocaust' and the Question of Genocide." *Journal of Genocide Research* 14.2 (2012): 215–238.

Mösken, Anne Lena. "'Die Täter im Blickpunkt": Neue Erinnerungsräume in den Bildern der Wehrmachtsausstellung." *NachBilder des Holocaust*. Ed. Inge Stephan and Alexandra Tacke. Cologne: Böhlau, 2007, 235–253.

Mouffe, Chantal. "An Agonistic Approach to the Future of Europe." *New Literary History* 43.4 (2012): 629–640.

Muchitsch, Wolfgang, ed. *Does War Belong in Museums? The Representation of Violence in Exhibitions*. Bielefeld: Transcript, 2013. Edition Museumsakademie Joanneum 4.

Muller, Adam. "Deterritorializing the Canadian Museum for Human Rights." To be published in *Museum & Society*. Manuscript 2019.

Muller, Anna, and Daniel Logemann. "War, Dialogue, and Overcoming the Past: The Second World War Museum in Gdańsk, Poland." *The Public Historian* 39.3 (2017): 85–95.

Müller, Siegfried. "Das Militärhistorische Museum der Bundeswehr in Dresden." *Geschichte in Wissenschaft und Unterricht* 57.12 (2006): 750–759.

Munslow, Alun. *Narrative and History*. Basingstoke: Palgrave Macmillan, 2007. Theory and History.

Muzeum Polaków Ratujących Żydów podczas II wojny światowej im. Rodziny Ulmów w Markowej. Website. https://muzeumulmow.pl/en/. Accessed 13 October 2019.

Muzeum Powstania Warszawskiego. *Przewofdnik po Muzeum Powstania Warszawskiego* [guide]. Warszawa: Muzeum Powstania Warszawskiego, 2011a.

Muzeum Powstania Warszawskiego. *Katalog: Muzeum Powstania Warszawskiego*. Warszawa: Muzeum Powstania Warszawskiego, 2011b.

Muzeum Powstania Warszawskiego. Website. https://www.1944.pl/en. Accessed 13 October 2019.

Nachama, Andreas. "Introduction." *Topography of Terror: Gestapo, SS and Reich Security Main Office on Wilhelm- and Prinz-Albrecht-Straße – a Documentation*. Berlin: Stiftung Topographie des Terrors, 2010. 6–9.

Nachama, Andreas, and Klaus Hesse, eds. *Vor aller Augen: Die Deportation der Juden und die Versteigerung ihres Eigentums – Fotografien aus Lörrach, 1940*. Berlin: Hentrich & Hentrich, 2nd ed. 2015 [2011].

National Museum of the United States Army. Website. https://armyhistory.org/. Accessed 13 October 2019.

National WWII Museum. *Museum Guide: A Pictorial Tour of America's WWII Museum*. New Orleans: National WWII Museum, 2016.

National WWII Museum. "Fiscal Year 2017 Annual Report." https://www.nationalww2museum.org/sites/default/files/2018-01/annual-report-2017-resize.pdf. Accessed 13 October 2019.

National WWII Museum. "Annual Report 2018." https://www.nationalww2museum.org/sites/default/files/2019-01/national-ww2-museum-annual-report-2018-compiled.pdf. Accessed 13 October 2019.

National WWII Museum. Website. https://www.nationalww2museum.org. Accessed 13 October 2019.

Nawrocki, Karol. "Foreword." Flyer *The Museum of the Second World War in Gdańsk*. Gdańsk: Muzeum II Wojny Światowej, 2018.

Neillands, Robin. *The Bomber War: Arthur Harris and the Allied Bomber Offensive*. London: Overlook Books, 2001.

Newsweek Polska. "Autorzy wystawy Muzeum II Wojny Światowej pozywają dyrekcję placówki" [The authors of the Museum of the Second World War exhibition are suing the institution's management], 30 January 2018. http://www.newsweek.pl/polska/polityka/zmiany-w-wystawie-muzeum-ii-wojny-swiatowej,artykuly,422571,1.html. Accessed 12 August 2018.

Noakes, Lucy. "Making Histories: Experiencing the Blitz in London's Museums in the 1990s." *The World War Two Reader*. Ed. Gordon Martel. London: Routledge, 2004. 422–434. Routledge Readers in History.

Nora, Pierre. "Between Memory and History: *Les Lieux de Mémoire*." Trans. Marc Roudebush. *Memory and Counter-Memory*. Spec. issue of *Representations* 26 (1989): 7–24.

NS-Dokumentationszentrum München. Website. https://www.ns-dokuzentrum-muenchen.de/en/documentation-center/about-us/. Accessed 13 October 2019.

Nünning, Ansgar. "Making Events – Making Stories – Making Worlds: Ways of Worldmaking from a Narratological Point of View." *Cultural Ways of Worldmaking. Media and Narratives*. Ed. Vera Nünning, Ansgar Nünning, and Birgit Neumann. Berlin: de Gruyter, 2010. 191–214. Concepts for the Study of Culture 1.

Nünning, Ansgar, and Vera Nünning. "Ways of Worldmaking as a Model for the Study of Culture: Theoretical Frameworks, Epistemological Underpinnings, New Horizons." *Cultural Ways of Worldmaking. Media and Narratives*. Ed. Vera Nünning, Ansgar Nünning, and Birgit Neumann. Berlin: de Gruyter, 2010. 1–25. Concepts for the Study of Culture 1.

Nünning, Vera, and Ansgar Nünning, eds. *Multiperspektivisches Erzählen: Zur Theorie und Geschichte der Perspektivenstruktur im englischen Roman des 18. bis 20. Jahrhunderts*. Trier: Wissenschaftlicher Verlag Trier, 2000.

Nugent, Christine R. "The Voice of the Visitor: Popular Reactions to the Exhibition *Vernichtungskrieg: Verbrechen der Wehrmacht 1941–1944*." *Journal of European Studies* 44.3 (2014): 249–262.

Orla-Burkowska, Annamaria: "Re-Presenting the Shoah in Poland and Poland in the Shoah." *Re-presenting the Shoah for the Twenty-First Century*. Ed. Ronit Lentin. New York: Berghahn, 2004. 179–194.

Pakier, Małgorzata, and Bo Stråth, eds. *A European Memory? Contested Histories and Politics of Remembrance*. New York: Berghahn, 2010. Studies in Contemporary European History 6.

Paver, Chloe. *Exhibiting the Nazi Past: Museum Objects Between the Material and the Immaterial*. Cham: Palgrave Macmillan, 2018. The Holocaust and its Contexts.

Pernau, Margrit. *Transnationale Geschichte*. Göttingen: Vandenhoeck & Ruprecht, 2011. Grundkurs neue Geschichte.

Perry, Rachel E. "Remediating Death at Yad Vashem's Holocaust History Museum." *Museums and Photography: Displaying Death*. Ed. Elena Stylianou and Theopisti Stylianou-Lambert. London: Routledge, 2017. 216–237. Routledge Research in Museum Studies.

Peschansky, Denis. "Foreword: Memory as the Object of History." *World War – Total War: The Caen Memorial*. Trans. Christopher Caines. New York: The New P / Mémorial de Caen, 2011 [French 2010]. xi–xiii.

Phillips, Mark Salber. "Relocating Inwardness: Historical Distance and the Transition from Enlightenment to Romantic Historiography." *PMLA* 118.3 (2003): 436–449.

Phillips, Mark. "Rethinking Historical Distance: From Doctrine to Heuristic." *Historical Distance: Reflections on a Metaphor*. Spec. issue of *History and Theory* 50 (2011): 11–23.

Phillips, Mark. *On Historical Distance*. New Haven, CT: Yale UP, 2013. The Lewis Walpole Ser. in Eighteenth-Century Culture and History.

Pieken, Gorch. "Concept and Structure of the Permanent Exhibition." *Militärhistorisches Museum der Bundeswehr / The Bundeswehr Museum of Military History: Exhibition Guide*. Ed. Gorch Pieken and Matthias Rogg. Dresden: Sandstein, 2012 [German 2011]. 21–29.

Pieken, Gorch. "Contents Space: New Concept and New Building of the Militärhistorisches Museum of the Bundeswehr." *Does War Belong in Museums? The Representation of Violence in Exhibitions*. Ed. Wolfgang Muchitsch. Bielefeld: Transcript, 2013. 64–82. Edition Museumsakademie Joanneum 4.

Pieken, Gorch, and Matthias Rogg, eds. *Militärhistorisches Museum der Bundeswehr / The Bundeswehr Museum of Military History: Exhibition Guide*. Dresden: Sandstein, 2012 [German 2011].

Pieper, Katrin. *Die Musealisierung des Holocaust: Das Jüdische Museum Berlin und das U.S. Holocaust Memorial Museum in Washington D.C.; ein Vergleich*. Cologne: Böhlau, 2006. Europäische Geschichtsdarstellungen 9.

Pirker, Eva Ulrike, and Mark Rüdiger. "Authentizitätsfiktionen in populären Geschichtskulturen: Annäherungen." *Echte Geschichte: Authentizitätsfiktionen in populären Geschichtskulturen*. Ed. Eva Ulrike Pirker, Mark Rüdiger, Christa Klein, Thorsten Leiendecker, Carolyn Oesterle, Miriam Sénécheau, and Michiko Uike-Bormann. Bielefeld: Transcript, 2010. 11–30. Historische Lebenswelten in populären Wissenskulturen 3.

Polonsky, Antony, Hanna Węgrzynek, and Andrzej Żbikowski, eds. *New Directions in the History of the Jews in the Polish Lands*. Boston, MA: Academic Studies P / Warsaw: POLIN Museum of the History of Polish Jews, 2018. Jews of Poland.

Powell, Raymond, and Jithendran Kokkranikal. "From History to Reality – Engaging with Visitors in the Imperial War Museum (North)." *Museum Management and Curatorship* 29.1 (2014): 36–49.

Prager, Brad. "On the Liberation of Perpetrator Photographs in Holocaust Narratives." *Visualizing the Holocaust: Documents, Aesthetics, Memory*. Ed. David Bathrick, Brad Prager, and Michael D. Richardson, Rochester, NY: Camden House, 2008. 19–37. Screen Cultures: German Film and the Visual.

Puttkamer, Joachim von. "Europäisch und polnisch zugleich: Das Museum des Zweiten Weltkriegs in Danzig." *Osteuropa* 67.1–2 (2017): 3–12.

Rauchensteiner, Manfred. "Von Beiräten, Hofräten und anderen Menschen." *Militärhistorisches Museum der Bundeswehr: Ausstellung und Architektur*. Ed. Gorch Pieken and Matthias Rogg. Dresden: Sandstein, 2011. 10–15.

Raupach-Rudnick, Wolfgang. "Die Gründung des Gedenkstättenreferates der Aktion Sühnezeichen Friedensdienste e.V." *GedenkstättenRundbrief* 100.4 (2001): 9–12.

Redlin, Jane, and Dagmar Neuland-Kizerow, eds. *Der Gefühlte Krieg: Emotionen im Ersten Weltkrieg*. Berlin: Verlag der Kunst/Museum Europäischer Kulturen: Staatliche Museen zu Berlin, 2014.

Reiter, Andrea. *Narrating the Holocaust*. Trans. Patrick Camiller. London: Continuum, 2000. Continuum Guide to Holocaust Studies.
Remes, Anastasia. "Memory, Identity and the Supranational History Museum: Building the House of European History." *Memoria e Ricerca* 54.1 (2017): 99–116.
Reynolds, Daniel P. *Postcards from Auschwitz: Holocaust Tourism and the Meaning of Remembrance*. New York: New York UP, 2018.
Richter, Peter. "Granatwerfer mit Kennzahl." *Süddeutsche Zeitung*, 7 December 2017, https://www.sueddeutsche.de/kultur/museum-granatwerfer-mit-kennzahl-1.3782097. Accessed 13 October 2019.
Ricœur, Paul. *Time and Narrative*, 3 vol. Chicago: Chicago UP, 1984–85 (French 1983–1985).
Rogg, Matthias. "The Architecture." *Militärhistorisches Museum der Bundeswehr / The Bundeswehr Museum of Military History: Exhibition Guide*. Ed. Gorch Pieken and Matthias Rogg. Dresden: Sandstein, 2012a [German 2011]. 7–13.
Rogg, Matthias. "The Architecture." *Militärhistorisches Museum der Bundeswehr / The Bundeswehr Museum of Military History: Exhibition Guide*. Ed. Gorch Pieken and Matthias Rogg. Dresden: Sandstein, 2012b [German 2011]. 15–19.
Rose, Julia. *Interpreting Difficult History at Museums and Historic Sites*. Lanham: Rowman & Littlefield, 2016. Interpreting History 8.
Rosenberg, Daniel. "Exhibiting Post-national Identity: The House of European History." *History and Belonging: Representations of the Past in Contemporary European Politics*. Ed. Stefan Berger and Caner Tekin. New York: Berghahn, 2018. 21–36. Making Sense of History: Studies in Historical Cultures.
Rothberg, Michael. *Multidirectional Memory: Remembering the Holocaust in the Age of Decolonization*. Stanford: Stanford UP, 2009. Cultural Memory in the Present.
Rozett, Robert. "Distorting the Holocaust and Whitewashing History: Toward a Typology." *Israel Journal of Foreign Affairs* 13.1 (2019): 23–36.
Rukszto, Katarzyna. "Haunted Spaces, Ghostly Memories: The Canadian War Museum." *Third Text* 22.6 (2008): 743–754.
Rürup, Reinhard, ed. *Topographie des Terrors: Gestapo, SS und Reichssicherheitshauptamt auf dem "Prinz-Albrecht-Gelände": Eine Dokumentation*. Berlin: Willmuth Arenhövel, rev. 14th ed. 2002 [1987].
Rüth, Axel. *Erzählte Geschichte: Narrative Strukturen in der französischen Annales-Geschichtsschreibung*. Berlin: de Gruyter, 2005. Narratologia 5.
Ryan, Marie-Laure, Kenneth Foote, and Maoz Azaryahu. *Narrating Space / Spatializing Narrative: Where Narrative Theory and Geography Meet*. Columbus, OH: Ohio State UP, 2016. Theory and Interpretation of Narrative.
Sabrow, Martin, and Achim Saupe: "Historische Authentizität: Zur Kartierung eines Forschungsfeldes." *Historische Authentizität*. Ed. Martin Sabrow and Achim Saupe. Göttingen: Wallstein, 2016. 7–28.
Scheerer, Thomas Eugen, ed. *Arsenal und Museum: Vergangenheit, Gegenwart, Zukunft*. Dresden: Militärhistorisches Museum der Bundeswehr, 2003a. Militärhistorisches Museum der Bundeswehr 5.
Scheerer, Thomas Eugen. "Vorbemerkung." *Arsenal und Museum: Vergangenheit, Gegenwart, Zukunft*. Ed. Thomas Eugen Scheerer. Dresden: Militärhistorisches Museum der Bundeswehr, 2003b. 4. Militärhistorisches Museum der Bundeswehr 5.

Schoder, Angelika. *Die Vermittlung des Unbegreiflichen: Darstellungen des Holocaust im Museum*. Frankfurt/M.: Campus, 2014.

Scholze, Jana. *Medium Ausstellung: Lektüren musealer Gestaltungen in Oxford, Leipzig, Amsterdam und Berlin*. Bielefeld: Transcript, 2004. Kultur- und Museumsmanagement.

Scholze, Jana. "Kultursemiotik: Zeichenlesen in Ausstellungen." *Museumsanalyse: Methoden und Konturen eines neuen Forschungsfeldes*. Ed. Joachim Baur. Bielefeld: Transcript, 2010. 121–148. Kultur- und Museumsmanagement.

Schröder, Vanessa. *Geschichte ausstellen – Geschichte verstehen: Wie Besucher im Museum Geschichte und historische Zeit deuten*. Bielefeld: Transcript, 2013. Kultur- und Medientheorie.

Schulz, Bernard."Große Pläne für 2018: Topographie des Terrors." *Der Tagesspiegel*, 12 January 2018, https://www.tagesspiegel.de/kultur/topographie-des-terrors-grosse-plaene-fuer-2018/20842970.html. Accessed 13 October 2019.

Seiter, Ines. *Holocausterinnerung im Museum: Zur Vermittlung zivilreligiöser Werte in nationalen Erinnerungskulturen im Vergleich*. Baden-Baden: Nomos, 2017.

Settele, Veronika. "Including Exclusion in European Memory? Politics of Remembrance at the House of European History." *Journal of Contemporary European Studies* 23.3 (2015): 405–416.

Shah, Nisha. "Death in the Details: Finding Dead Bodies at the Canadian War Museum." *Organization* 24.4 (2017): 549–569.

Shelby, Karen D. *Belgian Museums of the Great War: Politics, Memory, and Commerce*. London: Routledge, 2018. Routledge Research in Museum Studies.

Shore, Cris. "Inventing Homo Europaeus: The Cultural Politics of European Integration." *Ethnologia Europaea: Journal of European Ethnology* 29.2 (1999): 53–66.

Siddi, Marco, and Barbara Gaweda. "The National Agents of Transnational Memory and their Limits: the Case of the Museum of the Second World War in Gdańsk." *Journal of Contemporary European Studies* 27.2 (2019): 258–271.

Simon, Roger I. "The Pedagogical Insistence of Public Memory." *Theorizing Historical Consciousness*. Ed. Peter Seixas. Toronto: U of Toronto P, 2004. 183–201.

Simon, Roger I. "The Terrible Gift: Museums and the Possibility of Hope without Consolation." *Museum Management and Curatorship* 21 (2006): 187–204.

Simon, Roger I. "A Shock to Thought: Curatorial Judgment and the Public Exhibition of 'Difficult Knowledge'." *Memory Studies* 4.4 (2011): 432–449.

Snyder, Timothy. *Bloodlands: Europe between Hitler and Stalin*. New York: Basic Books, 2010.

Snyder, Timothy. "Poland vs. History." *The New York Review of Books* 3 May 2016, https://www.nybooks.com/daily/2016/05/03/poland-vs-history-museum-Gdańsk/. Accessed 18 August 2018.

Sodaro, Amy. *Exhibiting Atrocity: Memorial Museums and the Politics of Past Violence*. New Brunswick: Rutgers UP, 2018.

Springer, Philipp. "Auf Straßen und Plätzen: Zur Fotogeschichte des nationalsozialistischen Deutschland." *Vor aller Augen: Fotodokumente des nationalsozialistischen Terrors in der Provinz*. Ed. Klaus Hesse and Philipp Springer. Essen: Klartext, 2002. 11–33.

Stańczyk, Ewa. "Heroes, Victims, Role Models: Representing the Child Soldiers of the Warsaw Uprising." *Slavic Review* 74.4 (2015): 738–759.

Stiftung Topographie des Terrors, ed. *GedenkstättenRundbrief* 100.4 (2001).

Stiftung Topographie des Terrors. *Topography of Terror: Gestapo, SS and Reich Security Main Office on Wilhelm- and Prinz-Albrecht-Straße – a Documentation*. Berlin: Stiftung Topographie des Terrors, 2010a.
Stiftung Topographie des Terrors. *Site Tour Topography of Terror: History of the Site*. Berlin: Stiftung Topographie des Terrors, 2010b.
Stiftung Topographie des Terrors, ed. *Bericht April 2006–Mai 2010*. Berlin: Stiftung Topographie des Terrors, 2011.
Stiftung Topographie des Terrors. Website. https://www.topographie.de. Accessed 13 October 2019.
Stone, Dan. *Histories of the Holocaust*. Oxford: Oxford UP, 2010.
Studio Daniel Libeskind, Berlin. "Die Architektur des Arsenal-Hauptgebäudes (Konzeption)." *Arsenal und Museum: Vergangenheit, Gegenwart, Zukunft*. Ed. Thomas Eugen Scheerer. Dresden: Militärhistorisches Museum der Bundeswehr, 2003. 48–51. Militärhistorisches Museum der Bundeswehr 5.
Studio Libeskind. "Military History Museum Dresden, Germany." https://libeskind.com/work/military-history-museum/. Accessed 13 October 2019.
Stugu, Ola Svein. "Exhibiting the War: Approaches to World War II in Museum and Exhibitions." *Historicizing the Uses of the Past: Scandinavian Perspectives on History Culture, Historical Consciousness and Didactics of History Related to World War II*. Ed. Helle Bjerg, Claudia Lenz, and Erik Thorstensen. Bielefeld: Transcript, 2011. 189–206. Zeit – Sinn – Kultur 6.
Swick, Gerald D. "The National WWII Museum – 2015 and Beyond." Interview with Stephen Watson. 21 January 2015. http://www.historynet.com/the-national-wwii-museum-2015-and-beyond.htm. Accessed 13 October 2019.
Szczepanski, Joanna. "Romanticising and Revising the Second World War in Polish Museums." *Museum Management and Curatorship* 27.3 (2012): 273–289.
Tekin, Caner, and Stefan Berger. "Introduction: Towards a 'Europeanized' European History?" *History and Belonging: Representations of the Past in Contemporary European Politics*. Ed. Stefan Berger and Caner Tekin. New York: Berghahn, 2018. 1–20. Making Sense of History: Studies in Historical Cultures.
Terkel, Studs: *'The Good War': An Oral History of World War II*. New York: Pantheon, 1984.
Thamer, Hans-Ulrich. "Die Kulturgeschichte der Gewalt im Museum: Ein Konzept und seine Realisierung im Militärhistorischen Museum in Dresden." *Geschichte in Wissenschaft und Unterricht* 63.11/12 (2012): 658–668.
Thiele, Hans-Günther, ed. *Die Wehrmachtsausstellung: Dokumentation einer Kontroverse*. Bremen: Ed. Temmen, 1999.
Thiemeyer, Thomas. *Fortsetzung des Krieges mit anderen Mitteln: Die beiden Weltkriege im Museum*. Paderborn: Schöningh, 2010a. Krieg in der Geschichte 62.
Thiemeyer, Thomas. "Geschichtswissenschaft: Das Museum als Quelle." *Museumsanalyse: Methoden und Konturen eines neuen Forschungsfeldes*. Ed. Joachim Baur. Bielefeld: Transcript, 2010b. 73–94. Kultur- und Museumsmanagement.
Thiemeyer, Thomas. "Exhibiting the War: Heroes, Perpetrators, and Victims of the Two World Wars in German, French, and British Museums." *Out of the Tower: Essays on Culture and Everyday Life*. Ed. Monique Scheer, Thomas Thiemeyer, Reinhard Johler, and Bernhard Tschofen. Tübingen: Tübinger Vereinigung für Volkskunde, 2013. 288–307. Ludwig-Uhland-Institut für Empirische Kulturwissenschaft: Untersuchungen 114.

Thiemeyer, Thomas. "Politik des Zeigens: Das Museum als Medium der Weltkriegs-Erinnerung." *Krieg im Museum: Präsentationen des Zweiten Weltkriegs in Museen und Gedenkstätten des östlichen Europas.* Ed. Ekaterina Makhotina, Ekaterina Keding, Włodzimierz Borodziej, Étienne François, and Martin Schulze Wessel. Göttingen: Vandenhoeck & Ruprecht, 2015. 15–27. Veröffentlichungen des Collegium Carolinum 131.

Thiemeyer, Thomas. "Multi-Voiced and Personal: Second World War Remembrance in German Museums." Trans. Erin Johnston-Weiss. *Views of Violence: Representing the Second World War in German and European Museums and Memorials.* Ed. Jörg Echternkamp and Stephan Jaeger. New York: Berghahn, 2019. 27–51. Spektrum: Publications from the German Studies Association 19.

Till, Karen E. *The New Berlin: Memory, Politics, Place.* Minneapolis: U of Minnesota P, 2005.

Torgovnick, Marianna. *The War Complex World War II in Our Time.* Chicago: U of Chicago P, 2005.

Tripadvisor. Website. https://www.tripadvisor.com/TravelersChoice-Museums-cTop-g1. Accessed 13 October 2019.

Troebst, Stefan, and Johanna Wolf, eds. *Erinnern an den Zweiten Weltkrieg: Mahnmale und Museen in Mittel- und Osteuropa.* Leipzig: Leipziger Universitätsverlag, 2011. Schriften des Europäischen Netzwerks Erinnerung und Solidarität 2.

Tyndall, Andrea: "Memory, Authenticity and Replication of the Shoah in Museums: Defensive Tools of the Nation." *Re-presenting the Shoah for the Twenty-First Century.* Ed. Ronit Lentin. New York: Berghahn, 2004. 111–125.

Tyradellis, Daniel. *Müde Museen: Oder: Wie Ausstellungen unser Denken verändern könnten.* Hamburg: edition Körber-Stiftung, 2014.

Tyrrell, Ian. "Reflections on the Transnational Turn in United States History: Theory and Practice." *Journal of Global History* 4.3 (2009): 453–474.

Ukielski, Paweł. Interview by *Poland In English* with the Deputy Director of the Warsaw Rising Museum, Dr. Paweł Ukielski. 1 August 2018. https://polandinenglish.info/38321614/warsaw-rising-museum-exhibition-changes-thinking. Accessed 13 October 2019.

United States Holocaust Memorial Museum. 2019. *Holocaust Encyclopedia.* https://encyclopedia.ushmm.org. Accessed 13 October 2019.

Unsere Mütter, unsere Väter (engl. *Generation War*). Directed by Philipp Kadelbach. 2013. Chicago, IL: Music Box Films, 2014. DVD.

Vergo, Peter, ed. *The New Museology.* London: Reaktion Books, 1989.

Voorsanger Mathes LLC. "The National World War II Museum." http://www.archdaily.com/209361/the-national-world-war-ii-museum-voorsanger-architects. Accessed 13 October 2019.

Vovk van Gaal, Taja, and Christine Dupont. "The House of European History." *Entering the Minefields: the Creation of New History Museums in Europe.* Conference Proceedings *EuNaMus, European National Museums: Identity Politics, the Uses of the Past, and the European Citizen*, Brussels 25 January 2012. Ed. Bodil Axelsson, Christine Dupont, and Chantal Kesteloot. Linköping: Linköping U Electronic P, 2012. Linköping University Interdisciplinary Studies 83. 43–53.

Vovk van Gaal, Taja. "Step by Step towards the House of European History." *Creating the House of European History.* Ed. Andrea Mork and Perikles Christodoulou. Luxembourg: Publications Office of the European Union, 2018. 85–127.

Waterton, Emma, and Jason Dittmer. "The Museum as Assemblage: Bringing Forth Affect at the Australian War Memorial." *Museum Management and Curatorship* 29.2 (2014): 122–139.
Watson, Sheila: "'Death from the Skies': Photographs in Museums of the Aerial Bombing of Civilians During World War Two." *Museums and Photography: Displaying Death*. Ed. Elena Stylianou and Theopisti Stylianou-Lambert. London: Routledge, 2017. 62–83. Routledge Research in Museum Studies.
Weinberg, Jeshajahu. "A Narrative History Museum." *Curator* 37.4 (1994): 231–239.
Wellington, Jennifer. *Exhibiting War: the Great War, Museums, and Memory in Britain, Canada and Australia*. Cambridge: Cambridge UP, 2017. Studies in the Social and Cultural History of Modern Warfare.
Weiser, M. Elizabeth. *Museum Rhetoric: Building Civic Identity in National Spaces*. University Park, PA: Pennsylvania State UP, 2017. RSA Ser. in Transdisciplinary Rhetoric.
Westrate, J. Lee. *European Military Museums: a Survey of their Philosophy, Facilities, Programs, and Management*. Washington: Smithsonian Institution, 1961.
White, Hayden. *Metahistory: The Historical Imagination in Nineteenth-Century Europe*. Baltimore, MD: Johns Hopkins UP, 1973.
White, Hayden. *Tropics of Discourse: Essays in Cultural Criticism*. Baltimore, MD: Johns Hopkins UP, 1978.
White, Hayden. *The Content of the Form: Narrative Discourse and Historical Representation*. Baltimore, MD: Johns Hopkins UP, 1987.
Williams, Damien. "Once More, with Feeling: Commemorating Royal Air Force Bomber Command in Late Modern Britain." *Battlefield Events: Landscape, Commemoration and Heritage*. Ed. Keir Reeves, Geoffrey R. Bird, Laura James, Birger Stichelbaut, and Jean Bourgeois. London: Routledge, 2015. 90–106. Routledge Advances in Event Research Ser.
Williams, Paul. *Memorial Museums: The Global Rush to Commemorate Atrocities*. Oxford: Berg, 2007.
Wilms, Wilfried, and William Rasch, ed. *Bombs Away: Representing the Air War over Europe and Japan*. Amsterdam: Rodopi, 2006. Amsterdamer Beiträge zur neueren Germanistik 60.
Winter, Jay. *Remembering War: the Great War between Memory and History in the Twentieth Century*. New Haven: Yale UP, 2006.
Winter, Jay. "Museum and the Representation of War." *Does War Belong in Museums? The Representation of Violence in Exhibitions*. Ed. Wolfgang Muchitsch. Bielefeld: Transcript, 2013. 21–37. Edition Museumsakademie Joanneum 4.
Winter, Jay. "Afterword: The Memory Boom and the Commemoration of the Second World War." *Views of Violence: Representing the Second World War in German and European Museums and Memorials*. Ed. Jörg Echternkamp and Stephan Jaeger. New York: Berghahn, 2019. 252–260. Spektrum: Publications from the German Studies Association 19.
Witcomb, Andrea. *Re-imagining the Museum: Beyond the Mausoleum*. London: Routledge, 2003. Museum Meanings.
Wnuk, Rafał, Paweł Machcewicz, Oliwia Galka-Olejko, and Łukasz Jasinski. *Museum of the Second World War: Catalogue of the Permanent Exhibition*. Gdańsk: Muzeum II Wojny Światowej, 2016.

Yoshida, Takashi. *From Cultures of War to Cultures of Peace: War and Peace Museums in Japan, China, and South Korea*. Portland, ME: Merwin, 2014. Studies of the Weatherhead East Asian Institute, Columbia University.

Young, James E. *The Texture of Memory: Holocaust, Memorials and Meaning*. New Haven, CT: Yale UP, 1993.

Zolberg, Vera L. "Museums as Contested Sites of Remembrance: the Enola Gay Affair." *Theorizing Museums: Representing Identity and Diversity in a Changing World*. Ed. Sharon Macdonald and Gordon Fyfe. Oxford: Blackwell, 1996. 69–82. Sociological Review Monograph Ser. 43.

Zwach, Eva. *Deutsche und englische Militärmuseen im 20. Jahrhundert: Eine kulturgeschichtliche Analyse des gesellschaftlichen Umgangs mit Krieg*. Münster: Lit, 1999. Museen, Geschichte und Gegenwart 4.

Żychlińska, Monika, "Muzeum Powstania Warszawskiego jako wehikuł polskiej pamięci zbiorowej." *Kultura i Społeczeństwo* 3 (2009): 89–114.

Żychlińska, Monika, and Erica Fontana. "Museal Games and Emotional Truths: Creating Polish National Identity at the Warsaw Rising Museum." *East European Politics and Societies and Cultures* 30.2 (2016): 235–269.

Index

The index covers institutions, selected names, and selected concepts. The terms 'Europe,' 'memory,' 'museum,' 'Nazi,' 'remembrance,' 'Second World War,' 'visitor,' 'war,' and most countries and nationalities are not listed, unless the entries are further defined.

Adorno, Theodor W.   223, 293
aerial warfare   1, 7, 39, 46, 59, 69, 72, 134, 265, 267, 271f., 274–276, 280, 282, 290f., 310
aesthetic judgment   292
aesthetic response / aesthetic response theory   6, 43
affect   See emotion, emotional
agency   43f., 110, 186, 209, 260, 268
Air War (during the Second World War)   33, 47, 62, 66–73, 105, 130, 138, 144, 181, 191, 209f., 213, 224, 231, 265–269, 271, 273–278, 282, 284f., 288–291, 302, 308
Airborne Museum Hartenstein, Oosterbeek   54
Alba, Avril   226
Allies (Second World War)   66, 81f., 119, 191, 221, 253f., 259f., 267, 275–277, 290, 311f.
Altwinckle, Eric   294
Ambrose, Stephen E.   95f.
Andruchovych, Yuri   219
Annan, Kofi   76
anthropological   3, 7, 17, 37, 43, 64, 131, 135, 153f., 172, 186, 201, 223, 265, 269, 271, 282, 291, 297, 301, 306f.
anthropology of violence   131, 253
anti-heroic   133, 186
antisemitism, antisemitic   35, 140, 163, 168, 192, 222, 228, 243–246, 250, 253, 257, 261
Apor, Péter   45f.
architect (of museums)   3, 129, 161, 269
architecture (museum)   42, 44, 62, 96, 109f., 116, 130, 134, 150f., 154, 157, 161, 203, 218, 269, 277–279, 292, 299–303
Arendt, Hannah   223

Arnold-de Simine, Silke   14, 29, 32, 46, 52, 89, 133, 156, 158f., 246, 256, 269, 297
artwork (in history museums)   139, 151, 208, 213, 216–219, 231, 233, 258, 282, 292–305
– beautiful   292
– commissioned   247, 297–300
– self-referential   292f., 295
Asia-Pacific theater of the Second World War (see also War in the Pacific)   15, 34, 265
Assmann, Aleida   9f., 40, 222
Assmann, Jan   8
audio guide (museum)   80, 87, 121, 126, 272, 297f., 300, 309
audio station (in exhibition)   85, 152, 181
audio-visual (in museum installations)   54, 104, 107, 116, 156, 177–179
aura   10, 21, 55, 66, 282, 300, 302
Auschwitz   139, 167, 191, 225, 232, 234f., 247–252, 267
Auschwitz Concentration Camp Museum   216
Auschwitz Trial   144
Australian War Memorial, Canberra   43, 45
authenticity   4–6, 10, 25f., 31f., 45f., 54–56, 58, 66, 89, 109, 158, 163, 170f., 178, 226, 296
Azaryahu, Maoz   41

Babi Yar Massacre   148, 242, 256
Bagnall, Gaynor   150f., 230–232, 303
Bal, Mieke   42, 44, 46, 110
Barndt, Kerstin   58
Barthes, Roland   23
Bastogne Ardennes 44 Museum   31
Bastogne (bombardment)   54, 119, 123, 268
Bastogne (Sous-Lieutenant Heintz) Barracks   31

Bastogne War Museum   17, 33, 36, 38f., 94, 116–128, 154, 172, 184, 188, 229, 240f., 243, 254, 257, 260, 268–270, 288–291, 302, 312
Battle of Britain (also Blitz)   66, 89–93, 154, 158f., 231, 267f., 274f., 277, 282f., 296, 304
Battle of the Bulge   31, 97f., 117, 120, 124, 126, 235, 241, 259, 289
Baudrillard, Jean   51
Beck, Ulrich   15
Bednarek, Monika   107f., 111, 114
Beier-de Haan, Rosmarie   13, 15f., 22, 40, 42
Benjamin, Walter   302
Bergen-Belsen
– concentration camp   233f., 241
– Gedenkstätte   26
Bernard-Donals, Michael   24f., 226
Beutelsbacher consensus   13
Birkin, Edith   231
Blitz   See Battle of Britain
bloodlands   222, 253
'Bloody Sunday' (in Bydgoszcz, Poland) 190f.
Bogumił, Zuzanna   44, 77, 84
Bogunia-Borowska, Małgorzata   23, 108, 225
Bomber Command   67f., 70–72, 265, 274, 282
bombing, strategic   69, 71, 73, 99, 267, 283, 285f.
bombing war   See Air War (during the Second World War)
Bonnell, Jennifer   256
Borodziej, Włodzimierz   205
Bothwell, Robert   70f.
Brandon, Laura   294
Brandt, Willy   143
Braun, Wernher von   279, 281f.
Brecht, Bertolt   280
broad present   59
Brower, Benjamin Claude   266
Bruch, Klaus vom   280, 298–300, 302
Bryan, Julien   191
Buchenwald
– concentration camp   235f., 241

– Nationale Mahn- und Gedenkstätte Buchenwald   26, 241
Bundeswehr   130f., 282
Bundeswehr Military History Museum (Militärhistorisches Museum der Bundeswehr, MHM), Dresden   3f., 6, 11, 16f., 33, 36–39, 50, 56f., 117, 128–157, 159, 162f., 168, 170, 173, 186, 195, 203, 222f., 230, 232, 243, 246f., 254, 256, 258–262, 264, 269, 271, 277f., 280–285, 288, 291, 293, 295–299, 301f., 310f.
– Clash of Future: Myths of Nations   132
– Gender and Violence: War is for Men – Peace is for Women?   132, 301
– The Führer Adolf Hitler is Dead: Attempted Assassination and Coup d'État on 20 July 1944   132
Buschmann, Heike   41
Bush, George H.   76
bystander   12, 165–167, 233, 246, 258, 262

Cabinet War Rooms   See Churchill War Rooms
Canadian Museum for Human Rights, Winnipeg   59, 75, 140
Canadian Museum of History (Civilization), Ottawa   46, 62, 64, 73
Canadian War Museum (CWM), Ottawa   25, 33, 36, 38, 61–78, 87–89, 100, 131, 191, 229, 233–235, 254f., 257, 259, 269, 272f., 285, 288, 294f.
– debate Bomber Command exhibit   67, 69–71, 285
– debate Holocaust gallery   234
Carden-Coyne, Anna   224, 253f., 256
Center for Military History and Social Sciences of the Bundeswehr (Militärgeschichtliches Forschungsamt, MGFA), Potsdam   130
Cento Bull, Anna   16, 19f., 309
Cercel, Cristian   130f., 133, 309
characters, fictitious composite   49, 94, 117–120, 125f., 268, 302f., 306
children (in war)   2–4, 7, 57, 59, 75, 117, 123, 126, 152, 154, 156, 158f., 191, 193, 198, 212, 231, 233, 259, 307

chronosophic   3
chronosophic net   58, 240
Churchill, Winston   55, 86, 89, 213, 266, 276, 290
Churchill War Rooms (formerly Cabinet War Rooms), London   55, 89
– Churchill Museum   89
cinematic representation technique (museum)   108, 110, 147, 150
Clarke, David   172f., 182f., 201
close reading   35, 38, 44, 46, 60
clustering (museum technique)   58f., 163, 282, 306
Colburn, Martha   300
Cold War   65, 76, 217f., 231, 273, 280, 312
collaborators, collaboration   12, 14f., 35, 106, 119, 125, 177, 191–196, 209, 216, 221, 224, 241, 260, 269f., 277, 306, 308, 310
collection (of museums)   22, 33, 62, 96, 129, 151f., 156, 184, 219, 294
Cologne (bombing of)   69, 98, 101f., 165, 268, 274–276
colonialism   206, 270
'comfort women'   14, 34, 305
commemoration, to commemorate, commemorative   14, 24–26, 28, 31–33, 61, 63, 72–74, 77, 79f., 83–85, 87, 89, 93, 102, 142f., 182, 192, 224–226, 233, 242, 244, 251, 258, 265, 291, 308, 311
Commemorative Museum Pedagogy   53
Communism   79, 85, 187, 218
computer station (in exhibition)   6, 97f., 100, 109, 120f., 137, 162, 165, 192, 194, 236, 240f., 246f., 249, 271, 276, 278, 280, 288
concentration camp (Nazi)   26f., 53, 66, 98f., 104, 107, 109, 125, 167, 169, 186, 199, 201, 207–209, 216, 225, 228f., 234–241, 243, 246–250, 252, 254, 256–259, 261, 279, 305
constellations (created through museum techniques)   7, 17f., 20f., 58f., 126, 128, 135, 137, 139–141, 143, 152, 158, 174, 182, 184–186, 192, 194, 196, 199, 203f., 213f., 217, 247, 253, 271, 288f., 291, 297, 301, 311

Coventry (bombing of)   267, 275f., 301f.
Crane, Susan   46, 106
Cultural Projects Berlin (Kulturprojekte Berlin)   309
curator   6, 11, 37, 42f., 49, 64, 75, 93, 107, 131, 157, 163, 192, 204, 216, 273, 298, 306
curatorial   32, 35, 45, 64, 66, 83, 133, 163, 205, 239
Czuj, Łukasz   107

D-Day   31, 66f., 95f., 98, 105, 119, 125f., 155, 265, 267, 290, 294, 311
Dachau
– concentration camp   237f.
– KZ-Gedenkstätte Dachau   26, 225
Davenport, Nancy   299, 301
De-Nazification   119
death
– commemoration of   105, 124, 143, 145, 155, 192, 250
– depiction of   63, 72, 83, 142f., 174, 199, 253, 255, 287
death camp (also extermination camp)   23, 155, 181, 228, 242, 244, 248, 252
death march   177f., 199, 201, 228
democracy   63, 74, 105f., 136f., 160, 187, 206, 214, 217
Deutsch-Russisches Museum   See German-Russian Museum
Deutsches Historisches Museum (German Historical Museum), Berlin   16, 144, 229, 309
– Diversity Destroyed: Berlin 1933-1938-1945 (Zerstörte Vielfalt)   309
Dieker, Birgit   301
Dieppe   66
difficult heritage   10, 305
difficult knowledge   10, 27–29, 53, 256, 307, 311
digital   11, 55, 91, 175, 277
diorama   5, 10, 31f., 54f., 89, 114, 173, 300
discrimination
– during the time of National Socialism   163, 165f., 228, 236, 241, 243, 247, 257f., 290, 309
– in the United States   104f.

distantiation, distance   7, 9, 22, 29f., 32, 38, 41, 45–47, 51f., 56f., 80, 90f., 93f., 108, 113, 116, 119–122, 124f., 127–129, 143, 148, 159, 162, 175, 181, 189, 197f., 224, 232, 242, 252, 254, 257f., 263, 268, 276f., 303, 307, 311
Dittmer, Jason   44
Documentation Center Nazi Party Rallying Grounds (Dokumentationszentrum Reichsparteitagsgelände), Nuremberg   27
Doležel, Lubomír   109
Donnelly, Rachel   228
Dresden (bombing of)   3f., 98, 271, 275f., 278, 284f., 298f., 301f., 310
Duber, Paweł   182f., 201
Dunkirk   66, 153
Dupont, Christine   205

East Germany (also GDR)   26, 129, 136, 166, 215f., 299
economy of war   57, 246f., 262
Eichhorst, Franz   137f.
Eisenhower, Dwight D.   99f., 290
emotionalization   13, 66, 77, 106
empathetic unsettlement   53, 114, 226, 307, 311
empathy, to empathize (as museum visitor)   29f., 47, 49, 53, 56f., 62f., 67, 77f., 88f., 100, 103, 109, 114, 121–124, 128, 134, 152, 159–162, 179, 188f., 193, 195, 197–199, 212, 226, 230f., 243, 254, 256f., 261, 281, 289f., 296, 300, 303, 305, 311
– with perpetrators   179, 226
– with victims   20, 52, 134, 139, 145, 199, 212f., 223, 257, 263, 276, 284
enemy (representation of)   1, 16, 44, 84, 86, 113, 140, 181, 213, 230, 270, 307
Enola Gay   106, 209, 273, 312
Erll, Astrid   8f., 16, 55
ethnic cleansing   192f.
European identity   See identity, European
European memory   See memory, European
European migrant crisis (twenty-first century)   202
'euthanasia' program (Nazi)   145, 221f., 247

expellee (see also refugee)   200, 212
experience
– historical   38, 47–49, 51, 53, 89, 92, 100, 109f., 193, 204, 258, 265, 268, 289, 302
– structural   6, 21, 36, 56f., 61, 128, 148, 152, 154, 171, 173, 177, 199, 243, 249, 262, 308
– wartime   144, 158, 174, 182, 216, 274
experientiality   7, 12, 33, 38, 42, 47–50, 53–55, 57–62, 94, 128, 172, 178, 182, 202, 229, 245, 253, 274, 292f., 296, 305–308, 311f.
– primary   39, 54–57, 60–63, 71, 74, 78, 89, 97, 100–102, 107–109, 111, 127f., 161, 265, 289, 291
– restricted   38, 50f., 57, 60f., 94f., 107, 220, 234, 238, 244, 256, 263, 265, 272, 277, 291
– secondary   21, 32, 38f., 47, 50–53, 56–58, 60f., 71, 73f., 76, 94, 98, 108, 111, 114–116, 128f., 133f., 140, 142, 144, 146, 149–153, 156, 159, 162f., 166, 169, 173f., 177, 180, 182, 186f., 198, 202f., 211, 220f., 229, 233, 240, 243, 245, 253, 256, 263, 265, 268, 288, 291, 299
expulsion   See flight and expulsion
eyewitness   11, 13, 97, 106, 116f., 124, 126, 158, 165, 238, 261, 302

Fabryka Emalia Oskara Schindlera   See Oskar Schindler Enamel Factory
Failler, Angela   27
Falk, John H.   61
fascism   19, 187, 227f., 258
Fehr, Michael   29
Felix Nussbaum Haus, Osnabrück   139
fiction   48, 50, 117, 302f., 305
fictitious   See characters, fictitious composite
firebombing   107, 271, 276–278, 285, 288
First World War   14, 64, 67, 74, 76, 88f., 120, 136, 145, 154f., 158, 172, 187, 206, 219, 227, 232, 266, 270, 284, 296, 300, 303, 308
Fisher, Orville   294
Flacke, Monika   16

Fleurie, Sylvie   301
flight and expulsion   144, 181, 189, 191, 193, 199–201, 203, 209, 211, 277, 306
Fludernik, Monika   47–51
Fontana, Erica   77f., 80, 86f.
footage   65, 67, 76, 80, 90, 98, 104, 111, 123f., 153, 155f., 161, 177, 187, 195, 197, 209, 246, 254, 273f., 276, 278, 280, 298
Foote, Kenneth   41
forced labor, forced laborer   162, 165, 177–179, 186, 208–210, 242, 262, 280, 282
frame, narrative   188f., 200, 213, 255, 275, 302
Frank, Hans   84f., 112f., 169
Fränkel, Josef   216f.
Fränkel, Ritula   216, 258, 297
Fulda, Daniel   50f.
function (in museum representation)
– aesthetic   1, 226, 254, 256, 309
– authenticity   6, 226
– cognitive   22, 29f., 32
– commemorative   24f., 28, 31f., 61, 63, 223, 226, 233, 265
– comparative   226
– didactic   1, 25, 232
– documentary   226f., 254, 295–297
– educational (pedagogical)   31, 89, 226
– emotional (affective)   1, 30, 32, 296
– entertainment   31
– ethical   32
– experiential   1, 226
– historical   48, 63, 226f., 254
– illustrative   48, 92, 156, 162, 209, 231f., 282, 293, 295
– informational   109
– memory   1, 14
– meta-representational   1, 226, 289, 305
– narrative   1, 22, 46, 293
– political   32
– referential   302, 306
– remembrance   10, 311
– symbolic   301f.
futurity   28, 87

Gadolla, Josef Ritter von   146
Gaweda, Barbara   183, 185

Gedenkstätte   *See* memorial site (Gedenkstätte)
Geertz, Clifford   44
generation   76, 87, 93, 124, 140, 228, 233
generational remembrance   224
genocide   10, 31, 76, 84, 141, 148, 155, 170, 192, 206, 214, 224, 230, 235, 240f., 243, 256, 312
German Historical Museum   *See* Deutsches Historisches Museum
German Resistance Memorial Center   26
German-Russian Museum (Deutsch-Russisches Museum, DRM), Berlin-Karlshorst   11, 17, 33, 36–39, 50, 129, 170, 172–182, 203, 229, 240f., 256, 261, 264
Gestapo   112f., 160, 162f., 165–167, 169f., 243, 284
Goebbels, Joseph   180, 209, 266
Göring, Herrmann   84, 140, 282–284
Göth, Amon Leopold   261
Grethlein, Jonas   47
Gross, Jan T.   216, 262
Guerilla Girls   301
Guernica (bombing of)   267, 271, 275, 291
Gumbrecht, Hans-Ulrich   58f.
Günther, Ingo   297
Günther, Manuela   280, 300

Hackmann, Jörg   183, 249, 262
Halbwachs, Maurice   9
Hallmann, Heinz W.   161
Hamburg (bombing of)   98, 268, 273, 275
Hamburg Institute for Social Research (Hamburger Institut für Sozialforschung)   50
Hanks, Tom   103–106, 237
Hansen, Hans Lauge   19f.
Hansen, Randall   71
Hansen-Glucklich, Jennifer   11, 44, 225f., 232
Harris, Arthur   70
Heckner, Elke   134
Heeresmuseum (Military History Museum), Dresden   129
Heinemann, Monika   37, 77, 80, 83f., 107–110, 184, 188, 191, 193, 196–198, 242, 248
Heinze, Helmut   301f.

Heisig, Bernard   136
heritage   9, 25f., 40, 204, 213–215, 265, 299
hero, heroic, heroism   15, 25f., 32f., 47, 61, 63, 70–72, 78f., 81, 84f., 87f., 91, 93, 102f., 110, 118, 145–147, 183, 191f., 198, 201f., 239, 249f., 252, 259, 277, 279, 284, 290f.
'hero letters'   145f.
heroization   145, 147
Hesse, Klaus   163
Heydrich, Reinhard   167, 169, 178, 258
Himmler, Heinrich   167, 169f., 258
Hiroshima   140, 209, 267f., 272, 285, 287–289, 291, 297
Hiroshima Peace Memorial Museum, Tokyo   34
Historial of the Great War (Historial de la Grande Guerre), Péronne   24
historical knowledge   9f., 25, 58, 71, 100, 149, 203, 228
historical specificity, historically specific   7, 18, 21, 29, 47, 60, 128, 133, 142f., 148, 151, 155f., 182, 195, 201, 209, 211, 245, 252, 265, 268, 277, 291, 306
historical truth   27, 30, 61f., 71, 77, 86f., 94, 100, 198, 236, 253, 289
historiography   18, 22f., 48f., 166, 239
history of violence   245, 247, 264
Hitler, Adolf   16, 66f., 84, 99–101, 119f., 123, 126, 132, 136–138, 140, 144, 169, 177, 181, 194, 200, 238, 247, 258–260, 262, 271, 276, 284, 290
Hoffmann, Detlef   26
Hoffmann, Heinrich   111f.
Höll, Werner   295
Holocaust   9, 11, 13–15, 19, 23, 25, 37, 39, 52, 57–59, 62, 73, 75, 123, 141, 148, 154f., 163, 186, 193, 195f., 204, 206–209, 214–217, 220–259, 261–263, 265f., 268, 273, 293, 297, 311
– unrepresentability of   161, 223, 225f.
Holocaust exhibition   11, 167, 227, 230
Holocaust memorial museum   36, 221, 225, 257, 293
Holocaust museum   221–228, 230, 234

Holocaust representation   10, 33, 97, 221, 224, 226, 230, 233, 263, 308
hologram   224
home front (also war at home)   49, 62f., 66, 75f., 91f., 105, 128, 144, 155f., 158f., 228, 274
Horkheimer, Max   223
Höß, Rudolf   167, 258
House of European History (HEH), Brussels   2, 6, 16f., 19, 24, 33, 36, 38f., 57, 172, 186, 203–220, 223, 229, 243, 245, 258, 260f., 268, 270f., 288, 291, 294, 296, 300, 302, 308
House of Terror (Terror Háza), Budapest   23, 45f., 78, 189, 239
human rights   25, 27, 37, 59, 72, 100, 140, 219, 225, 235, 307
humiliation (during time of National Socialism)   59, 111, 149, 163f., 166f., 169, 171, 233, 242, 257, 262
Huyssen, Andreas   8

Iché, René   208, 302
identity
– affective   34
– Canadian   35, 62–64, 70, 74, 76f., 233f.
– collective   26, 181, 200
– European   35, 205, 214, 217
– Jewish   238f.
– national   14–16, 20f., 23, 32, 35, 61, 63f., 103, 244, 308
– perpetrator   166
– Polish   77f., 86, 183
– regional   20
– US American   35
– visitor   44
Illinois Holocaust Museum and Education Center, Skoke   26, 224
imagination (of museum visitor)   45, 55f., 145, 149, 153, 193, 212f., 231f., 305
immersion, to immerse, immersive   5f., 22, 52, 55, 89, 94, 97f., 100f., 103, 107f., 111, 116, 134, 159, 161f., 196, 223f., 226, 230, 236f., 257f., 263, 307, 311

Index — 347

Imperial War Museum, London (IWML)   11, 33, 36, 38 f., 62, 88–93, 172, 225, 227 f., 230, 243 f., 256, 278–282, 295
– A Family in Wartime (exhibition)   62, 90–92, 291
– Blitz Experience (installation)   89 f., 93
– The Holocaust Exhibition   11, 89, 225, 227, 230, 279
Imperial War Museum North (IWMN), Manchester   11, 16, 33, 36, 38 f., 57, 59, 117, 128 f., 150–160, 188, 198, 210, 229–232, 244, 252, 258 f., 269, 274, 277 f., 288, 293, 296 f., 300, 303 f.
– Big Picture Show   152, 154–160, 231, 269, 274, 278
– TimeStack   151, 154, 231
'in situ' vs. 'in context' (style in museums)   5 f., 22
International Museum of World War II, Natick, Massachusetts   33
interwovenness   See networking
Iser, Wolfgang   43
Ives, Andrew   63 f.

Jackson, Anthony   25 f.
Jacob, George   27 f.
Jähn, Sigmund   280
Japanese-Canadian relocation (internment)   70, 72 f., 75
Jedwabne (pogrom)   191, 216, 262 f.
Jewish Museum Berlin (Jüdisches Museum Berlin)   157, 225, 278
Jewish Museum Sydney   226
Jews, Jewish citizens (representation of)   78, 94, 104, 108 f., 111 f., 119, 128, 148 f., 162 f., 165, 167–170, 178, 186, 192, 210, 216 f., 221, 225, 229, 237–253, 257, 262 f.
John Paul II (Pope)   78, 87
Johnston-Weiss, Erin   141, 143, 162, 246, 254, 257
Jong, Steffi de   25, 80, 124
Judt, Tony   217, 219

Kaiser, Wolfram   14, 19, 205, 220
Kansteiner, Wulf   58, 224, 240, 309 f.

Kant, Immanuel   292 f.
– Critique of Judgement   292
Kästner, Erich   3, 188
Katyń   218, 297
Kazerne Dossin: Memorial, Museum and Documentation Centre on the Holocaust and Human Rights, Mechelen   225
Kesteloot, Chantal   205, 215
Kidd, Jenny   26
Kindertransport   152, 158 f., 230
Kirshenblatt-Gimblett, Barbara   5, 22, 41, 225
Korff, Gottfried   22
Koselleck, Reinhart   8, 58 f., 142
Krankenhagen, Stefan   19, 205 f.
Kristeva, Julia   214, 217
Kula, Marcin   184

LaCapra, Dominick   52 f., 226
Landsberg, Alison   30, 52, 80
Lang, Anne   20
laughter   163, 167, 195, 304
Law and Justice (Prawo i Sprawiedliwość = PiS), Polish political party   183, 192
Le Goff, Jacques   219
Lee, Jooyoun   34
Lees, Diane   227
Leggewie, Claus   20
Lehrer, Erica   28
Leiderman, Yuri   218, 297
Leningrad, Siege of   148, 179 f., 193
Lentin, Ronit   223 f.
Leoni, Claudio   161
Levy, Daniel   15, 223
liberation   66, 96, 108, 112, 125 f., 146, 181, 228, 235–238, 240, 247, 254, 256, 260, 267, 312
Libeskind, Daniel   3, 116, 129–134, 150 f., 157, 225, 269, 277–279, 297–300, 302 f.
linear (representation)   19, 23, 25, 27, 58, 61, 63, 76, 79, 94, 110, 135, 149, 204, 217 f., 227, 240
Logemann, Daniel   184, 192
London (bombing of)   See Battle of Britain (also Blitz)
Loxham, Angela   151

Lübbe, Herrmann 8
Lübbert, Fritz 284
Luhmann, Susanne 258
Luke, Timothy W. 258

MacArthur, Douglas 287 f.
Macdonald, Sharon 19, 43 f., 305
Machcewicz, Paweł 20, 117, 183 f., 186, 189, 196, 202, 248, 255, 270
MacKay, Donald 294
MacLeod, Suzanne 42, 157
MacMillan, Margaret 71
Majewski, Piotr M. 22 f., 77, 184
Makhotina, Ekaterina 8
Malmedy Massacre 259
Manchester Blitz 231
Mann, Roger 273
martyr, matyrdom 77, 239
master narrative 9, 23, 25, 27 – 29, 34 f., 45, 49, 61 – 64, 66 f., 70 f., 73 f., 76, 80, 83, 86 f., 94, 103, 105 f., 128, 133 f., 166, 172, 182, 186 f., 189, 191 f., 195, 200, 202 – 204, 209, 217 – 219, 236 – 238, 245, 253, 256, 265 f., 272, 276, 285, 287 f., 291, 312
Max Planck Institute for Human Development (Bildungsforschung), Berlin 308
McLuhan, Marshall 45, 105, 171
media, hot versus cool 45 f., 171
medium of the museum 38, 40, 42, 44 f., 50 f., 60, 295, 305 – 307
Melnik, Timofey 175
Memorial and Educational Site House of the Wannsee Conference (Gedenk- und Bildungsstätte Haus der Wannseekonferenz), Berlin 26, 225
Mémorial de Caen 11, 33, 186, 230, 243 – 245, 255 f., 264, 266 – 268, 291
Memorial Hall of the Victims in Nanjing Massacre by Japanese Invaders 34
memorial museum See museum, memorial
memorial site (Gedenkstätte) 11 – 13, 21, 23, 25 – 28, 36, 40 f., 53, 87, 163, 224, 226, 258
memory
– agonistic 13, 17, 20 f., 25, 27, 304, 307, 309 f.
– antagonistic 16, 20, 310
– collective 6, 9, 15, 20, 35, 62, 93, 106, 116, 134, 173, 204, 228, 235, 270, 311
– communicative 8, 13, 77, 93
– cosmopolitan 15, 19 f., 25, 27, 173, 205, 223, 244, 310
– cultural 6 – 16, 34 – 36, 50, 56, 60 – 62, 71, 74, 77, 87 f., 93 f., 97, 100, 178, 187, 195 f., 198, 203 f., 206, 211, 213, 222, 285, 306 – 308, 311 f.
– East European memory of the Second World War 12, 15, 19, 185, 216, 222
– living 8 f., 11, 224, 293 f., 312
– multidirectional 13, 17, 20 f., 201, 307
– prosthetic 30, 52
– public 12, 50, 144
– transnational 13, 17, 20, 57, 182, 196, 199, 203, 213, 265
– traveling 17
– West European memory of the Second World War 14, 19
memory battle 14, 35, 182 f., 203, 218, 308
memory debate 12, 14, 23, 34, 50, 63, 67, 69 f., 73, 86, 131 f., 182 f., 192, 234, 285, 312
memory politics 9, 11 f., 15, 35, 57, 183, 217 f., 262, 265, 307 f.
Mengele, Josef 167, 236, 258
Merkel, Angela 311
Metropolitan Museum of Art (MET), New York 95
Meyer, Wilhelm 175
migration, migrant 108, 154, 189, 200, 202, 212
Mikuska-Tinman, Emma 199, 201, 309
Militärhistorisches Museum der Bundeswehr See Bundeswehr Military History Museum
Military History Museum (Heeresgeschichtliches Museum), Vienna 32
Milton, Cynthia E. 28
mimesis
– non-mimetic 6
mimesis, mimetic 6, 10, 12, 44 f., 48 f., 51 – 54, 56, 58, 61, 94, 108, 128, 134, 158, 226, 255, 293 f.

Mittelbau-Dora concentration camp   247, 279–281
Molotov-Ribbentrop Pact (also Nazi-Soviet Pact)   174, 189
montage (image, photograph, multimedia)   76, 81, 129, 158, 162f., 165, 181, 198, 209, 240f., 289
Morin-Pelletier, Mélanie   75
Moriyama, Raymond   62
Mork, Andrea   204–208, 219
Morré, Jörg   173
Morris, Nicholas   216, 258, 297
Mouffe, Chantal   20
mourning   118, 124, 141–143, 145, 147, 233, 307f.
Mueller, Gordon H. 'Nick'   96
Mueller, Gustav Alfred   136
Muller, Adam   43
Muller, Anna   184, 192f.
multimedia installation   80, 97, 101–103, 107, 122, 151, 158, 184, 192, 206, 230, 237, 285
multiperspectivity, multiperspectival   19, 121f., 205
multisensory (sensory)   9, 30, 80, 121, 158f.
Munich Documentation Centre for the History of National Socialism   27f.
Muschg, Adolf   219
Musée de la Bataille des Ardennes, Clervaux   31
Museum for European Culture (Museum Europäischer Kulturen), Berlin Dahlem
– Feeling War (Der gefühlte Krieg)   308f.
Museum of the Great Patriotic War, Moscow   25
Museum of the Second World War (Muzeum II Wojny Światowej, MIIWŚ), Gdańsk   1f., 14, 17, 23, 33, 36–39, 56, 78, 117, 140, 172, 182–203, 207–211, 220, 222, 229, 239, 243, 247, 250f., 253, 255, 259f., 262, 264, 269–271, 274–277, 285, 287f., 291
– Museum of Westerplatte and the War of 1939   202
– Seven Looks at Westerplatte   202
museum temple   59, 130, 189

museum (type, genre)
– collector   21, 30–32, 55
– experiential   21, 29–31, 52
– history   12, 21f., 24, 28, 31, 36f., 40f., 44, 47, 57, 61, 63, 75, 77f., 88f., 95, 101, 106f., 130, 132, 172, 184, 205, 219, 221, 228, 233, 292f., 299, 302, 306f.
– ideas   21, 24f., 27f., 31, 59, 184
– memorial   21f., 24–26, 28, 30f., 36, 46, 61, 63, 77f., 95, 101, 107, 116, 161, 224f.
– military history   5, 31f., 36, 129, 131f., 208, 221, 225f., 229f., 263
– narrative   22f., 25, 27, 31, 78, 107
– transnational   12, 17, 25, 172, 175, 182–184, 204
music (in relation to war)   75, 132, 134, 140, 193
Muzeum II Wojny Światowej   See Museum of the Second World War
Muzeum Powstania Warszawskiego   See Warsaw Rising Museum
myth   1, 14, 25, 56, 61, 72, 74, 86f., 90, 93f., 96, 144f., 153, 220, 226, 245, 300, 307, 310, 312

Nachama, Andreas   161f.
Nagasaki   125, 140, 267, 272, 285–289, 291
Nagel, Wilfried   137f.
Najewitz, Jens   300
Nanjing Massacre   34, 275
narrativity   45, 47f., 50f., 170
narratology   40, 47, 50
nation state   15–17, 182, 187, 206, 217
National Air Space Museum, Washington, DC
– The Crossroads: The End of World War II, the Atomic Bomb and the Cold War (Enola Gay exhibition)   106, 273, 312
National Museum of the United States Army, Fort Belvoir, VA   97
National Socialism (see also Nazism)   19, 49, 129, 145, 166, 208, 246, 309
National WWII Museum, New Orleans   10, 25, 33, 36–39, 66, 94–107, 109, 125, 128, 159, 191, 229, 235–237, 254, 257, 259f., 272f., 279, 285–287, 289–291, 303
– Anne Frank: A History for Today   237

- Beyond All Boundaries: a 4D Jouney through the War that Changed the World 103, 106, 237f., 285
- Dog Tag Experience 97f., 100, 103, 106, 236, 238
- Final Mission: USS Tang Submarine Experience 101f.
- L.W. 'Pete' Kent Train Car Experience 102f.
- State of Deception: The Power of Nazi Propaganda 237

nationalism 14, 24, 74, 120, 192, 207
NATO 76, 282
Nawrocki, Karol 183, 250
Nazi Documentation Center Ordensburg Vogelsang (Vogelsang NS-Dokumentationszentrum) 27
Nazism (see also National Socialism) 120, 174, 187f., 235, 244, 247, 259
Netherlands (liberation of) 66, 294
networking (museum technique) 21, 57–60, 62, 126, 133, 140f., 149, 152, 159, 163, 167, 211, 227–230, 240, 243, 245, 247, 253, 256, 282, 296, 304
new museology 42, 44
Nicolai, Carsten 300
Noakes, Jeff 64
Noakes, Lucy 89
Nora, Pierre 9
nuclear bomb, nuclear bombing 34, 97, 104, 106, 125, 140, 209, 265, 268, 272f., 277, 285f., 288, 297, 301
Nünning, Ansgar 40
Nuremberg Trials 241, 260
Nussbaum, Felix 139, 247, 297

occupation (German, of European countries during the Second World War) 14f., 37, 49, 78–80, 107–111, 114, 168, 176, 180–182, 190–196, 198, 239, 241–243, 248–250, 259f.
'occupation,' Soviet (1945–1989) 15, 79, 109, 194
Ohrdruf concentration camp 99, 235, 241
Okinawa Prefectural Peace Park 34
Oliver, Dean 64

open versus closed museum representation of the past 17, 19, 76, 79, 129, 172, 201, 203, 289, 293, 304
Operation Barbarossa 147, 170, 242, 256
oral history 10, 94f., 97, 236
Oskar Schindler Enamel Factory (Fabryka Emalia Oskara Schindlera, OSF), Kraków 17, 33, 36–39, 49, 55f., 94, 107–116, 128f., 229, 240, 242f., 257, 261
Osthofen concentration camp memorial site (Gedenkstätte KZ Osthofen) 27
'otherness' 20, 59, 166
Overlord Museum, Colleville-sur-Mer 55

Paris Uprising 196f.
Patton, George S. 99, 121
Paver, Chloe 246
peace 25, 27, 31, 34, 74, 76, 120, 135, 159, 184, 204, 233, 265
performative (museum style) 5, 12, 22, 25, 29, 40–42, 44, 46f., 58, 109f., 112
perpetration 3, 10, 15f., 20, 26, 35–37, 39, 50, 124, 139, 142f., 146, 162, 180, 182, 191–193, 211, 216, 226, 229f., 245, 252, 254, 256, 258f., 261–263, 266, 270f., 276f., 282, 299, 305f., 308
perpetrator 4, 12, 16, 20, 26f., 35, 84f., 141, 161–163, 165–167, 170f., 178f., 200, 203, 211, 223, 226, 228, 230, 233, 240, 242f., 245f., 253, 256, 258–265, 269f., 274f., 284, 296
Perry, Rachel E. 253
perspective
- collective 16, 49, 57, 61, 63, 66, 72, 94, 100, 109f., 125, 128f., 158, 161, 172–175, 180, 198f., 203, 229, 233, 235, 242f., 257, 263, 266, 287, 311
Petrucci, Mario 303f.
Phillips, Mark 46, 89f.
photography 10, 45, 50, 166, 171, 175, 253, 256, 294f.
Picasso, Pablo 271
Pieken, Gorch 129, 131–134, 141, 262
Pirker, Eva Ulrike 5, 55
Plaszów concentration camp 109, 243, 257
play (and war) 132, 140, 153, 159, 193, 280, 300f.

Plötzensee Memorial Center (Gedenkstätte Plötzensee), Berlin 26
poetry (in the museum) 303–306
pogrom 143, 191f., 203, 241f., 247, 262f.
poiesis, poietic 42, 44, 56, 110, 149, 162, 182
POLIN Museum of the History of Polish Jews (Muzeum Historii Żydów Polskich), Warsaw 225
Prague Uprising 196
prisoner of war (POW) 66, 111, 123, 148, 152, 162f., 173, 175–180, 193, 203, 222, 233, 241f., 255, 259, 267, 295
progress, progressive development (of history) 8, 17, 19, 23, 25, 27, 58f., 79, 87, 135, 204, 206, 218, 233, 282
propaganda 153, 300
– Allies 253, 267
– German 145
– Nazi 109, 111–114, 120, 137, 145–147, 163f., 166, 168, 171, 175, 177, 180f., 188, 190, 194, 253, 267, 295
– Polish 190
– Soviet 79, 179, 181, 188
– US American 106, 171
proximity See distantiation, distance
Putin, Vladimir 312

Raab, Imre Párkányi 14
race, racism, racial 73, 101, 104f., 120, 140, 145, 170, 177, 188, 192, 206f., 221, 236, 238, 242–246, 250, 257, 261, 271, 290
rape 181, 199–201, 305
Ravensbrück
– concentration camp 231, 234, 296
– Mahn- und Gedenkstätte 26, 258
reconciliation 73, 124, 172, 265, 268, 278, 302
Red Army (also Soviet army) 108, 173, 177f., 181, 187, 196, 199, 295
reenactment 1, 5, 10, 29, 40, 53, 57, 77, 144, 147, 297
refugee 74f., 155, 175, 212, 222, 295
Reichspogromnacht 241
Reims 99
Remes, Anastasia 205
replica 5, 46, 78

resistance (during war, dictatorships, and occupation) 15, 49, 85, 93, 110, 114, 117, 119, 125, 147, 174, 181, 186, 188f., 192–196, 198, 203, 209, 211, 216, 232, 239, 246, 252f., 258, 277, 296, 311
Resistance Museum (Verzetsmuseum), Amsterdam 110
Rhineland-Palatinate National Socialist Documentation Centre (NS-Dokumentationszentrum Rheinland-Pfalz) 27
Richthofen, Manfred von 145, 284
Ricœur, Paul 23, 42
Rigney, Ann 55
Rogg, Matthias 130–134, 141
Rohde, Maik 300
Roosevelt, Franklin D. 266, 290
Rosenzweig, Chava 231, 233, 258, 297
Rosoman, Leonard Henry 296
Rothberg, Michael 17, 20f., 213, 223
Rotterdam (bombing of) 267, 271, 275
Rougier Lecoq, Violette 231, 296
Rowland, Antony 150f., 230–232, 303
Royal Army Museum of Military History (Musée royal de l'Armée et d'Histoire militaire), Brussels 32
Rüdiger, Mark 5, 55
Ruhr Museum, Essen 16, 58, 309
– Krieg. Macht. Sinn: War and Violence in European Memory (Krieg und Gewalt in der europäischen Erinnerung) 16, 309–311
Ryan, Marie-Laure 41

Sachsenhausen
– concentration camp 27
– Gedenkstätte und Museum Sachsenhausen 26
Sandison, Charles 297
Santayana, George 214
scenographic (museum style) 51, 128, 184, 225, 266
scenography (museum) 11, 22f., 29, 57, 292
scenovision 117, 119–121, 123–125, 241
Schindler's List (film) 108
Schulze-Wessel, Martin 8
SD (Security Service, Sicherheitsdienst) 162, 169, 178

self-reflexivity; self-reflection   38, 55, 233, 307 f.
September 11 (9/11)   76, 158, 303
Shah, Nisha   255
Shoah   *See* Holocaust
shock (through representation)   254, 256, 284 f.
Shokeikan Museum for Wounded Soldiers, Tokyo   34
Siddi, Marco   183, 185
Simon, Roger I.   27 f., 256
simulate, simulating (the past)   5 – 7, 10, 21, 29 f., 34, 45, 48 – 50, 52 – 54, 56 f., 61 f., 74, 80, 89 f., 94, 97, 103, 105, 108 – 112, 126, 128, 134, 149, 159, 173, 182, 186, 188, 198 f., 265, 272, 274, 277, 289, 291, 300, 308, 310
simulation   51
– of the past   5, 40 f., 49, 51 – 53, 57, 61, 93 f., 110, 117, 127, 173, 180, 192, 274, 302 f.
– structural   53, 173, 308, 311
simultaneity   40, 58, 174
Sinti and Roma (persecution)   222, 242, 247
Slovak Uprising   196
social engineering   200, 247
Sodaro, Amy   24, 225
sound, soundscape (in museums)   43, 54, 78, 80, 89 f., 103, 107, 109 f., 112, 121, 124, 147, 156, 158, 179, 196, 274, 300, 307
source (historical)   3, 16, 22, 37, 48, 50, 66, 159, 162, 254, 288, 292, 295
Soviet Union   15, 67, 104, 120, 147, 163, 167 f., 172 – 174, 176, 178 f., 185 f., 188, 191, 193, 200, 207, 209, 211, 219, 221 f., 235, 239, 242, 244, 249, 262, 265, 271, 275, 286
space (museum)   5, 7, 9, 11 f., 25, 29, 35, 38, 40 – 44, 46 – 49, 52, 55 f., 60 f., 108 – 112, 115, 117, 133, 148 f., 154, 156 f., 159 f., 162, 174, 225, 233, 242, 257, 273, 278, 292 f., 297, 304, 306, 308 f.
Spanish Civil War   208
Sparks, Felix   237 f.
specificity, historical   *See* historical specificity, historically specific

spectacle   45, 138, 159, 165, 168, 224, 253, 272, 277
Spielberg, Steven   108
SS mobile killing unit (Einsatzgruppe)   148, 167
SS (Schutzstaffel)   16, 27, 84, 113, 146, 148, 160, 162, 164, 167, 169 f., 177, 199, 237, 240, 259, 261
101st Airborne Museum Le Mess, Bastogne   53
staging, to stage (museum style)   5 f., 22, 38, 40, 42, 48, 51, 55 f., 87, 90, 98, 106, 109, 112 f., 116, 125 f., 128, 135, 164, 167, 179, 198, 242, 302 – 304, 308
Stalin, Joseph Vissarionovich   81, 83, 86, 181, 197, 200, 247, 260, 266, 271
Stalingrad   175, 181, 275
Steel, Nigel   273
Stimson, Henry L.   287 f.
Stöppler, Wilhelm   140
Stroop, Jürgen   170, 240, 258
sublime, the, sublimity   72, 138, 292
suffering
– civilian   66, 125, 184, 186, 193, 203, 211, 213, 217, 243, 247, 249, 253, 255, 265, 268
– German   200, 311
– Jewish   216, 249, 252
– Polish   247, 252 f.
– Soviet   200
survivor
– Air War   273, 301
– German war crimes   124
– Holocaust   154, 216, 223 f., 231, 233, 238, 244, 279
– Polish   249
– war crimes   260
– Warsaw Uprising   77
Syrian Civil War (twenty-first century)   202, 287
Szpilman, Władysław   239

tablet (as exhibition guide)   3, 206, 208 – 211, 213 f.
tangencies   174

temporality, temporalization (of past, present, and future)   6, 8, 24, 28 f., 31, 58, 87, 97, 133, 147, 170, 213, 226
terror   69, 72, 108, 161, 164, 166–171, 193, 195, 200, 203, 205–208, 214, 219, 243, 247, 255 f., 270, 275, 285, 291
Thamer, Hans-Ulrich   131
Thatcher, Margaret   153
theatrical (representational technique museum)   29, 41, 55, 94, 108–111, 150, 299
'thick description'   44
Thiemeyer, Thomas   11, 13, 15 f., 22 f., 30, 37, 45 f., 50, 106, 266, 294
time travel, time traveler   49, 94, 108, 110, 115, 117, 128, 242, 257
Tokyo (firebombing)   269, 272 f., 275, 285, 287
Tolson, Roger   273
Topography of Terror (Topographie des Terrors, ToT), Berlin   17, 27, 33 f., 36–39, 50, 59, 129, 160–173, 179, 203, 209, 225, 229 f., 243, 245, 256 f., 259–261, 264
'total war'   3, 6, 14 f., 39, 140, 155, 167, 182, 186, 188, 191–193, 208 f., 211, 217, 243–245, 261, 265–273, 275, 277, 282, 286, 308
totalitarianism/totalitarian   104, 120, 185–189, 191–194, 198, 200, 202, 204, 206–209, 211, 221, 245, 253, 255, 270 f., 275–277, 285, 291, 312
tourism   31, 108, 116
Traavik, Morton   301
transnational   12 f., 16 f., 19–21, 25, 31, 34–36, 39, 57, 60, 76, 172–175, 179, 182–184, 186 f., 189, 191–193, 195 f., 198–203, 205, 209, 211, 213 f., 217–220, 223, 242, 253, 260, 263, 265, 277
trauma (traumatic)   10, 28, 30, 52 f., 73, 77, 124, 141, 143, 145, 212, 224 f., 244 f., 249, 254, 260, 266, 271, 278, 296 f., 300, 304
– structural   52, 308
– vicarious   52
– virtual   52 f.
– wartime   93

trials (post Second World War)   79, 147, 161, 178, 221, 228, 247, 259–261
Tucholsky, Karl   188
Tyradellis, Daniel   41

Ukielski, Paweł   78
Ulma Family Museum of Poles Saving Jews in World War II, Markowa   249
United States Holocaust Memorial Museum (USHMM), Washington, DC   22–25, 52, 59, 78, 167, 221, 223–227, 230, 232, 237–239, 252, 254 f., 257 f.
universality   23, 60, 203, 219 f., 276
University of Southern California Institute for Creative Technologies   224
University of Southern California Shoah Foundation   224
UNREST (Unsettling Remembrance and Social Cohesion in Transnational Europe)   16, 309
Unsere Mütter, unsere Väter (Generation War, TV miniseries)   220
Urban, Michał   107

V weapons (V1, V2)   88, 132, 191, 228, 247, 276, 278–282, 300 f.
Valkyrie (film)   144
valor   15, 25, 77, 83, 202, 224, 294
Versailles, Treaty of   64, 121, 187, 189
veterans (war)   30 f., 36, 70–72, 74, 80, 95 f., 105 f., 118, 232, 234, 273, 284, 296
victimhood   10, 15 f., 26, 35, 46, 53, 95, 109, 139, 182, 192, 194, 216, 252, 285, 299, 306, 310
visitor (of museum)
– active   29, 59, 129, 134, 140 f., 145, 149, 152, 172, 309–311
– concept as experiencer / consciousness   7, 10, 48–50, 53, 61 f., 100, 302, 306, 310
– empirical / actual   12, 43 f., 50, 61, 149, 307
– 'ideal'   35, 38, 44
– manipulation of   12, 44 f., 85, 106, 109, 159, 171, 202, 263, 268, 275, 290, 307
– overwhelming of   13, 30, 46, 91, 106, 150, 238, 255, 263, 278, 292

visualization 59, 106, 125 f., 129, 163, 165, 170 f., 256
'Volk Community' ('Volksgemeinschaft') 162–164, 166, 171, 245
Volksdeutsche 112 f., 211
Volkssturm 99 f., 146, 181
Voorsanger Mathes LLC 96
Vovk van Gaal, Taja 204 f.

war crimes 50, 85, 120, 123 f., 142 f., 167, 170 f., 179, 191, 196, 222, 237, 241 f., 255 f., 259–261
war in the East (Eastern Europe) 67, 172, 176, 222, 312
War in the Pacific (Second World War; see also Asia-Pacific Theater of the Second World War 66, 75, 95, 101, 118, 266, 289
war of annihilation (see also 'total war') 6, 105, 123, 137, 147, 186, 242, 266 f., 270 f., 273
war toy 1–8, 140, 153, 270, 307
Warsaw (bombing/destruction of) 2 f., 82, 170, 191, 198, 239, 272
Warsaw Ghetto Uprising 143, 196 f., 199, 239
Warsaw Rising Museum (Muzeum Powstania Warszawskiego, WRM) 5, 16, 18, 23, 33, 36–38, 49, 57, 62, 77–88, 100, 107, 110, 189, 197 f., 229, 238 f., 257, 260, 272
Warsaw Uprising 36, 77 f., 84, 86 f., 169, 196 f., 239 f., 252, 261
Waterton, Emma 43 f.
Watson, Sheila 284

Watson, Stephen 106
Wehrmacht 31, 50 f., 113, 117, 129, 143, 145–148, 169 f., 177, 190
Wehrmacht Exhibition (War of Annihilation
 – Crimes of the Wehrmacht 1941 to 1944 = Vernichtungskrieg
 – Verbrechen der Wehrmacht 1941 bis 1944) 50
Weinberg, Jeshajahu 22 f.
Weiser, M. Elizabeth 130, 157, 205
Weiss, Charlotte 236
Weissenborn, Helmuth 296
West Germany 3, 118, 144, 165, 215
Westerplatte 183, 191, 202
Wewelsburg 1933–1945 Memorial Museum (Erinnerungs- und Gedenkstätte Wewelsburg 1933–1945) 27
White, Hayden 23, 42
Wielun (bombing of) 270 f.
Wiesel, Elie 213
Wilhelm Gustloff (ship) 199
Wilms, Ursula 161
Wilson, Woodrow 187
Winter, Jay 51, 219, 270
Wóycicka, Zofia 172 f., 182
Wundshammer, Benno 175

Yad Vashem: The World Holocaust Remembrance Center, Jerusalem 224–226
Young, James E. 161

Zolberg, Vera L. 273
Zumthor, Peter 161
Żychlińska, Monika 77 f., 80, 86 f.

www.ingramcontent.com/pod-product-compliance
Lightning Source LLC
Chambersburg PA
CBHW061930220426

43662CB00012B/1859